SQL Server 2017 Integration Services Cookbook

Powerful ETL techniques to load and transform data from almost any source

Christian Cote
Matija Lah
Dejan Sarka

BIRMINGHAM - MUMBAI

SQL Server 2017 Integration Services Cookbook

First published: June 2017

Production reference: 1300617

Published by Packt Publishing Ltd.
Livery Place
35 Livery Street
Birmingham
B3 2PB, UK.
ISBN 978-1-78646-182-7

www.packtpub.com

Credits

Authors

Christian Cote
Matija Lah
Dejan Sarka

Reviewers

Jasmin Azemovic
Marek Chmel
Tomaz Kastrun
Ruben Oliva Ramos

Commissioning Editor

Amey Varangaonkar

Acquisition Editor

Vinay Agrekar

Content Development Editor

Cheryl Dsa

Technical Editor

Dinesh Pawar

Copy Editor

Safis Editing

Project Coordinator

Nidhi Joshi

Proofreader

Safis Editing

Indexer

Pratik Shirodkar

Graphics

Tania Dutta

Production Coordinator

Deepika Naik

About the Authors

Christian Cote is a database professional from Montreal, Quebec, Canada. For the past 16 years, he's been involved in various data warehouse projects and business intelligence projects. He has contributed to business intelligence solutions in various domains like pharmaceutical, finance, insurance, and many more. He's been a Microsoft Most Valuable Professional since 2009 and leads the Montreal PASS chapter.

Matija Lah has more than 15 years of experience working with Microsoft SQL Server, mostly from architecting data-centric solutions in the legal domain. His contributions to the SQL Server community have led to the Microsoft Most Valuable Professional award in 2007 (data platform). He spends most of his time on projects involving advanced information management, and natural language processing, but often finds time to speak at events related to Microsoft SQL Server where he loves to share his experience with the SQL Server platform.

Dejan Sarka, MCT and SQL Server Most Valuable Professional, is an independent trainer and consultant who focuses on the development of database and business intelligence applications, located in Ljubljana, Slovenia. Besides his projects, he spends around half of his time on training and mentoring. He is the founder of the Slovenian SQL Server and .NET users group. Dejan is the main author and coauthor of many books and courses about databases and SQL Server. He is a frequent speaker at many worldwide events.

About the Reviewers

Jasmin Azemovic is a university professor, active in the areas of database systems, information security, data privacy, forensic analysis, and fraud detection. His PhD degree was in the field of modeling design and developing an environment for the preservation of privacy inside database systems. He is the author of many scientific-research papers and two books: *Writing T-SQL Queries for Beginners Using Microsoft SQL Server 2012* and *Securing SQL Server 2012*. He is an active member of the professional IT world: Microsoft MVP (Data Platform—eight years so far) and a security consultant. He is an active speaker at many IT professional and community conferences.

Marek Chmel is an IT consultant and trainer with more than 10 years of experience. He's a frequent speaker with a focus on Microsoft SQL Server, Azure ,and security topics. Marek writes for Microsoft's TechnetCZSK blog, and since 2012 he's an MVP: Data Platform. Marek is also recognized as a Microsoft Certified Trainer: Regional Lead for Czech Republic for a few years in a row, he holds many MCSE certifications, and on the top of that he's an ECCouncil Certified Ethical Hacker and holder of several eLearnSecurity certifications. Marek earned his MSc (Business and Informatics) degree from Nottingham Trent University. He started his career as a trainer for Microsoft Server courses. Later, he joined AT&T, as a sr. database administrator with a specialization in MSSQL Server, Data Platform, and Machine Learning.

Tomaz Kastrun is an SQL Server developer and data analyst. He has more than 15 years of experiences in the field of business warehousing, development, ETL, database administration, and query tuning. He also has more than 15 years of experience in the fields of data analysis, data mining, statistical research, and machine learning. He is Microsoft SQL Server MVP for data platforms and has been working with a Microsoft SQL Server since version 2000. Tomaz is a blogger, the author of many articles, the coauthor of a statistical analysis book, speaker at community and Microsoft events, and an avid coffee drinker.

> *Thanks to people who inspired me, the community, and the SQL family. Thank you, dear reader, for doing this. For endless inspiration, thank you Rubi.*

Ruben Oliva Ramos is a computer systems engineer with a master's degree in computer and electronic systems engineering, teleinformatics, and networking specialization from University of Salle Bajio in Leon, Guanajuato, Mexico. He has more than five years of experience in developing web applications to control and monitor devices connected with Arduino and Raspberry Pi using web frameworks and cloud services to build IoT applications.

He is a mechatronics teacher at University of Salle Bajio and teaches students on the master's degree in Design and Engineering of Mechatronics Systems. He also works at Centro de Bachillerato Tecnologico Industrial 225 in Leon, Guanajuato Mexico, teaching subjects like: electronics, robotics and control, automation and microcontrollers at mechatronics technician career, consultant and developer projects in areas like: monitoring systems and datalogger data using technologies: Android, iOS, Windows Phone, HTML5, PHP, CSS, Ajax, JavaScript, Angular, ASP, .NET databases: SQlite, mongoDB, MySQL, web servers: Node.js, IIS, hardware programming: Arduino, Raspberry pi, Ethernet Shield, GPS and GSM/GPRS, ESP8266, control and monitor systems for data acquisition and programming.

I would like to thank God for helping me reviewing this book; my wife, Mayte, my sons, Ruben and Dario, for their support while writing this book and in general for their support in all my projects. To my parents and my brother and sister, whom I love.

www.PacktPub.com

For support files and downloads related to your book, please visit www.PacktPub.com.

Did you know that Packt offers eBook versions of every book published, with PDF and ePub files available? You can upgrade to the eBook version at www.PacktPub.com and as a print book customer, you are entitled to a discount on the eBook copy. Get in touch with us at service@packtpub.com for more details.

At www.PacktPub.com, you can also read a collection of free technical articles, sign up for a range of free newsletters and receive exclusive discounts and offers on Packt books and eBooks.

https://www.packtpub.com/mapt

Get the most in-demand software skills with Mapt. Mapt gives you full access to all Packt books and video courses, as well as industry-leading tools to help you plan your personal development and advance your career.

Why subscribe?

- Fully searchable across every book published by Packt
- Copy and paste, print, and bookmark content
- On demand and accessible via a web browser

Customer Feedback

Thanks for purchasing this Packt book. At Packt, quality is at the heart of our editorial process. To help us improve, please leave us an honest review on this book's Amazon page at https://www.amazon.com/dp/178646182X.

If you'd like to join our team of regular reviewers, you can e-mail us at customerreviews@packtpub.com. We award our regular reviewers with free eBooks and videos in exchange for their valuable feedback. Help us be relentless in improving our products!

Table of Contents

Preface

SQL Server Integration Services is a tool that facilitates data extraction, consolidation, and loading options (ETL), SQL Server coding enhancements, data warehousing, and customizations. With the help of the recipes in this book, you'll gain hands-on experience of SSIS 2017 as well as the new 2016 features, design and development improvements including SCD, tuning, and customizations. At the start, you'll learn to install and set up SSIS as well other SQL Server resources to make optimal use of this business intelligence tool. We'll begin by taking you through the new features in SSIS 2016/2017 and implementing the necessary features to get a modern scalable ETL solution that fits the modern data warehouse. Through the course of the book, you will learn how to design and build SSIS data warehouses packages using SQL Server Data Tools. Additionally, you'll learn how to develop SSIS packages designed to maintain a data warehouse using the data flow and other control flow tasks. You'll also go through many recipes on cleansing data and how to get the end result after applying different transformations. Some real-world scenarios that you might face are also covered and how to handle various issues that you might face when designing your packages. At the end of this book, you'll get to know all the key concepts to perform data integration and transformation. You'll have explored on-premises big data integration processes to create a classic data warehouse, and will know how to extend the toolbox with custom tasks and transforms.

What this book covers

Chapter 1, *SSIS Setup*, contains recipes describing the step by step setup of SQL Server 2016 to get the features that are used in the book.

Chapter 2, *What Is New in SSIS 2016*, contains recipes that talk about the evolution of SSIS over time and what's new in SSIS 2016. This chapter is a detailed overview of Integration Services 2016, new features.

Chapter 3, *Key Components of a Modern ETL Solution*, explains how ETL has evolved over the past few years and will explain what components are necessary to get a modern scalable ETL solution that fits the modern data warehouse. This chapter will also describe what each catalog view provides and will help you learn how you can use some of them to archive SSIS execution statistics.

Chapter 4, *Data Warehouse Loading Techniques*, describes many patterns used when it comes to data warehouse or ODS load. You will learn how to effectively load a data warehouse and process a tabular model, maintain data partitions and modern data refresh rates.

Chapter 5, *Dealing with Data Quality*, focuses on how SSIS can be leveraged to validate and load data. You will learn how to identify invalid data, cleanse data and load valid data to the data warehouse.

Chapter 6, *SSIS Performance and Scalability*, will talk about how to monitor SSIS package execution. It will also provide solutions to scale out processes by using parallelism. You will learn how to identify bottlenecks and how to resolve them using various techniques.

Chapter 7, *Unleash the Power of SSIS Script Task and Component*, covers how to use scripting with SSIS. You will learn how script tasks and script components are very valuable in many situations to overcome the limitations of stock toolbox tasks and transforms.

Chapter 8, *SSIS and Advanced Analytics*, talks about how SSIS can be used to prepare the data you need for further analysis. Here, you will learn how you can make use of SQL Server Analysis Services (SSAS) and R models in the SSIS data flow.

Chapter 9, *On-Premises and Azure Big Data Integration*, describes the Azure feature pack that allows SSIS to integrate Azure data from blob storage and HDInsight clusters. You will learn how to use Azure feature pack components to add flexibility to their SSIS solution architecture and integrate on-premises Big Data can be manipulated via SSIS.

Chapter 10, *Extending SSIS Tasks and Transformations*, talks about extending and customizing the toolbox using custom developed tasks and transforms and security features. You will learn the pros and cons of creating custom tasks to extend the SSIS toolbox and secure your deployment.

Chapter 11, *Scale Out with SSIS 2017*, talks about scaling out SSIS package executions on multiple servers. You will learn how SSIS 2017 can scale out to multiple workers to enhance execution scalability.

What you need for this book

This book was written using SQL Server 2016 and all the examples and functions should work with it. Other tools you may need are Visual Studio 2015, SQL Data Tools 16 or higher and SQL Server Management Studio 17 or later.

In addition to that, you will need Hortonworks Sandbox Docker for Windows Azure account and Microsoft Azure.

The last chapter of this book has been written using SQL Server 2017.

Who this book is for

This book is ideal for software engineers, DW/ETL architects, and ETL developers who need to create a new, or enhance an existing, ETL implementation with SQL Server 2017 Integration Services. This book would also be good for individuals who develop ETL solutions that use SSIS and are keen to learn the new features and capabilities in SSIS 2017.

Sections

In this book, you will find several headings that appear frequently (Getting ready, How to do it, How it works, There's more, and See also). To give clear instructions on how to complete a recipe, we use these sections as follows:

Getting ready

This section tells you what to expect in the recipe, and describes how to set up any software or any preliminary settings required for the recipe.

How to do it...

This section contains the steps required to follow the recipe.

How it works...

This section usually consists of a detailed explanation of what happened in the previous section.

There's more...

This section consists of additional information about the recipe in order to make the reader more knowledgeable about the recipe.

See also

This section provides helpful links to other useful information for the recipe.

Conventions

In this book, you will find a number of text styles that distinguish between different kinds of information. Here are some examples of these styles and an explanation of their meaning. Code words in text, database table names, folder names, filenames, file extensions, pathnames, dummy URLs, user input, and Twitter handles are shown as follows: "The last characters CI and AS are for case insensitive and accent sensitive, respectively." A block of code is set as follows:

```
USE DQS_STAGING_DATA;
SELECT CustomerKey, FullName, StreetAddress, City, StateProvince,
CountryRegion, EmailAddress, BirthDate, Occupation;
```

New terms and **important words** are shown in bold. Words that you see on the screen, for example, in menus or dialog boxes, appear in the text like this: "Click on the **Sign in** visible at the right (top) to log into Visual Studio Dev Essentials."

Warnings or important notes appear in a box like this.

Tips and tricks appear like this.

Reader feedback

Feedback from our readers is always welcome. Let us know what you think about this book-what you liked or disliked. Reader feedback is important for us as it helps us develop titles that you will really get the most out of. To send us general feedback, simply e-mail feedback@packtpub.com, and mention the book's title in the subject of your message. If there is a topic that you have expertise in and you are interested in either writing or contributing to a book, see our author guide at www.packtpub.com/authors .

Customer support

Now that you are the proud owner of a Packt book, we have a number of things to help you to get the most from your purchase.

Downloading the example code

You can download the example code files for this book from your account at http://www.packtpub.com. If you purchased this book elsewhere, you can visit http://www.packtpub.com/support and register to have the files e-mailed directly to you. You can download the code files by following these steps:

1. Log in or register to our website using your e-mail address and password.
2. Hover the mouse pointer on the **SUPPORT** tab at the top.
3. Click on **Code Downloads & Errata**.
4. Enter the name of the book in the **Search** box.
5. Select the book for which you're looking to download the code files.
6. Choose from the drop-down menu where you purchased this book from.
7. Click on **Code Download**.

You can also download the code files by clicking on the **Code Files** button on the book's webpage at the Packt Publishing website. This page can be accessed by entering the book's name in the **Search** box. Please note that you need to be logged in to your Packt account. Once the file is downloaded, please make sure that you unzip or extract the folder using the latest version of:

- WinRAR / 7-Zip for Windows
- Zipeg / iZip / UnRarX for Mac
- 7-Zip / PeaZip for Linux

The code bundle for the book is also hosted on GitHub at https://github.com/PacktPublishing/SQL-Server-2017-Integration-Services-Cookbook. We also have other code bundles from our rich catalog of books and videos available at https://github.com/PacktPublishing/. Check them out!

Downloading the color images of this book

We also provide you with a PDF file that has color images of the screenshots/diagrams used in this book. The color images will help you better understand the changes in the output. You can download this file from https://www.packtpub.com/sites/default/files/downloads/SQLServer2017IntegrationServicesCookbook_ColorImages.pdf.

Errata

Although we have taken every care to ensure the accuracy of our content, mistakes do happen. If you find a mistake in one of our books-maybe a mistake in the text or the code-we would be grateful if you could report this to us. By doing so, you can save other readers from frustration and help us improve subsequent versions of this book. If you find any errata, please report them by visiting http://www.packtpub.com/submit-errata, selecting your book, clicking on the **Errata Submission Form** link, and entering the details of your errata. Once your errata are verified, your submission will be accepted and the errata will be uploaded to our website or added to any list of existing errata under the Errata section of that title. To view the previously submitted errata, go to https://www.packtpub.com/books/content/support and enter the name of the book in the search field. The required information will appear under the **Errata** section.

Piracy

Piracy of copyrighted material on the Internet is an ongoing problem across all media. At Packt, we take the protection of our copyright and licenses very seriously. If you come across any illegal copies of our works in any form on the Internet, please provide us with the location address or website name immediately so that we can pursue a remedy. Please contact us at copyright@packtpub.com with a link to the suspected pirated material. We appreciate your help in protecting our authors and our ability to bring you valuable content.

Questions

If you have a problem with any aspect of this book, you can contact us at questions@packtpub.com, and we will do our best to address the problem.

1
SSIS Setup

In this chapter, we will cover the following recipes:

- SQL Server 2016 download
- Installing JRE for PolyBase
- Installing SQL Server 2016
- SQL Server Management Studio installation
- SQL Server Data Tools installation
- Test SQL Server connectivity

Introduction

This chapter will cover the basics of how to install SQL Server 2016 to properly go through the examples in this book. The version of SQL Server used through out this book is the Developer edition of SQL Server 2016. It's available for free as long as you subscribe to Visual Studio Dev Essentials.

SQL Server 2016 download

Following are the steps to download and install SQL Server 2016.

Getting ready

You need to have access to the internet for this recipe.

How to do it...

1. Open your browser and paste this link: `https://www.visualstudio.com/dev-es sentials/`. The following page appears in your browser:

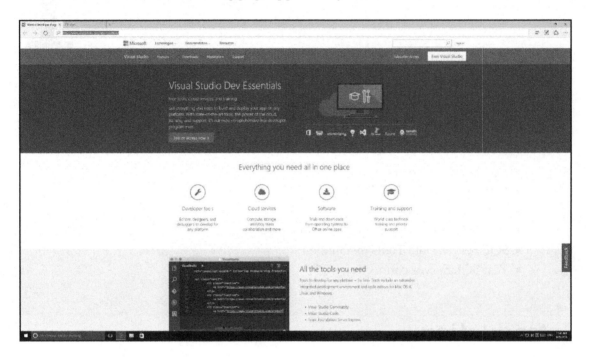

2. Click on **Sign in** visible at the right (top) to log in Visual Studio Dev Essentials. If you don't have an existing subscription, you can create one by clicking on the **Join or access now** button in the middle of the page, as shown in the following screenshot:

3. You are directed to the **My Information** page. Click on **My Benefits** at the top of the page to access the download section as shown in the following screenshot:

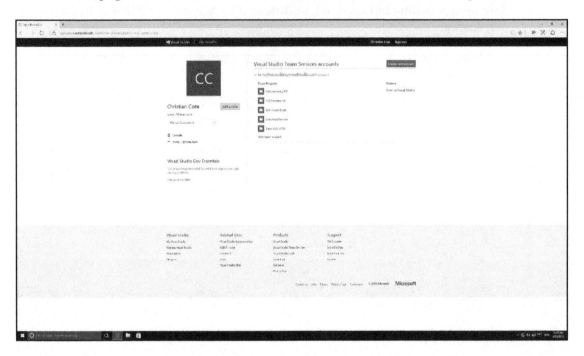

4. Click on the **Download** link in the **Microsoft SQL Server Developer Edition** tile as highlighted in the following screenshot:

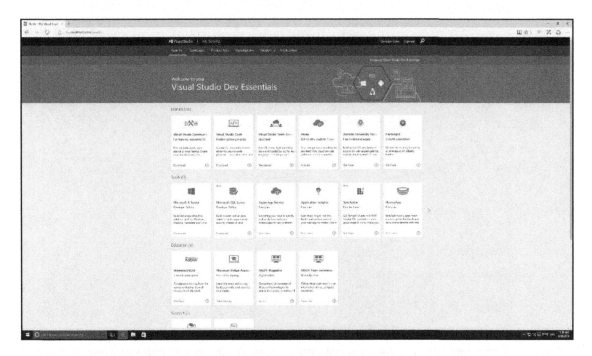

5. This will redirect you to the **SQL Server 2016 Developer Edition** page. Click on the green arrow to start downloading the ISO file as shown in the following screenshot:

6. Due to its pretty large size, the file may take some time to download. The following screenshot is shows 44% done and 10 seconds left to download. This is due to the fact that the file is being downloaded on an Azure VM. It might take longer for you to download it. Depending on your browser, you should see the file downloading as in the following screenshot:

7. Don't mount the ISO file for now. We have to install an external component described in the next section before we proceed with the installation of SQL Server.

Installing JRE for PolyBase

Java Runtime Engine (JRE) is required for PolyBase installations. SQL Server PolyBase is the technology that allows data integration from other sources other than SQL Server tables. PolyBase is used to access data stored in **Hadoop File System (HFS)** or **Windows Azure Storage Blob (WASB)**.

As you will see later in this book, SSIS can now interact with these types of storage natively but having PolyBase handy can save us valuable time in our ETL.

Getting ready

For this recipe you will need to have access to the internet and have administrative rights on your PC to install JRE.

How to do it...

1. To download JRE, follow this link:
   `http://www.oracle.com/technetwork/java/javase/downloads/index.html`.
   You will see the screen shown in the following screenshot:

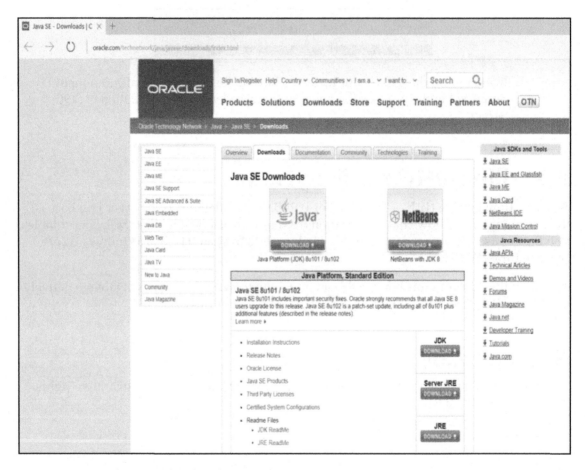

This directs you to the **Java SE Download** at Oracle.

2. Click the download link in the JRE section as shown in the following screenshot:

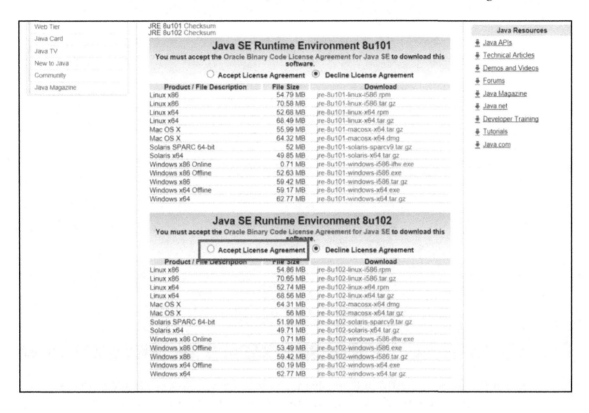

3. You must accept the license agreement to be able to select a file to download. Select **Accept License Agreement** as indicated in the following screenshot:

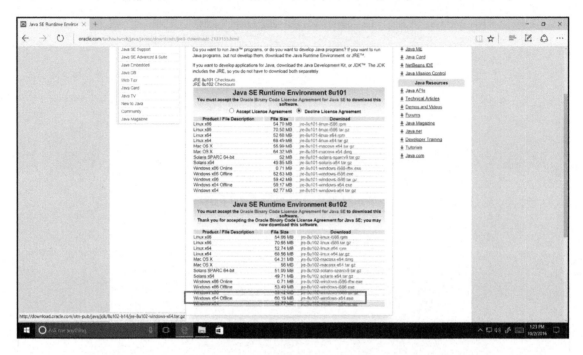

4. Since SQL Server 2016 only exists in a 64-bit version, download the 64-bit JRE. The version of Java SE runtime environment might be different from the one show in the screenshot, which is the one available at the time this book was written:.

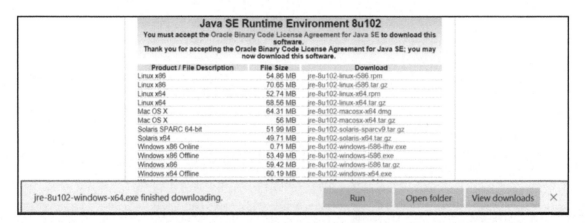

5. Once downloaded, launch the installer. Click on **Run** as shown in Edge browser. Otherwise, go to your `Downloads` folder and double-click on the file you just downloaded (`jre-8U102-windows-x64.exe` in our case); you will see the following window:

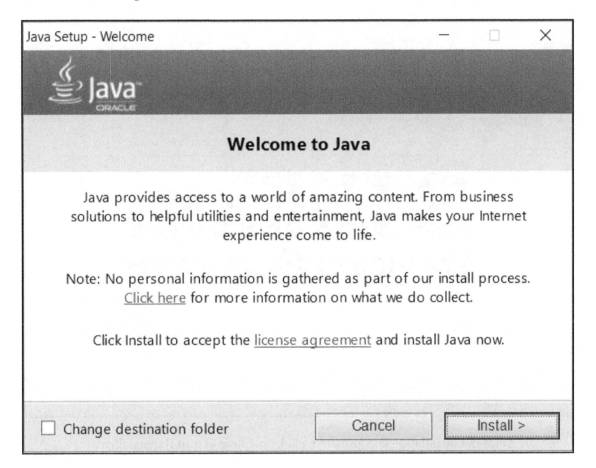

6. The Oracle JRE installation starts. Click on **Install**. The following screen appears. It indicates the progress of the JRE installation.

7. Once the installation is completed, click on **Close** to quit the installer:

You are now ready to proceed to install SQL Server 2016. We'll do that in the next section.

How it works...

Microsoft integrated PolyBase in SQL Server 2016 to connect almost natively to the Hadoop and NoSQL platforms. Here are the technologies it allows us to connect to:

- HDFS (Hortonworks and Cloudera)
- Azure Blob Storage

Since Hadoop is using Java technology, JRE is used to interact with its functionalities.

Installing SQL Server 2016

This section will go through the installation of SQL Server engine, which will host the database objects used throughout this book.

These are the features available for SQL Server setup:

- **Database engine**: It is the core of SQL Server. It manages the various database objects such as tables, views, stored procedures, and so on.
- **Analysis services**: It allows us to create a data semantic layer that eases data consumption by users.
- **Reporting services (native)**: It allow us to create various reports, paginated, mobile, and KPI's for data consumption.
- **Integration services**: It is the purpose of this book, SQL Server data movement service.
- **Management tools**: We'll talk about these in the next section.
- **SQL Server Data Tools**: We'll talk about these in the next section.

Getting ready

This recipe assumes that you have downloaded SQL Server 2016 Developer Edition and you have installed Oracle JRE.

How to do it...

1. The first step is to open the ISO file that you downloaded from the Microsoft Visual Studio Dev Essentials website as described in the *SQL Server 2016 download* recipe. If you're using Windows 7, you'll need to extract the ISO file into a folder. Third-party file compression utilities such as WinRAR, WinZip, or 7-Zip (and there are many more) can handle ISO file decompression. The setup files will be uncompressed in the folder of your choice. In other versions of Windows such as Windows 8.1, Windows 10, or Windows Server 2012 and beyond, simply double-click on the ISO file that you have downloaded previously and a new drive will appear in Windows Explorer.

2. Double-click on the file named `Setup.exe` to start the SQL Server installation utility. The features we're going to install are as follows:

    - **New SQL Server stand-alone installation or adding features to an existing installation**: This will install a local instance (service) of SQL Server on your PC

    - **SQL Server Management Tools**: The tools used to create, query, and manage SQL Server objects

    - **Install SQL Server Data Tools**: This contains Visual Studio templates to develop and deploy SQL Server databases, integration services packages, analysis service cubes, and reporting services

3. From the installation utility, select the **New SQL Server stand-alone installation...** option as shown in the following screenshot. A new SQL Server setup window opens.

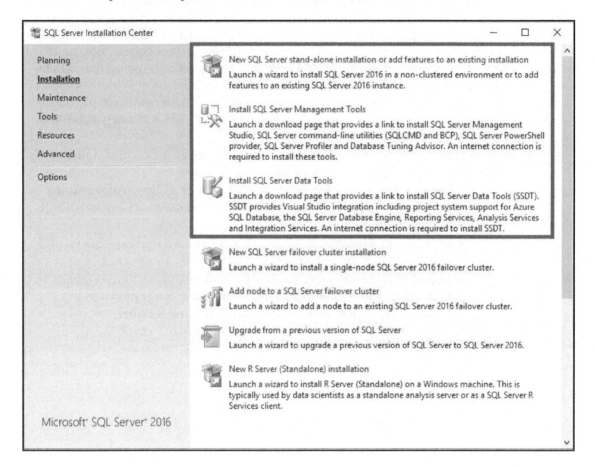

4. The **Product Key** page allows us to specify an edition to install. Since we're going to use the free Developer Edition, click **Next** to go to the next page, as shown in the following screenshot:

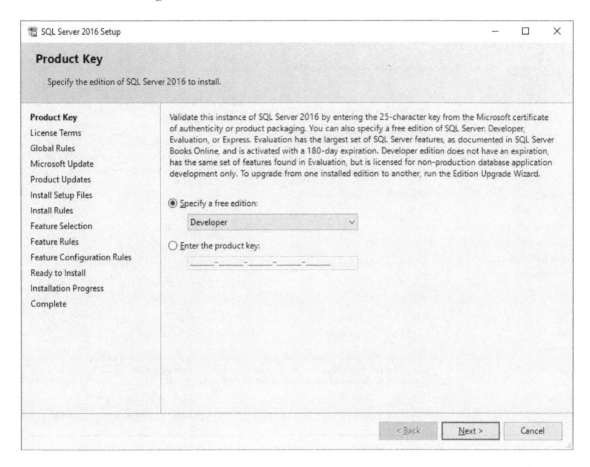

5. Accept the license terms and click **Next** to go to the next page, as shown in the following screenshot:

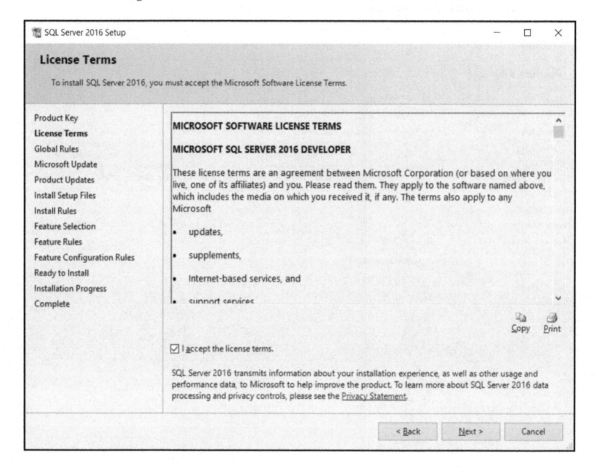

6. In this step, the SQL Server setup will check for product updates and will integrate itself into Windows update checks that are done regularly on your machine. This step is not mandatory but it's better to use the latest code. Check **Use Microsoft Update...** and click **Next**, as shown in the following screenshot:

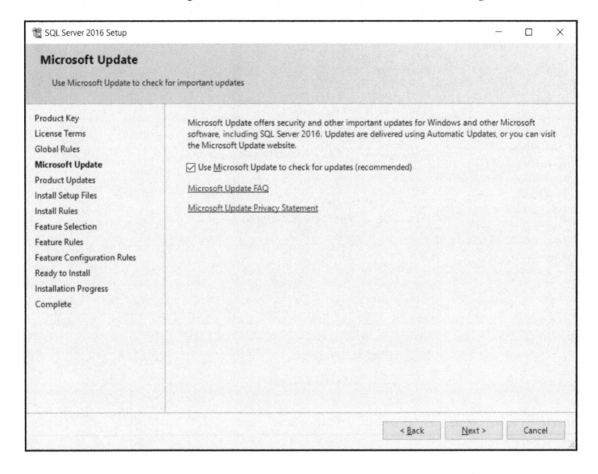

7. Some updates might be found during setup. You can get more information on these updates by clicking the link in the **More Information** column. Click **Next** to install the updates, as shown in the following screenshot:

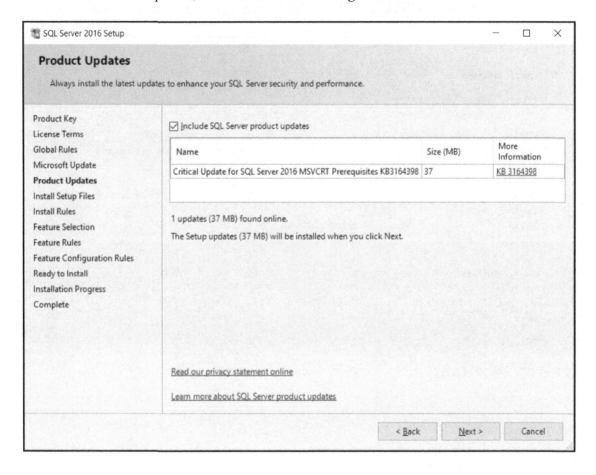

8. This step simply checks to make sure that the latest version of SQL Server is installed. Click **Next** once the setup files are installed, as shown in the following screenshot:

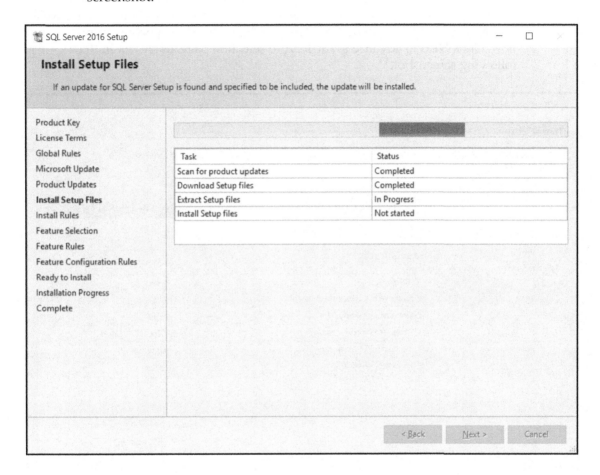

9. SQL Server setup will check several rules to ensure that the computer where we want to install it is setup properly. You might get a warning due to Windows firewall rules. This tells you that the port (1433 by default) is not open and SQL Server won't be available from outside your PC. Don't worry about it. Since we'll be using SQL Server from our PC only, we do not need to open any ports for now. Click **Next** to advance to the feature selection page, as shown in the following screenshot:

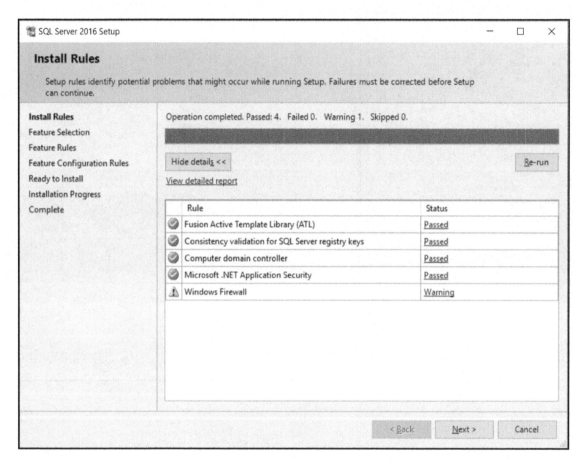

10. Select all features checked in the preceding screenshot and click **Next**, as shown in the following screenshot:

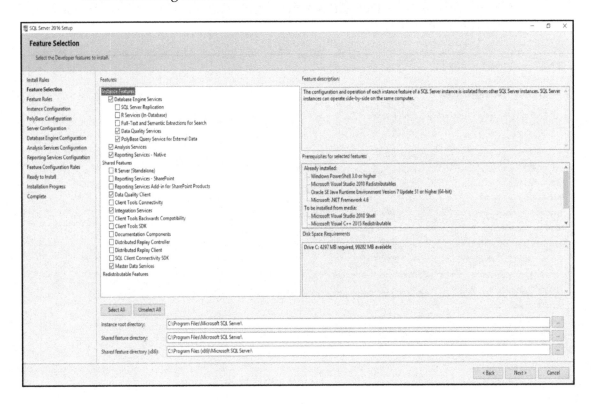

11. Instance configuration allows to specify a name for the SQL Server service. This is done by selecting the **Named instance** radio button. Since we'll only use one SQL Server instance, leave **Default instance** selected and click **Next**, as shown in the following screenshot:

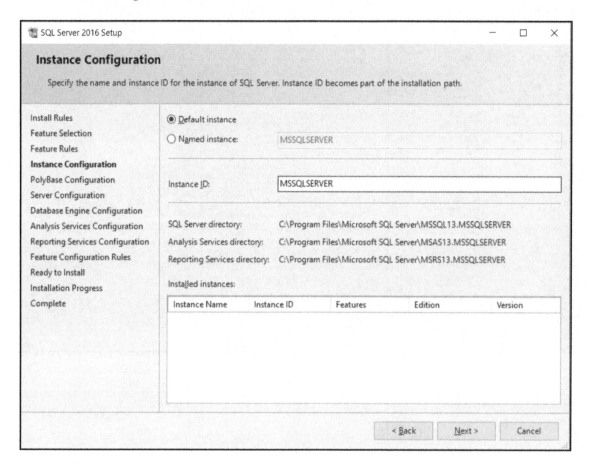

12. This page allows SQL Server to be part of a PolyBase scale out group. Since we're only setting up SQL Server PolyBase to be used by one instance, leave the default **Use this SQL Server as standalone PolyBase-enabled instance** and click **Next**, as shown in the following screenshot:

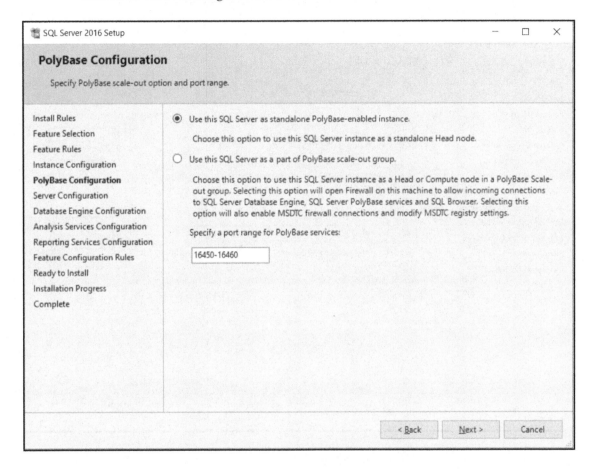

13. Now for server configuration. This step allows us to specify distinct or specific service accounts. Since we're installing SQL Server on a single development machine, we'll use the default accounts, as shown in the following screenshot:

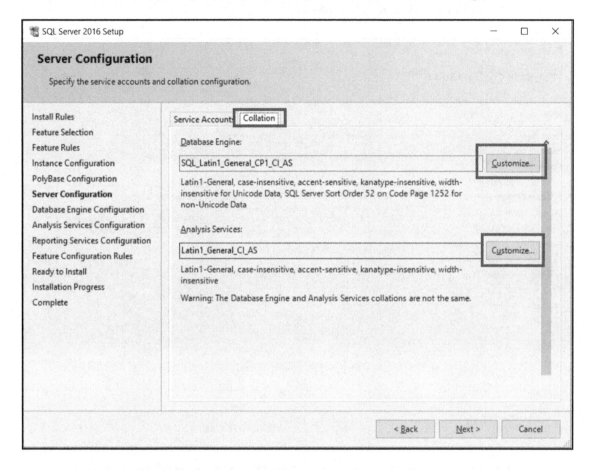

14. Click on the **Collation** tab as highlighted on the preceding screenshot. The default collation used by SQL server is SQL Latin1_General_CP1_CI_AS. This is a legacy collation. The choice of the collation is important for character string columns. The latest (fewer bugs) collation is Latin1_General_100. The last characters CI and AS are for case-insensitive and accent-sensitive, respectively.

15. We'll change the collation defaults. Click **Customize...** at the end of SQL Latin1_General_CP1_CI_AI, as shown in the following screenshot:

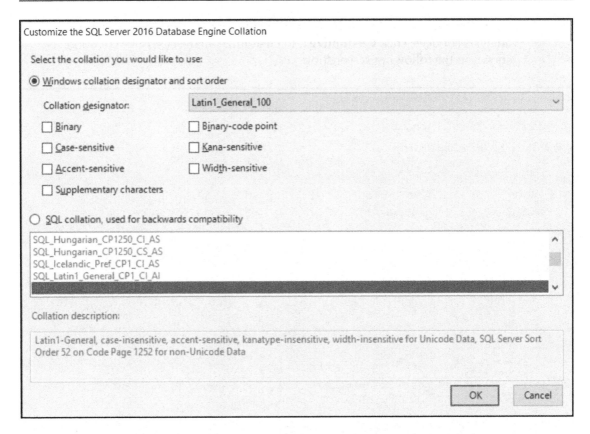

16. As stated previously, we'll use the Windows collation designator `Latin1_General_100`. Uncheck **Accent-sensitive**. This allows SQL Server to sort character columns without using accentuated characters. For example, suppose that our application has a `FirstName` column and we have the following first names:
    - `Joel`
    - `Joël`

17. If we query SQL Server filtering on `FirstName = 'Joel'` with the **Accent-sensitive** collation option, we end up retrieving the value `Joel` only. If we do not select the **Accent-sensitive** collation option, we will get both values.

18. Click **OK** when done to return to the previous screen. We'll do the same for analysis services; click **Customize...** to customize analysis service collation, as shown in the following screenshot:

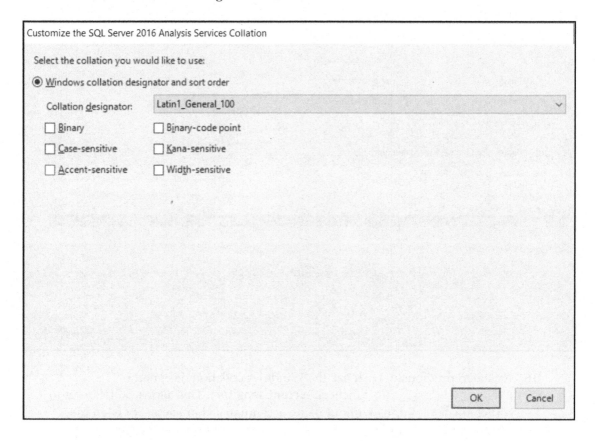

19. Again, choose `Latin1_General_100` in Collation designator and uncheck the **Accent-sensitive** checkbox. Click **OK** to return to the previous screen. Click on **Next**, as shown in the following screenshot:

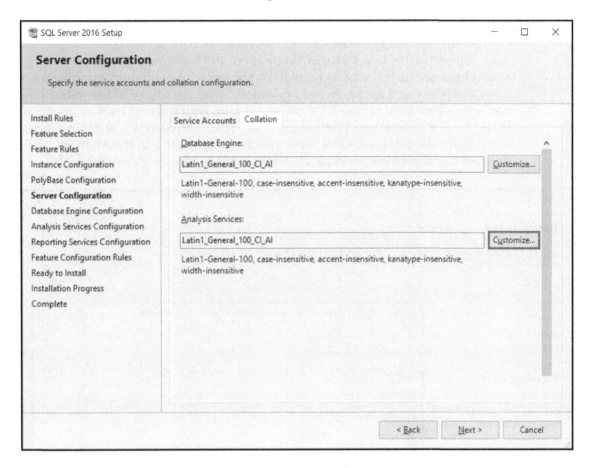

20. This will direct you to the following screen. For the database engine configuration, we'll use **Mixed Mode** to allow us to use SQL Server logins and Windows logins. The default authentication is **Windows authentication mode**, which is more secure than SQL Server authentication because it uses the Kerberos security protocol, password, and account lockout policies, and password expiration. Make sure you use strong passwords for SQL Server logins. By default, password policy, password expiration, and user must change password at next login are turned on also for SQL Server login. You should not disable the password policy and the password expiration. Select the **Mixed Mode** radio box and enter a password for the SA account. Click on **Add Current User** as shown in the screenshot to add your Windows account as an administrator of the instance. You'll have all rights on it. Click **Next**, which will direct you to the **Analysis Services Configuration** window, as shown in the following screenshot:

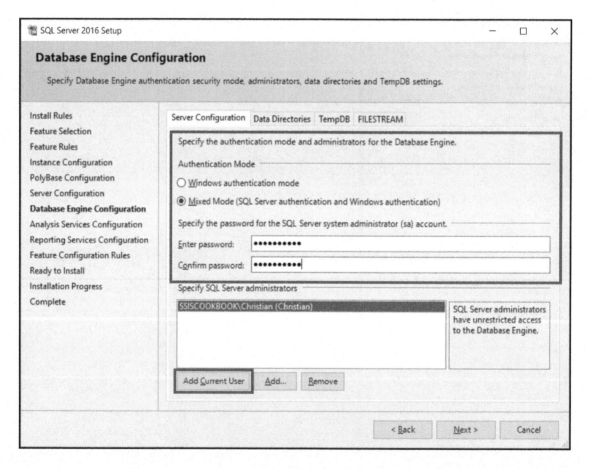

21. For analysis services configuration, the **Server Mode** we'll use is **Tabular Mode** and again click on **Add Current User** as shown in the following screenshot to add your Windows account as an administrator of the service. Click **Next.**

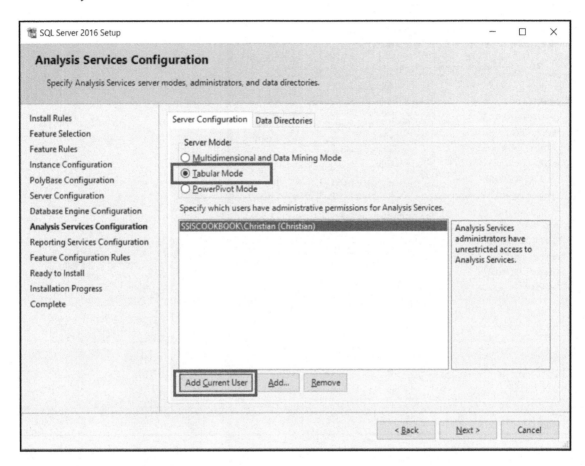

22. For the Reporting services configuration, leave the default values and click **Next**, as shown in the following screenshot:

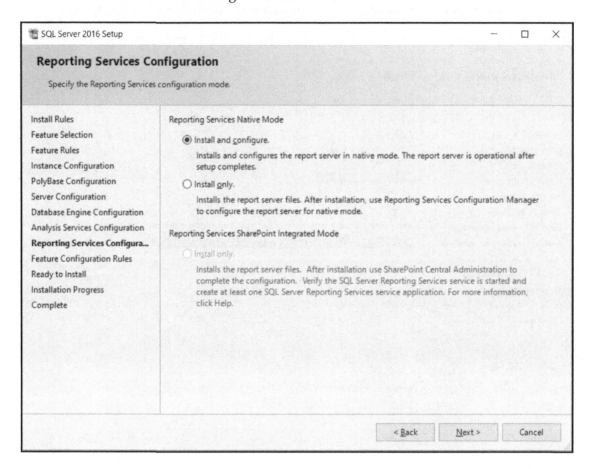

23. We're finally ready to install. Click **Install** to start the installation process, as shown in the following screenshot:

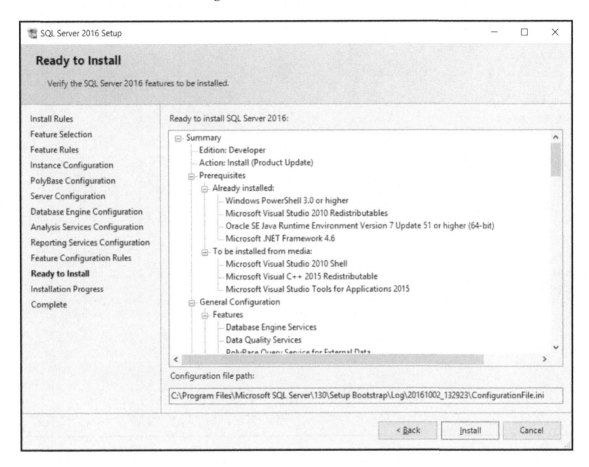

24. The following screenshot shows the installation progress:

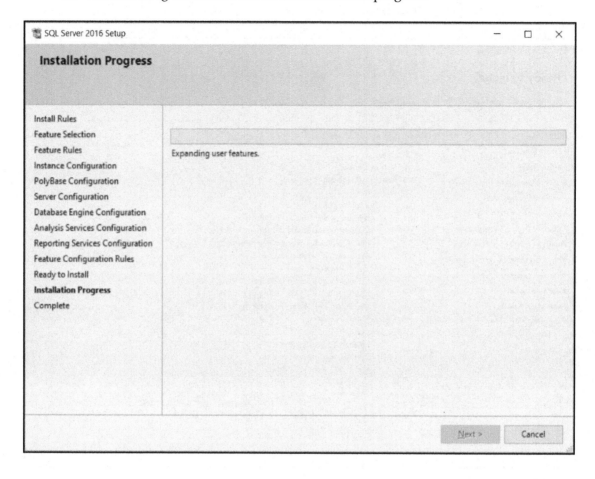

25. Once the installation is complete, you get the following screen:

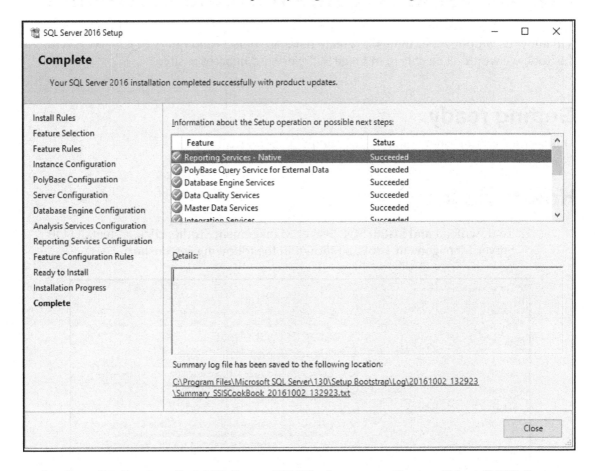

We're done. We just installed SQL Server 2016! In the next section, we'll install SQL Server Management Studio.

The number, the order, and the appearance of the setup screens change slightly with every version of SQL Server, or even with a service pack. If you encounter a new screen not mentioned here, just use the default settings and proceed with the installation.

SQL Server Management Studio installation

SQL Server Management Studio is a separate download from SQL Server. This program will allow us, among other things, to create database objects and query SQL Server. Without this tool, we wouldn't be able to manage SQL Server databases easily.

Getting ready

This section assumes that you have installed SQL Server 2016.

How to do it...

1. To download and install SQL Server Management Studio, click on Install SQL Server Management Tools, as shown in the following screenshot:

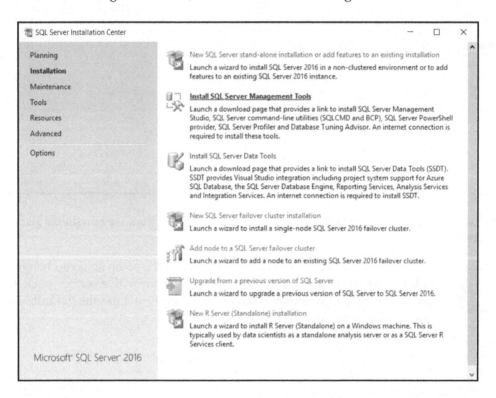

2. The SSMS download page opens in your browser. Click **Download SQL Server Management Studio** (the latest version) to start the download process. Once downloaded, run the installation as shown in the following screenshot:

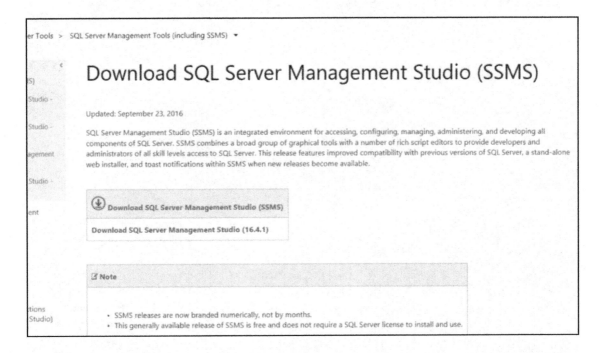

3. Click **Install**, as shown in the following screenshot:

4. This will direct you to the Microsoft SQL Server Management Studio installation screen as follows. The installation is in progress; it may take several minutes to complete.

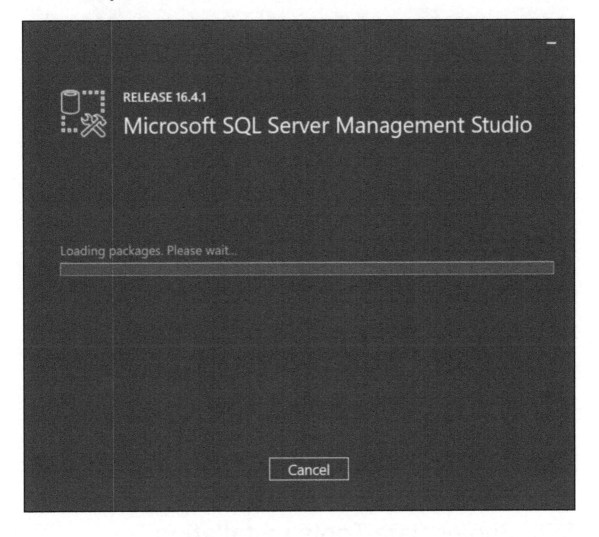

5. Click **Close** to close the installation wizard, as shown in the following screenshot:

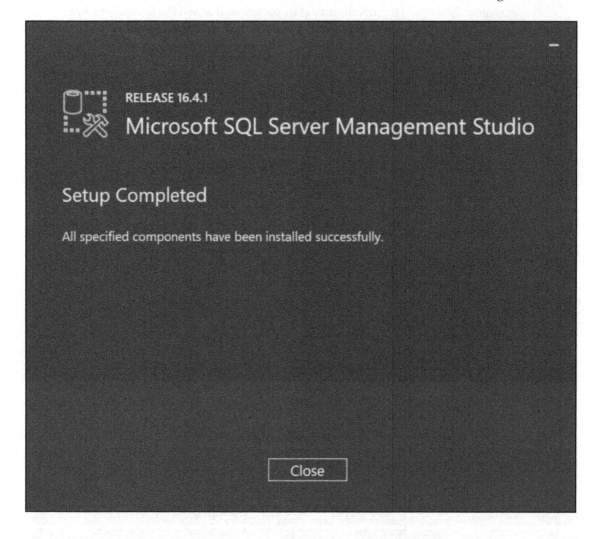

SQL Server Data Tools installation

The last part of our SQL Server 2016 setup is to install SQL Server Data Tools. This will install a Visual Studio Shell that contains BI templates necessary for the following:

- SQL Server integration services
- SQL Server analysis services

- SQL Server reporting services
- Database object management

Getting ready

We'll use SSDT throughout this book to create, deploy, and maintain our SSIS packages and some databases.

How to do it...

1. From the SQL Server 2016 setup utility, click on **SQL Server Data Tools (SSDT)**. This will open the **Download SQL Server Data Tools (SSDT)** download page in your browser as shown in the following screenshot:

Here, there are two choices:

> **Install SSDT only**: This is the simplest scenario. It only installs SSDT and a development shell.

Install Visual Studio and SSDT: You choose this if you plan to use source control inside Visual Studio or when you want to implement different types of development (.NET, Python, and so on) such as SSIS/SSAS/SSRS development. Since we'll talk about custom components in this book, we'll install Visual Studio Community Edition. This version is free for individuals.

2. Click on the **Download Visual Studio Community 2015** link to download the Visual Studio installer.

3. Once downloaded, click on **Run** to launch the Visual Studio installer.

4. Accept the default installation type and click **Install** to start the installation process. This will give you the following window:

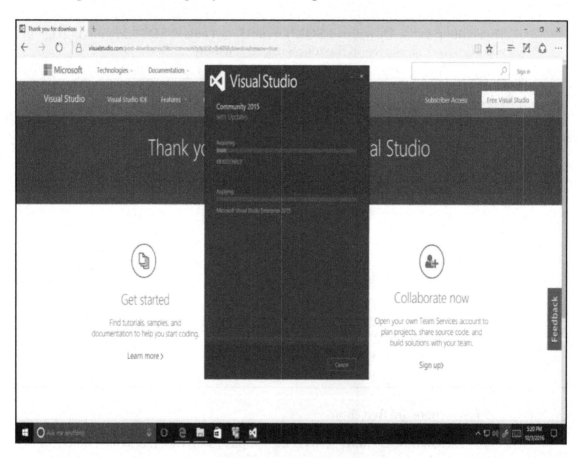

5. Once the installation is completed, since we haven't installed SSDT, don't launch Visual Studio yet. Close this window. We'll install SQL Server Data Tools first. Return to the browser window and click **Download SQL Server Data Tools for Visual Studio 2015** as shown in the following screenshot:

6. This will direct you to the SSDT download screen shown as follows:

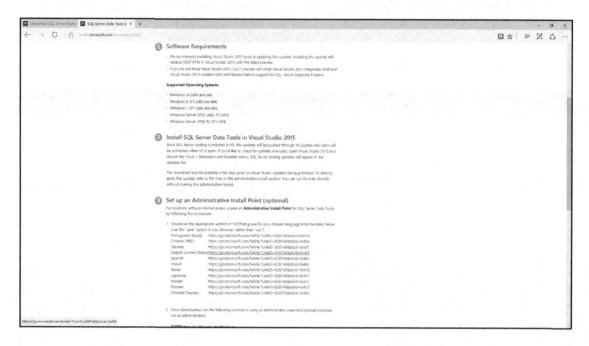

7. From the browser page that opens, choose **English (United States)**. The SSDT setup executable file download starts. Since it's a small file, it takes only a few seconds to download. Once the download completes, click **Run** or double-click on the newly downloaded file to start SSDT installation. Accept the defaults and click **Next** to proceed to the next step, as shown in the following screenshot:

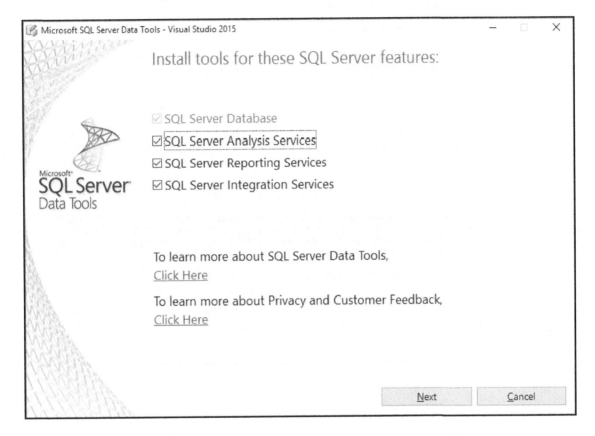

8. Accept the license agreement by checking the **I agree to the license terms and conditions** and click **Install**, as shown in the following screenshot:

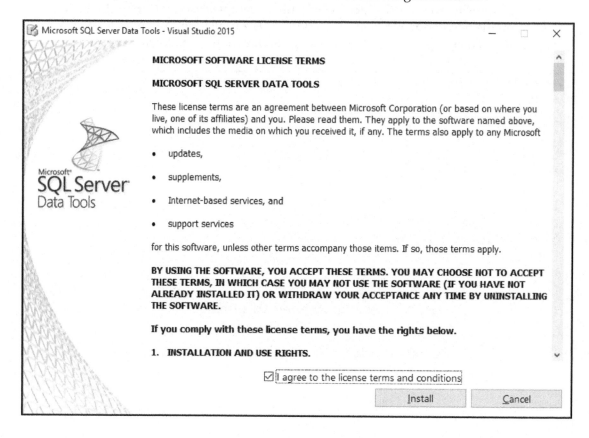

9. The SSDT installer will download the necessary files and proceed to the installation, as shown in the following screenshot:

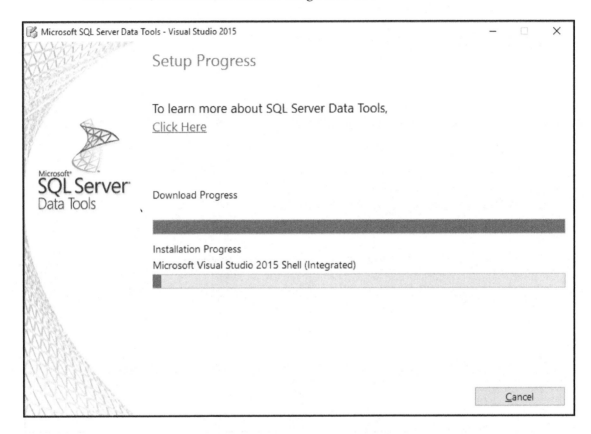

10. Once the installation completes, you might have to restart your computer. If that's the case, restart it, as shown in the following screenshot. Once that's done, look for SQL Server Data Tools in your Start menu and launch it.

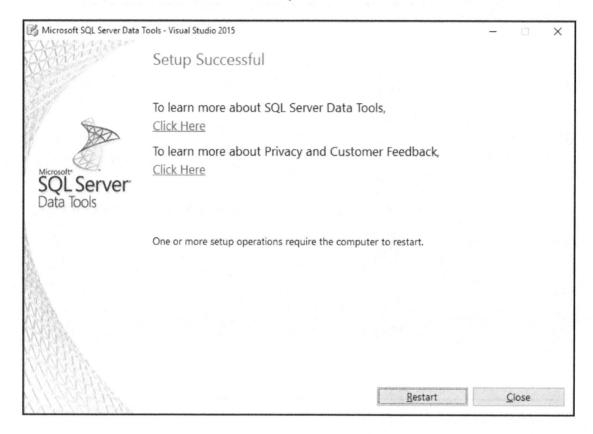

11. From the **File** menu, select **New Project**. Once the **New Project** window appears, you will see **Business Intelligence** in the project templates, as shown in the following screenshot:

12. Close SSDT; we're done with it for now.

Testing SQL Server connectivity

SQL Server Management Studio has been installed in this chapter in the *SQL Server Management Studio installation* recipe. We'll now test whether we're able to connect to our local instance.

Getting ready

This recipe assumes that you have successfully installed SQL Server 2016 Developer Edition as well as SQL Server Management Studio.

How to do it...

1. Look for SQL Server Management Studio in your Start menu and launch it.
2. Once the application opens, you should see your PC's name in the **Server Name** field. Click on **Connect**. SSMS will now connect to your local SQL Server instance, as shown in the following screenshot:

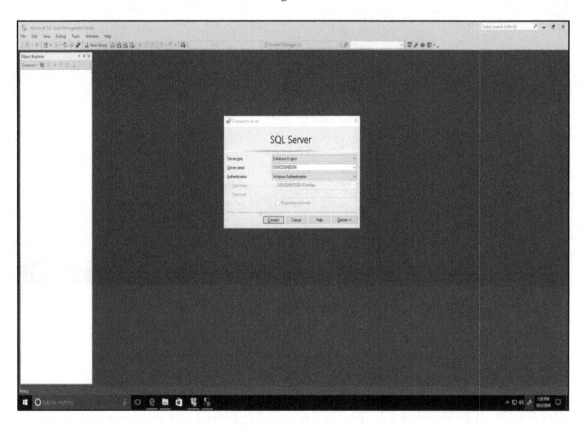

3. You are now able to connect to your local SQL Server instance, and we're now ready to begin work! You will get the following screen:

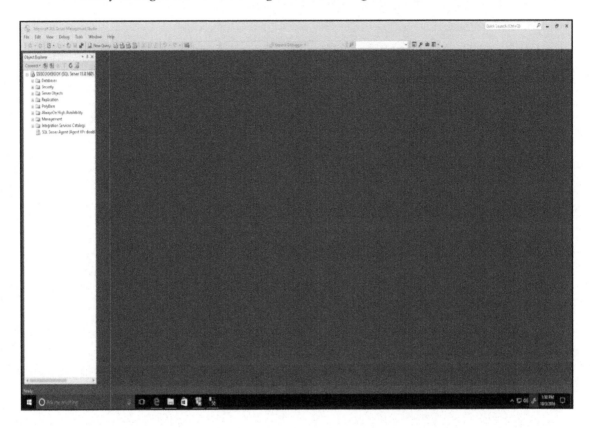

2

What Is New in SSIS 2016

This chapter will cover the following recipes:

- Creating an SSIS Catalog
- Custom logging
- Azure tasks and transforms
- Incremental package deployment
- Multiple version support
- Error column name
- Control flow templates

Introduction

The 2016 release of SQL Server Integration Services is a major revision of the software. But, instead of being a complete re-write of the product, it's more an evolution of the product. Here is the SSIS timeline since its beginning in SQL Server 7.0 (1998):

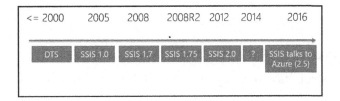

In the early years of SQL Server, Microsoft introduced a tool to help developers and **database administrator (DBA)** to interact with the data: **Data Transformation Services (DTS)**. The tool was very primitive compared to SSIS and it mostly relied on ActiveX and T-SQL to transform the data. SSIS V1.0 (2005) appeared in 2005. The tool was a game changer in the ETL world at the time. It was a professional and (pretty much) reliable tool for 2005. 2008/2008 R2 versions were much the same as 2005 in the sense that they didn't add much functionality, but they made the tool more scalable.

In 2012, Microsoft enhanced SSIS in many ways. They rewrote the package XML to ease source control integration and make the package code easier to read. They also greatly enhanced the way packages are deployed by using an SSIS Catalog in SQL Server. Having the catalog in SQL Server gives us execution reports and many views that allow us access to metadata or metaprocess information in our projects.

Version 2014 didn't have anything for SSIS. Version 2016 brought other set of features, as you will see in the remainder of this chapter. We now also have the ability to integrate with big data, which we'll talk about in some later sections of the book.

Creating SSIS Catalog

This section will walk you through the various steps to create an SSIS Catalog in SSMS. As mentioned before, the SSIS Catalog contains information about the package components and their execution. As we will see later in the book, SSIS projects are deployed into this catalog. It can be easily queried for custom reports as well, allowing us to create SSIS executions using T-SQL. This is very useful for on-demand executions of SSIS packages.

SSIS versions prior to 2012 did not have these capabilities since the catalog appeared with 2012. It is still possible to bypass the deployment to an SSIS Catalog by using a special mode: the *package deployment model*. This is mostly used for backward compatibility with previous SSIS frameworks.

Getting ready

This section assumes you have already installed **SQL Server Management Studio (SSMS)**.

How to do it...

1. We'll first create the SSIS Catalog in SSMS. Open SSMS and connect to your local instance:

2. Look for the `Integration Services Catalogs` folder in **object explorer**.
3. Right-click on it and select the option **Create Catalog....**

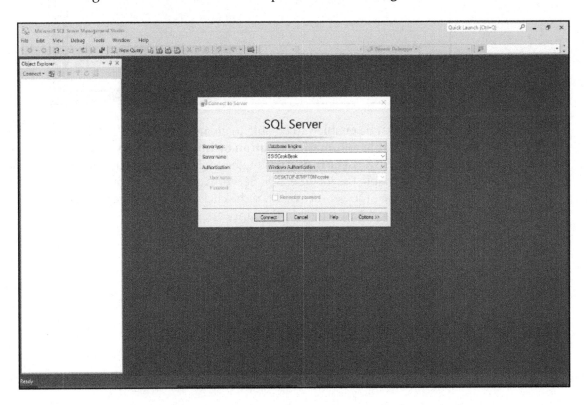

4. If the **Create Catalog...** option is not available (disabled - greyed out), it means that a catalog has already been created. Even if the folder is called `Integration Services Catalogs` - plural, only one Integration Services Catalog can be created by the SQL Server instance. The **Create Catalog** dialog box appears:

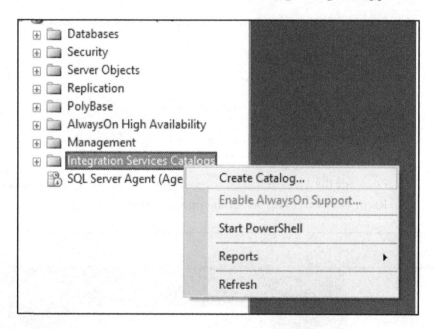

5. SQL Server CLR must be enabled to be able to create a catalog. It's also a good practice to check **Enable automatic execution of Integration Services stored procedures at SQL Server startup**. This creates a job that cleans up the SSIS Calalog tables. To enable the job, the SQL Server Agent must be enabled and started. To enable the SQL Server Agent, right-click on **SQL Server Agent** and select **Start** from the contextual menu that appears.

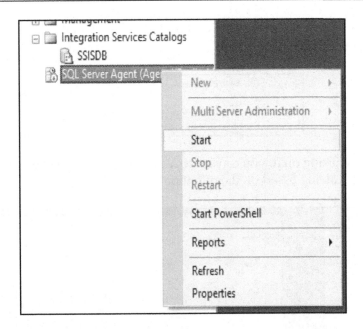

6. A confirmation screen appears to confirm that we want to start the Agent:

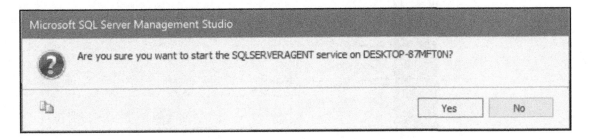

7. Once the Agent has successfully started, we can see in the `Jobs` folder a job called **SSIS Server Maintenance Job**:

8. Double-clicking on it, you can see that this job is running every day to clean up the SSIS Catalog based on the retention window:

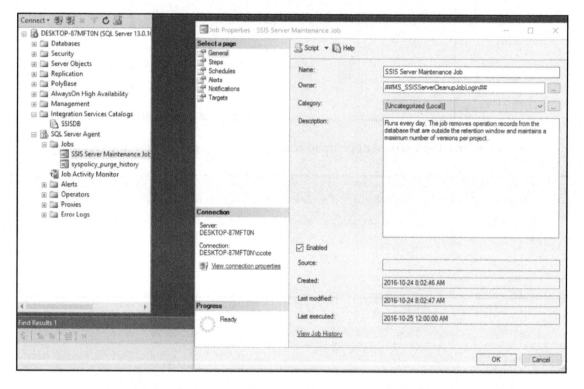

9. By default, the retention window is set to 365 days. We don't have to change it for the recipes we're going to implement from this book. But you should adjust the retention window setting to ensure that the catalog doesn't get filled with too many execution logs.

10. One of the benefits of this job is to execute clean up log entries in the catalog. As all executions are logged (we'll talk about logging in a later section), the catalog tables can fill up fast.

11. To manage the retention window, in SSMS object explorer right-click on the catalog (SSISDB) and select **Properties** from the drop-down menu. The following window appears:

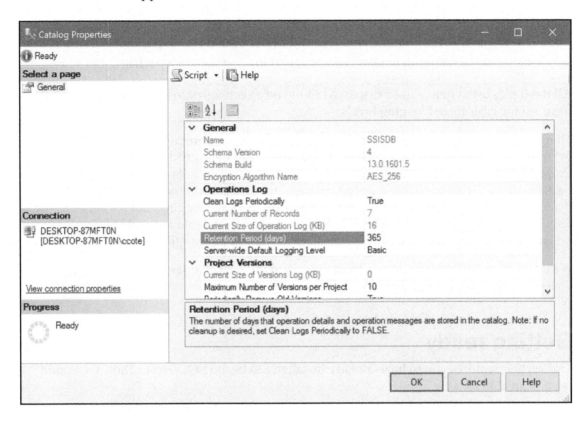

12. You can now modify the **Retention Period (days)** property, as shown in the preceding screenshot. Notice that you also have the ability to stop the clean logs schedule by setting the **Clean Logs Periodically** to **False**.

Custom logging

This section will talk about various loggings and how we can customize logging to suit our needs in terms of logging information. The reason why we need logging is because we want to retrieve some information on our package executions.

Here are some examples of logging info we might be interested in getting:

- How much time it took to execute a specific package
- How many rows have been transferred from one transform to another in our data flows
- What were the warnings or errors that were issued by the package execution
- The new values that have been assigned to a variable in a package, and so on

All the topics listed here will be discussed in the next sections of the book. For now, we'll focus on the customized logging levels.

There are various ways that we can log package execution information in SSIS. In versions prior to 2012 (or if we opt for a **Package Deployment Mode** instead of the default one, the **Project Deployment Mode**), the only way to enable logging was to enable it in each package. If we forgot to enable it in one package, the latter would not log anything. The default Project Deployment Mode can also log using package logging, but it's better to use SSIS Catalog logging, since it's integrated with projects once deployed and SSIS built-in execution reports will use it to display package execution information.

We'll talk about the various deployment models in the next chapter, Chapter 3, *Key Components of a Modern ETL Solution*.

Getting ready

This section requires you to have already installed SSMS and SQL Server Data Tools, and created an SSIS Catalog.

How to do it...

1. We'll start SQL Server Management Studio and connect to our local instance. We'll then expand the Integration Services Catalogs:

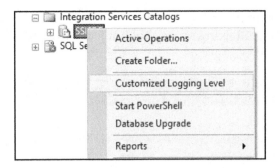

2. The following screen appears. Click on the **Create** button to create a custom logging level:

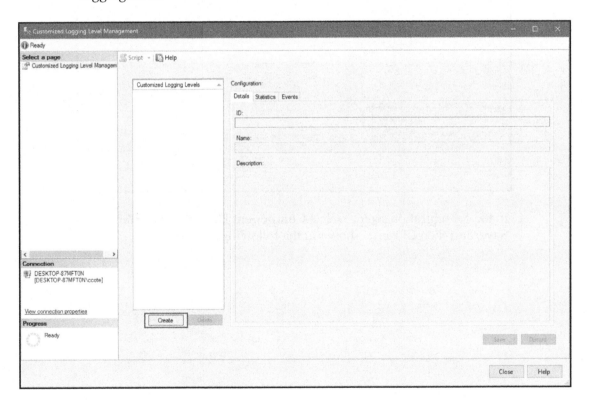

3. The **Create Customized Logging Level** screen appears. Set the various properties as shown in the following screenshot but leave the **Create from existing logging level** unchecked:

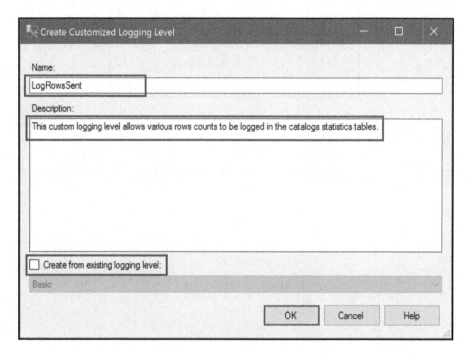

4. In the configuration screen, select **Component Data Volume Statistics**, click **Save,** and then **Close,** as shown in the following screenshot:

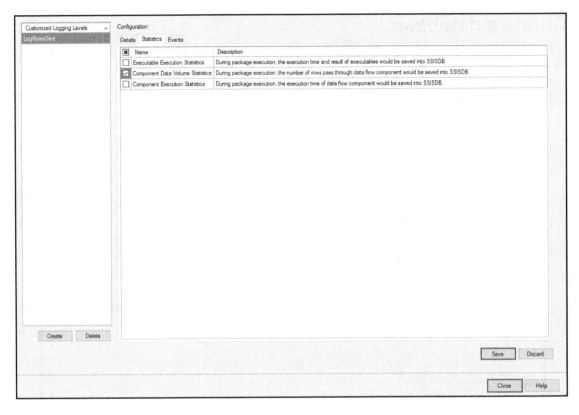

That's it for now! We have created our custom logging level.

How it works...

Using logging while executing our SSIS packages creates entries in the SSIS Catalog table called `execution_data_statistics` in the `internal` schema. This table is meant to record data movement statistics in SSIS packages.

We never use tables in the internal schema, as they are seen as system tables. That's the reason we use the view `[catalog].[ execution_data_statistics]` instead.

There's more...

Creating our logging level in SSMS will allow us to use it when our SSIS project will be deployed in the SSIS Catalog. We'll do that in the next recipe, *Azure tasks and transforms*; we'll create a simple SSIS package that will use this logging level when we execute it.

Create a database

This recipe, like many others in this book, requires a database to be created. It can be done by using SQL Server Management Studio. Start SSMS, connect to your local instance and right-click on the database folder. From the contextual menu, choose **New Database...**. The following window appears:

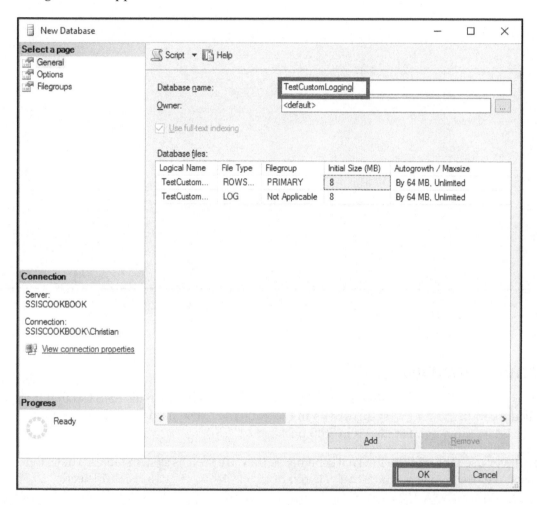

Fill in the **Database name** and click **OK** as we don't need to change the **Owner** and **Database files** information. You should now see the database under the Databases folder in SSMS. We're now ready to create an SSIS package that'll use it.

Create a simple project

This recipe will show you how to create an SSIS project to be able to use the custom logging level that we just created in the previous part of the recipe.

First, start SQL Server Data Tools and create a new Integration Services project: **File** | **New** | **Integration Services Project**. The following screenshot suggests how the project can be named:

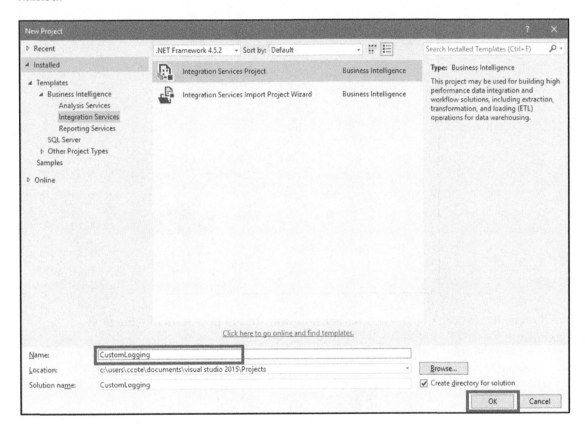

Once the project has been created, we should see a package called `Package.dtsx`. We'll right-click on it and select **Rename,** as shown in the following screenshot:

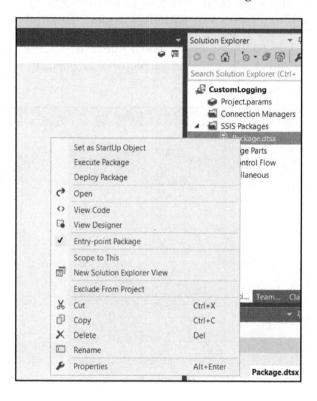

We'll name it `CustomLogging.dtsx`. The solution should now look like the next screenshot:

We will now add a **Data Flow Task** in our package. A **Data FlowTask** is a container that will allow us to do data transformations. Its toolbox has a rich set of data transformation tools.

From the **SSIS Toolbox**, drag a **Data Flow Task** to the package's control flow as shown in the following screenshot:

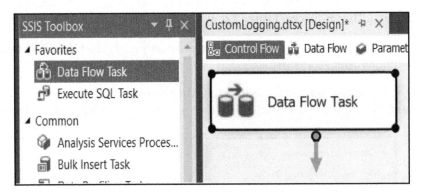

Rename the **Data Flow Task** dft_dbo_CustomLogging, as shown in the following screenshot:

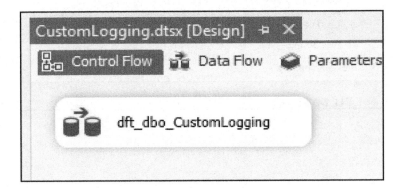

In the next chapter, we'll talk about the way we name our SSIS tasks and transforms.

In the next few steps, we'll start customizing our SSIS toolbox. Double-click on the `dft_dbo_CustomLogging` **Data Flow Task** to go into it.

Throughout the book, we'll often customize the **SSIS Toolbox** to suit our needs. You'll notice that the toolbox has sections such as: **Favorites**, Common, Azure (this will be covered in the next recipe), **Other Sources**, **Other Transforms**, and **Other Destinations**.

For now, we remove the source and destination assistants and add **OLE DB Source** and destination to the favorites transforms:

1. In the **SSIS Toolbox**, scroll down to **Other Sources** and right-click on **OLE DB Source**. From the contextual menu that appears, select **Move to Favorites**.

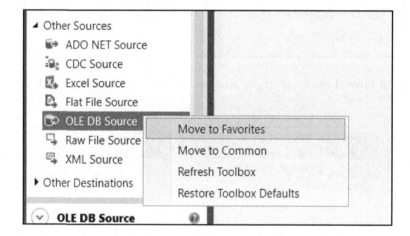

2. Next, scroll down again to **Other Destinations**, right-click on **OLE DB Destination**, and select **Move to Favorites** as shown in the following screenshot:

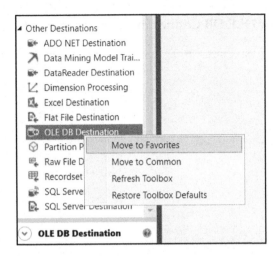

3. Now scroll up to the **Favorites** group at the top. We'll remove the source and destination assistants from the **Favorites**. As the following screenshot demonstrates, right-click on the **Destination Assistant** and select **Move to Other Destinations**. Repeat the same process for the **Source Assistant**:

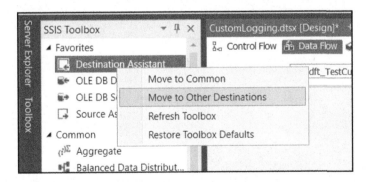

4. Repeat same process for the **Source Assistant**. We'll move it to the **Other Sources** group.

5. Now, we're ready to create a connection manager. We'll use it to read or insert data into the `TestCucstomLogging` database that we created earlier. As shown in the following screenshot, right-click in the **Connection Managers** area and select **New OLE DB Connection** from the menu that appears.

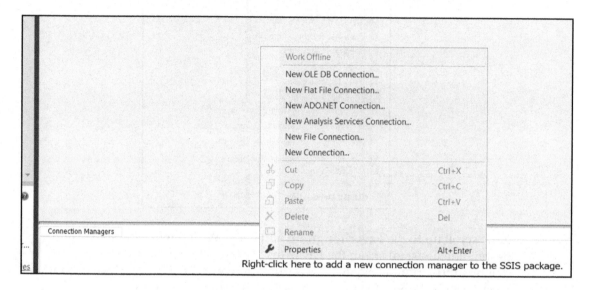

6. Click on **New** in the **Configure OLE DB Connection** window that appears and the following screen will appear. Set the **Server Name** to the name of your machine or the named instance you might have chosen when you set up SQL Server. Select `TestCustomlogging` as the **Database Name**. The following screenshot shows the two properties set up for my PC. Click **OK** once finished.

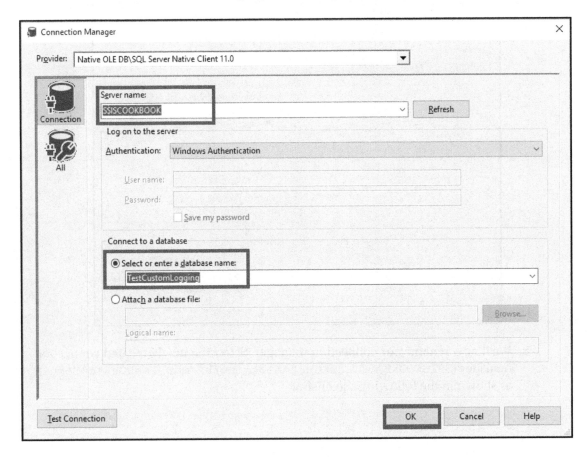

7. You're back on click **OK** in **the Configure OLE DB Connection Manager** window as shown in the following screenshot:

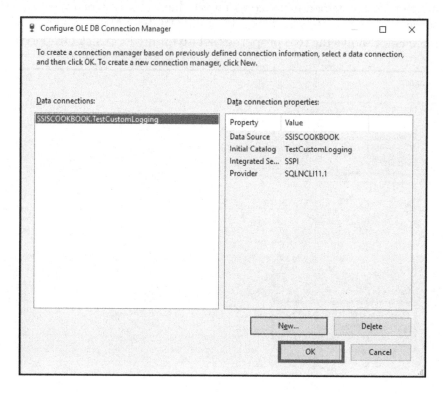

8. We'll now rename our connection manager. Select the newly created connection manager (SSISCOOKBOOK TestCustomLogging) to cmgr_TestCustomLogging as shown in the following screenshot:

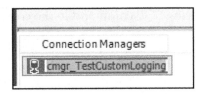

9. Now, from the favorite section of the SSIS toolbox, drag and drop an OLEDB source on the surface of the **Data Flow**. Now, as shown in the following screenshot, rename it to `ole_src_SELECT_1`. Double-click on it to get to the **OLE DB Source Editor** window. Set the **OLE DB connection manager** to `cmgr_TestCustomLogging` as demonstrated in the screenshot. Set the **Data access mode** to **SQL command**.

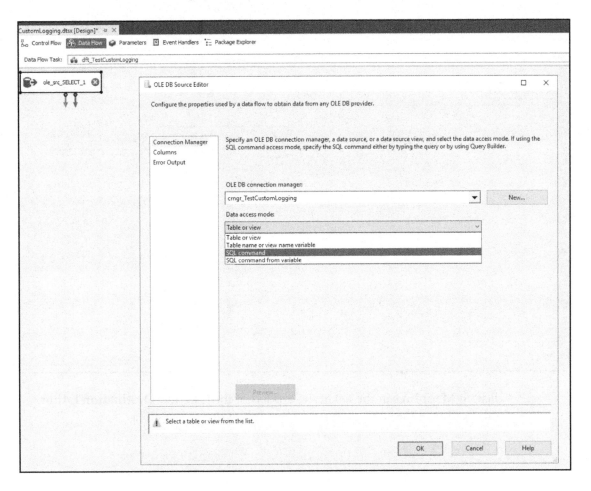

10. Now, enter the following SQL command in the command text and click on **OK**:

```
SELECT 1 AS LogID
UNION ALL
SELECT 2 AS LogID
```

11. Again, from the **Favorites** section of the **SSIS Toolbox**, drag an **OLE DB Destination** in the **Data Flow**. Connect the source to the destination and rename the **OLE_DB Destination** ole_dst_dbo_CustomLogging. Double-click on it, assign the **OLEDB connection manager** property, and click **OK** on the **New** button at the right of the name of the table or the view property. The Create Table window appears. Modify the command as shown in the following screenshot and click on **OK**:

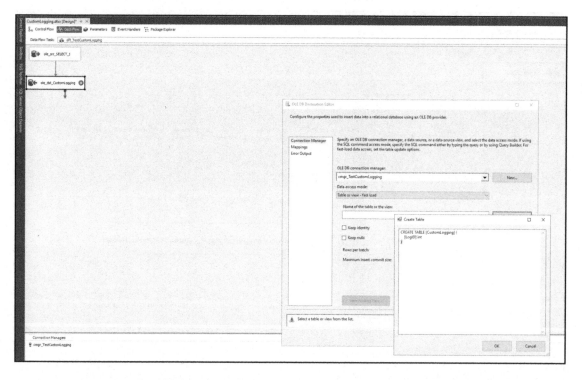

12. Click on **Mappings** in the list at the top left of the **OLE DB Destination Editor**. You should get the same screen as in the following screenshot:

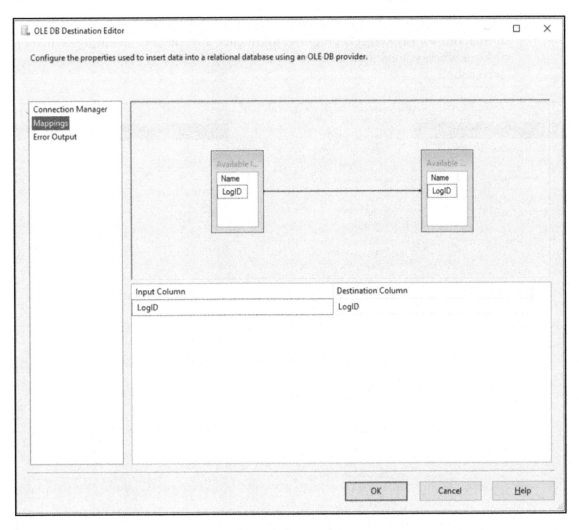

13. Click on **OK** to close the **OLE DB Destination Editor**.

14. Now, we'll bring in the **Layout** toolbar. We'll use it throughout this book to format our package objects properly. Right-click anywhere in an empty section of the quick access toolbar and select **Layout**, as highlighted in the following screenshot:

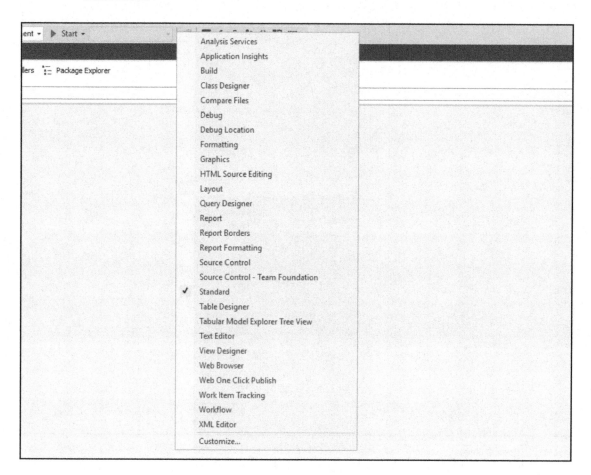

15. Now, from the **Edit** menu, select **Select All** or press *Ctrl + A* to select the entire Data Flow content. In the **Layout** toolbar, click on the *, **Make Same Width** button, as shown in the following screenshot:

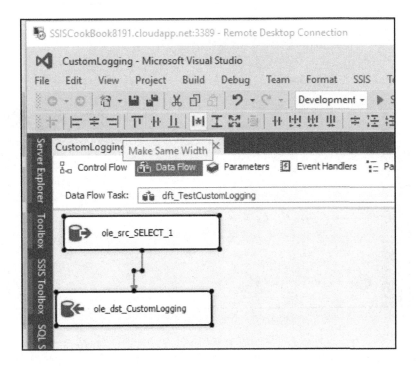

16. From the menu, select **Auto Layout | Diagram**. This will format the data flow objects, as shown in the following screenshot:

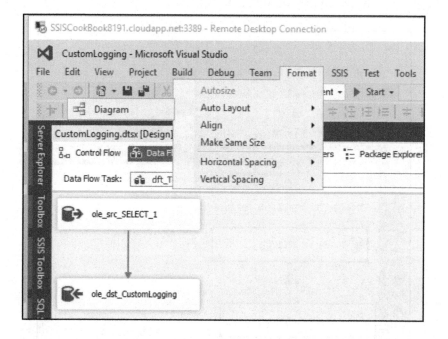

17. Now, right-click anywhere in the data flow task background and select **Execute Task** from the contextual menu that appears. The data flow should execute successfully as follows.

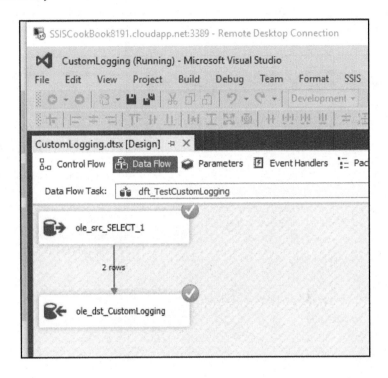

18. Now, we're ready to deploy our project to the SSIS Catalog that we created at the beginning of the chapter, in the recipe *Creating an SSIS Catalog*. Right-click on the CustomLogging project in the **Solution Explorer** at the top right of SSDT and hit **Deploy**. The project deployment wizard starts, as shown in the following screenshot:

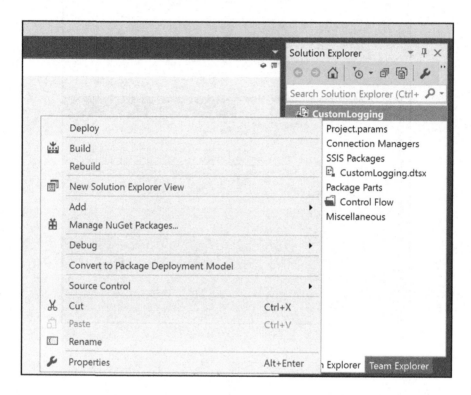

19. The first page explains the step performed by the wizard. Check **Do not show this page again** as in the following screenshot if you want to skip this step in future deployments of the project or individual packages, as we'll see later in this chapter.

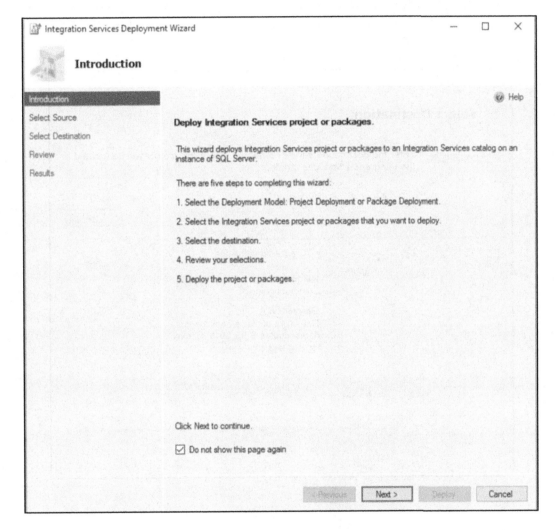

20. The wizard is now asking for an SSIS Catalog and folder. Since we don't have any folder yet in the catalog, we'll create one called CustomLogging, as shown in the following screenshot:
    1. Select the **Server name** by clicking on the **Browse** button. Select your machine name from the list and click on **OK**.

2. The **Path** property specifies where the project will be deployed in the SSIS Catalog. To assign a path to the project deployment, click on **Browse** at the right of it. The **Browse for Folderor Project** window appears. We're going to create a folder for our project. Click on **New folder**. From the **Create New Folder** window that appears, fill the text boxes as shown in the following screenshot. Click **OK** to save and close the window.

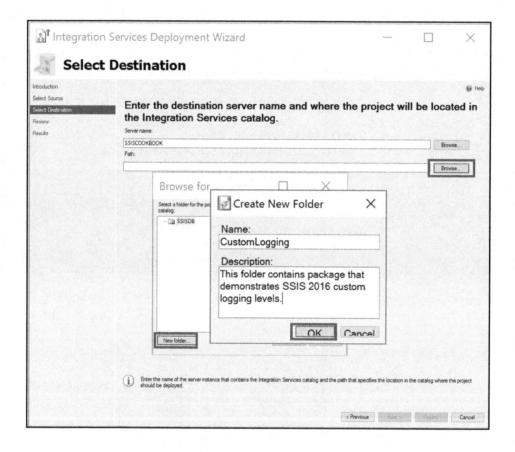

21. Your screen will look like the following screenshot. Click **OK** again to close the **Browse for Folder or Project** window.

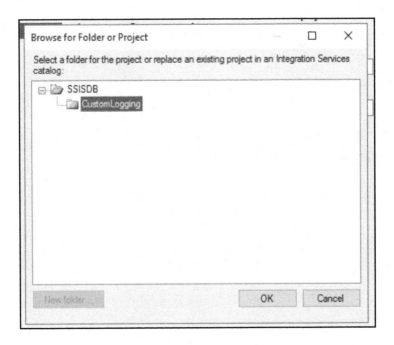

22. Back on the **Integration Services Deployment Wizard,** click on the **Next** button to go to the next deployment step. You should have a window similar to the following screenshot:

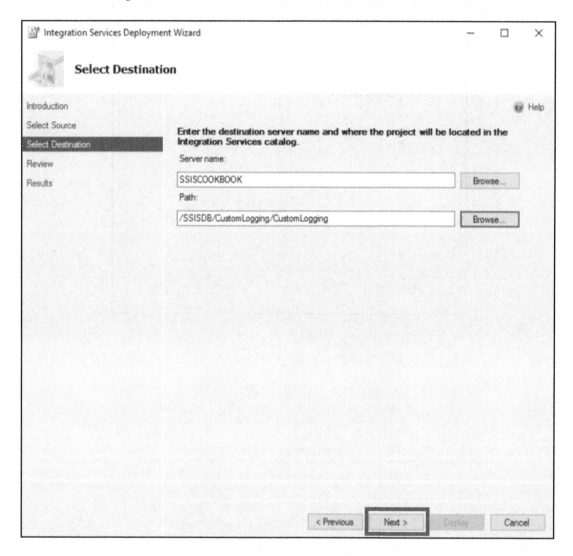

23. Click on **Deploy**, as shown in the following screenshot:

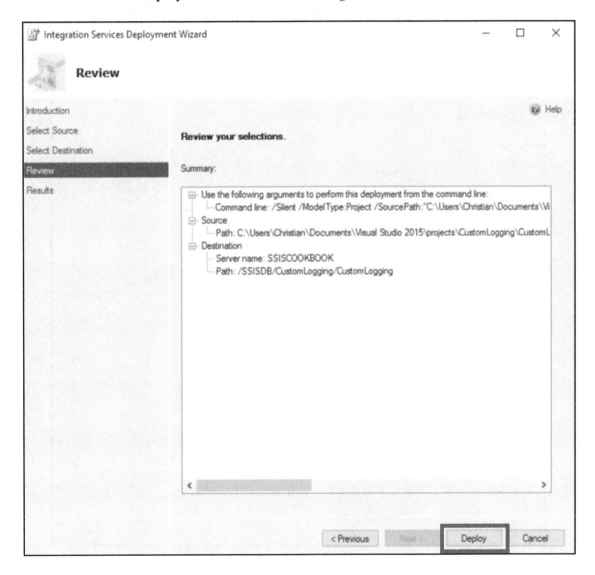

24. As the following screenshot shows, the project is deployed in the SSIS Catalog. If this fails, click on the **Report** button to investigate the error details. Whenever deployment errors occur, you can click on **Previous** to make a correction. Click **Close** to terminate the deployment wizard.

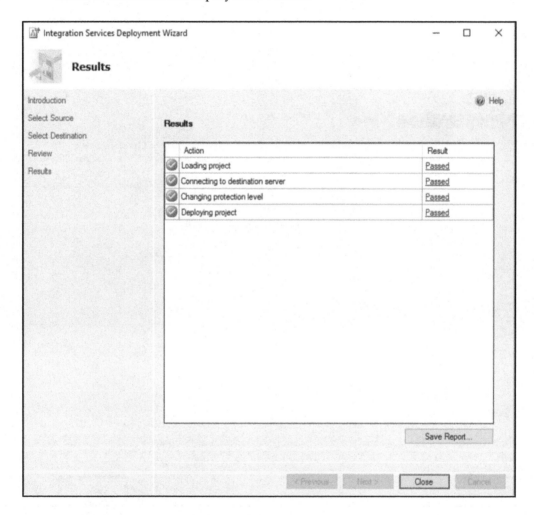

Testing the custom logging level

This part of the recipe will guide you through the steps to execute our sample package on the server (the SSIS Catalog on the local machine). We will use the custom logging level that we created previously in the recipe.

1. Open SSMS and expand the `Integration Services Catalogs` as shown in the following screenshot. Expand the `CustomLogging` folder and navigate to the package as shown in the following screenshot:

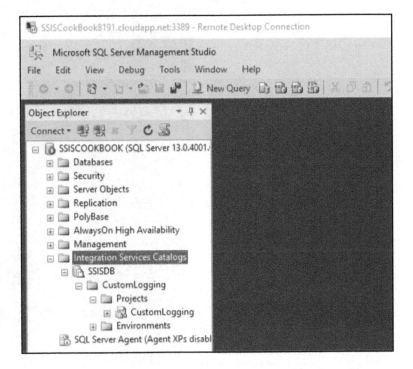

2. When you expand the **SSISDB** catalog, you'll notice that there is a folder called `CustomLogging`; it has been created previously in this recipe when we deployed the SSIS project.

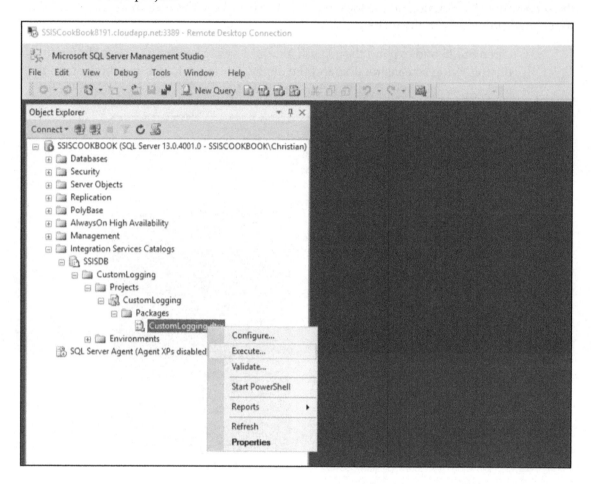

3. Click on the dropdown list near the **Logging level property and select Select customized logging level...** as shown in the following screenshot:

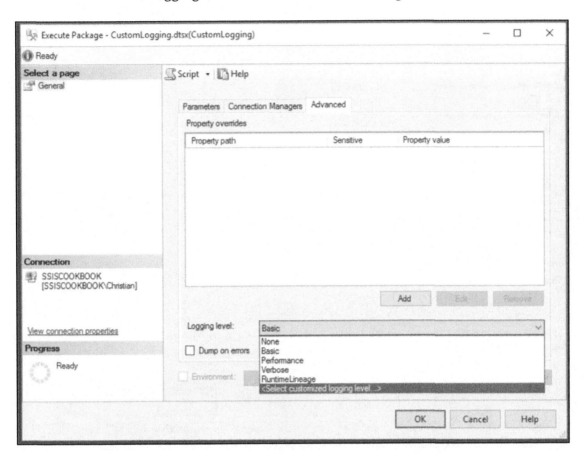

4. Make sure that our custom logging level, **CustomLogging,** is selected and click **OK** as shown in the following screenshot:

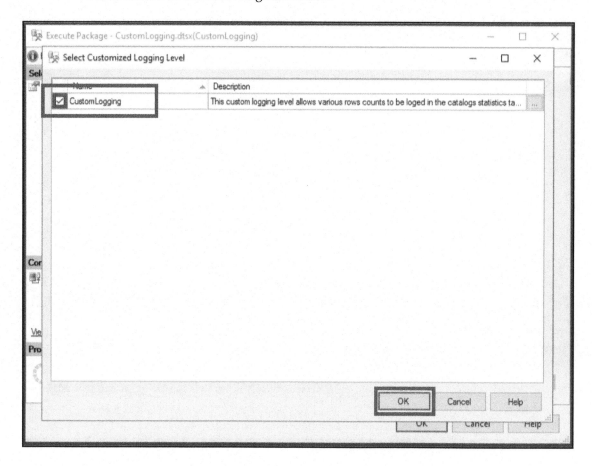

5. Make sure that the **Logging level** property is set to **Customized: CustomLogging** and click on **OK** to close the window and start package execution as in the following screenshot.

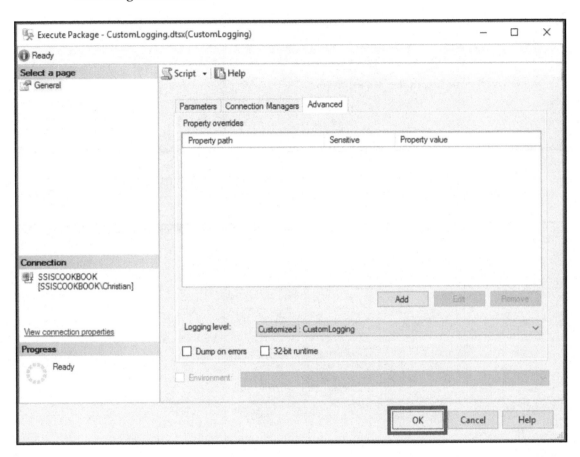

6. The following screen appears. Click on **Yes** to see the execution report.

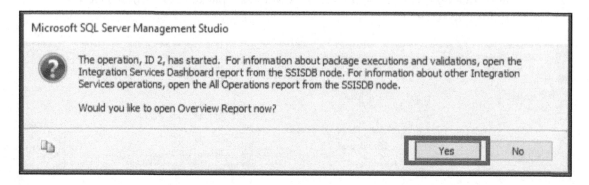

7. The execution report tells us that the package executed properly, as shown in the following screenshot:

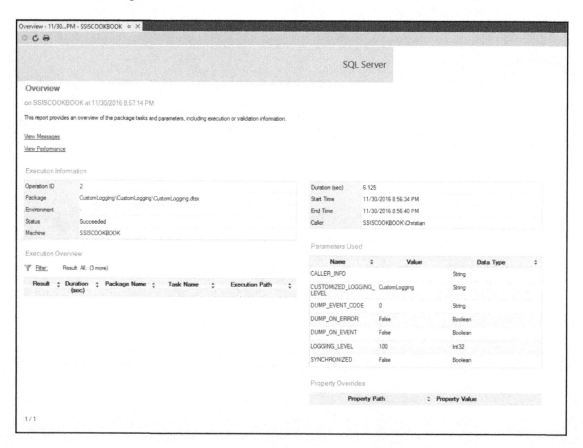

8. Click on **New Query** in SSMS and type the following query. Click on **Execute** or *F5* to execute the query. You should see that the package read and inserted two rows.

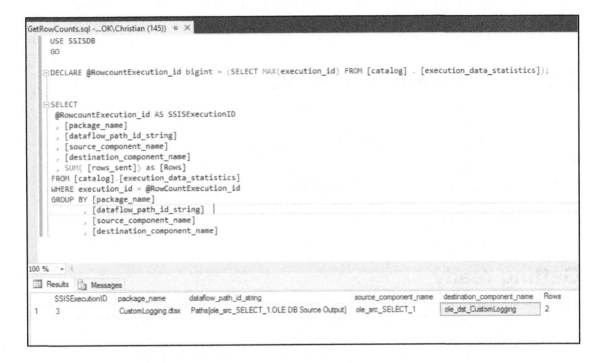

See also

We'll talk more about logging in the next chapter where we'll talk about an SSIS framework. In the meantime, this recipe introduced you to logging in SSIS but there's much more to be covered later in the book.

Azure tasks and transforms

This section will guide you on how to install the Azure Feature Pack that, in turn, will install Azure control flow task and data flow components. The Azure ecosystem is becoming predominant in Microsoft ecosystems and SSIS has not been left over in the past few years.

The Azure Feature Pack is not an SSIS 2016 specific feature. It's also available for SSIS version 2012 and 2014. It's worth mentioning that it appeared in July 2015, a few months before the SSIS 2016 release.

Getting ready

This section assumes that you have installed SQL Server Data Tools 2015.

How to do it...

We'll start SQL Server Data Tools, and open the `CustomLogging` project if not already done:

1. In the SSIS Toolbox, scroll to the **Azure** group. Since the Azure tools are not installed with SSDT, the **Azure** group is disabled in the toolbox. Thee toolss must be downloaded using a separate installer. Click on the **Azure** group to expand it and click on **Download Azure Feature Pack** as shown in the following screenshot:

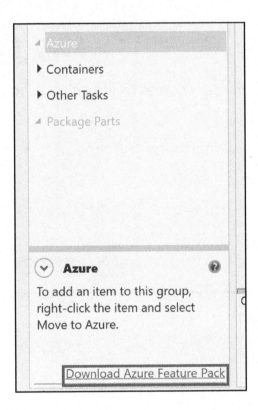

2. Your default browser opens and the **Microsoft SQL Server 2016 Integration Services Feature Pack for Azure** opens. Click on **Download** as shown in the following screenshot:

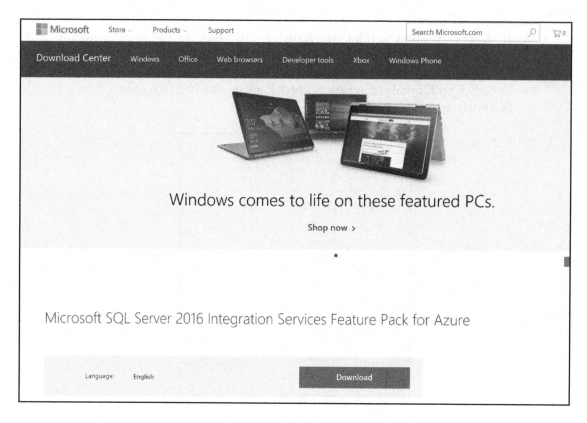

3. From the popup that appears, select both the 32-bit and 64-bit versions. The 32-bit version is necessary for SSIS package development since SSDT is a 32-bit program. Click **Next** as shown in the following screenshot:

4. As shown in the following screenshot, the files are downloaded:

5. Once the download completes, run one the installers downloaded. The following screen appears. In this case, the 32-bit (**x86**) version is being installed. Click **Next** to start the installation process.

6. As shown in the following screenshot, check the box near **I accept the terms in the License Agreement**and click **Next**. The installation starts.

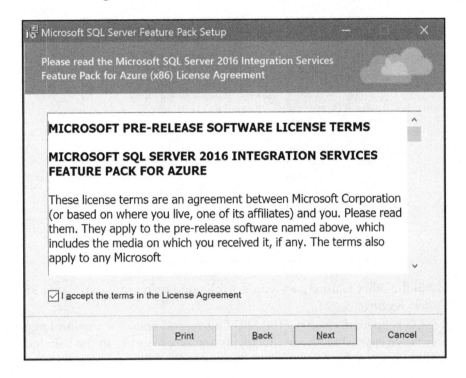

7. The following screen appears once the installation is completed. Click **Finish** to close the screen.

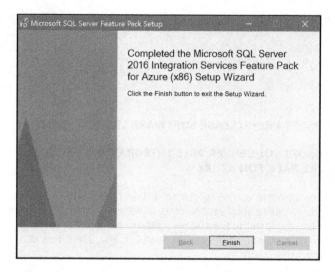

8. Install the other feature pack you downloaded using previous recipe steps in *Custom logging*.
9. If SSDT is opened, close it. Start SSDT again and open the **CustomLogging** project we created in another recipe. In the **Azure** group in the SSIS toolbox, you should now see the Azure tasks as shown in the following screenshot:

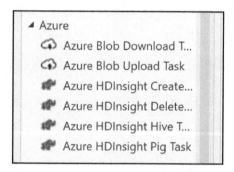

See also

This book contains a dedicated chapter on Azure tasks and transforms: Chapter 9, *On-Premises and Azure Big Data Integration*. They will be explained in more detail with useful examples.

Incremental package deployment

Prior to SSIS 2012, packages needed to be deployed one by one. We were usually downloading all packages from the source control software, such as **Team Foundation Server (TFS)**, Visual Source Safe, SVN, and so on. Once downloaded, packages were moved to their destination. At that time, the person who deployed the packages had the choice to overwrite or skip existing packages. Usually, they overwrote all the packages since they were using the source control.

For those who didn't use the source control, they had all the necessary flexibility to deploy what needed to be deployed. Usually, they were keeping a backup somewhere on a file share of all packages. The reason why they chose what to deploy was mainly because they had doubts about the consistency of the packages in the file share. They were simply not sure of the state of the packages because they were using a manual process to maintain their solution. The source control software helps a lot with this. We have the possibility to compare versions between packages committed in the source control, and when and who pushed the package, among other benefits.

Enter SSIS 2012 with Project Deployment. The only way to deploy a package was to deploy the entire project, and thus, all packages in it. If the source control was in place to manage the package code, this was barely an issue. But, not everybody is using the source control and Microsoft recognized it. With SSIS 2016, we can now deploy part of your project packages. You're not forced to deploy the entire project.

Getting ready

This recipe assumes that you have created and deployed the **CustomLogging** recipe.

How to do it...

1. With the **CustomLogging** project opened, right-click on the
   CustomLogging.dtsx package and select **Copy** as shown in the following
   screenshot:

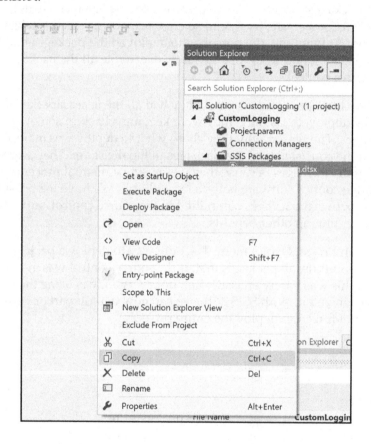

2. Now, right-click on the `SSIS Packages` folder and select **Paste** as shown in the following screenshot:

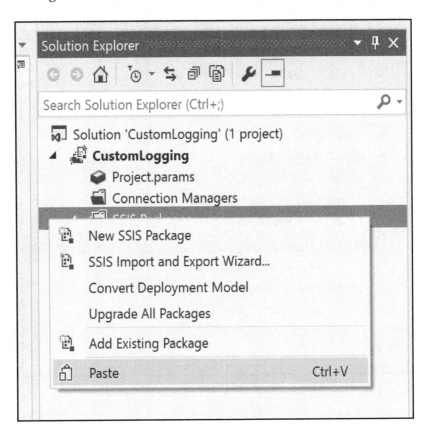

3. A copy of the package is created and named `CustomLogging 1.dtsx` as shown in the following screenshot:

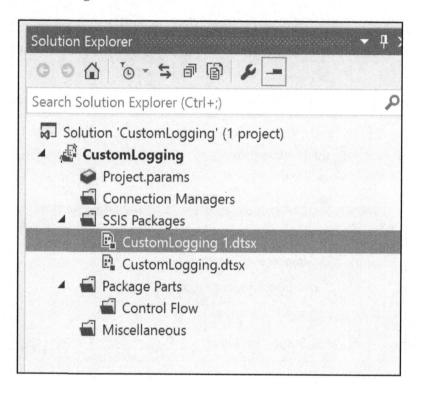

4. Right-click on the newly created package, `CustomLogging 1.dtsx`, and **select Deploy Package** from the menu as shown in the following screenshot:

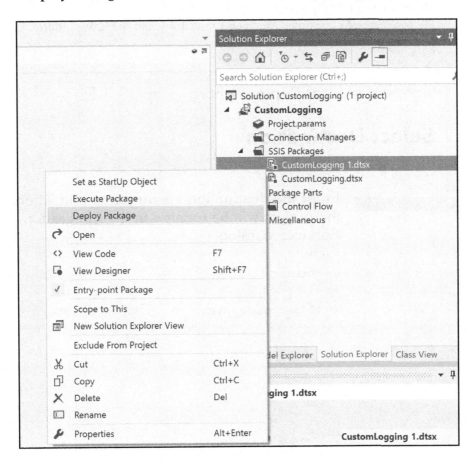

5. As shown in the following screenshot, the **Server name** is already selected since we've deployed the project there before. It can be changed if necessary. The **Path** is where the deployed package will be located; the `SSISDB/CustomLogging/CustomLogging` folder in the SSIS Catalog. Click **Next** to advance to the next step.

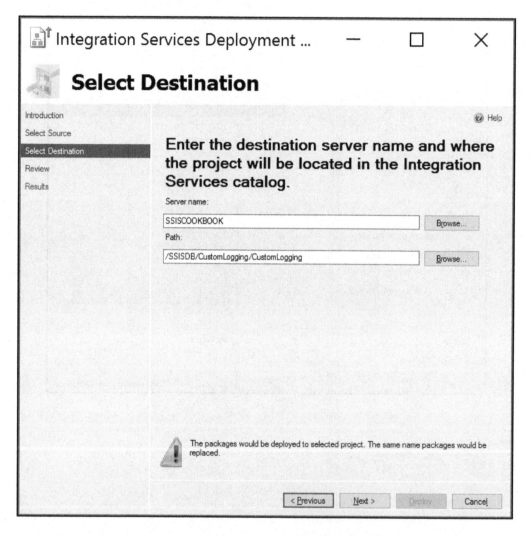

6. Now we are at the **Review** screen as shown in the following screenshot.

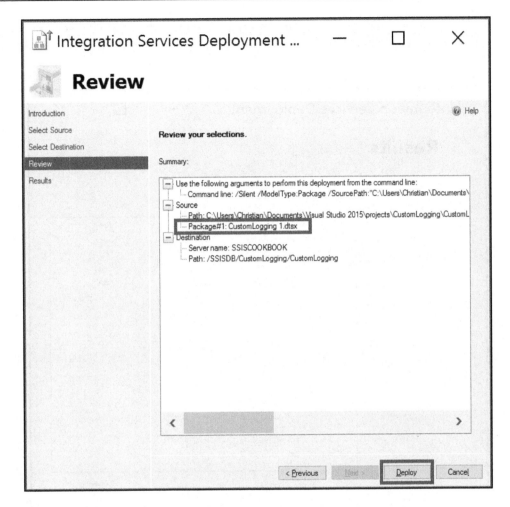

 Notice that the package to be deployed is `CustomLogging 1.dtsx`. It is tagged as **Package#1** since we might have selected multiple packages to deploy. Click **Deploy** to proceed to the deployment.

7. If everything goes well, you should get a screen like the following screenshot meaning that the package has been successfully deployed. Click on **Close** to get rid of it.

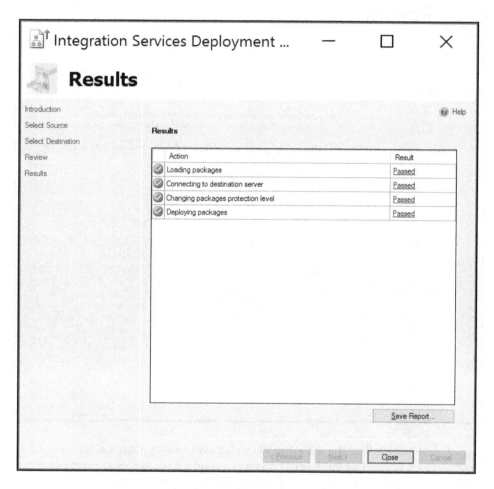

8. Now, go to SSMS and open the SSIS Catalog as shown in the following screenshot. You will see that the package has been deployed. We won't execute it for now as we only wanted to demonstrate how single package deployment works.

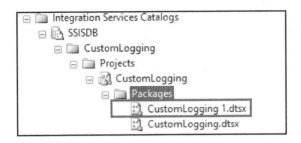

There's more...

The capability to deploy individual packages is possible with SSIS 2016 only. If we have tried to deploy to a SSIS Catalog of a previous version of SSIS (2012-2014), the deployment would have failed. So, to reinforce the point here, SSDT can show you the option that you can deploy individual packages but you'll need SSIS 2016 to be able to use it.

Multiple version support

Since its inception, SSIS designer never supported backward compatibility. For example, if you developed a package in SSIS 2014 and tried to deploy it in a SSIS 2012 catalog, you would not be able to do it. Or worse, if you opened a package developed with SSIS 2012 with a SSDT that was used with SSIS 2014, the package was upgraded. When another developer tried to open it with SSDT used for SSIS 2012, he/she was not able to do it. The package was upgraded, period.

With SSIS 2016, SSDT had the following enhancements:

- Backward compatibility to prior SSIS versions down to SSIS 2012.
- Unified SSDT: as we'll see later in the book, SSDT can be used for BI components development as well as database development. Prior to SSDT for Visual Studio 2015, it was confusing whether we were using SSDT-BI for BI development or SSDT-SQL for database development.

Getting ready

This recipe assumes that you have created an SSIS project in SSDT. We'll be using the CustomLogging SSIS project developed in a previous recipe in this chapter.

How to do it...

1. With SSDT and **CustomLogging** SSIS project opened, right-click on the project and select **Properties** as shown in the following screenshot:

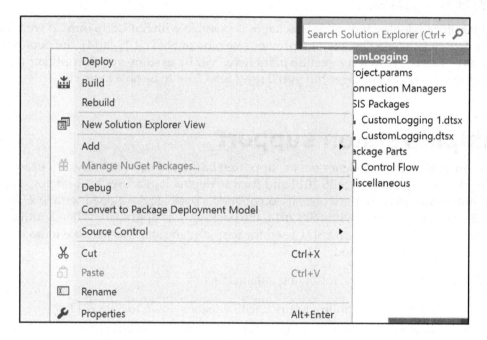

2. The **CustomLogging Property Pages** dialog box opens. Select **Configuration Properties** and you'll notice a drop-down list near the property **TargetServerVersion**. In our case, the selected version is **SQL Server 2016**. You'll notice that you can select prior versions as shown in the following screenshot. Click on **OK** to close this window.

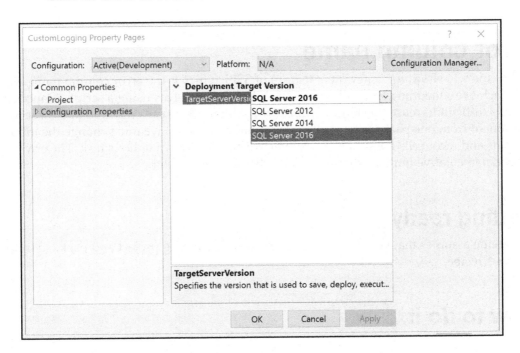

There's more...

This simple recipe shows you how easily we can now use SSDT for Visual Studio 2015 with prior SSIS versions. If you open an existing SSIS project that is developed in the SQL Server 2012 or 2014 SSDT version, the designer (SSDT) will be smart enough to select the right target version (2012 or 2014) without upgrading your project or packages.

The default Target Server version is SQL Server 2016. If you created your SSIS project without setting this property and try to deploy it on a prior version to 2016, the deployment will fail. Also, if you change this property from, for example, SQL Server 2016 down to SQL Server 2014 and your package uses new SSIS functionality, the project won't build and therefore you will not be able to deploy it.

Error column name

This recipe will show you a new neat feature of SSIS, which is the error column name. We could achieve something similar before SSIS 2016 but it involves using a script component and it is difficult to reuse this kind of transform. Although we can copy and paste a script component from one package to another, every time we do so, we must change the input columns and recompile the script. It's not very difficult but it's a tedious task. The error column name native implementation in SSIS 2016 is very welcome.

Getting ready

This recipe assumes that you have created the **CustomLogging** project and package from previous recipe.

How to do it...

1. In the CustomLogging.dstx package, navigate to the dft_dbo_CustomLogging by double-clicking on the Data Flow task. Click on the path (blue arrow) between the ole_src_SELECT_1and the ole_dst_dbo_CustomLogging transform to select it. Right-click on it and select **Delete** to delete it.

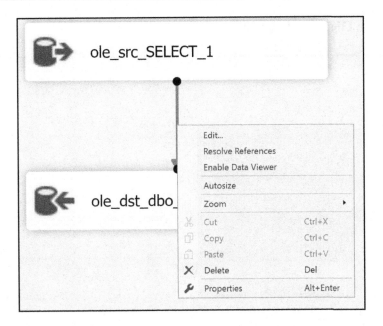

2. Drag and drop a derived column transform from the SSIS Toolbox onto the data flow. Link it to the `ole_src_SELECT_1` and double-click on it to open the derived column transformation. As shown in the following screenshot, do the following:
   - **Derived Column Name**: **DateToConvert**
   - **Derived Column**: leave it as **<Add as new column>**
   - **Expression**: Type `1600-01-00`. This is not a valid date; it will cause an error and that's precisely what we want.

3. Click on **OK** when finished.

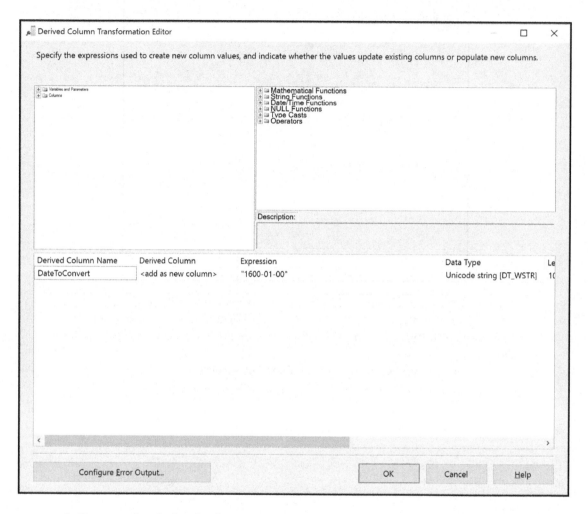

4. Rename the derived column der_AddDate.
5. Now, drag and drop a data conversion transform onto the dataflow task. Attach it to the der_AddDate derived column created previously and double-click on it to open the **Data Conversion Transformation Editor**. Enter the values as shown in the following screenshot:
    - **Input Column**: Check the column **DateToConvert** in the Available Input Columns.
    - **Output Alias**: Change it to **DateConverted**.
    - **Data Type**: Select **date [DT_DATE]** from the drop-down list.

It is also shown in the following screenshot:

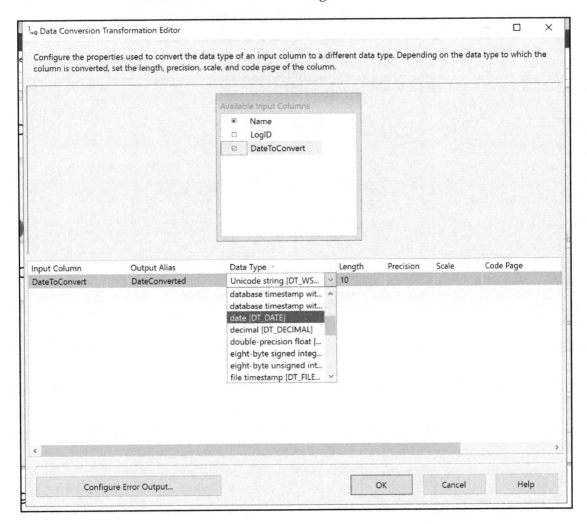

6. The **Data Conversion Transformation Editor** should now look like the following screenshot. Click on the **Configure Error Output...** button.

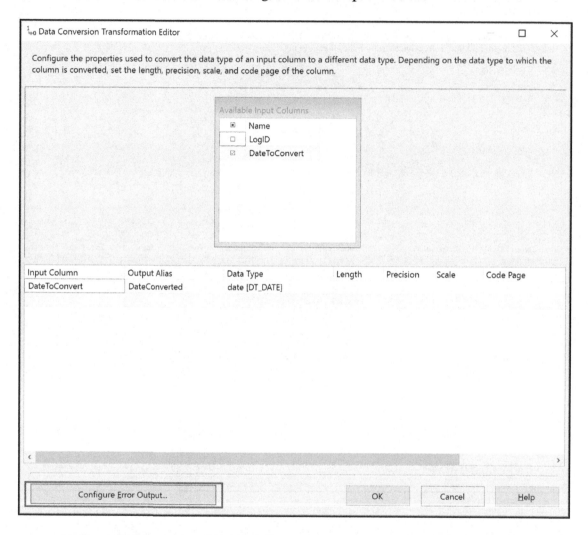

7. You will get a screen like the following screenshot. By default, the **Error** and **Truncation** errors will fail the component.
   1. Select both columns and from the drop-down list near **Set this value to select cells**, select **Redirect row**. Click **Apply**.
   2. You should now see that both column values are now set to **Redirect row**.

3. Click **OK** to close the editor and rename the transform as `dcnv_DateConverted`.

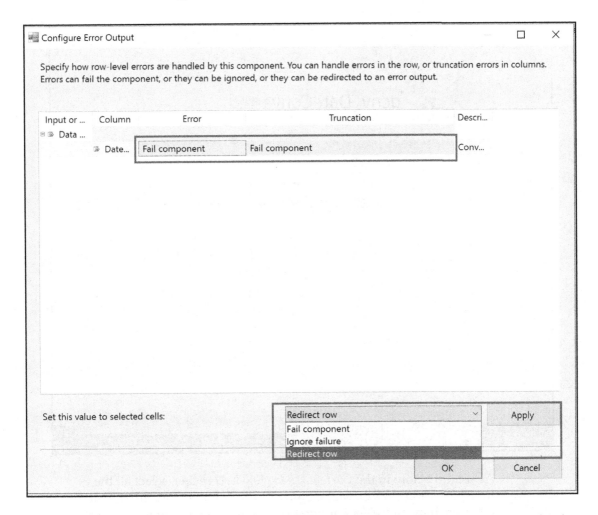

8. Now, bring an audit transform from other transforms onto the dataflow task. The following steps detail what's in the following screenshot:
     1. Attach the **Data Conversion Error Output** (red path or arrow) to it.

2. Right-click on the error path and **select Enable Data Viewer** from the menu that appears.

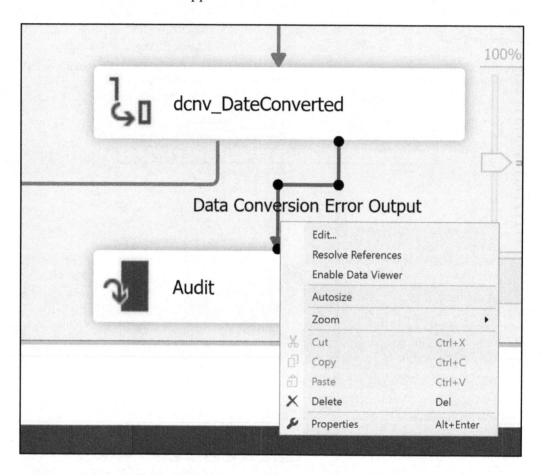

 As we did before in the *Customized logging level* recipe, select all the transforms and click on **Make Same Width** from the **Layout** toolbar. From the **Format** menu, select **Format Auto Layout à Diagram** to format the data flow task objects properly.

9. Your data flow task should look like the following screenshot. Now, right-click anywhere in the background of the data flow task and select **Execute Task** from the menu.

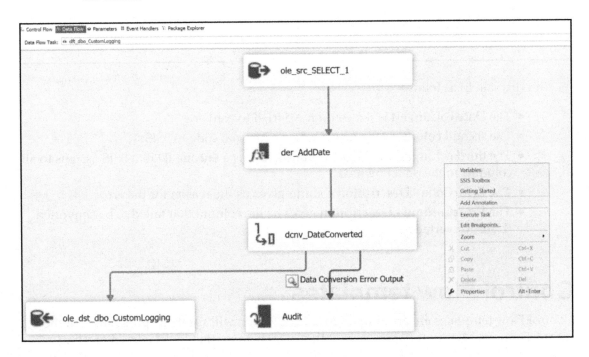

10. You should see a data viewer like the following screenshot:

LogID	DateToConvert	Error...	Error...	ErrorCode - Description	ErrorColumn - Description
1	1600-01-00	-107...	9	The data value cannot be converted for reasons other than sign mismatch or data overflow.	dcnv_DateConverted.Outputs[Data Conversion Output].Columns[DateConverted]
2	1600-01-00	-107...	9	The data value cannot be converted for reasons other than sign mismatch or data overflow.	dcnv_DateConverted.Outputs[Data Conversion Output].Columns[DateConverted]

Data Conversion Error Output Data Viewer at dft_dbo_CustomLogging

Detach Copy Data

It is explain in as follows:

- The **DateToConvert** is the column we tried to convert.
- The second column is the **ErrorCode**, an internal code to SSIS.
- The third column is the **ErrorColumn** which is a lineage ID that SSIS assigns to all columns in the data flow task.
- **The ErrorCode - Description** column gives us the reason for the error.
- **The ErrorColumn - Description** gives us the column that failed to be converted (**DateConverted**).

Control Flow templates

Control Flow templates are an addition to SSIS 2016 that will surely be promising...in the future. For now, Microsoft put the foundation of something that looks very interesting.

If there's one thing missing with SSIS it is the reusability of custom components without doing .NET code. We'll see how to achieve custom task and transforms later in this book using .NET and you'll see that it's tedious to achieve even for something simple. Let's say that we would like to create a truncated table task; that is, a task that we would use to solely erase a table's content. This task would then appear in the SSIS toolbox and be available to all packages in your projects. This recipe is exactly what we will do using Control Flow templates.

Getting ready

This recipe assumes that you have done all previous recipes in this chapter or you have your own SSIS project open.

How to do it...

1. In SSDT, with your project open, right-click on the `Control Flow` folder in the *Package Parts* section of the solution explorer. As shown in the following screenshot, select **New Control Flow Package Part** from the contextual menu. Rename it `Chapter2Part.dtsxp`.

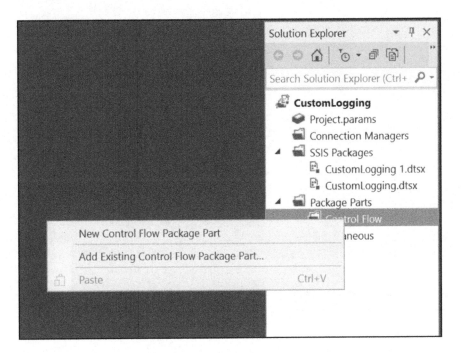

2. Drag and drop an **Execute SQL** task on it:
   1. Rename it `sql_Truncate_dbo_CustomLogging`.
   2. Click anywhere in the **Control Flow**. Set its description property to **This is a simple template that is meant to truncate the table [dbo].[CustomLogging]**.
   3. As shown in the following screenshot, right-click in the Connection Managers area and choose **New OLE DB Connection...** from the menu that appears:

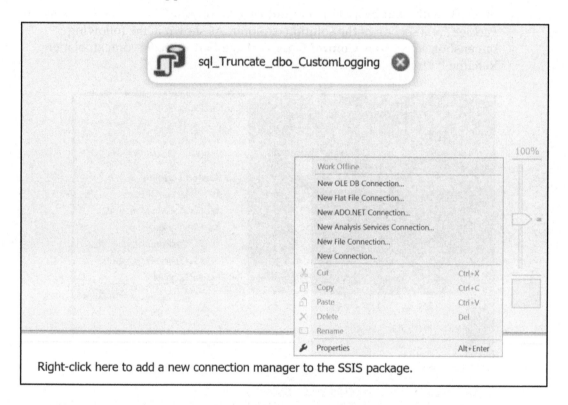

Right-click here to add a new connection manager to the SSIS package.

3. As shown in the following screenshot, select the existing connection
    (**SSISCOOKBOOK\TestCustomLogging** in this case) in the top left or create a
    new one by clicking on **NEW....** Click on **OK** when done to close the **Configure
    OLE DB Connection Manager** window.

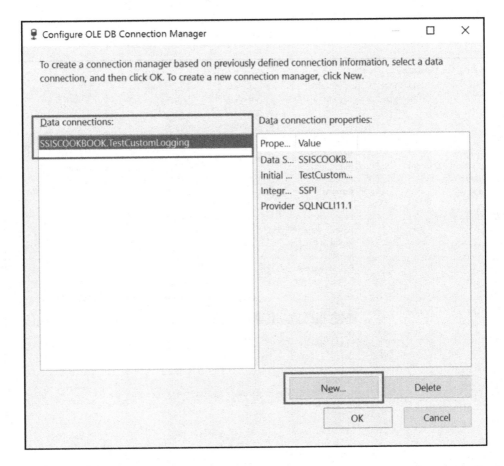

4. Double-click on the `sql_Truncate_dbo_CustomLogging` task to open the
    Execute SQL Task Editor. Set the properties in the **SQL Statement** section as
    follow:

    - **ConnectionType: OLE DB**, the default value
    - **Connection**: Set it to the connection manager created in the previous
      step.

- **SQLSourceType**: Leave the default value, **Direct input** type the following SQL DML statement in the **SQL Statement** property:

```
TRUNCATE TABLE [dbo].[CustomLogging];
```

It is also shown in the following screenshot:

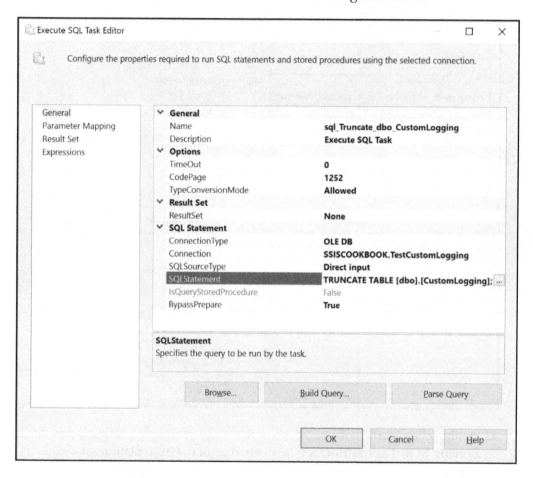

5. Save and close the Chapter2Part.dtsxp package part.

6. Now, open the `CustomLogging` package from the solution explorer. As shown in the following screenshot, there is now a new component in the *Package Parts* section of the **SSIS Toolbox**: the **Chapter2Part** created in the previous steps. Also, notice the description below the *Package Parts* section. This is the one that we assigned at the **Control Flow** level of the package part when it was created.

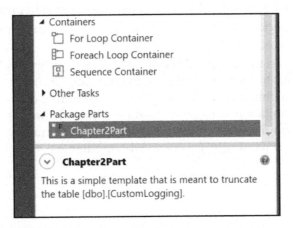

7. Drag and drop a **Chapter2Part** onto the **Control Flow** of the `CustomLogging` package. Now to get the same as in the following screenshot:

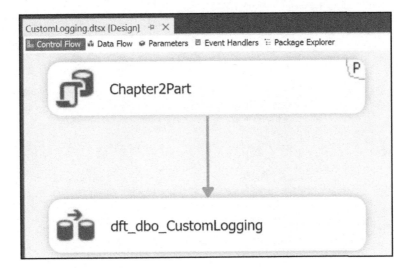

Execute the following steps:

8. Connect it to the **dft_dbo_CustomLogging** data flow task.

9. Select all **Control Flow** components

10. In the **Layout** toolbar, click Make Same Size

11. From the Format menu, select **Auto Layout Diagram** to properly align the tasks

12. Execute the package to make sure that the package part is properly working and stop the package execution when done.

13. Double-click on the **Chapter2Part** to view its properties as shown in the following screenshot. Go to the **Connection Managers** tab. Locate the **ConnectionString** property as highlighted in the screenshot. Notice that it has a fixed value. This is the biggest limitation of these parts; there is no way for now to alter any of the property at runtime. We cannot use package configurations or parameters to alter these values dynamically as we can with regular tasks.

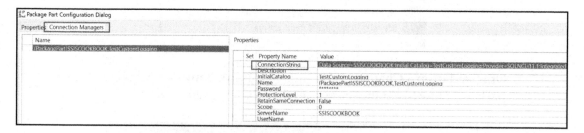

3

Key Components of a Modern ETL Solution

This chapter will cover the following recipes:

- Installing the sample solution
- Deploying the source database with its data
- Deploying the target database
- SSIS projects
- ETL framework

Introduction

Now, let's go for the real stuff! This chapter will cover many topics that will lay out the foundations of a simple and effective ETL solution. Over the years, I have seen many SSIS implementations and one of the goals of this chapter is to give the readers the following:

- A simple but effective SSIS framework
- SSIS development best practices
- New data source integrations

All remaining chapters assume that we want to load a data warehouse that is a star schema with its staging area.

The source (operational) database used is `AdventureWorksLT,` an old well-known database. The following diagram describes the source database that we're going to use:

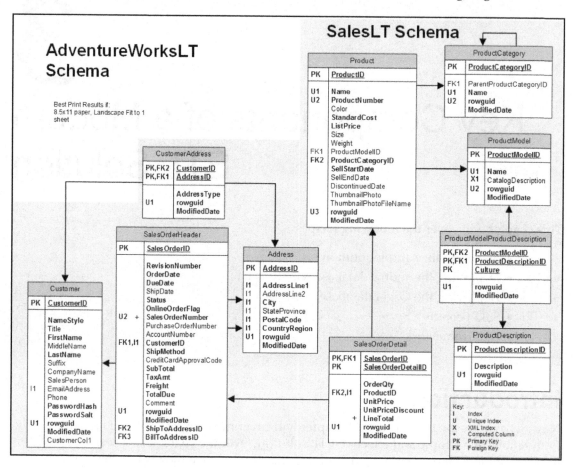

From this database, we'll insert data in a staging area and finally into a data warehouse. The staging area and the data warehouse will be separated in schemas in a database that we'll manage using SSDT.

The following diagram is the representation that describes the staging schema of the `AdventureWorksLTDW` database:

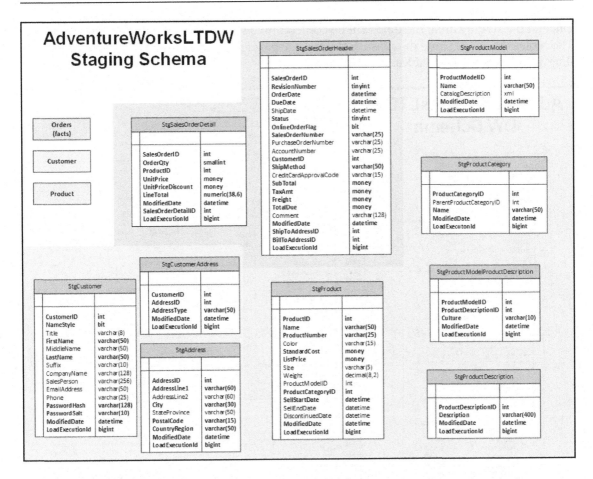

Not all tables are copied in the staging area and three sections have been identified:

- **Orders**: These tables contain order information as well as dates related information. In the data warehouse section, these sections have their own tables.

- **Customer**: These tables contain information related to a customer and their addresses. In the data warehouse, these tables are grouped.

- **Product**: These tables contain the product information such as model, description in multiple languages, and so on. Like customer data, these tables are grouped in the data warehouse.

Once in the staging area, the data will be copied into a star schema database representation. The tables are in the same database, but have a separate schema called DW. The following diagram shows the DW tables:

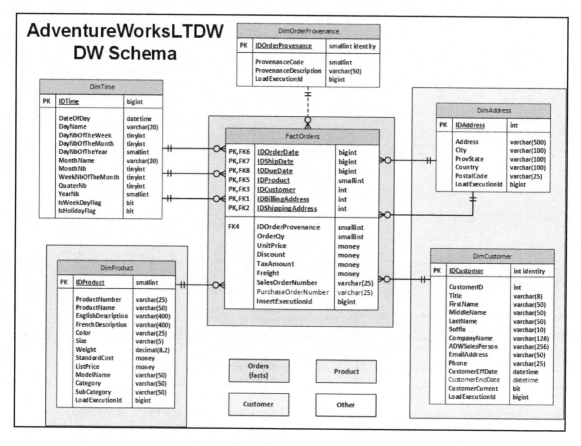

The goal of the data warehouse is to ease data consumptions. It's easy to understand by most users and data is categorized into areas (tables) that represent the subjects that the end users will base their analysis on.

The customer information has been regrouped into two tables, DimCustomer and DimAddress. The DimAddress table has two links to the fact table. These relationships represent the multiple addresses, two in our case: the billing and shipping address of the customer.

The product information has been flattened into one dimension: DimProduct. Although the base model allowed for more than one language when it comes to the product descriptions, only two are retained in the dimension: French and English - EnglishDesctiption and FrenchDescription.

The orders tables have been merged into one fact table: FactOrders. The DimTime dimension has been added to allow better querying of the orders using various dates: order, shipped, and due dates. The SalesOrderNumber and PurchaseOrderNumber are considered derived dimensions and stay in the fact table. We don't have enough information that can be derived from these columns and they are strongly tied to the facts.

The remaining dimension, DimOrderProvenance, has no source in the AdventureWorksLT operational database. It has been added and is managed by Master Data Services, another service that comes with SQL Server 2016 Developer Edition. We'll talk about this service and this dimension later in this book.

In the next few recipes, we'll deploy these databases and the ETL's (SSIS packages) that load these tables.

Installing the sample solution

This section will walk you through the deployment of the databases contained in the sample solution.

Getting ready

This section assumes that you have downloaded the solution files.

How to do it...

1. We'll first create a folder that will hold the solution files. In our case, we created a folder called `C:\Projects\SSISCookbook` and we uncompressed the solution file in it, as shown in the following screenshot:

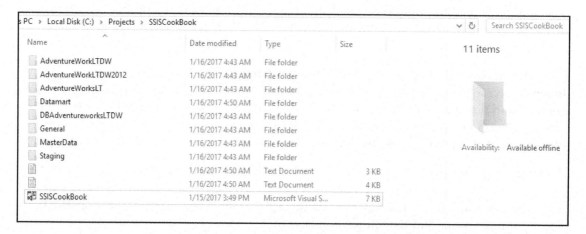

2. Now, we open the solution in Visual Studio by double-clicking on the `SSISCookBook` solution file, as highlighted in the preceding screenshot.

3. The solution opens and you will see its projects, as shown in the following screenshot:

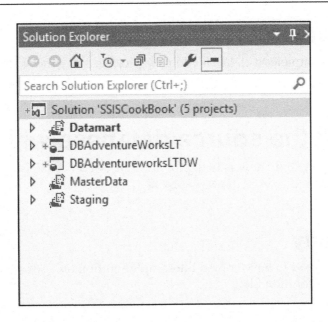

The following point will describe the projects that are shown in the **Solution Explorer** in SQL Server Data Tools (Visual Studio):

- `DB.AdventureWorksLT`: This is an SQL Server database project that contains the `AdventureWorksLT` database objects.
- `DB.AdventureWorksLTDW`: This is the SQL Server database project that contains the staging, DW, the framework database objects. We'll talk about the framework in a subsequent recipe.
- `ETL.DW`: This is an SSIS project that fills the tables in the DW schema.
- `ETL.MasterData`: This is an SSIS project that connects to Master Data Services and loads the `DW.DimOrderProvenance` table in the `AdventureWorksDW` database.
- `ETL.Staging`: This is an SSIS project that loads the tables in the staging schema in the `AdventureWorksDW` database.

There's more...

The solution is not completed yet. We'll add new projects as we move forward in the chapter's recipes.

Deploying the source database with its data

The first thing we have to do now is to deploy the SQL Server database, which are AdventureWorksLT and AdventureWorksLTDW.

Getting ready

This section requires you to have copied the sample solution on your PC and opened the SSISCookBook.sln solution file.

How to do it...

1. In SQL Server Data Tools (Visual Studio), right-click on the DB.AdventureWorksLT project and select **Publish...**, as shown in the following screenshot:

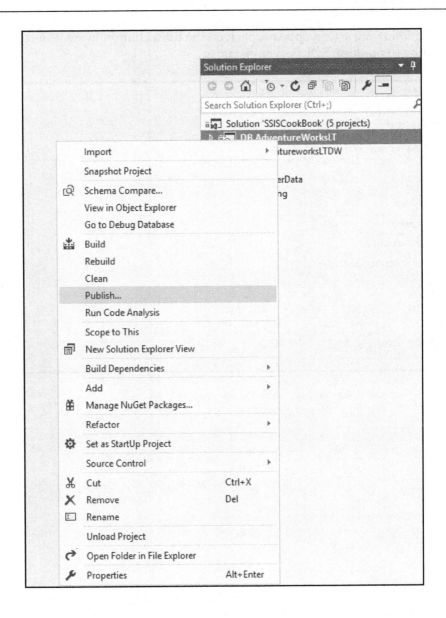

2. The following screen appears; click on the **Edit...** button to create a connection string to our local SQL Server instance:

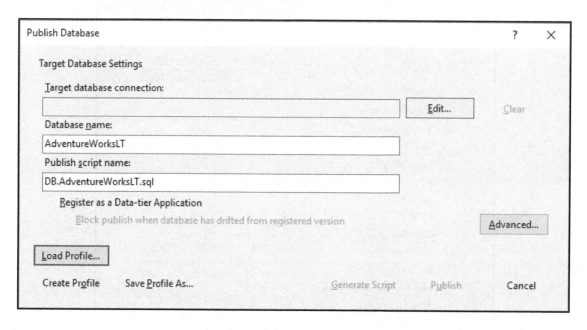

3. As shown in the following screenshot, clicking on the **Browse** tab brings up a screen where we can choose the SQL Server instance location. In our case, we'll choose `Local`. Expand the `Local` label and choose your SQL Server instance, in our case `SSISCOOKBOOK`. The **Server Name** textbox will display the server you chose. Click **OK** to return to the previous screen.

4. Back in the **Publish Database** screen, click on the **Advanced...** button, and the following screen appears. This screen allows us to manage many options when we deploy a database. Check the **Always re-create database** option and click on **OK** to close the screen.

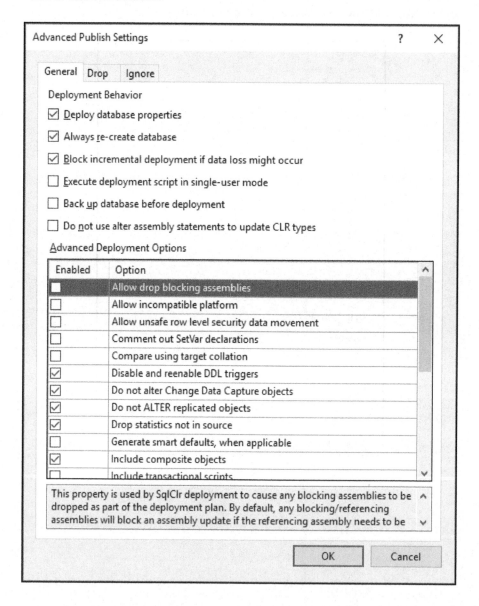

5. Back in the **Publish Database** screen, fill the textboxes as follows:
   - **Database name**: `AdventureWorksLT`
   - **Publish script name**: `DB.AdventureWorksLT.sql`

It is also shown in the following screenshot:

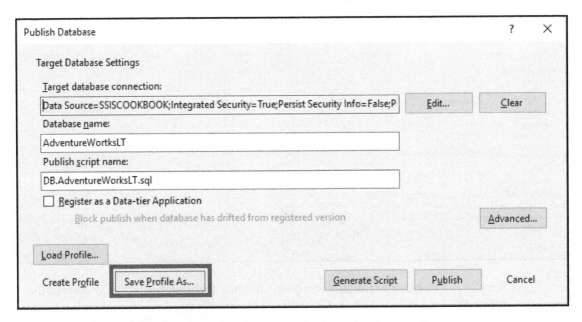

6. Click on the **Save Profile As...** button.

7. We're going to save these settings as a publish profile for this database project. That will allow us to reuse it in the future without having to repeat the preceding steps. Fill in the filename as shown in the following screenshot. It will create a publish profile in the project. As shown in the following screenshot, name the publish profile `DB.AdventureWorksLT` and click on **Save**.

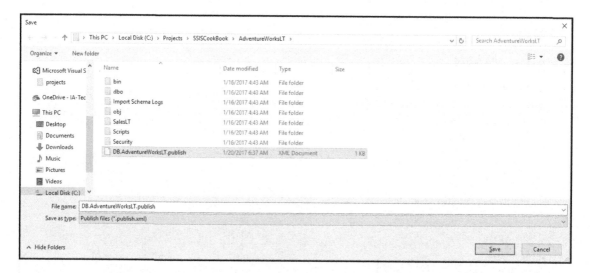

8. Back in the **Publish Database** window, click the **Publish** button as shown in the following screenshot. The **Generate Script** option is used when we want to only create a deployment script without deploying the database immediately. A good example of this is when we create a script to handle it to a DBA that will be responsible for the database deployment.

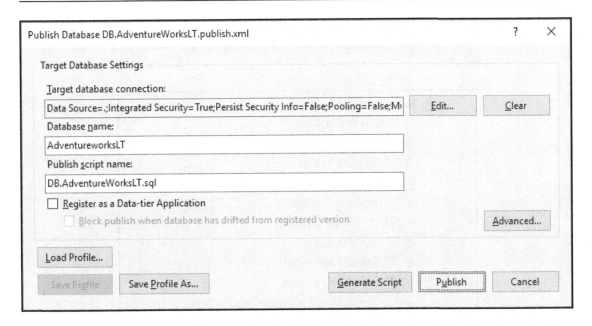

9. The **Data Tools Operations** window opens and displays the steps required that are executed to deploy the database. You should get something very similar to the following screenshot:

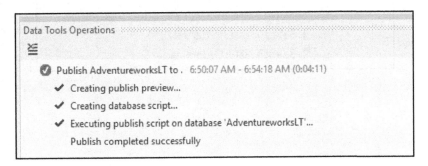

10. Start **SQL Server Management Studio (SSMS)** and look for the
    AdventureWorksLT database in the object explorer, as shown in the following
    screenshot:

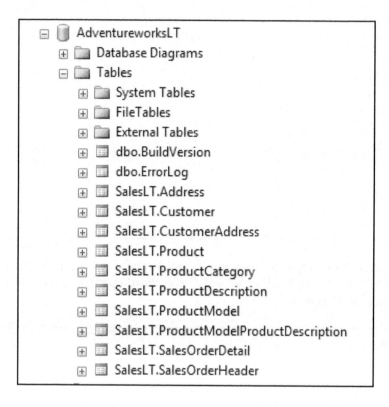

11. Right-click on any table and choose **Select Top 1000 Rows**, as shown in the following screenshot:

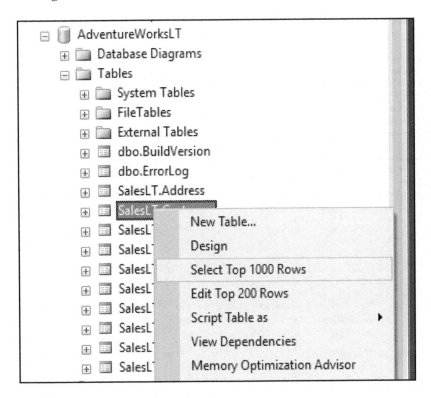

12. This command will generate an SQL statement and execute it. The right pane will show that the table has data, as shown in the following screenshot:

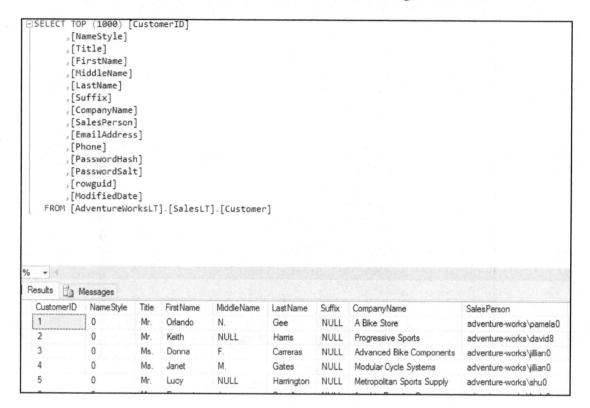

There's more...

Usually, SSDT database projects only create empty database shells when we select the option that always recreates the database. The reason why we have data in the newly deployed database is because we added a script to the database project, as shown in the following screenshot (`AdventureWorksLTData.sql`):

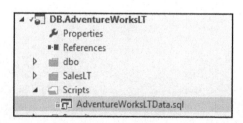

This file contains `INSERT` statements that load the different tables. You can glimpse its content in the following screenshot:

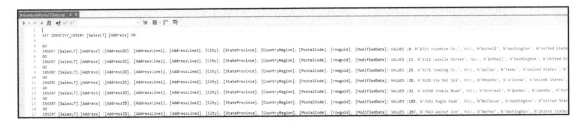

This SQL file is called via a special script in SSDT: a post deployment script. To create it, we simply need to add a script in the project, as shown in the following screenshot. This dialog box appears when we right-click on a folder and select **Add** | **New** | **Script**.

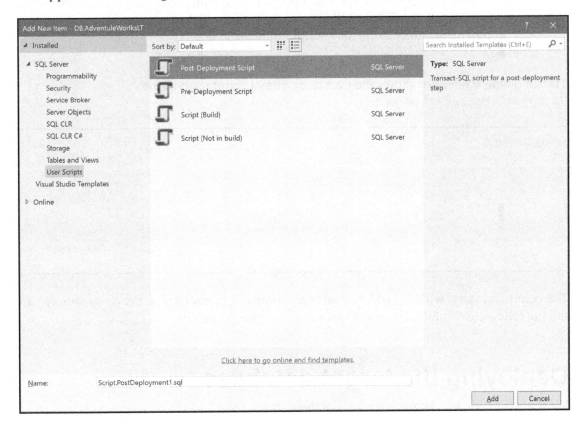

Several scripts are available. The following list describes them and how they can be used:

- **Post-deployment script**: This script is executed after all the database objects have been deployed. This is what we've used to load the `AdventureWorksLT` database tables.
- **Pre-deployment script**: This script is executed before the database objects are created. It might be used to back up certain data from tables or views before altering a table structure.
- **Script (build)**: These scripts are SQLCMD scripts that are parsed for errors by SSDT when it builds the database project.
- **Script (not in build)**: These scripts are not included in the build, meaning that their content is not validated by SSDT when the project is built, only their existence will be checked, that is, that the scripts really exist. There can be any SQL in these scripts. It's the developer's responsibility to make sure that the SQL is valid inside the scripts. Otherwise, the script will throw an error at deployment. An example of a script not in build is `ADVentureWorksLTData.sql`.

The following screenshot shows the post deployment script used in the `DB.AdventureWorksLT` project:

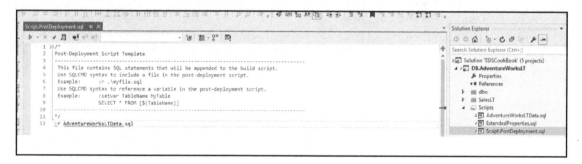

The command starts with `:r`, which is an SQL command that tells SQL Server to simply run the file following command, in our case, `AdventureWorksLTData.sql`.

Deploying the target database

We'll now deploy the data warehouse database that is called `AdventureWorksLTDW2016`.

Getting ready

This recipe assumes that you have access to the sample solution that is available for this book and you have read and executed all the steps to deploy the source database.

How to do it...

The steps will be essentially similar to the ones used to deploy the source database. Since we explained most of the steps previously, this recipe will be more concise:

1. The DB.AdventureWorksDW project contains the following schemas:
   - Cube: This contains specific database objects, mainly views that can be used by an SSAS cube.
   - dbo: This the default schema.
   - DW: This folder contains database objects that belong to the DW schema, that is, the data warehouse star schema objects.
   - Scripts: This is a folder that holds pre or post-deployment scripts, as well as utility scripts.
   - Staging: This folder contains database objects used by the Staging schema.
   - SystemLog: This folder contains database objects used by the SSIS framework. We'll talk about it in a section later in this book.

   It is also shown in the following screenshot:

   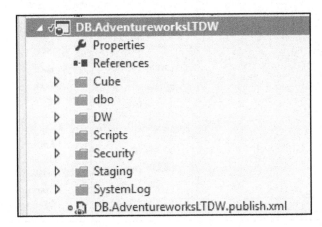

2. Right-click on the `DB.AdventureWorksLTDW` project in the solution and select **Publish...** as shown in the following screenshot:

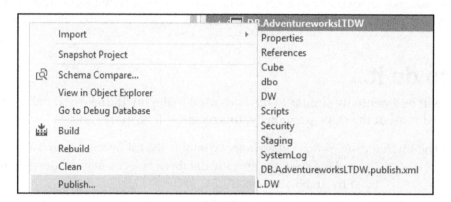

3. The **Publish Database** window appears. Click on **Load Profile...** and select the `DB.AdventureWorks2016.publish.publish` profile from the **Publish Settings** window that appears. Click on **Open,** as shown in the following screenshot:

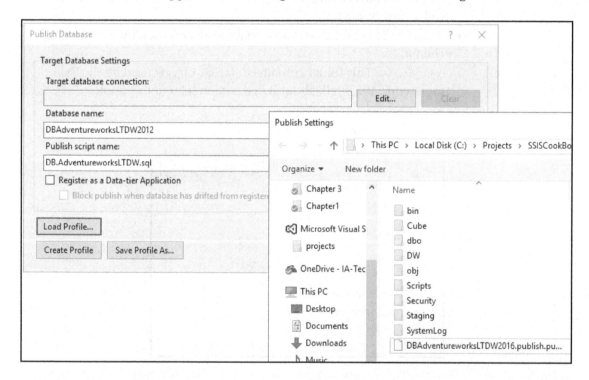

4. Back in the **Publish Database** window, click on **Publish** to deploy the database, as shown in the following screenshot:

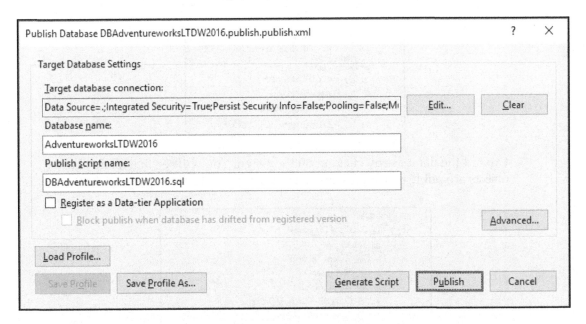

5. The database starts deploying. You can see its progress in the **Data Tools Operations** window, located at the bottom of the screen. It should look like the following screenshot:

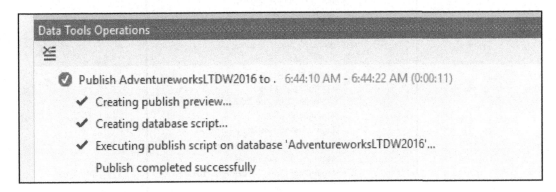

6. Once the deployment has completed, open SSMS and verify that
AdventureWorksLTDW2016 is in the object explorer, as shown in the following
screenshot:

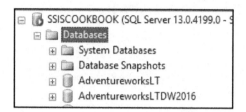

7. Expand the database by clicking on the + sign. You will see that all database
objects are published successfully, as shown in the following screenshot:

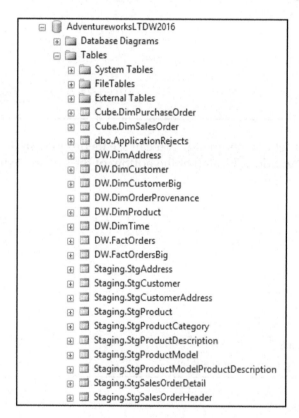

8. As with the `AdventureWorksLT` database, there are some tables that contain data: the dimensions. There's a post-deployment script that calls another not in build script: `DimensionsUnknownMembers.sql`. This script contains SQL `INSERT` statements, one for each table. These SQL statements insert one entry in the dimensions with a `-1` value for the primary key column, `N/A` for the codes, and `Not available` for longer text entries. They are referred to as unknown members and we'll talk about them in a later chapter of this book covering data warehouse loads.

9. If you right-click on a dimension table -- they're all prefixed with `Dim`.

SSIS projects

This section will now focus on the SSIS projects that move the data from various locations. There are several SSIS projects in the solution:

- `ETL.Staging`: This contains SSIS packages that transfer data from `AdventreWorksLT` to the `Staging` schema in `AdventureWorksLTDW2016`
- `ETL.DW`: This contains packages that transfer and transform data from the `Staging` schema to the `DW` schema in `AdventureWorksLTDW2016`

We'll have recipes in this section that will explain how the packages are structured and how we'll deploy and run them to load data from the source database to the data warehouse.

There are two types of SSIS packages in the projects:

- Entry-point packages: These packages orchestrate the **Extract, Transform, and Load** (ETL) flow of the solution. It's in these packages that other packages call and in what order they are called. In the solution, there's only one entry-point package per project.

- Regular (child) packages: These packages are doing the ETL work, that is, extracting the data from the source system and loading it in the destination tables. There is one child package for each destination table. For example, the `StgAddress.dtsx` package will only load the `AdventureWorksLTDW2016.Staging.StgAddress` table. Doing so gives better flexibility in terms of orchestration of packages in the entry-point packages. As we will see later, we can make good use of parallelism since our child package does only one task. It also makes the naming of the packages more straightforward: we give them the same name as the destination table that they load.

This project contains packages that load the `Staging` schema of the `AdventreWorksLTDW2016` database. The following screenshot shows the structure of the project:

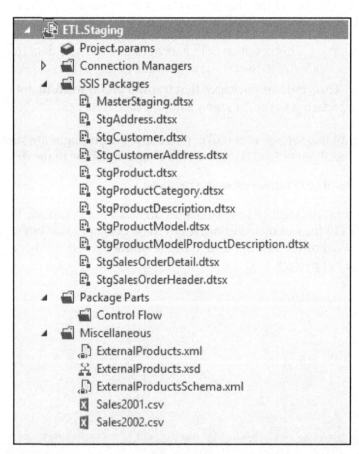

In project deployment mode, the following sections are present in the project:

- `Project.params`: This project artifact contains parameters that are passed by the calling program or job of any of the packages in the project. Most of the time, a project's connection manager's connection strings are part of it. The following screenshot shows a glimpse of the `ETL.Staging` project parameters:

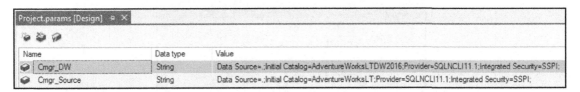

- `Connection Managers`: The project's level connection managers are available to all packages in the project. In `ETL.Staging`, the following project's connection managers have been created:
  - `cmgr_DW`: Connection to the `AdventureWorksLTDW2016` database
  - `cmgr_MDS_DB`: Connection to the Master Data Services database
  - `cmgr_Source`: Connection to the source database `AdventureWorksLT`

  It is also shown in the following screenshot:

- `SSIS Packages`: This folder contains all the packages necessary to load the `Staging` schema of the `ADVentureWorksLTDW2016` database. As stated previously, there's one package per table loaded, as shown in the following screenshot:

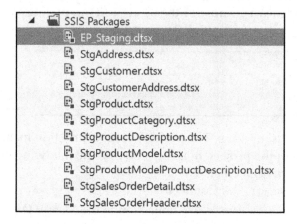

- As shown in the following screenshot, the package called `EP_Staging.dtsx` is the main package of the project. It is tagged as **Entry-point Package**. We'll see later what it does when the project will be deployed. So `EP` stands for entry-point in that case. There's usually one entry-point package per project.

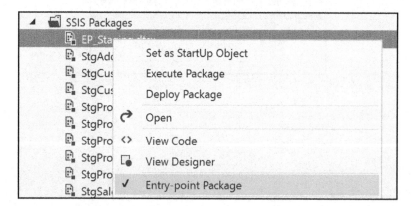

We'll now deploy the project and load the staging tables from the sources.

Getting ready

This recipe assumes that you have access to the companion solution and have the
ETL.Staging SSIS project handy.

How to do it...

1. From SSDT, right-click on the ETL.Staging project and choose **Deploy** from the
contextual menu, as shown in the following screenshot:

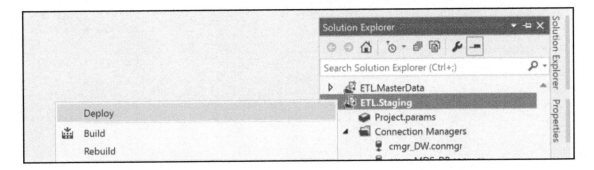

2. From the **Integration Services Deployment Wizard**, create
   SSISCookBookSolution, as shown in the following screenshot:

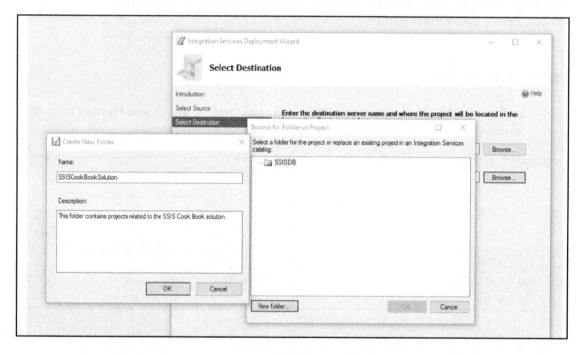

3. Click on **OK** twice to dismiss both the **Create New Folder** and the **Browse for Folder in Project** windows. Make sure that the path is named /SSISDB/SSISCookBookSolution/ETL.Staging and click on **Next** and then **Deploy** to deploy the project.

4. Once deployed, go back to SSMS; we're going to configure the project. Navigate to the project and right-click on it. As shown in the following screenshot, select **Configure**:

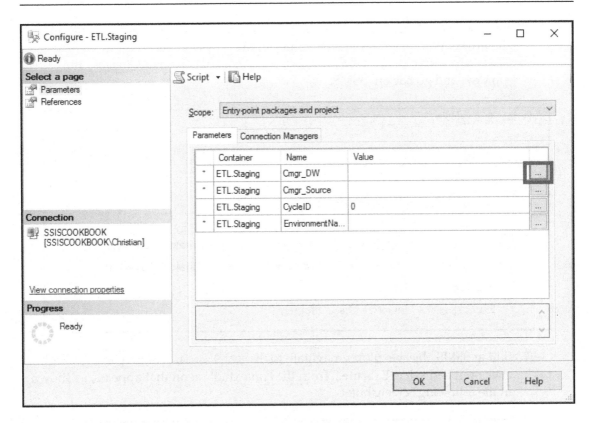

5. As shown in the preceding screenshot, click on the ellipsis (...) button for each parameter and set the property as follows:

- Cmgr_DW: Data Source=.;Initial Catalog=AdventureWorksLTDW2016;Provider=SQLNCLI11.1;Int egrated Security=SSPI

- Cmgr_Source: Data Source=.;Initial Catalog=AdventureWorksLT;Provider=SQLNCLI11.1;Integrate d Security=SSPI

- CycleID: No need to change it

- EnvironmentName: Staging

6. Once set, you should have something like the following screenshot. Configuring the project parameters stores the values in the project's catalog view `[SSISDB].[catalog].[object_parameters]`. Click on **OK** to close the window and go back to SSMS.

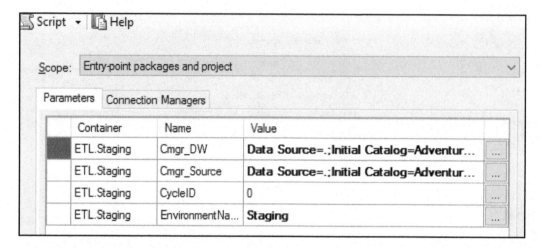

7. Still in SSMS object explorer, navigate to the `EP_Staging.dtsx` package. Right-click on it and select **Execute...** from the contextual menu that appears, as shown in the following screenshot:

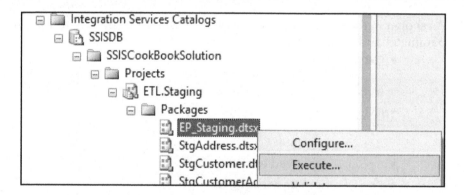

8. Click on **Yes** when asked to view the execution report. Your screen should look like the following screenshot:

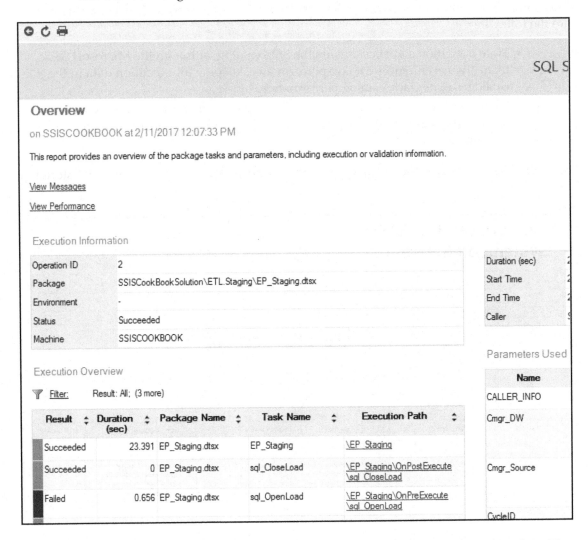

9. Still in SSMS, right-click on any table in the `Staging` schema to view its data. The `Staging` schema is now loaded.

Framework calls in EP_Staging.dtsx

This section of the book introduces an ETL framework. The purposes of such a framework are the following:

- Store execution statistics outside the SSIS catalog: although the Microsoft SSIS team always enhances catalog performance, keeping all execution data in the catalog will degrade catalog performance.
- Align the data in such a way to be able to do some analytics on the execution data. In that case, think of the framework as an SSIS package execution data warehouse.

The following diagram is the ER diagram of the framework tables. These tables are stored in the SystemLog schema:

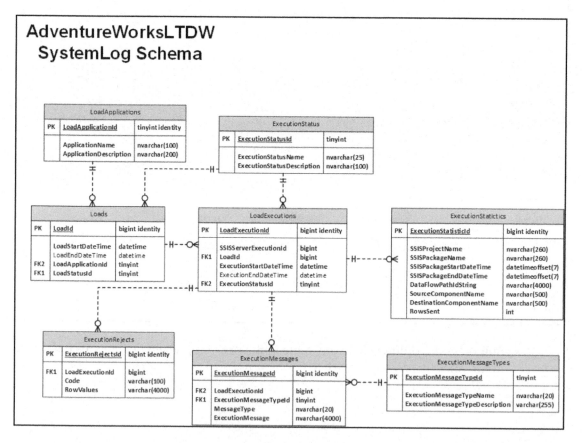

Here's the table list and their purposes:

- LoadApplications: This table contains one value: SSISCookBook sample solution. The purpose of this table, coupled with the Loads table that we'll describe next, is to group many SSIS executions together into a common solution. For example, in this book, we'll have an entry-point package that will call the execution of the entry-point packages of both ETL.Staging and ETL.DW projects.

- Loads: Using this table is not mandatory. The purpose of this table is to group many SSIS executions together to know how much time it took to execute all related projects. It can also be used to determine if all related projects finished successfully or not.

- LoadExecutions: This table contains information related to a specific SSIS execution. The execution start and end time allow us to calculate the execution time, while the execution status will tell us what happened for this execution.

- ExecutionStatistics: Now we're as detailed as possible in SSIS package components. This table contains various row counts and/or execution times for each component in the SSIS package.

- ExecutionStatus: This table shows SSIS execution statuses according to the product's documentation:
    - Execution created
    - Running
    - Cancelled
    - Failed
    - Pending
    - Ended unexpectedly
    - Succeeded
    - Stopping
    - Completed

- ExecutionRejects: This table will hold row that have failed to load properly in a target table. The Code column can contain error code as well as business keys. The rows values hold the column values for a specific row from the source. We'll talk about this table's usage later in the book.

- ExecutionMessages: This table is mainly used to hold various warnings and errors that occur during packages execution.

- `ExecutionMessageTypes`: This table contains the possible message types used by the framework:
    - Errors
    - Warnings
    - Information

These tables have been deployed as part of the `ADVentureWorks2016` database. They are used with stored procedures called **Execute SQL Tasks** from the entry-point packages.

These stored procedures are in the `SystemLog` schema. The following list describes the various stored procedures used to load these tables:

- `OpenLoad`: This procedure inserts a row in the `Systemlog.Loads` table and it returns the `LoadId` column value to the calling program; in our case, an entry-point package. The newly created row status is set to `Running` and the `LoadStartDateTime` is set to the system date and time of the machine where the code is executed.
- `CloseLoad`: This procedure takes a `LoadId` parameter and does the following updates on the table `SystemLog.Loads` table:
    - Check if all related `LoadExecutions` entries have run successfully. If that's the case, the status will change from `Running` to `Success`. Otherwise, the status will be set to `Failed`.
    - In any case, set the `LoadEndDateTime` value to the system date and time of the machine where the code is executed.

- `OpenLoadExecution`: This procedure has the following parameters:
    - `@ServerExecutionId`: The SSIS execution ID that is sent from the calling SSIS package.
    - `@LoadId`: The `SystemLog.Loads` table's `LoadId` value. Since this value is optional, the parameter has a default value of -1.

    It then inserts a row in the `SystemLog.LoadExecutions` table with parameters values and system date and time. It also returns the `LoadExecutionId` column value that has been assigned by the insertion of the row to the calling program (SSIS entry-point package).

- `CloseLoadExecution`: This is one of the most complex procedures. It receives a single parameter, `@LoadExecutionId` and does the following:
  - It retrieves the status for the `SSISExecutionId` column value for the `@LoadExecutionId` value
  - It retrieves the row counts of various packages components for the `SSISExecutionId` and inserts them into the `ExecutionStatistics` table
  - It assigns the `@ExecutionEndDatetime` column to system date and time

- `LogExecutionMessage`: This procedure receives three parameters: `@LoadExecutionId`, `@ExecutionMessageType`, and `@ExecutionMessage`. It simply inserts a row into the `SystemLog.ExecutionMessages` table.
- `LogExecutionRejects`: This procedure is used to log rows that have been rejected by the package executions. It has three parameters: `@LoadExecutionId`, `@RejectCode`, and `@RowValues`.

This constitutes the basics of an ETL framework. As well see in future recipes, we'll use the preceding procedures in the entry-point packages.

The `Loads`, `ExecutionStatus`, and `ExecutionMessageTypes` tables have some predefined data inserted via a `ScriptPostDeployment`.

Now we're going to insert the framework procedure calls into the `EP_Staging` package.

Getting ready

This recipe assumes that you have access to this book's companion solution.

How to do it...

1. With the solution opened, expand the ETL.Staging SSIS project. Select the EP_Staging.dtsx package and open it. Navigate to the **Event Handler** tab and select the OnPreExecute event handler from the drop-down list, as shown in the following screenshot:

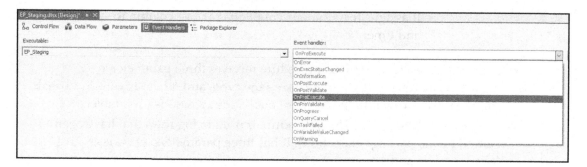

2. As shown in the following screenshot, click the hyperlink to create the OnPreExecute event handler:

Click here to create an 'OnPreExecute' event handler for executable 'EP_Staging'

3. If you look at the **Variable** pane, you'll notice that there are is a variable in that package that is called LoadExecutionId. This variable will hold the value returned by the OPenLoadExecution stored procedure call. From the SSIS toolbox, drag and drop an **Execute SQL Task** onto the designer surface and name it sql_OpenLoadExecution.

4. Double-click on the SQL task (or right-click on it and select **Edit**) and set the following properties on the **General** tab:
   - **ResultSet**: Choose **None** from the drop-down list. This is the default value.
   - **Connection**: From the drop-down list, choose cmgr_DW.
   - **SQLStatement**: Enter EXECUTE [SystemLog].[OpenLoadExecution] ?,?,? OUTPUT.The ? marks correspond to parameters. We'll set them up next in this recipe.

5. Now, click on the **Parameter Mapping** tab in the list at the left of the **Execute SQL Task Editor** and add the following parameters:
   - First parameter:
     - **Variable Name**: System::ServerExecutionID
     - **Direction**: Inpu
     - **Data Type**: Long
     - **Parameter Name**: 0
     - **Parameter Size**: -1

   - Second parameter:
     - **Variable Name**: $Project::LoadId
     - **Direction**: Input
     - **Data Type**: Long
     - **Parameter Name**: 1
     - **Parameter Size**: -1

   - Third parameter:
     - **Variable Name**: SystemLog::LoadExecutionId
     - **Direction**: Output
     - **Data Type**: Long
     - **Parameter Name**: 2
     - **Parameter Size**: -1

6. Now, right-click on the task and select **Execute Task** from the contextual menu that appears. The task should execute successfully.

7. In SSMS, right-click on the SystemLog.LoadExecutions table and click on the **Select Top 1000 Row** to see the data. You should have one row in the table.

8. Now, let's move to the OnPostExecute event handler. Click the hyperlink to create an OnPostExecute event handler and drag an SQL task onto its surface. Assign the following properties on the **General** tab:
   - **ResultSet**: Choose **None** from the drop-down list. This is the default value.
   - **Connection**: From the drop-down list, choose cmgr_DW.
   - **SQLStatement**: Enter EXECUTE [SystemLog].[CloseLoadExecution] ? Again. The ? marks correspond to parameters. In this case, we have only one.

9. Now, click on the **Parameter Mapping** tab in the list at the left of the **Execute SQL Task Editor** and add the following parameters:
   - First parameter:
     - **Variable Name:** SystemLog::LoadExecutionId
     - **Direction:** Output
     - **Data Type:** Long
     - **Parameter Name:** 0
     - **Parameter Size:** -1

10. That's it! All framework objects are set up for the ETL.Staging SSIS project! In the next chapter, we'll have a look at the project integration with SQL jobs and automation.

There's more...

The issue faced many times with SSIS load applications is that collecting execution statistics and messages are not built up front. In the past, before the SSIS catalog facilities, developers needed to add substantial elements, such as **Execute SQL Tasks** in the various event handlers or add row counts and variables in every child package. This was most of the time accomplished by using template packages, packages that contained all the necessary plumbing. They were then adapted to the load tasks necessary to load data. When these templates were not used up front, developers needed to open all developed packages and modify them. With medium to large sized project's that had 50+ packages, this task was tedious and most of the time not done.

Creating framework calls in SSIS entry-point packages is the simplest way to collect row counts and execution messages while the package is executing. The framework shown here is both simple and efficient at doing it. Nothing special must be set in the called (child) package to record execution information.

4
Data Warehouse Loading Techniques

This chapter will cover the following recipes:

- Designing patterns to load dimensions of a data warehouse
- Loading the data warehouse using the framework
- Near real-time and on-demand loads
- Using parallelism

Introduction

Once the framework is set up, it's time to focus on the different layers of our data warehouse. There are various architectural schools of thought when it comes to data warehouses:

- **Corporate Information Factory (CIF)**
- The Kimball Group dimensional data warehouse
- Data vault

The main difference between the Kimball Group and the others is the way a datamart is loaded. The Kimball Group approach loads data into a staging area and from there, refreshes the data warehouse. The latter is modeled as a dimensional data warehouse. It is also known as a **datamart** or **star schema**. The Kimball Group approach uses denormalized tables in its data warehouse.

A typical data warehouse using the Kimball Group method has the following components:

- Data sources that can be in different formats such as text files, databases, Excel, and so on
- A staging area that can be either persistent (contains all history of data loaded) or transient (emptied every time data is loaded)
- One or more datamarts that are tied to business processes such as sales in the samples of this book

It is also shown in the following screenshot:

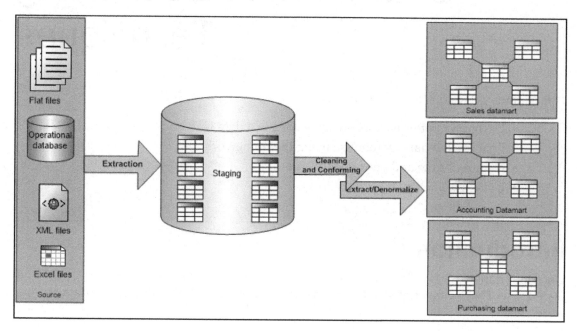

The two other approaches load data into a staging area and transfer it to another layer. The CIF approach uses a data warehouse that consists of tables modeled at third normal form. The data vault approach requires loading data into special entities such as hubs, satellites, and links. Once the data is loaded in this layer, it is most often loaded into a datamart for ease of consumption.

As stated in the previous chapter, the adventureworksLTDW2016 database uses the Kimball Group architecture. The reason for this is that it's a simpler architecture, especially since our sample database has only data source.

Designing patterns to load dimensions of a data warehouse

The difference between these patterns is the way historical data is stored in the dimensions. We call them **Slowly Changing Dimensions (SCD)**. The following points give an overview of various SCD types:

- **Type 0**: This retains the original. This means that any changes to a specific member of the dimension will result in a new member inserted with new values. As opposed to SCD type 2, there's no concept of the current version or start and end date of a row. This SCD type is rarely used.

- **Type 1**: This overwrites changes, no history is kept. For example, let's say we have a person's `marital status` attribute in a `claimant` dimension. If the initial value at insertion was `Single`, the attribute value is updated to `Married` when the person gets married.

- **Type 2**: This keeps history (versioning). A bunch of system columns are added to the dimension:

  - The start and end date of the dimension member (row). Usually, the start date equals the date when the row was first inserted in the dimension, and the end date is set to a value that is very far in the future (for example, December 31, 9999). This allows us to report using a specific date as the interval and see the member value with its historical value.

  - Often, a Boolean column, `IsCurrent`, is used in conjunction with the dates. It eases the retrieval of the latest dimension value without using dates.

  - For the preceding example, a person's marital status, instead of overwriting the person `marital status` attribute, a new row is inserted. The previous row (where the person marital status was single) sees its `IsCurrent` value set to false while the new row becomes current.

- **Type 3**: A column is added to the dimension n to hold the previous value. For the person marital status example, we would have the `marital previous status` and the `marital status` columns. The first column would be added to the dimension structure.

- **Type 4**: Adds a mini dimension. It is mainly used for large dimensions, this pattern allows the update of dimensions members that change frequently without having to query or update a very large table. An example of this would be the demographic attributes of a large `ClubMember` dimension for a company that sells shows (circus, festivals, and so on). If the organization has a promotion for a certain type of member (frequent assistance, high salary, age group), it would be easier to link these dimension attributes in a separate table attached to the fact table. The following screenshot shows an example of this modeling technique:

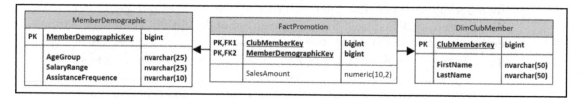

- **Type 5**: Adds a mini dimension and type 1 outrigger. When the `DimMemberDemographic` dimension becomes large, we might need to filter the current attributes against the base dimension. This is exactly what the SCD type 5 does. The following screenshot shows that a small outrigger is used to better slice the `DimClubMember` dimension by bringing the current demographic attributes of each member into a more manageable dimension table:

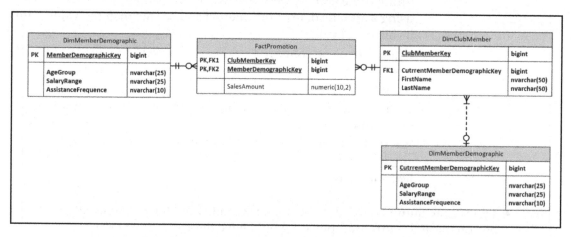

- **Type 6**: This is a combination of SCD types 1, 2, and 3. Basically, the dimension has date ranges to preserve history, some attributes (columns) are overwritten, and there may be some denormalization of attributes (type 3).

In the sample solution, we've implemented SCD types 1 and 6 only.

This recipe discusses type 1 implementation. We'll go through an existing package and explain how to complete it. All the type 1 dimension's packages have been completed except one: `DimProduct_Incomplete.dtsx`. As a reference, you can always look at the completed package: `DimProduct.dtsx`. The incomplete package is shown in the following screenshot:

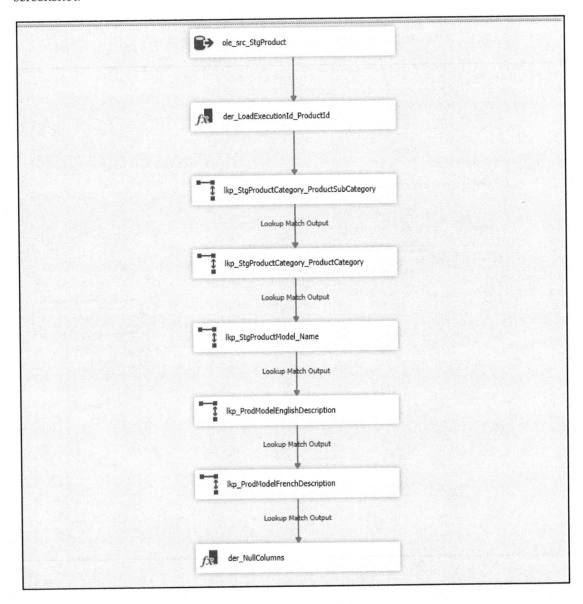

The `ole_src_StgProduct` contains a query from the `Staging.StgProduct` table:

```
SELECT ProductID, Name ProductName, ProductNumber, Color, StandardCost,
ListPrice, [Size], Weight, ProductModelID, ProductCategoryID
FROM Staging.StgProduct
WHERE LoadExecutionId = ?
```

The `LoadExecutionId` is parameterized with the package parameter
(`SourceLoadExecutionId`), as shown in the following screenshot:

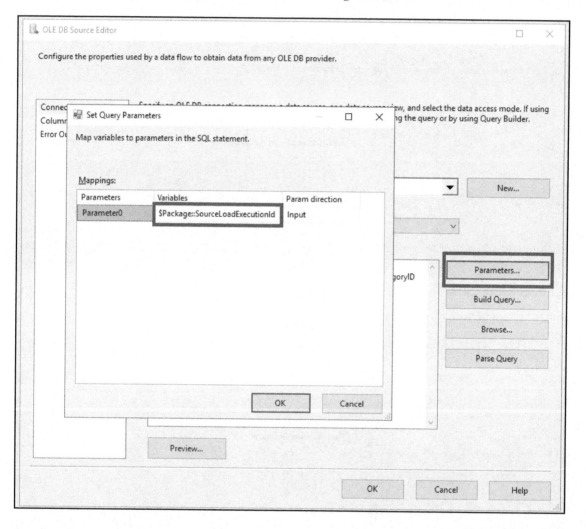

This parameter is given by a framework-stored procedure call (`OpenLoadExecutionId`). It allows you to query the latest slice of staging data that has not been inserted in the data warehouse yet.

A derived column is used to add the data warehouse `LoadExecutionId` to the pipeline. It also converts the integer source product ID from an integer to a small integer, as shown in the following screenshot:

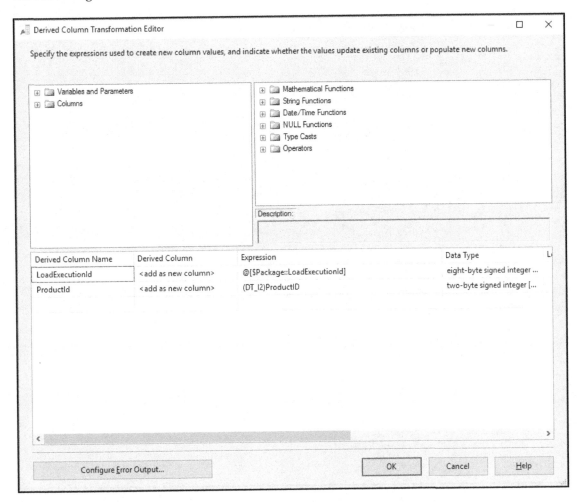

Then, there are a bunch of lookups that bring attributes to the pipeline. For example, the following screenshot shows how we retrieve the `SubCategory` column from the `Staging.StgProductCategory` table using the product category ID from the OLE DB source. At the same time, the `ParentProductCategoryID` column is retrieved to get the category in a subsequent lookup:

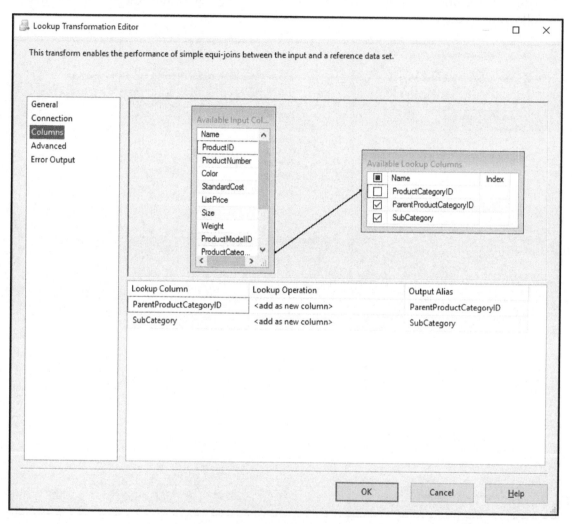

All the lookups use what is called **lookup expressions**. This means that the lookup cache is built with only the latest `LoadExecutionId` available for the staging area environment. To set the lookup expression, we click anywhere in the background of the data flow task and go to the **Properties** pane. We scroll down to **Expressions** and we set the `lkp_StgProductCategory` SQL command, as shown in the following screenshot:

Clicking on the ellipsis button (...) will produce the following dialog box:

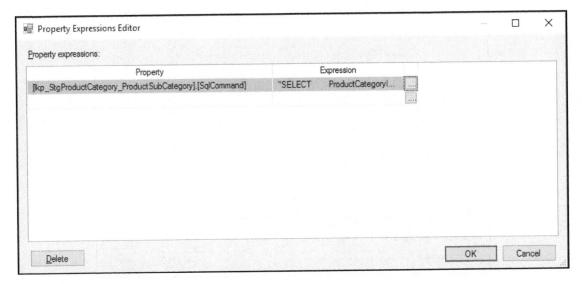

To set the expression, we click on the ellipsis button again. The **Expression Builder** appears as shown in the following screenshot:

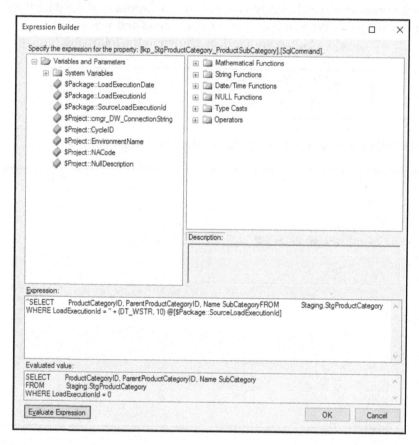

The SELECT SQL statement is filtered using the package SourceExecutionId parameter. This filtering is used to cache only the necessary rows in memory as lookups with full cache might use lots of memory if we're not careful.

After all the lookups, we have a derived column that replaces all the nullable columns with default values.

Doing so has the following benefits:

- Simplifies the dimension usage when querying. A null value cannot be compared to another value even if it's null. Using default values simplifies the queries.
- Null values cannot be indexed. Having a value instead of a null will surely help querying performances.
- Null values have to be handled differently in many SSIS transforms. Using non-null values simplifies the code.

The following screenshot shows the content of the der_NULL columns:

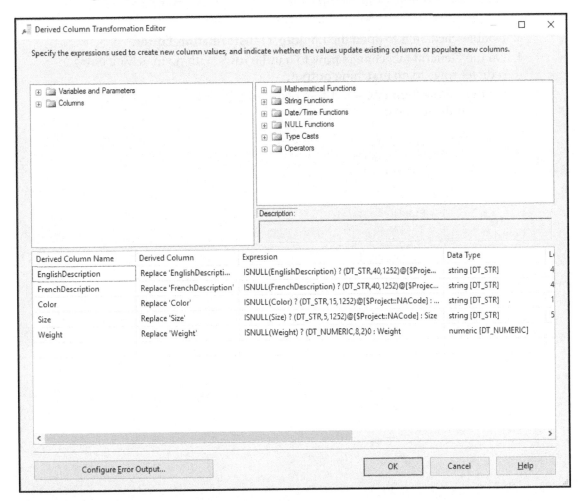

All right, enough talk now. Let's complete the package.

Getting ready

You will need to have access to the sample solution to follow this recipe.

How to do it...

1. Open the DimProduct_Incomplete if not done and go into the data flow task (dft_DimProduct_ups).
2. Add a lookup transform after the der_NULLColumns and rename it lkp_DimProduct_productid.
3. Double-click on it to open the **Lookup Transformation Editor**.
4. On the **General** tab, change how to handle rows with no matching entry to redirect rows to no matching output.
5. On the **Connection** tab, select **Use result of SQL** query and paste the following query in the textbox:

```
SELECT   [IDProduct]
       , [ProductName]
       , [EnglishDescription]
       , [FrenchDescription]
       , [Color]
       , [Size]
       , [Weight]
       , [StandardCost]
       , [ListPrice]
       , [ModelName]
       , [Category]
       , [SubCategory]
       , [LoadExecutionId]
FROM     [DW].[DimProduct];
```

6. On the **Columns** tab, select all the columns except `IDProduct` and rename them as shown in the following screenshot:

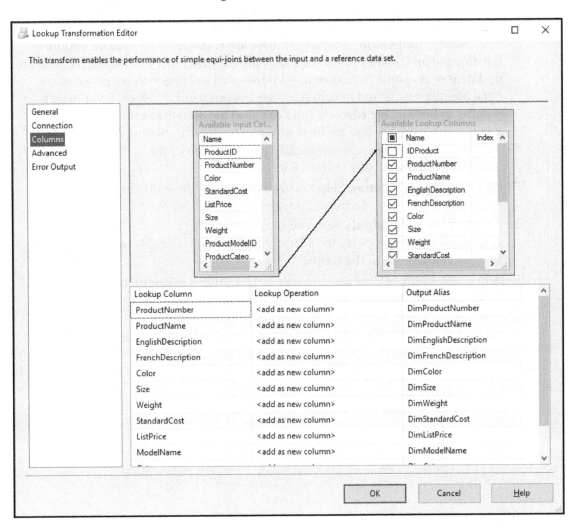

7. Click **OK** to close the **Lookup Transformation Editor**.

8. From the SSIS toolbox, insert a script component transform. Select transformation script type and rename it `scr_CheckForDifferentColumns`. This script will be used to enhance performance of the data flow. If the product exists in the `DimProduct` dimension, we check if there are real differences before updating the dimension. Updates in the data flow are executed row by row. Every time an update is sent to an `oledb` command transform, a connection is opened to the database, the row is updated, and a `Commit` command is issued. So, if there's nothing to update, the row will not be sent to the dimension, saving us unnecessary updates, and performance will be greatly enhanced.

9. Tie the script component to the lookup match output of the `lkp_DimProduct_productid` lookup.

10. Go to the **Input Columns**. Select everything except the following columns: `ProductID`, `Product Number`, `ProductModelID`, and `ProductCategoryID`.

11. Go to **Inputs and Outputs**. Rename `Output0` to `DifferentColumns`. Set its `ExclusionGroup` property to `1`. This will allow us to use this output selectively later, as you will see in the script.

12. Add a new output called `SameColumns`. This output is useful to debug the script component. Set its `SynchronousInoutID` to `scr_CheckForColumnDifference`. Also set its `ExclusionGroup` property to `1`.

13. Now, go back to the **Script** tab and click on the **Edit Script...** button. The VSTA editor opens. Type the script as shown in the following screenshot:

```
       2 references
16  ⊟  public override void Input0_ProcessInputRow(Input0Buffer Row)
17     {
18         bool _RowIsDifferent = false;
19
20         if ((!_RowIsDifferent) && (Row.Category != Row.DimCategory))
21             _RowIsDifferent = true;
22
23         if ((!_RowIsDifferent) && (Row.Color != Row.DimColor))
24             _RowIsDifferent = true;
25
26         if ((!_RowIsDifferent) && (Row.EnglishDescription != Row.DimEnglishDescription))
27             _RowIsDifferent = true;
28
29         if ((!_RowIsDifferent) && (Row.FrenchDescription != Row.DimFrenchDescription))
30             _RowIsDifferent = true;
31
32         if ((!_RowIsDifferent) && (Row.DimListPrice!= Row.DimListPrice))
33             _RowIsDifferent = true;
34
35         if ((!_RowIsDifferent) && (Row.ModelName != Row.DimModelName))
36             _RowIsDifferent = true;
37
38         if ((!_RowIsDifferent) && (Row.ProductName!= Row.DimProductName))
39             _RowIsDifferent = true;
40
41         if ((!_RowIsDifferent) && (Row.ProductNumber != Row.DimProductNumber))
42             _RowIsDifferent = true;
43
44         if ((!_RowIsDifferent) && (Row.Size != Row.DimSize))
45             _RowIsDifferent = true;
46
47         if ((!_RowIsDifferent) && (Row.StandardCost != Row.DimStandardCost))
48             _RowIsDifferent = true;
49
50         if ((!_RowIsDifferent) && (Row.SubCategory != Row.DimSubCategory))
51             _RowIsDifferent = true;
52
53         if ((!_RowIsDifferent) && (Row.Weight != Row.DimWeight))
54             _RowIsDifferent = true;
55
56         if (_RowIsDifferent == true)
57             Row.DirectRowToDifferentColumns();
58         else
59             Row.DirectRowToSameColumns();
60     }
```

14. Then declare a Boolean variable and every `if` statement. Check if there's a difference between a column in the source and its matching component in the dimension. At the end of the script, if there's a difference, we need to update the row and the method `Row.DirectRowToDifferentColumns` is called. This is possible because we previously set the `ExclusionGroup` property of the output to `1`. If no difference has been found, the row is sent to the `SameColumns` output.

15. Now, we'll do the final wiring of the data flow task. Add an OLE DB destination from the SSIS toolbox and rename it `ole_dst_DimProduct`.

16. From the `lkp_DimProduct_productid` lookup, drag the green path (arrow) to it. Double-click on it to open the **OLE DB Destination Editor** and set the properties as shown in the following screenshot:

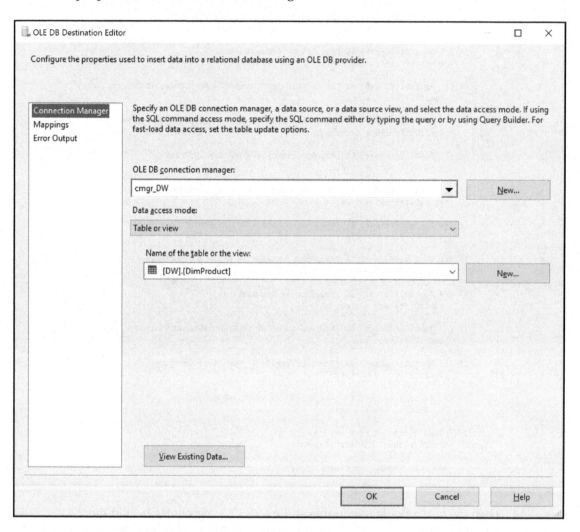

17. Click on the **Mappings** tab and map the columns as shown in the following screenshot. Click **OK** to close the **OLE DB Destination Editor**:

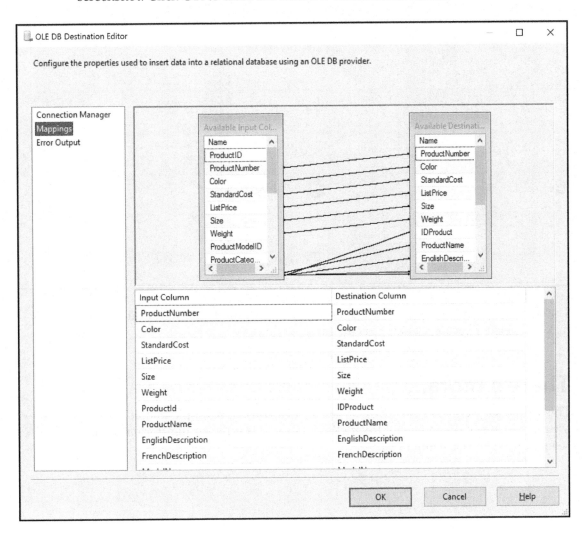

18. The final version of the package should end up looking like the following screenshot:

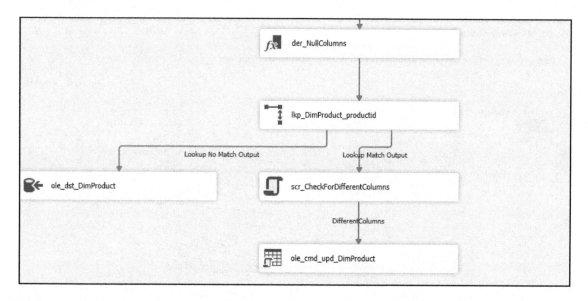

The package is now complete! You can now right-click on the background of the data flow task and select **Execute Task** to execute the data flow.

There's more...

This recipe showed you how a SCD type 1 dimension can be implemented in SSIS. There are many ways of doing so, but the method we used is quite straightforward and we've seen many solutions using it.

Loading the data warehouse using the framework

This section of the chapter will focus on data warehouse refresh types. The recipes we'll be working through will show you how data is usually refreshed in a data warehouse. This section will basically cover the following topics:

- **Full historical load**: This type of loading technique is usually used once to initialize the data warehouses when they are empty
- **Incremental loads**: This only loads changes in the source into the data warehouse
- **Near real-time loads (on demand)**: This is usually used to refresh specific tables with the latest changes for reporting

This recipe will show how the data warehouse loads data in batches. The load programs (SSIS packages) are triggered via a schedule. You'll see that all the packages use the framework to filter the data loaded into the staging. This is the basis of the incremental load that we're going to implement in the data warehouse packages.

Getting ready

This section assumes you have downloaded the solution files and you are the administrator of your PC.

How to do it...

1. Open SSMS and go to **Security | Credentials**. Right-click on the folder and select **New Credential** from the contextual menu.
2. Set the different properties as shown in the following screenshot:

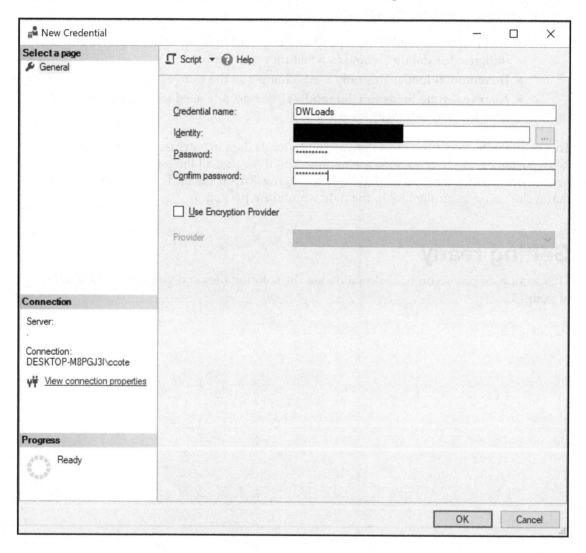

3. For the **Identity** textbox, use your domain (or machine name) login. This information can easily be found if you open a command prompt and execute the command WhoAmI.

4. Once the credential is set, we'll create a SQL Agent proxy. Expand the SQL Server Agent node as shown in the following screenshot. If the agent is not started, right-click on it to start the service.

5. Right-click on the Proxies/SSIS Package Execution folder and select **New Proxy** from the contextual menu that appears. The **New Proxy Account** window appears. To set the **Credential name**, click on the ellipsis button at the right of the textbox and select the DWLoads credential created in an earlier step. Set the properties similar to those that are shown in the following screenshot:

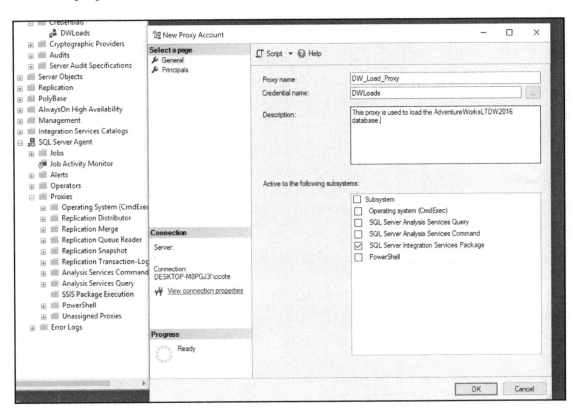

6. Click on **OK** to save the proxy and close the window.
7. We'll create the SQL job now. Right-click on the `Jobs` folder and select **New Job** from the menu that appears. The **New Job** window appears. Set the properties like those in the following screenshot:

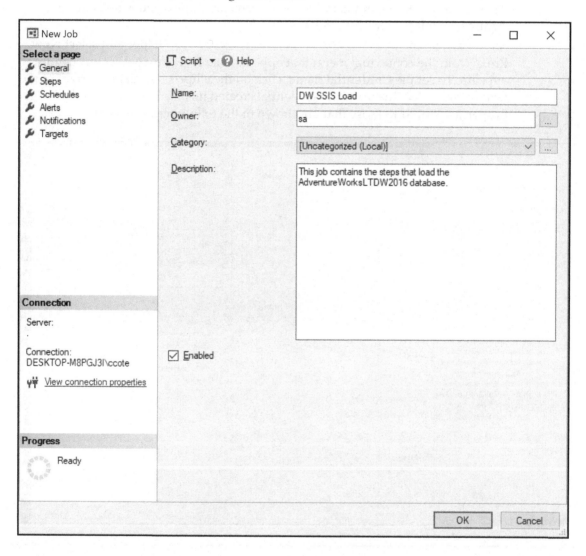

8. Click on the **Steps** in the left menu. The left pane appears. Click on the **New...** button at the bottom of the window. The **Job Step Properties** window appears. Fill the textboxes as shown in the following screenshot:

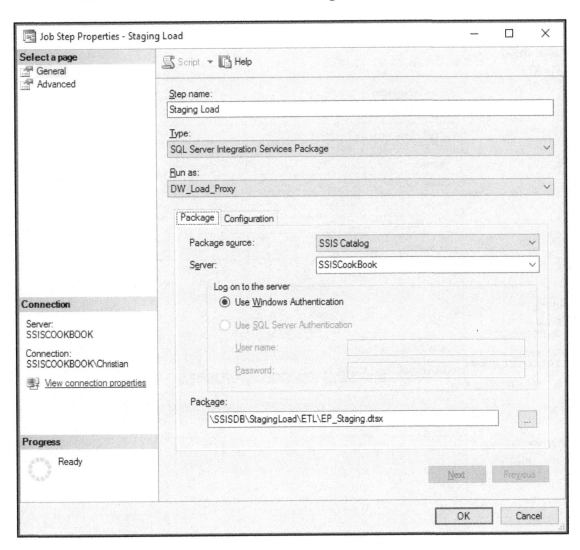

9. Click on the **Configuration** tab beside the package one. The parameters' configuration is now visible. For each parameter, click on the ellipsis button (...) to set the value of the parameters as shown in the following screenshot:

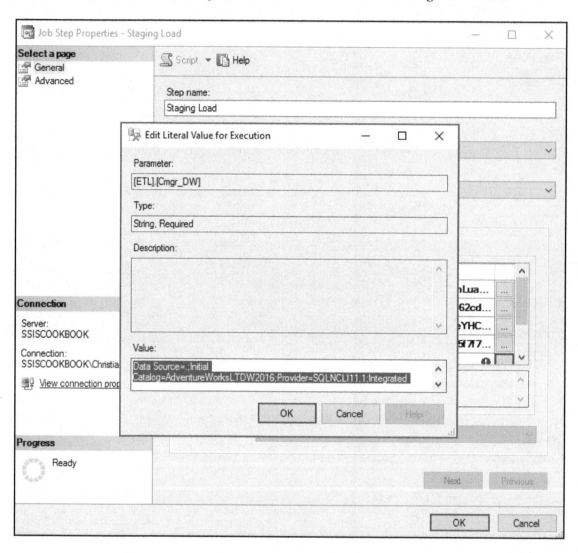

10. Click **OK** to close the **Edit Literal Value for Execution** window. Still in the **Configuration** tab, click on the **Advanced** tab. From there, select the custom logging level we created in `Chapter 2`, *What Is New in SSIS 2016*. Your screen should look like the following screenshot. Click **OK** to close the **Job Step Properties** windows and save your changes:

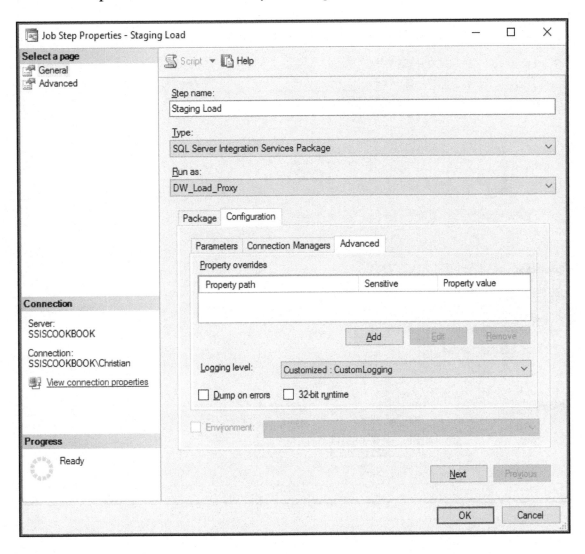

11. Repeat the same steps for the `EP_Datamart` entry-point package.

12. Your job window should now look like the following screenshot. Click on **OK** to close the **New Job** window and create the job:

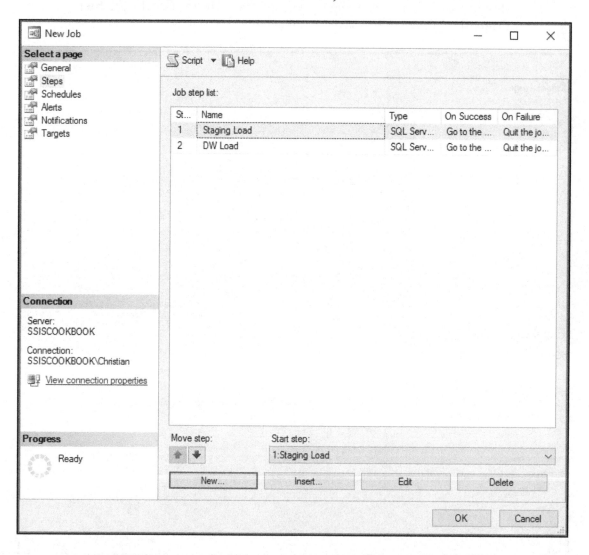

13. Right-click on the job and select **Start Job at Step**. A window like the one in the following screenshot appears. Click on **Start** to start the job execution:

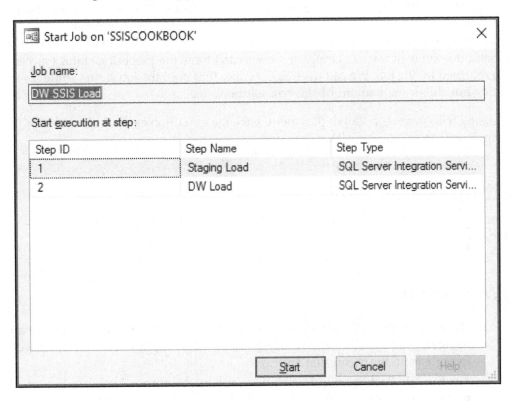

The database AdventureWorksLTDW2016 is now completely loaded.

Near real-time and on-demand loads

Triggering loads using SQL Server Agent has some limitations. For one, we cannot run the job more than once at a time. Another limitation is that it is hard to trigger jobs programmatically. There is a stored procedure called `sp_Start_Job` that can do it. It starts the job but doesn't wait for it to complete, so we can't have the execution status (success, failed) returned by the job. We can use TSQL scripts that pool the job status while it's executing but still, it's not an out-of-the-box solution.

When using SSIS project-model deployment, package execution can be called via TSQL. This recipe will show you how it can be done.

Getting ready

This recipe assumes that you have deployed the two sample SSIS projects in the SSIS catalog.

How to do it...

1. Open SSMS if not already open and go to the SSIS catalog node. Expand it and navigate to the `EP_Staging` entry-point package. Right-click on it and select **Execute** from the menu that appears.
2. The **Execute Package** window opens. Click on the ellipsis button (...) to set all parameter values, and accept the default that is used in the project.
3. As shown in the following screenshot, click on script and select **New Query Editor Window**:

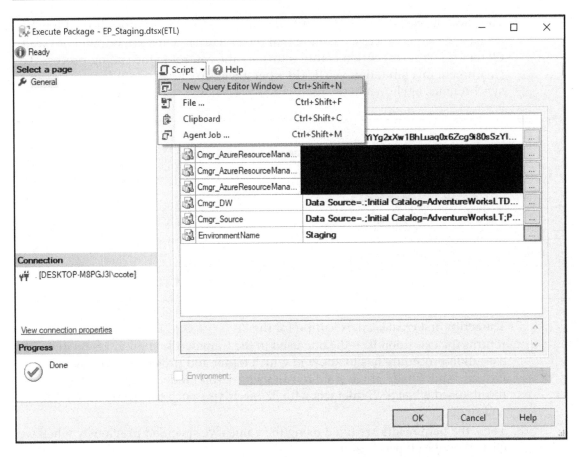

4. The execution script is created into a **New Query Editor Window**. Click on **Cancel** to close the **Execute Package** window.

5. Going back to SSMS, you can see that all execution steps have been scripted.

6. The package execution will run but, like the `sp_Start_Job` procedure, it will be an asynchronous process, meaning that the execution will start, but will not wait till the end of the execution before returning the control to the calling process. To circumvent this limitation, we'll add a parameter to the set execution synchronous, as shown in the following screenshot:

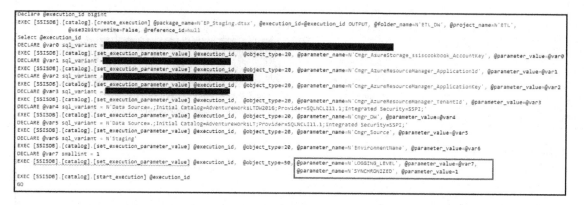

7. The script first creates an execution for the `EP_Staging.dtsx` package and returns the execution ID—the one used in the framework in previous recipes. The execution procedure has to know in which folder and project the package is located. And, finally, if we want to run using 32-bit mode, this parameter is mostly used when SSIS interacts with 32-bit drivers such as Oracle, Excel, Access, and so on.

8. Then, the parameters are filled using the values we specified previously when we clicked on the ellipsis buttons.

9. The parameters are then associated to the execution. Notice the highlighted parameter that specifies that we want the execution to be synchronous.

10. Finally, the execution is triggered. It will return the control to the calling process once the execution terminates.

11. To grab the execution status, we need to run the following query once the execution is completed:

```
SELECT [Status]
FROM SSISDB.[catalog].[executions]
WHERE execution_id = @execution_id
```

There's more...

That's all that is needed to run the package in TSQL. This technique is sometimes used by certain schedulers to call SSIS execution. This method could also be used in reports to refresh certain tables in a near real-time approach.

Using parallelism

This section will now focus on how we can enhance the performance of our package execution. Using parallelism in SSIS is very easy. A simple use of parallelism is in the entrypoint packages. Other parallelism can be implemented in the data flow tasks by using multiple source and destination components. In fact, every source we use in a data flow task has its own thread in SSIS, meaning that SSIS will try to execute all source transforms at once using different hardware resources.

In this recipe, we'll complete the entry-point package for the DW schema load. In this package, we have linked the dimensions together first. We now think that there are no dependencies between them and we'll separate them.

Getting ready

This recipe assumes that you have access to this book's sample solution.

How to do it...

1. From the SSIS.Etl project, open the EP.D_Sequential package from the solution explorer.

2. You'll see that all dimensions are called in sequence, one after the other. An execute package task has to complete before the other starts, as shown in the following screenshot:

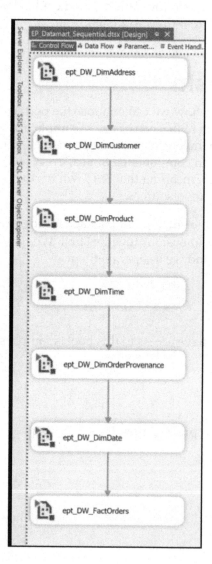

3. From the SSIS toolbox, add a sequence container to the package's control flow and name it `seq_Dimensions`.

4. Delete the link between the fact-tables container and the dimension.

5. Select all the dimensions and drag them into the newly added sequence container.

6. Delete all the links between the dimensions.

7. Now, link the `seq_Dimensions` sequence contained in the fact sequence container.

8. That's it; now SSIS will call the dimension table package execution in parallel. The following screenshot shows the completed package:

There's more...

The solution is not completed yet. We'll add packages as we move forward in the book's recipes.

5
Dealing with Data Quality

n this chapter, we will cover the following recipes:

- Profiling data with SSIS
- Creating a DQS knowledge base
- Data cleansing with DQS
- Creating a MDS model
- Matching with DQS
- Using SSIS fuzzy components

Introduction

Business intelligence projects often reveal previously unseen issues with the quality of the source data. Dealing with data quality includes data quality assessment, or data profiling, data cleansing, and maintaining high quality over time.

In SSIS, the data profiling task helps you find unclean data. The data profiling task is not like the other tasks in SSIS because it is not intended to be run over and over again through a scheduled operation. Think about SSIS as being the wrapper for this tool. You use the SSIS framework to configure and run the data profiling task, and then you observe the results through the separate data profile viewer. The output of the data profiling task will be used to help you in your development and design of the ETL and dimensional structures in your solution. Periodically, you may want to rerun the data profile task to see how the data has changed, but the package you develop will not include the task in the overall recurring ETL process.

SQL Server **Data Quality Services (DQS)** is a knowledge-driven data-quality solution. This means that it requires you to maintain one or more **knowledge base (KB)**. In a KB, you maintain all knowledge related to a specific portion of data—for example, customer data. In DQS projects, you perform cleansing, profiling, and matching activities. You can also use an intermediate staging database to which you copy your source data and export DQS project results. DQS includes server and client components. Before you can use DQS, you must start by installing the DQS components.

The following diagram shows the DQS architecture:

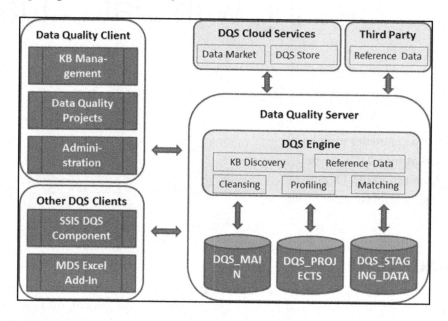

The **Data Quality Server** component includes three databases:

- DQS_MAIN: This includes DQS stored procedures. The DQS stored procedures make up the actual DQS engine. In addition, DQS_MAIN database includes published KBs. A published KB is a KB that has been prepared for use in cleansing projects.
- DQS_PROJECTS: This includes data for KB management and data needed during cleansing and matching projects.
- DQS_STAGING_DATA: This provides an intermediate storage area where you can copy source data for cleansing and where you can export cleansing results.

You can prepare your own knowledge bases locally, including reference data. However, you can also use reference data from the cloud. You can use Windows Azure Marketplace data market to connect to reference data providers. You can also use a direct connection to a third-party reference data provider through a predefined interface.

With the data quality client application, you can manage knowledge bases; execute cleansing, profiling, and matching projects; and administer DQS. SQL Server includes two tools to assist with these tasks. You can use the SSIS DQS cleansing transformation to perform cleansing inside a data flow of your SSIS package. This allows you to perform batch cleansing without the need for interactivity required by the data quality Client. With the free **master data services (MDS)** add-in for Microsoft Excel, you can perform master data matching in an Excel worksheet. The DQS components must be installed together with MDS in order to enable DQS/MDS integration.

Many companies or organizations do regular data cleansing. When you cleanse the data, the data quality goes up to some higher level. The data quality level is determined by the amount of work invested in the cleansing. As time passes, the data quality deteriorates, and you need to repeat the cleansing process. If you spend an equal amount of effort as you did with the previous cleansing, you can expect the same level of data quality as you had after the previous cleansing. Then the data quality deteriorates over time again, and the cleansing process starts over and over again.

The idea of data quality Services is to mitigate the cleansing process. While the amount of time you need to spend on cleansing decreases, you will achieve higher and higher levels of data quality. While cleansing, you learn what types of errors to expect, discover error patterns, find domains of correct values, and so on. You don't throw away this knowledge. You store it, and use it to find and correct the same issues automatically during your next cleansing process.

The idea of master data management, which you can perform with MDS, is to prevent data quality from deteriorating. Once you reach a particular quality level, the MDS application—together with the defined policies, people, and master data management processes—allows you to maintain this level permanently.

There are four main parts of the MDS application. In the MDS database, the master data is stored along with MDS system objects. MDS system objects include system tables and many programmatic objects such as system stored procedures and functions. The MDS service performs the business logic and data access for the MDS solution. Master data manager is a web application for MDS users and administrators. In addition, advanced users can use the master data services add-in for Microsoft Excel.

The following diagram shows the MDS architecture:

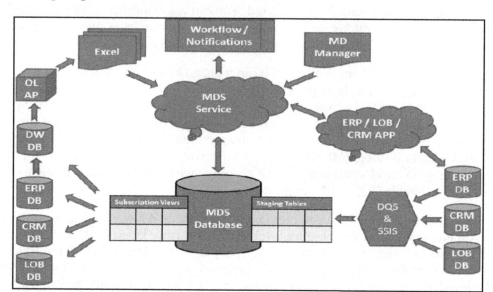

Profiling data with SSIS

The objective of this task is to work with SSIS to profile the data to find the potentially wrong values. In this exercise, you will create an SSIS package with a single task, the data profiling task. Then you will execute the package to profile a set of data. Finally, you will check the results with the data profile viewer application.

Getting ready

You need to have installed the AdventureWorkDW2014 demo database for this exercise.

You can download the full database backup ZIP file `Adventure Works DW 2014 Full Database Backup.zip` from this link:
`https://msftdbprodsamples.codeplex.com/releases`. In addition, the backup file is provided with the source code for this book. Assuming that you copied the `AdventureWorksDW2014.bak` file to the `C:\SSIS2016Cookbook` folder, you can use **SQL Server Management Studio (SSMS)** to execute the following command to restore the database:

```
USE master;
RESTORE DATABASE AdventureWorksDW2014
 FROM  DISK = N'C:\SSIS2016Cookbook\AdventureWorksDW2014.bak'
 WITH  FILE = 1,
 MOVE N'AdventureWorksDW2014_Data'
  TO N'C:\SSIS2016Cookbook\AdventureWorksDW2014_Data.mdf',
 MOVE N'AdventureWorksDW2014_Log'
  TO N'C:\SSIS2016Cookbook\AdventureWorksDW2014_Log.ldf',
 STATS = 5;
GO
```

Then you need to prepare the table you are going to profile. In SSMS, execute the following code:

```
USE AdventureWorksDW2014;
SELECT CustomerKey, FirstName,
MiddleName, LastName,
EmailAddress, MaritalStatus,
Gender, TotalChildren, NumberChildrenAtHome,
EnglishEducation AS Education,
EnglishOccupation AS Occupation,
HouseOwnerFlag, NumberCarsOwned,
CommuteDistance, Region,
BikeBuyer, YearlyIncome,
Age - 10 AS Age
INTO dbo.Chapter05Profiling
FROM dbo.vTargetMail;
GO
```

 For your convenience, the T-SQL code needed for this chapter is provided in the `Chapter05.sql` file.

How to do it...

1. Open **SQL Server Data Tools (SSDT)** and create a new project using the Integration Services Project template. Place the solution in the C:\SSIS2016Cookbook folder and name the project Chapter05.

2. Rename the default package to DataProfiling.dtsx.

3. From the SSIS toolbox, drag the data profiling task onto the control flow work area.

4. Double-click the task to open the **Data Profiling Task Editor**.

5. On the **General** page of the **Data Profiling Task Editor**, select **FileConnection** in the drop-down list for the **DestinationType** property. Select **New File Connection** from the **Destination** property drop-down list. In the File Connection Manager Editor that appears, select **Create File** and enter C:\SSIS2016Cookbook\DataProfiling.xml. Click **Open**, and then click **OK**.

6. Back in the **Data Profiling Task Editor** set the **OverwriteDestination** property to **True**. Your **Data Profiling Task Editor** should look like the following screenshot:

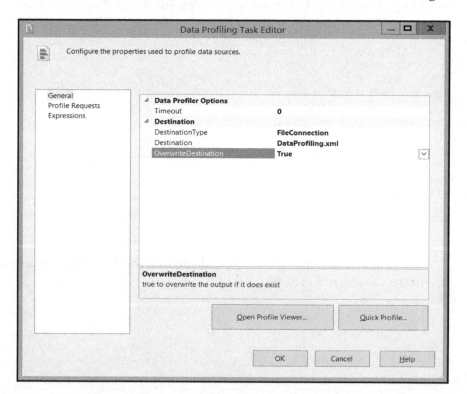

7. Go to **Profile Requests** page. Click somewhere in the first row of the **Profile Type** column and select the **Column Length Distribution Profile Request**. Click the **Request ID** column to finish creating this request.

8. Fill in the **Request Properties** section in the lower half of the window. For the **ConnectionManager** property, create a new ADO.NET connection to connect to the `AdventureWorksDW2014` database on the local SQL Server instance. Select the `dbo.Chapter05Profiling` table for the **TableOrView** property. Select the **MiddleName** column.

9. Add another profile request, but this time create a **Functional Dependency Profile Request**. Use the same ADO.NET connection manager and the same table. Use `Education`, `HouseOwnerFlag`, `MaritalStatus`, and `NumberCarsOwned` for the **DeterminantColumns** property. Use `Occupation` for the **DependentColumn** property. Lower the **FDStrengthThreshold** property to `0.3` so that slightly lower strength dependencies are included.

10. Add a **Candidate Key Profile Request**. For the **KeyColumns** property, select all the columns from the `dbo.Chapter05Profiling` table.

11. Add a **Column Null Ratio Profile Request**. Select the `MiddleName` column.

12. Add a **Column Pattern Profile Request**. Select the `EmailAddress` column.

13. Add a **Column Statistics Profile Request**. Select the `Age` column.

14. Add a **Column Value Distribution Profile Request**. Select the `NumberCarsOwned` column.

15. Your **Data Profiling Task Editor** window should resemble the one shown in the following screenshot. Click **OK** to close the **Data Profiling Task Editor**:

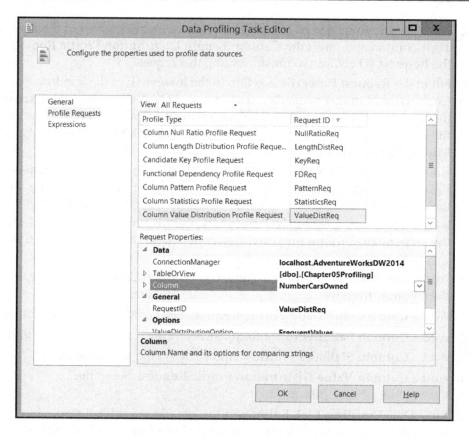

16. Save the package and execute it in debug mode. When the execution is finished, exit the debugging mode. Review the XML file that was created during execution with Visual Studio, Notepad, or Internet Explorer. Close SSDT.

17. Start the **Data Profile Viewer**.

18. In the **Data Profile Viewer** window, click the **Open** button in the upper-left corner.

19. Navigate to the `C:\SSIS2016Cookbook` folder and open the `DataProfiling.xml` file.

20. Click the **Candidate Key Profiles** option in the left-hand pane. Check which columns are suitable to be used as keys (these are the columns that have more unique values than the threshold **Percentage** property for the profile).

21. Click the **Column Length Distribution Profiles** option in the left-hand pane. Check the `MiddleName` distribution. In the middle area of the right-hand pane, click the row that shows the distribution for length `10`. In the right-hand corner of this middle area, click the drill down button to show the source row, as shown in the following screenshot:

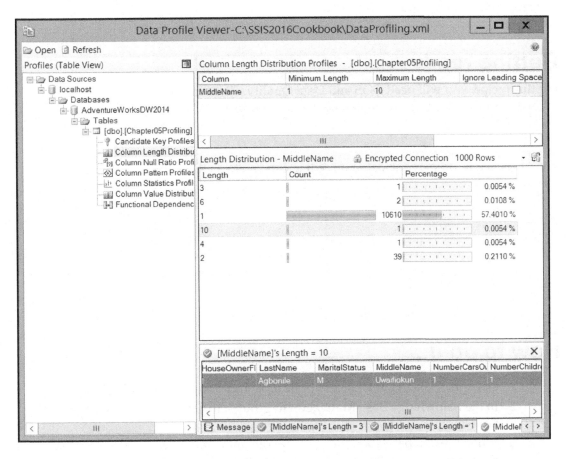

22. Check the **Column Pattern Profiles**. Note the patterns extracted from the `EmailAddress` column. The patterns are expressed as regular expressions. You can use these regular expressions in a rule for the column in a DQS knowledge base domain.

23. Check the other profiles. After you have finished, close the **Data Profile Viewer**. If it is still open, close SSDT as well.

Creating a DQS knowledge base

A DQS KB is the place where you store the knowledge about the data and the cleansing in order to speed up the regular cleansing process. In a real-life scenario, you constantly add knowledge to the KB, and thus improve the cleansing process over time. In this recipe, you will create a basic DQS KB.

Getting ready

For this recipe, you will need DQS and Data Quality Client installed. Please refer to the following link to learn how to install the DQS components:
https://docs.microsoft.com/en-us/sql/data-quality-services/install-windows/install-data-quality-services.

You also need to prepare the data you will use to create a DQS KB. In SSMS, execute the following code:

```
USE AdventureWorksDW2014;
SELECT DISTINCT
City, StateProvinceName AS StateProvince,
EnglishCountryRegionName AS CountryRegion
INTO dbo.AWCitiesStatesCountries
FROM dbo.DimGeography;
GO
```

How to do it...

1. Open the Data Quality Client application and connect to your DQS instance.
2. In the **Knowledge Base Management** group, click the **New KnowledgeBase** button.
3. Name the database AWCustomers. If you want, add a description. Make sure that the **None** option is selected in the **Create Knowledge Base from** drop-down list. Select the **Knowledge Discovery** option in the **Select Activity** list in the lower-right corner of the screen. Click **Next**.
4. On the **Map** tab of the **Knowledge Base Management** screen, select **SQL Server** as your data source. Select the AdventureWorksDW2014 database and the dbo.AWCitiesStatesCountries table.

5. In the **Mappings** section, click the **Create a domain** button (the third button from the left in the group of buttons above the **Mappings** grid, marked with a circle with a yellow star) to create a domain.

6. In the dialog box that appears, enter `City` as the **Domain Name**, and use **String** as the **Data Type**. Make sure that the **Use Leading Values**, **Normalize String**, and **Disable Syntax Error Algorithms** options are checked, and that the **Enable Speller** option is not checked. Make sure that the **Format Output to** option is set to **None** and that the **Language** selected is **English**, as shown in the following screenshot. Click **OK**:

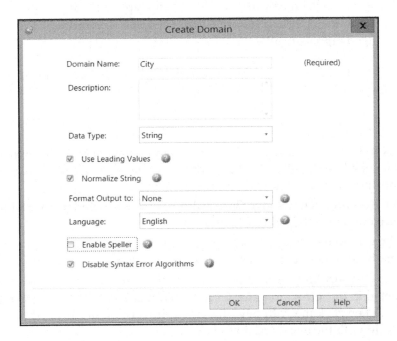

7. Create two additional domains, named `State` and `Country`, with the same settings you used for the `City` domain in step 6.

8. In the **Mappings** grid, select the `City` column from the source in the left-hand column of the first row and map it to the `City` domain in the right-hand column of the first row in the grid.

9. Repeat step 8 twice to add a mapping from the `StateProvince` source column to the `State` domain, and from the `CountryRegion` source column to the `Country` domain. Click Next.

10. On the **Discover** tab, click the **Start** button to start the knowledge discovery. Wait until the process is finished, then review all of the information in the **Profiler** section. This section gives you a quick profile of your data. When you are finished reviewing the profiler information, clickan class="packt_screen">Next.

11. On the **Manage Domain Values** tab, make sure that the City domain is selected in the left-hand pane. Then click the **Add new domain value** button (the button with a small green plus sign on a grid) in the right-hand pane above the grid listing the extracted domain values.

12. In the Value cell, enter Munich. Change the type to **Error** (a red cross). Enter München in the Correct to cell. Press the *Enter* key and note that the data is rearranged alphabetically.

To write ü, hold the *Alt* key and type *0252* or *129* on the numeric keyboard.

13. Click the other two domains in the left-hand pane to check the extracted values. Then click **Finish**. Select **No** in the pop-up window because you are not ready to publish the KB yet. You will edit the domains.

14. Click the **Open Knowledge Base** button in the **Knowledge Base Management** group on the Data Quality Client main screen.

15. In the grid in the left-hand pane, select the AWCustomers KB. Make sure that the **Domain Management** activity is selected. Click **Next**.

16. In the **Domain Management** window, make sure that the City domain is selected in the left-hand pane. Click the **Domain Values** tab in the right-hand pane. Then click the **Add new domain value** button in the right-hand pane above the grid with the extracted domain values.

17. In the Value cell, enter Muenchen. Change the type to **Error** (a red cross). Enter München in the Correct to cell. Press the *Enter* key and note that the data is rearranged alphabetically.

18. Find the **München** value in the grid. Note that this is now the leading value for two additional synonyms, Munich and Muenchen.

19. In the left-hand pane, click the **Create a domain** button. Name the domain StreetAddress and use **String** as the data type. Make sure that the **Use Leading Values**, **Normalize String**, and **Disable Syntax Error Algorithms** options are checked, and that the **Enable Speller** option is not checked. Also make sure that the **Format Output to** option is set to **None** and that the language selected is **English**. Click **OK**.

20. Click the **Term-Based Relations** tab for the `StreetAddress` domain. You will add a term-based relation to correct all occurrences of a term in the domain values.

21. Click the **Add new relation** button. Enter `Ct.` in the `Value` cell and `Court` in the `Correct to` cell. Press *Enter*. The **Apply Changes** button should be unavailable because you do not have any domain values yet.

22. Add a new domain called `BirthDate`. Select **Date** as the data type. Use the leading values and do not format the output. Click **OK**.

23. Click the **Domain Rules** tab for the `BirthDate` domain. In the right-hand pane, click the **Add a new domain rule** button.

24. In the rules grid, enter `MinBirthDate` in the `Name` cell.

25. In the **Build a Rule: MinBirthDate** section, make sure that the **Value is greater than** option is selected in the drop-down condition list. Then enter `1/1/1900` in the textbox and press *Enter*. Check whether this was successfully changed to `Monday, January 01, 1900`.

26. Add a new domain, `Occupation`. Use **String** as the data type. Make sure that the **Use Leading Values** and **Normalize String** options are checked. However, this time **Enable Speller** should be checked and uncheck **Disable Syntax Error Algorithms**. Do not format the output, and use the English language. Click **OK**.

27. Add a new domain, `EmailAddress`. Use **String** as the data type. Make sure that the **Use Leading Values**, **Normalize String**, and **Disable Syntax Error Algorithms** options are checked, and that the **Enable Speller** option is not checked. Do not format the output, and use the English language. Click **OK**.

28. Click the **Domain Rules** tab for the `EmailAddress` domain. Add a new rule called `EmailRegEx`.

29. Select the **Value matches regular expression** option in the **Build a Rule: EmailRegEx Conditions** drop-down list. Then enter `\p{L}+\d\d@ADVENTURE-WORKS\.COM` as the expression. Click outside the textbox.

30. Click the **Add a new condition to the selected clause** button (the leftmost button in the upper-right part of the **Build a Rule area**).

31. Select the **OR** operator to connect the conditions. Select the **Value matches regular expression** option for the second condition from the drop-down list in the **Build a Rule: EmailRegEx Conditions** drop-down list. Then enter `\p{L}+\d@ADVENTURE-WORKS\.COM` as the expression. Click outside the textbox.

The regular expressions needed for this exercise were extracted with the data profiling task in the previous recipe.

32. Click **Finish** to complete domain management. Then click the **Publish** button in the pop-up window. Finally, click **OK** in the next pop-up window. Your knowledge base is now prepared for use.

Data cleansing with DQS

In this recipe, you will create a view with some dirty data and use a DQS cleansing project to cleanse it. You will use the DQS knowledge base prepared in the previous exercise.

Getting ready

This recipe assumes that you have built the DQS knowledge base from the previous recipe. In addition, you need to prepare some demo data in advance. In SSMS, use the following query to prepare the data:

```
USE DQS_STAGING_DATA;
SELECT C.CustomerKey,
C.FirstName + ' ' + c.LastName AS FullName,
C.AddressLine1 AS StreetAddress,
G.City, G.StateProvinceName AS StateProvince,
G.EnglishCountryRegionName AS CountryRegion,
C.EmailAddress, C.BirthDate,
C.EnglishOccupation AS Occupation
INTO dbo.CustomersCh05
FROM AdventureWorksDW2014.dbo.DimCustomer AS C
INNER JOIN AdventureWorksDW2014.dbo.DimGeography AS G
ON C.GeographyKey = G.GeographyKey
WHERE C.CustomerKey % 10 = 0;
GO
```

How to do it...

1. The data prepared in the previous section is clean. For the DQS cleansing project, use the following code to add two rows with incorrect data:

```
USE DQS_STAGING_DATA;
SELECT CustomerKey, FullName,
 StreetAddress, City,
 StateProvince, CountryRegion,
 EmailAddress, BirthDate,
 Occupation
INTO dbo.CustomersCh05DQS
FROM dbo.CustomersCh05
UNION
SELECT -11000,
 N'Jon Yang',
 N'3761 N. 14th St',
 N'Munich',                               -- incorrect city
 N'Kingsland',                            -- incorrect state
 N'Austria',                              -- incorrect country
 N'jon24#adventure-works.com',           -- incorrect email
 '18900224',                             -- incorrect birth date
 'Profesional'                            -- incorrect occupation
UNION
SELECT -11100,
 N'Jacquelyn Suarez',
 N'7800 Corrinne Ct.',                    -- incorrect term
 N'Muenchen',                             -- another incorrect city
 N'Queensland',
 N'Australia',
 N'jacquelyn20@adventure-works.com',
 '19680206',
 'Professional';
GO
```

2. Open the Data Quality Client application if necessary, and connect to your DQS instance.

3. In the **Data Quality Projects** group, click the **New Data Quality Project** button.

4. Name the project `AWCustomersCleansing`. Use the `AWCustomers` knowledge base you created in the previous exercise. Make sure that the **Cleansing** activity is selected. Click **Next**.

5. The **Data Quality Project** window will open with the **Map** tab as the active tab. Select **SQL Server** as the data source, choose the `DQS_STAGING_DATA` database, and select the `dbo.CustomersCh05DQS` table in the **Table/View** drop-down list.

6. In the **Mappings** area, click the button with the small green plus sign above the **Mappings** grid twice to add two rows to the **Mappings** grid. (Five mappings are provided by default, but you need seven.)

7. Use the drop-down lists in the **Source Column** and **Domain** cells to map the following columns and domains:

Column	Domain
BirthDate	BirthDate
StreetAddress	StreetAddress
City	City
StateProvince	State
CountryRegion	Country
EmailAddress	EmailAddress
Occupation	Occupation

8. The following screenshot shows the correct mappings of columns to domains. When your mappings are correct, click **Next**:

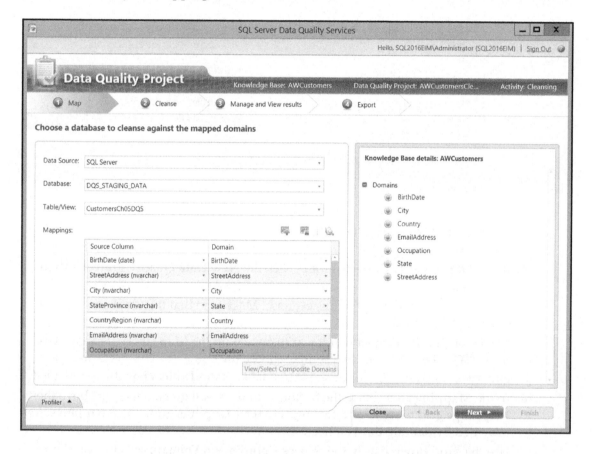

9. On the **Cleanse** tab, click **Start**. Wait until the computer-assisted cleansing is finished, then review the results of the profiling. Click **Next**.

10. On the **Manage and View results** tab, check the results, one domain at a time. Start with the `BirthDate` domain. There should be one invalid value. Make sure that the `BirthDate` domain is selected in the left-hand pane, and click the **Invalid** tab in the right-hand pane. Note the invalid value that was detected. You could write a correct value now in the **Correct to** cell of the grid with invalid values, but this action is not needed for this exercise. Note that all correct values were suggested as new.

11. Select the `StreetAddress` domain in the left-hand pane. One value should be corrected. However, because only the term-based relation (and not the whole value) was corrected, it does not appear among the corrected values. It should appear among the new values. Click the **New** tab in the right-hand pane. Search for the value `7800 Corrinne Ct.` and note that it was corrected with 100 percent confidence to `7800 Corrinne Court`.

12. Clear the **Search Value** textbox. Select the `State` domain in the left-hand pane. Click the **New tab** in the right-hand pane. Note that one value (`Kingsland`) was found as new. The similarity threshold to the original value (`Queensland`) was too low for DQS to automatically correct or even suggest the value. You could correct this value manually, but this is not needed in this exercise.

13. Select the `City` domain in the left-hand pane. Two values should be corrected. Click the **Corrected** tab in the right-hand pane. Note the corrections of the synonyms for `München` (`Munich` and `Muenchen`) to the leading value (`München`). Note also that the confidence for these two corrections is 100 percent. All other values already existed in the KB, and therefore DQS marked them as correct.

14. Select the `Country` domain in the left-hand pane. One value should be suggested. Click the **Suggested** tab in the right-hand pane. Note that DQS suggests replacing `Austria` with `Australia` with 70 percent confidence. You can approve a single value by checking the **Approve** option in the grid. However, don't approve it, because, of course, this is a wrong suggestion. Note that DQS identified all other countries as correct.

15. Select the `EmailAddress` domain in the left-hand pane. One value should be invalid. Click the **Invalid** tab in the right-hand pane. DQS tells you that the `jon24#adventure-works.com` email address does not comply with the `EmailRegEx` rule. Note that all other values are marked as new.

16. Select the `Occupation` domain in the left-hand pane. Note that all values are new. Click the **New** tab in the right-hand pane. Note that the value `Profesional` is underlined with a red squiggly line. This is because you enabled the spelling checker for the `Occupation` domain. Enter `Professional` in the `Correct to` field for the incorrect row. Note that, because you corrected the value manually, the confidence is set to `100` percent. Select the **Approve** checkbox for this row. The row should disappear and appear among the corrected values. Click the **Corrected** tab. Observe the corrected value along with the reason. Click **Next**.

17. On the **Export** tab, look at the output data preview on the left-hand side of the window. You could export the results to a SQL Server table and then correct the original data. However, you don't need to export the results in this lab. Just click **Finish**.

18. Close SSMS and the Data Quality Client application.

Creating a MDS model

In this recipe, you are going to create an MDS model with the entities, attributes, and hierarchies needed for a customer's entity set. Then you will populate the entities and check your business rules.

Getting ready

In order to test this recipe, you need to have MDS installed. Please refer to the following link to learn how to install the MDS components:
`https://docs.microsoft.com/en-us/sql/master-data-services/install-windows/insta ll-master-data-services.`

How to do it...

1. You need to open the Master Data Manager application. Open your web browser, navigate to your Master Data Manager site, and log in. Navigate to the home page.
2. Click the **System Administration** link.
3. In the **Manage Models** page, click **Add**.

4. Name the model `AWCustomer`. Make sure that the option **Create entity with the same name as model** is checked. Leave the **Description** textbox empty, and **Log Retention** drop-down list to the default, **System Setting**, as the shown in the following screenshot. Click the **Save** button:

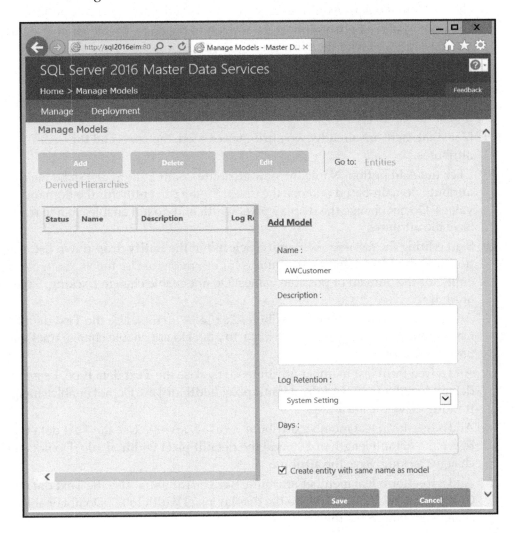

5. On the **Manage Models** page, click the **Entities** link in the **Go to** section.

6. On the **Manage Entities** page, click the **Add** button. Name the entity StateProvince. Check the **Create code values automatically** option. Write 1 in the **Start with** text box. Make sure that the **Enable data compression** checkbox is checked and the **Approval Required** is not checked. Click the **Save** button.

7. Click the **Manage Entities** link at the top left of the page. Create another entity, CountryRegion, with the same settings as the StateProvince created in the previous step. Save it.

8. Click the **Manage Entities** link at the top left of the page. Click the StateProvince entity in the list of entities to highlight it. Click the **Attributes** link in the **Go to** section.

9. Note that there are already two attributes created, the Name and the Code attributes.

10. Click the **Add** button. Name the new attribute CountryRegion. Make the new attribute domain-based and use the CountryRegion entity for the domain values. Do not change the display pixel width and do not enable change tracking. Save the attribute.

11. Start editing the AWCustomer entity. Select it in the **Entity** drop-down list. Add a domain-based leaf member attribute, StateProvince. Use the StateProvince entity for the domain of possible values. Do not enable change tracking. Save the attribute.

12. Add a free-form leaf member attribute, StreetAddress. Use the **Text** data type. Change the Display Width (Pixel) to 200. Do not enable change tracking. Save the attribute.

13. Add a free-form leaf member attribute, City. Use the **Text** data type. Leave the default length of 100 and the default pixel width of 100. Do not enable change tracking. Save the attribute.

14. Add a free-form leaf member attribute, EmailAddress. Use the **Text** data type. Leave the default length of 100 and the default pixel width of 100. Do not enable change tracking. Save the attribute.

15. Add a free-form leaf member attribute, MaritalStatus. Use the **Text** data type. Change the length to 1. Change the display pixel width to 20. Do not enable change tracking. Save the attribute.

16. Add a free-form leaf member attribute, BirthDate. Use the **DateTime** data type. Use the default pixel width of 100. Use the yyyy/MM/dd input mask. Do not enable change tracking. Save the attribute.

17. Add a free-form leaf member attribute, `YearlyIncome`. Use the **Number** data type with two decimals. Use the default pixel width of `100`. Use the `-####` input mask. Do not enable change tracking. Save the attribute.

18. Navigate to the **Manage Entities** page (**Home | AWCustomer Model | Manage Entities**). Select the `AWCustomer` entity.

19. Click the **Attribute Groups** link. Click **Add**. Name the group `Demography`.

20. In the **Attributes** section, add the `MaritalStatus`, `BirthDate`, and `YearlyIncome` attributes to this attribute group, as shown in the following screenshot, and then save the attribute group:

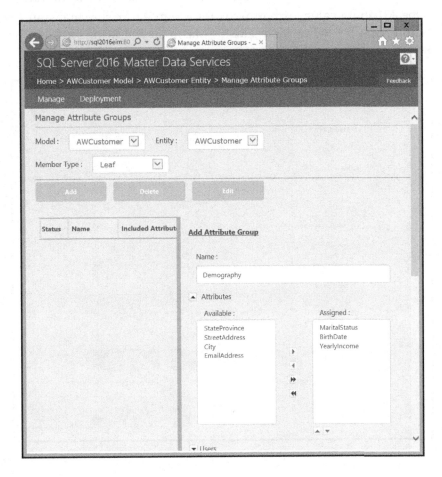

21. Navigate to the **Manage Entities** page (**Home | AWCustomer Model | Manage Entities**). Select the AWCustomer entity.

22. Click the **Business Rules** link. Click **Add**. Name the rule EmailAt.

23. In the **Add Business Rule** pop-up window, click the **Add** link in the **Then** section.

24. In the **Create Action** pop-up window, select the EmailAddress attribute in the **Attribute** drop-down list.

25. In the **Operator** drop-down list, select the **must contain the pattern** operator.

26. In the **Must contain the pattern** drop-down list, select **Attribute value**.

27. In the **Attribute value** textbox, write the @ sign. Make sure that your **Create Action** pop-up window looks like the one in the following screenshot, then click **Save**:

28. In the **Add Business Rule** window, click **Save**.

29. In the **Business Rules** window, click the **Publish All** button to activate all business rules.

30. Navigate to the home page. Make sure that the AWCustomer model is selected in the **Model** drop-down list. Then click **Explorer**.

31. Click the **Entities** button at the top-left of the screen, and select the CountryRegion entity. In the editor, click the **Add Member** button.

32. In the **Details** pane on the right, enter Australia as the value of the Name field. Note that the value for the Code field is assigned automatically. Click **OK**.

33. Add another member with the value United States as the Name field.

34. Using the **Entities** button, select the StateProvince entity. In the editor, click the **Add Member** button.

35. In the **Details** pane, enter Queensland as the value of the Name field. Note that the value for the Code field is assigned automatically. In the CountryRegion drop-down list, select 1 {Australia}. Click **OK**.

36. Add another member with the value Washington for the Name field. Click the button to the right of the CountryRegion drop-down list to open another window with a list of members of the CountryRegion entity. Check the code for the United States member. Go back to the window where you are editing the StateProvince entity and insert the appropriate CountryRegion code. Click **OK**.

37. Using the **Entities** button, select the AWCustomer entity. Note that there are two views: one with the attributes from the Demography attribute group only and another one with all the attributes. Click the **[All Attributes]** tab to see all of the attributes. You are going to add two members with data based on two customers from the dbo.DimCustomer table in the AdventureWorksDW2014 sample database. In the editor, click the **Add Member** button.

38. Insert the following information and then click **OK**:

Parameters	Values
Name	Jon Yang
Code	1
StateProvince	1 {Queensland}
StreetAddress	3761 N. 14th St
City	Rockhampton
EmailAddress	jon24@adventure-works.com
MaritalStatus	M
BirthDate	1970/04/08
YearlyIncome	90000

39. Add another customer with the following information:

Parameters	Values
Name	Lauren Walker
Code	2
StateProvince	2 {Washington}
StreetAddress	4785 Scott Street
City	Bremerton
EmailAddress	lauren41#adventure-works.com
MaritalStatus	M
BirthDate	1970/01/18
YearlyIncome	100,000.00

40. Before clicking **OK** to save the member, try to change the value of the MaritalStatus field to UNKNOWN. You should get an error immediately notifying you that the length of this field cannot be greater than one. Correct the value back to M.

41. Try to insert the birth date in a different format.

42. Note that the EmailAddress field contains the # character instead of the @ character. Click **OK** to save the member anyway.

43. Note that in the grid showing all customers, there is a red exclamation point near the `Lauren Walker` entry. Point to it and read the message. Note also the message about validation errors in the **Details** pane on the right, as shown in the following screenshot:

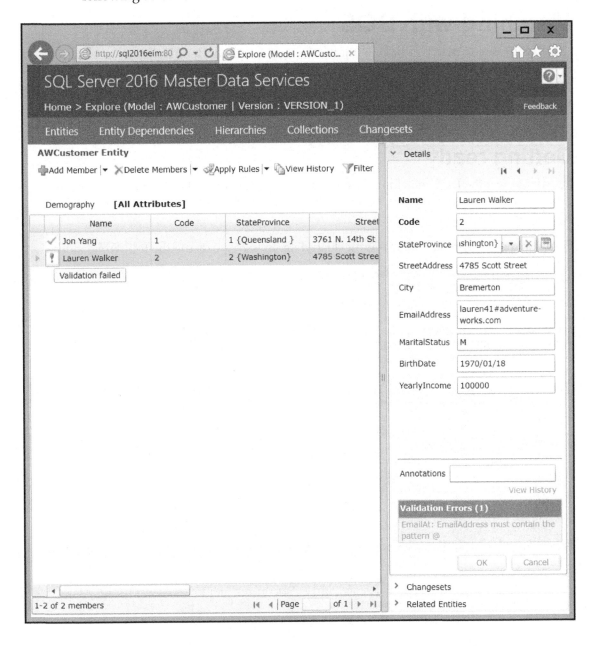

44. In the **Details** pane, correct the value in the `EmailAddress` field and click **OK**. Now the validation should succeed.

Matching with DQS

Often, you need to match entities without having a common identification. For example, you might get data about customers from two different sources. Then you need to do the matching based on similarity of attributes, for example, names and addresses. Matching is a very complex task. In SQL Server, DQS is one of the tools that can help you with this task.

Getting ready

In order to test the DQS matching, you need to prepare some data. The following section contains a lot of code; therefore, you might want to use the code provided in the book's companion content.

First, you need to prepare a table with clean data. In SSMS, execute the following code:

```
-- Preparing the clean data table
USE DQS_STAGING_DATA;
CREATE TABLE dbo.CustomersClean
(
CustomerKey INT NOT NULL PRIMARY KEY,\
FullName NVARCHAR(200) NULL,
StreetAddress NVARCHAR(200) NULL
);
GO
-- Populating the clean data table
INSERT INTO dbo.CustomersClean
(CustomerKey, FullName, StreetAddress)
SELECT CustomerKey,
FirstName + ' ' + LastName AS FullName,
AddressLine1 AS StreetAddress
FROM AdventureWorksDW2014.dbo.DimCustomer
WHERE CustomerKey % 10 = 0;
GO
```

Then you create a similar table for the dirty data, and also initially populate it with clean data:

```
-- Creating and populating the table for dirty data
CREATE TABLE dbo.CustomersDirty
(
```

```
CustomerKey INT NOT NULL PRIMARY KEY,
FullName NVARCHAR(200) NULL,
StreetAddress NVARCHAR(200) NULL,
Updated INT NULL,
CleanCustomerKey INT NULL
);
GO
INSERT INTO dbo.CustomersDirty
(CustomerKey, FullName, StreetAddress, Updated)
SELECT CustomerKey * (-1) AS CustomerKey,
FirstName + ' ' + LastName AS FullName,
AddressLine1 AS StreetAddress,
0 AS Updated
FROM AdventureWorksDW2014.dbo.DimCustomer
WHERE CustomerKey % 10 = 0;
GO
```

The next step is the most complex one. You need to make random changes in the dirty data table. Note that in this table, the original `CustomerKey` column is multiplied by –1, and that there is a space for the clean `CustomerKey`. This way, you will be able to check the quality of the matches. Nevertheless, the following code makes somehow random changes in the table, mimicking human errors:

```
-- Making random changes in the dirty table
DECLARE @i AS INT = 0, @j AS INT = 0;
WHILE (@i < 3) -- loop more times for more changes
BEGIN
SET @i += 1;
SET @j = @i - 2; -- control here in which step you want to update
-- only already updated rows
WITH RandomNumbersCTE AS
(
SELECT CustomerKey
,RAND(CHECKSUM(NEWID()) % 1000000000 + CustomerKey) AS RandomNumber1
,RAND(CHECKSUM(NEWID()) % 1000000000 + CustomerKey) AS RandomNumber2
,RAND(CHECKSUM(NEWID()) % 1000000000 + CustomerKey) AS RandomNumber3
,FullName, StreetAddress, Updated
FROM dbo.CustomersDirty
)
UPDATE RandomNumbersCTE SET
FullName = STUFF(FullName,
CAST(CEILING(RandomNumber1 * LEN(FullName)) AS INT), 1,
CHAR(CEILING(RandomNumber2 * 26) + 96))
,StreetAddress = STUFF(StreetAddress,
CAST(CEILING(RandomNumber1 * LEN(StreetAddress)) AS INT), 2, '')
,Updated = Updated + 1
WHERE RAND(CHECKSUM(NEWID()) % 1000000000 - CustomerKey) < 0.17
```

```
AND Updated > @j;
WITH RandomNumbersCTE AS
(
SELECT CustomerKey
,RAND(CHECKSUM(NEWID()) % 1000000000 + CustomerKey) AS RandomNumber1
,RAND(CHECKSUM(NEWID()) % 1000000000 + CustomerKey) AS RandomNumber2
,RAND(CHECKSUM(NEWID()) % 1000000000 + CustomerKey) AS RandomNumber3
,FullName, StreetAddress, Updated
FROM dbo.CustomersDirty
)
UPDATE RandomNumbersCTE SET
FullName = STUFF(FullName,
CAST(CEILING(RandomNumber1 * LEN(FullName)) AS INT), 0,
CHAR(CEILING(RandomNumber2 * 26) + 96))
,StreetAddress = STUFF(StreetAddress,
CAST(CEILING(RandomNumber1 * LEN(StreetAddress)) AS INT), 2,
CHAR(CEILING(RandomNumber2 * 26) + 96) +
CHAR(CEILING(RandomNumber3 * 26) + 96)) ,Updated = Updated + 1
WHERE RAND(CHECKSUM(NEWID()) % 1000000000 - CustomerKey) < 0.17
AND Updated > @j;
WITH RandomNumbersCTE AS
(
SELECT CustomerKey
,RAND(CHECKSUM(NEWID()) % 1000000000 + CustomerKey) AS RandomNumber1
,RAND(CHECKSUM(NEWID()) % 1000000000 + CustomerKey) AS RandomNumber2
,RAND(CHECKSUM(NEWID()) % 1000000000 + CustomerKey) AS RandomNumber3
,FullName, StreetAddress, Updated
FROM dbo.CustomersDirty
)
UPDATE RandomNumbersCTE SET
FullName = STUFF(FullName,
CAST(CEILING(RandomNumber1 * LEN(FullName)) AS INT), 1, '')
,StreetAddress = STUFF(StreetAddress,
CAST(CEILING(RandomNumber1 * LEN(StreetAddress)) AS INT), 0,
CHAR(CEILING(RandomNumber2 * 26) + 96) +
CHAR(CEILING(RandomNumber3 * 26) + 96))
,Updated = Updated + 1
WHERE RAND(CHECKSUM(NEWID()) % 1000000000 - CustomerKey) < 0.16
AND Updated > @j;
END;
GO
```

You can compare the data after the changes with the original data using the following query:

```
SELECT C.FullNameD.FullNameC.StreetAddressD.StreetAddress, D.Updated
FROM dbo.CustomersClean AS C
INNER JOIN dbo.CustomersDirty AS D
ON C.CustomerKey = D.CustomerKey * (-1)
WHERE C.FullName <> D.FullName
OR C.StreetAddress <> D.StreetAddress
ORDER BY D.Updated DESC;
GO
```

There should be more than 700 rows updated. The exact number changes with every execution. When executing the code as an example for this chapter, I got 756 rows updated. This means 756 customers that need to be matched with the clean data table.

How to do it...

1. In SSDT, open the `Chapter05` solution from the first recipe of this chapter.
2. Add a new package to the solution and rename it to `DataMatching.dtsx`.
3. Create a new package OLE DB connection manager to your local SQL Server instance, the `DQS_STAGING_DATA` database.
4. In the control flow of the package, add a data flow task. Open the data flow editor for this task.
5. Add an OLE DB source. Rename it to `CustomersDirty`. Open the **OLE DB Source Editor** and select the `dbo.CustomersDirty` table as the source table. Click the **Columns** tab to check the columns. Click **OK** to close the editor.
6. The next step in the preparation for identity mapping (or matching) is to perform the exact matches. Drag the lookup transformation to the working area and connect it with the blue data flow path using the OLE DB source. Name it `Exact Matches` and double-click it to open its editor.

7. In the **Lookup Transformation Editor**, select the **Connection** tab in the left-hand pane. Use the connection manager for the DQS_STAGING_DATA database. Select the dbo.CustomersClean table. Click the **Columns** tab.

8. Drag the FullName and StreetAddress columns from the **Available Input Columns** onto the columns with the same name in the **Available Lookup Columns** table. Select the checkbox next to the CustomerKey column in the **Available Lookup Columns** table. In the **Lookup Operation** field in the grid in the bottom part of the editor, select the Replace 'CleanCustomerKey' option. Rename the output alias CleanCustomerKey, as shown in the following screenshot:

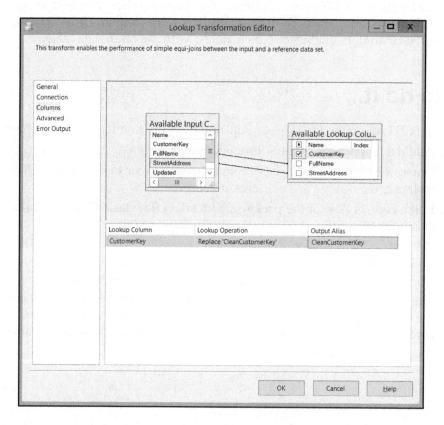

9. Click the **General** tab. In the **Specify how to handle rows with no matching entries** drop-down list, select the **Redirect rows to no match output** option. Click **OK** to close the **Lookup Transformation Editor**.

10. Drag two multicast transformations to the working area. Rename the first one `Match` and the second one `NoMatch`. Connect the lookup transformation with them, the first by using the lookup match output and the second by using the lookup no match output. You do not need to multicast the data for this recipe. However, you are going to expand the package in the next recipe.

11. In SSMS, create a new table in the `DQS_STAGING_DATA` database in the `dbo` schema and name it `CustomersDirtyMatch`. Use the following code:

```
CREATE TABLE dbo.CustomersDirtyMatch
(
    CustomerKey INT NOT NULL PRIMARY KEY,
    FullName NVARCHAR(200) NULL,
    StreetAddress NVARCHAR(200) NULL,
    Updated INT NULL,
    CleanCustomerKey INT NULL
);
```

12. Add another new table in the `dbo` schema and name it `CustomersDirtyNoMatch`. Use the following code, which uses the same schema as the previous table:

```
CREATE TABLE dbo.CustomersDirtyNoMatch
(
    CustomerKey INT NOT NULL PRIMARY KEY,
    FullName NVARCHAR(200) NULL,
    StreetAddress NVARCHAR(200) NULL,
    Updated INT NULL,
    CleanCustomerKey INT NULL
);
```

13. In the data flow in SSDT, add a new OLE DB destination and rename it `CustomersDirtyMatch`. Connect it to the match multicast transformation. Double-click it to open the editor. Select the `dbo.CustomersDirtyMatch` table. Click the **Mappings** tab to check the mappings. Click **OK**.

14. Add a new OLE DB destination and rename it `CustomersDirtyNoMatch`. Connect it to the no match multicast transformation. Double-click it to open the editor. Select the `dbo.CustomersDirtyNoMatch` table. Click the **Mappings** tab to check the mappings. Click **OK**.

15. Save the project. Execute the package in debug mode. After the execution has completed, review the contents of the dbo.CustomersDirtyMatch and dbo.CustomersDirtyNoMatch tables.

16. Stop debugging. Do not exit SSDT.

17. In the DQS_STAGING_DATA database in SSMS, create a table that unions clean and dirty customer data by using the following code:

```
SELECT CustomerKey, FullName, StreetAddress
INTO dbo.CustomersDQSMatch
FROM dbo.CustomersClean
UNION
SELECT CustomerKey, FullName, StreetAddress
FROM dbo.CustomersDirtyNoMatch;
```

18. Start the Data Quality Client and connect to your DQS server.

19. Create a new knowledge base. Name it AWCustomersMatching. Make sure that the **Matching Policy** activity is selected. Click **Next**.

20. In the **Knowledge Base Management** window, on the **Map** tab (the first one), select **SQL Server** as the data source. Select the DQS_STAGING_DATA database and the CustomersDQSMatch table.

21. Create a domain named FullName. Use the data type **String**, and select the **Use Leading Values**, **Normalize String**, and **Disable Syntax Error Algorithms** checkboxes. Clear the **Enable Speller** checkbox. Set the **Format Output to** option to **None** and select **English** as the language. Click **OK**.

22. Create another domain named StreetAddress with the same settings as for the FullName domain.

23. Map the FullName column to the FullName domain, and map the StreetAddress column to the StreetAddress domain.

24. Create a new composite domain (click the second icon from the right, above the column/domain mappings grid in the left-hand pane). For matching, you typically use a composite domain, which encompasses all columns involved in an approximate match. Name the domain `NameAddress` and add the `FullName` and `StreetAddress` columns from the **Domain List** listbox to the **Domains in Composite Domains** listbox. Click **OK**. Your screen should resemble the one shown in the following screenshot. After you have made sure that you have the correct domains and mappings, click **Next**.

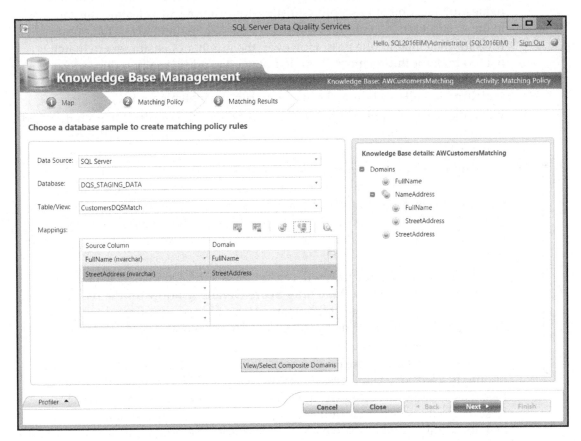

25. On the **Matching Policy** tab, click the **Create a matching rule** button in the left-hand pane. In the **Rule Details** pane on the right-hand side, change the name of the rule to Composite100.

26. In the **Rule Editor** area on the right, click the **Add a new domain element** button in the upper-right corner. The NameAddress domain should appear. Scroll to the right of the Similarity column (leave the value Similar in it) to show the Weight column. Change the weight to 100% for the NameAddress composite domain. You could also start matching with exact matches for one domain by requesting this domain as a prerequisite—for example, by selecting the checkbox in the Prerequisite column for the FullName domain to lower the number of rows for matching in one pass. However, the number of customers to match is not too high for this recipe, so you do not need to additionally reduce the matching search space. When you are done defining the rule, click **Start** in the **Matching Results** section of the screen to run the matching policy.

27. When the matching policy run has finished, review the results. Filter on matched or unmatched records by selecting the appropriate option in the **Filter** drop-down list.

28. You should test multiple rules. Therefore, create a new rule. Name it Name60Address40. In the **Rule Editor** section, click the **Add a new domain element** button. Scroll to the right of the Similarity column (leave the value Similar in it) to show the Weight column. Change the weight to 60% for the FullName domain and 40% for the StreetAddress domain. Click Start to test this rule.

29. When the rule testing has finished, review the results. Double-click a few of the matched records to get the **Matching Score Details** window for the records. Check how much the name and how much the address contributed to the score. Then close the window. When you are done with your review, click **Next**.

30. In the **Matching Results** window, you can check all the relevant rules at once. Make sure that the **Execute on previous data** option (which is below the **Start** button) is selected. Click the **Start** button. Wait until DQS finishes the process, then check the **Profiler**, **Matching Rules**, and **Matching Results**. In **Matching Results**, double-click a few of the matched records to show the **Matching Score Details** window, and check which rule was used. The composite domain should be used more often than the single domains.

31. When you are done with your review and have closed the **Matching Score Details** window, click **Finish**. Then click **Publish** in the pop-up window to publish the KB. When it is published, click **OK** in the next pop-up window.

32. The next step is to create a DQS matching project. Click the **New Data Quality Project** button in the Data Quality Client main screen.

33. Name the project `AWCustomersMatchingProject`. Select the `AWCustomersMatching` KB. Make sure that the **Matching** activity is selected. Click **Next**.

34. On the **Map** tab (the first one) in the **Knowledge Base Management** window, select **SQL Server** as the data source. Select the `DQS_STAGING_DATA` database and the `CustomersDQSMatch` table. Note that in a real project, you would have a separate table with sample data for learning during the KB creation and another table for the actual matching.

35. Map the `FullName` column to the `FullName` domain and the `StreetAddress` column to the `StreetAddress` domain, unless they have already been mapped automatically. Click **Next**.

36. On the **Matching** tab, click **Start**. Wait until the matching process finishes, then review the results. When you are finished, click **Next**.

37. On the **Export** page, choose **SQL Server** as the destination type and choose the `DQS_STAGING_DATA` database. Select both the **Matching Results** and **Survivorship Results** checkboxes. Export the matching results to a table named `DQSMatchingResults` and the survivorship results to a table named `DQSSurvivorshipResults`. Do not add schema names to table names; the tables will be created in the `dbo` schema. Select the **Most complete and longest record** survivorship rule. Click the **Export** button.

38. When the export is finished, click **Close** in the **Matching Export** pop-up window and then click **Finish**.

39. In SSMS, review the exported results. You can quickly see that the survivorship policy is not sophisticated enough because many customers with negative `CustomerKey` values are selected as survivors. You should use the matching results and define your own survivorship rules, or select the survivors manually.

40. Close the Data Quality Client.

Using SSIS fuzzy components

SSIS includes two really sophisticated matching transformations in the data flow. The fuzzy lookup transformation is used for mapping the identities. The fuzzy grouping transformation is used for de-duplicating. Both of them use the same algorithm for comparing the strings and other data.

Identity mapping and de-duplication are actually the same problem. For example, instead for mapping the identities of entities in two tables, you can union all of the data in a single table and then do the de-duplication. Or vice versa, you can join a table to itself and then do identity mapping instead of de-duplication. This recipe shows how to use the fuzzy lookup transformation for identity mapping.

Getting ready

This recipe assumes that you have successfully finished the previous recipe.

How to do it...

1. In SSMS, create a new table in the DQS_STAGING_DATA database in the dbo schema and name it dbo.FuzzyMatchingResults. Use the following code:

```
CREATE TABLE dbo.FuzzyMatchingResults
(
   CustomerKey INT NOT NULL PRIMARY KEY,
   FullName NVARCHAR(200) NULL,
   StreetAddress NVARCHAR(200) NULL,
   Updated INT NULL,
   CleanCustomerKey INT NULL
);
```

2. Switch to SSDT. Continue editing the **DataMatching** package.
3. Add a fuzzy lookup transformation below the no match multicast transformation. Rename it FuzzyMatches and connect it to the no match multicast transformation with the regular data flow path. Double-click the transformation to open its editor.
4. On the **Reference Table** tab, select the connection manager you want to use to connect to your DQS_STAGING_DATA database and select the dbo.CustomersClean table. Do not store a new index or use an existing index.

When the package executes the transformation for the first time, it copies the reference table, adds a key with an integer data type to the new table, and builds an index on the key column. Next, the transformation builds an index, called a match index, on the copy of the reference table. The match index stores the results of tokenizing the values in the transformation input columns. The transformation then uses these tokens in the lookup operation. The match index is a table in a SQL Server database. When the package runs again, the transformation can either use an existing match index or create a new index. If the reference table is static, the package can avoid the potentially expensive process of rebuilding the index for repeat sessions of data cleansing.

5. Click the **Columns** tab. Delete the mapping between the two CustomerKey columns. Clear the checkbox next to the CleanCustomerKey input column. Select the checkbox next to the CustomerKey lookup column. Rename the output alias for this column to CleanCustomerKey. You are replacing the original column with the one retrieved during the lookup. Your mappings should resemble those shown in the following screenshot:

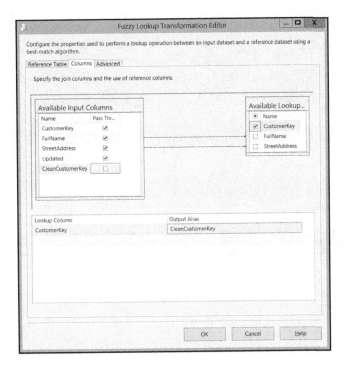

6. Click the **Advanced** tab. Raise the **Similarity threshold** to 0.50 to reduce the matching search space. With similarity threshold of 0.00, you would get a full cross join. Click **OK**.

7. Drag the union all transformation below the fuzzy lookup transformation. Connect it to an output of the matchmulticast transformation and an output of the FuzzyMatches fuzzy lookup transformation. You will combine the exact and approximate matches in a single row set.

8. Drag an OLE DB destination below the union all transformation. Rename it FuzzyMatchingResults and connect it with the union all transformation. Double-click it to open the editor.

9. Connect to your DQS_STAGING_DATA database and select the dbo.FuzzyMatchingResults table. Click the **Mappings** tab. Click **OK**. The completed data flow is shown in the following screenshot:

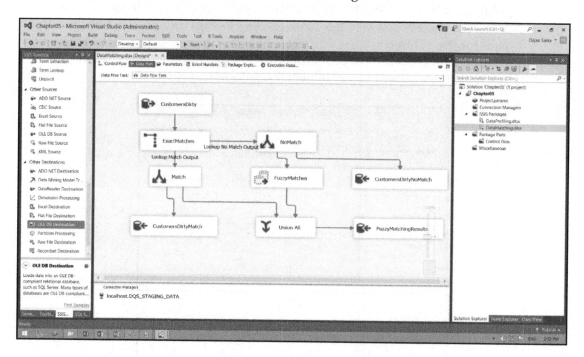

10. You need to add restart ability to your package. You will truncate all destination tables. Click the **Control Flow** tab. Drag the execute T-SQL statement task above the data flow task. Connect the tasks with the green precedence constraint from the execute T-SQL statement task to the data flow task. The execute T-SQL statement task must finish successfully before the data flow task starts.

11. Double-click the execute T-SQL statement task. Use the connection manager to your DQS_STAGING_DATA database. Enter the following code in the T-SQL statement textbox, and then click **OK**:

```
TRUNCATE TABLE dbo.CustomersDirtyMatch;
TRUNCATE TABLE dbo.CustomersDirtyNoMatch;
TRUNCATE TABLE dbo.FuzzyMatchingResults;
```

12. Save the solution. Execute your package in debug mode to test it. Review the results of the fuzzy lookup transformation in SSMS. Look for rows for which the transformation did not find a match, and for any incorrect matches. Use the following code:

```
-- Not matched
SELECT * FROM FuzzyMatchingResults
WHERE CleanCustomerKey IS NULL;
-- Incorrect matches
SELECT * FROM FuzzyMatchingResults
WHERE CleanCustomerKey <> CustomerKey * (-1);
```

13. You can use the following code to clean up the AdventureWorksDW2014 and DQS_STAGING_DATA databases:

```
USE AdventureWorksDW2014;
DROP TABLE IF EXISTS dbo.Chapter05Profiling;
DROP TABLE IF EXISTS dbo.AWCitiesStatesCountries;
USE DQS_STAGING_DATA;
DROP TABLE IF EXISTS dbo.CustomersCh05;
DROP TABLE IF EXISTS dbo.CustomersCh05DQS;
DROP TABLE IF EXISTS dbo.CustomersClean;
DROP TABLE IF EXISTS dbo.CustomersDirty;
DROP TABLE IF EXISTS dbo.CustomersDirtyMatch;
DROP TABLE IF EXISTS dbo.CustomersDirtyNoMatch;
DROP TABLE IF EXISTS dbo.CustomersDQSMatch;
DROP TABLE IF EXISTS dbo.DQSMatchingResults;
DROP TABLE IF EXISTS dbo.DQSSurvivorshipResults;
DROP TABLE IF EXISTS dbo.FuzzyMatchingResults;
```

14. When you are done, close SSMS and SSDT.

6

SSIS Performance and Scalability

This chapter covers the following recipes:

- Using SQL Server Management Studio to execute an SSIS package
- Using T-SQL to execute an SSIS package
- Using the DTExec command-line utility to execute an SSIS package
- Scheduling an SSIS package execution
- Using the cascading lookup pattern
- Using the lookup cache
- Using lookup expressions
- Determining the maximum number of worker threads in a data flow
- Using the master package concept
- Requesting an execution tree in SSDT
- Establishing a performance monitor session
- Configuring a performance monitor data collector set

Introduction

This chapter discusses the various methods of SSIS package execution, how to monitor the performance of running SSIS packages, and how to plan the utilization of resources for a given SSIS package. You will also learn how to use different techniques of acquiring reference data (also referred to as data look ups), and their impact on SSIS execution performance.

One of the objectives followed in the design of the SSIS execution engine is to maximize the use of resources on the system hosting SSIS package executions. In part, this is reflected in the capabilities of parallel execution of various operations; for instance, using multiple threads to perform data movements and transformations in the data flow, parallelizing the execution of operations in the control flow, or even scaling out the execution of packages to multiple hosting servers. Some of the techniques that you can use to improve resource utilization for SSIS executions are also discussed in this chapter.

SSIS execution techniques can be divided into two groups:

- **On-demand execution is performed through intervention**: A user creates, configures, and starts, the execution of an SSIS package. Typically, on-demand execution is used for SSIS solutions that only need to run when a user has decided that the work needs to be performed. Alternatively, SSIS packages are executed on demand when they have been integrated into existing systems, or tools, that the organization is using to perform its data management operations. In such cases, the execution is created, configured, and started, by a client application or a service.

- **Scheduled execution is performed automatically**: An administrator configures the execution of an SSIS package, where the execution starts automatically (in absence of user intervention). Typically, automated execution is performed on a schedule prepared in advance; for instance, using the SQL Server Agent, or another similar scheduling tool. Alternatively, the execution can also be started automatically based on certain other criteria defined in advance, the state of which can be determined automatically; for instance, a scheduled operation checks whether these criteria are met, and either starts the execution of an SSIS package, or completes without starting it.

When SSIS packages designed under the project deployment model are executed, the following three steps are performed:

1. An execution instance is created for the given SSIS package with the selected SSIS environment. If an environment is not associated with this execution, design-time values for any parameters, or any other configurable settings, are used.

2. After the execution has been created successfully, further settings can be configured; for instance, the logging level, the operational mode, or any other accessible property of the SSIS package. In this step, any configurable design-time settings can be overridden.

3. After all the execution properties have been set, the execution is started. This step actually invokes the execution of the package. Two modes of operation are supported:

   - In synchronous mode, the control is not returned to the caller until the execution of the package has completed (either successfully or with errors); this mode is useful for situations where the next operation in a sequence should not start until the preceding one has finished. When SSIS packages are set up as individual steps of an SQL Server Agent job, the next step must not begin until the preceding step has completed; therefore, SQL Server Agent uses synchronous executions.

   - In asynchronous mode, the control is returned to the caller immediately after the execution has started, allowing the caller to perform other work concurrently. This mode is useful when multiple packages, or multiple instances of the same package, need to be executed in parallel. In order to monitor the asynchronous execution of packages, the caller application needs to check the current state of the executions by querying the SSIS catalog. Typically, asynchronous executions are used when SSIS packages are integrated in the organization's existing systems, where other operations might need to be executed at the same time.

Steps 1 and 3 are mandatory, step 2 is optional. Both mandatory steps must be performed; otherwise, the execution cannot start. Step 2 needs to be performed for each additional setting, and can therefore be performed multiple times in a single execution.

SSIS deployment models

The project deployment model has been the default deployment model since SQL Server 2012; it perceives all packages of the same SSIS project as a single unit of work from design, deployment, configuration, and administration aspects.

The deployment model used in SSIS 2005, 2008, and 2008 R2, where individual packages are deployed, configured, and administered, independently even if they were developed as part of the same project, is now referred to as the package deployment model.

Several methods are available for on-demand execution of SSIS packages:

- At design time, the SSIS package can be executed in debug mode from within **SQL Server Data Tools (SSDT)**. You should already be familiar with design-time package execution from previous chapters.
- After the packages have been deployed to the target environment, they can be executed using the DTExec utility, provided by the SQL Server installation, by using Windows PowerShell, or through the integration services API. Starting with SQL Server 2012, SSIS packages deployed to the SSIS catalog can also be executed using T-SQL. As you have seen in previous chapters, SSIS execution is also fully integrated into SQL Server Management Studio. Depending on the deployment model used, this can either be achieved by accessing the SSIS catalog (under the project deployment model), or by connecting to the legacy SSIS service (when the packages have been deployed to the msdb database, or the managed SSIS package store—both under the package deployment model).

Connecting to the legacy SSIS service in SQL Server 2012 and later versions

Starting with SQL Server 2012, special Windows operating system privileges are required to access the SSIS service. By starting SSMS as an administrator, members of the administrators users group are allowed to connect to the SSIS service.

You can find more information about the legacy SSIS service in the book's online article entitled *Integration Services Service (SSIS Service)*, at https://docs.microsoft.com/en-us/sql/integration-services/servic e/integration-services-service-ssis-service.

This chapter assumes that you have completed Chapter 2, *What Is New in SSIS 2016*, and that you have deployed at least the CustomLogging project to the SSISDB catalog.

If, for some reason, you were not able to complete the exercises in Chapter 2, *What Is New in SSIS 2016*, follow these steps to prepare the environment:

1. In SSMS, open the Chapter06_Preparation.sql script located in the C:\SSIS2016Cookbook\Chapter06\Scripts folder.

2. Carefully review the script, and then execute it. Any missing database objects used in the CustomLogging.dtsx package will be created.

3. Use Windows Explorer to navigate to the C:\SSIS2016Cookbook\Chapter06\Scripts folder, and locate the Chapter06_ProjectDeployment.bat command file.

4. Double-click the file to start the deployment. After it completes, you will be prompted to press any key to close the Command Prompt window.

Using SQL Server Management Studio to execute an SSIS package

In this recipe, you are going to use **SQL Server Management Studio (SSMS)** to prepare, and invoke, the execution of an SSIS package deployed to the SSISDB catalog.

Getting ready

Even if you have successfully completed the exercises in Chapter 2, *What Is New in SSIS 2016*, follow these steps to create an SSIS environment, and configure the CustomLogging project:

1. In SSMS, open the Chapter06_Configuration.sql script located in the C:\SSIS2016Cookbook\Chapter06\Scripts folder.

2. Carefully review the script, and then execute it. The script will create the Chapter06 environment with a single environment variable, and associate it with the CustomLogging project. The cmgr_TestCustomLogging_CS variable will allow you to configure the connection manager used by the project.

How to do it...

1. Start SSMS, unless it is already running, and make sure that the **Object Explorer** is connected to the local SQL Server instance on your machine.

2. In the **Object Explorer**, locate the Integration Services Catalogs node, and expand it fully to locate the CustomLogging.dtsx package in the CustomLogging project of the CustomLogging folder, as shown in the following screenshot:

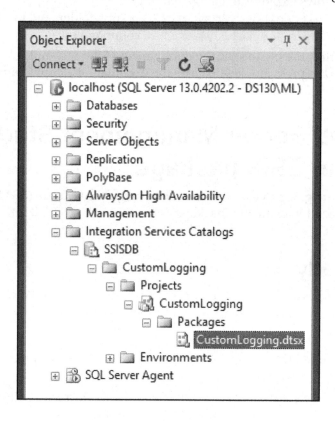

3. Right-click the package, and in the shortcut menu select **Execute...** to open the **Execute Package** dialog, as shown in the following screenshot:

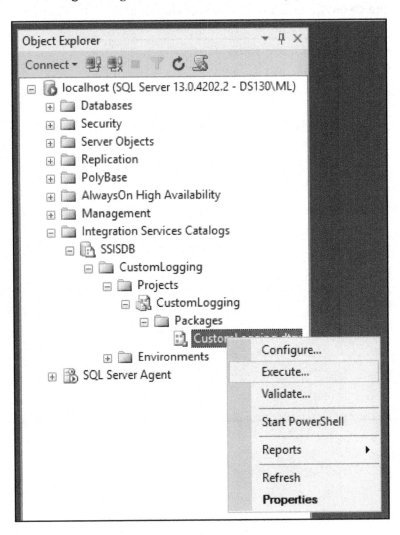

4. On the **General** page of the **Execute Package** dialog, on the **Parameters** tab, check the **Environment** option at the bottom of the dialog, and make sure that the **Chapter06** environment is selected, as shown in the following screenshot:

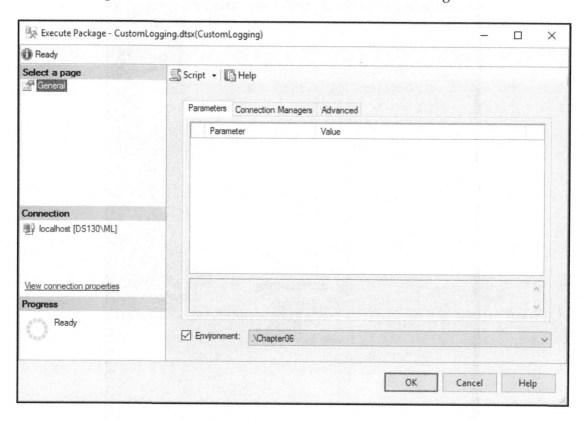

5. On the **Connection Managers** tab, you will see that the
   cmgr_TestCustomLogging_CS variable is used to set the value of the
   connection string of the cmgr_TestCustomLogging connection manager.

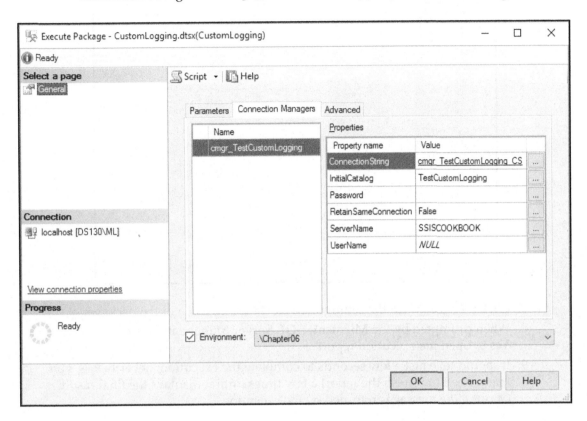

6. On the **Advanced** tab, observe the **Logging level** setting, and make sure that it is set to **Basic**, as shown in the following screenshot:

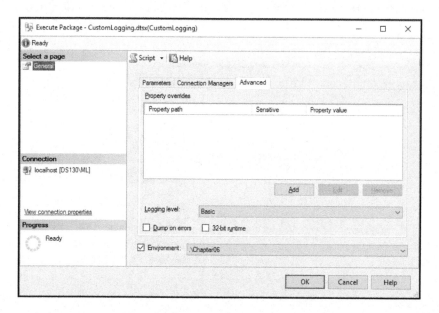

7. Click **OK** to confirm the settings and start the execution of the package.
8. When prompted by the **Microsoft SQL Server Management Studio** dialog, click **Yes** to open the execution report.
9. It should take just a few seconds to complete the execution; nevertheless, you might need to refresh the report a few times until it displays the final result. Observe the messages returned by the execution.

How it works...

When using SSMS to execute packages, the **Execute Package** wizard queries the SSISDB Catalog to access the package properties, and the properties of the associated environments, which allows you to configure the execution. When you start the execution, SSMS invokes the stored procedures used to create, configure, and start the execution of a package, as explained earlier.

In brief: SSMS uses Transact-SQL to execute SSIS packages deployed to the SSISDB Catalog; this is explained in more detail in the following recipe.

Using T-SQL to execute an SSIS package

In this recipe, you are going to perform all three steps of SSIS package execution by using three special stored procedures in the SSISDB database.

This procedure can be used only on packages deployed to the SSISDB Catalog.

How to do it...

1. In SSMS, connect to the SSISDB database; that is, the user database hosting the SSISDB catalog. You can use the following command:

   ```
   USE SSISDB;
   ```

   For your convenience, the T-SQL code needed for this chapter is provided in the Chapter06.sql script, located in the C:\SSIS2016Cookbook\Chapter06\Scripts folder.

2. Use the following query to retrieve the identifier of the environment reference, and assign the value to a variable:

   ```
   DECLARE @reference_id INT;
   SET @reference_id = (
     SELECT environment_references.reference_id
     FROM catalog.folders
       INNER JOIN catalog.projects
       ON projects.folder_id = folders.folder_id
       INNER JOIN catalog.environment_references
       ON environment_references.project_id = projects.project_id
     WHERE (folders.name = N'CustomLogging')
       and (projects.name = N'CustomLogging')
       and (environment_references.environment_name = N'Chapter06')
   );
   ```

   All of the queries in this recipe actually need to be executed as a single batch; for now, review them without executing them.

3. The following query is used to create the execution, and it uses the environment reference identifier determined using the first query:

```
DECLARE @execution_id BIGINT;
EXEC catalog.create_execution
    @package_name = N'CustomLogging.dtsx',
    @execution_id = @execution_id OUTPUT,
    @folder_name = N'CustomLogging',
    @project_name = N'CustomLogging',
    @use32bitruntime = False,
    @reference_id = @reference_id;
```

4. When the execution is created, its identifier (returned by the `@execution_id` output parameter) is also assigned to a variable; it will be needed in two more procedure calls.

5. The following invocation of the `catalog.set_execution_parameter_value` procedure sets the `logging_level` of the execution; the value of 1 represents the **Basic** logging level:

```
DECLARE @logging_level SMALLINT;
    SET @logging_level = 1;
    EXEC catalog.set_execution_parameter_value
    @execution_id = @execution_id,
    @object_type = 50,
    @parameter_name = N'LOGGING_LEVEL',
    @parameter_value = @logging_level;
```

SSISDB catalog logging levels are shown in the following table:

Value	Name	Description
0	None	Logging is turned off. Only the package execution status is logged.
1	Basic	All events are logged, except custom and diagnostic events. This is the default value.
2	Performance	Only performance statistics and `OnError` and `OnWarning` events are logged.
3	Verbose	All events are logged, including custom and diagnostic events.

6. Note the execution identifier being passed into the `catalog.set_execution_parameter_value` procedure; the setting must be associated with the correct execution instance.

7. By default, SSIS package executions are started asynchronously, meaning that the control is returned to the caller immediately. To start an execution synchronously, so that the caller will wait for the execution to complete, invoke the `catalog.set_execution_parameter_value` procedure once more:

```
DECLARE @is_synchronized BIT;
SET @is_synchronized = 1;
EXEC catalog.set_execution_parameter_value
 @execution_id = @execution_id,
 @object_type = 50,
 @parameter_name = N'SYNCHRONIZED',
 @parameter_value = @is_synchronized;
```

8. After all the required settings have been determined, the execution should be started using the following command (once more, the correct execution identifier needs to be passed into the procedure):

```
EXEC catalog.start_execution
 @execution_id = @execution_id;
```

9. To execute the package, use the mouse, or the keyboard, to highlight and execute all of the preceding statements as a single batch. Afterwards you can observe the execution progress by right-clicking the package name in the **Object Explorer** in SSMS, and selecting the **Reports | Standard Reports | All Executions** command from the shortcut menu, as shown in the following screenshot:

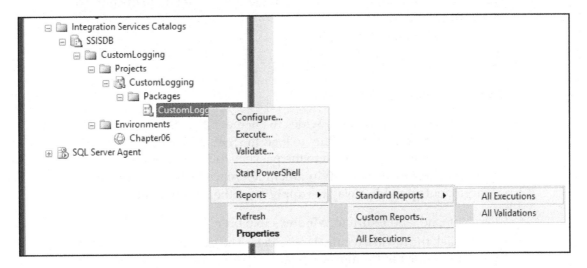

How it works...

When using T-SQL to execute SSIS packages, all the individual steps of the operation are performed using the corresponding stored procedures. Certain steps depend on a value determined in a preceding step, or query; therefore, it is necessary to store these values in variables.

Using the DTExec command-line utility to execute an SSIS package

In this recipe, you are going to execute an SSIS package using the DTExec command-line utility. This utility supports not only packages deployed to the SSISDB catalog, but also packages managed by the legacy SSIS Service (stored in the msdb system database, or in the managed SSIS package store), and even packages stored in the filesystem.

How to do it...

1. Using Windows Explorer, locate the Chapter06_Execution_DTExec.bat command file in the C:\SSIS2016Cookbook\Chapter06\Scripts\ folder.
2. Right-click the file, and select **Edit** from the shortcut menu to open the file in Notepad.
3. Inspect the DTExec command line:

```
DTExec /Server localhost /ISServer
"\SSISDB\CustomLogging\CustomLogging\CustomLogging.dtsx" /Env 1 /Par
$ServerOption::LOGGING_LEVEL(Int32);1
```

> The /Server argument provides the name of the SSIS Server, the /ISServer argument instructs the utility to load the SSIS package from the SSISDB Catalog (the complete path to the package must be provided), the /Env argument provides the environment reference identifier, and the /Par arguments provide a way to supply any other runtime settings.

4. Close Notepad, and return to Windows Explorer.
5. Double-click the file to execute the package. The execution results should be listed in a Command Prompt window.
6. When the execution finishes, close the Command Prompt window.

How it works...

When using the DTExec command-line utility you need to provide all the configuration settings in the command line; for instance, if you want to use a specific environment, you need to query the SSISDB database first to retrieve it.

In the background, the DTExec utility also uses T-SQL procedures in the SSISDB database to create, configure, and start SSIS package executions, and also to receive any messages from the execution engine.

There's more...

Alternatively, SSIS packages can be executed from Windows PowerShell, or from DOT.NET applications, by using the **SSIS Managed API**. The complete object model is accessible through the classes available in the `Microsoft.SqlServer.Management.IntegrationServices` namespace. By using the API, SSIS packages can be even more closely integrated into your existing client applications, or services.

 More information about the SSIS Managed API is available on the **Microsoft Developer Network (MSDN)** website, at `https://msdn.microsoft.com/en-us/library/microsoft.sqlserver.man agement.integrationservices.aspx`.

Scheduling an SSIS package execution

In this recipe, you are going to create an SQL Server Agent job with a single step using an SSIS package, configured with a specific SSIS environment. You are going to assign a schedule to the job so that it can be executed automatically.

SQL Server Agent is a special SQL Server feature, hosted on the SQL Server instance, which supports the automation of a variety of operations and processes. One of them is the execution of SSIS packages; these can be configured as one or more steps of an SQL Server Agent job.

SQL Server Agent and SQL Server Agent jobs

SQL Server Agent is available in SQL Server 2016 Enterprise, Standard, and Web editions; it is not available in the Express, nor Express with Advanced Services editions.

SQL Server Agent Job is a collection of one or more operations that represent a complete unit of work to be performed automatically, for example, on a schedule. Multiple steps of an SQL Server Agent job are executed in sequence.

In addition to facilitating automation, SQL Server Agent includes additional functionalities to provide a complete automated environment experience:

- **Schedules**: SQL Server Agent jobs can be executed automatically, on a schedule.
- **Alerts**: In case of errors, or even after successful executions, alerts can be configured so that the administrators of the hosting environments can be notified via email or through a paging system.
- **Operators**: Responses to certain events during SQL Server Agent job executions can also be configured. An operator can, for instance, be used to start another job in case the originating job has failed.

Getting ready

If you haven't performed any of the preceding recipes yet, you need to perform the same preparatory steps described at the beginning of this chapter.

How to do it...

1. In SSMS, in the **Object Explorer**, locate the **SQL Server Agent** node. Expand it to show its contents, and locate the Jobs folder.

If the SQL Server Agent of the selected SQL Server instance is not running, right-click its node in the Object Explorer, and select **Start** from the shortcut menu to start it.

2. Right-click the `Jobs` folder in the **Object Explorer**, and select the **New Job...** command from the shortcut menu to open the **New Job** wizard, as shown in the following screenshot:

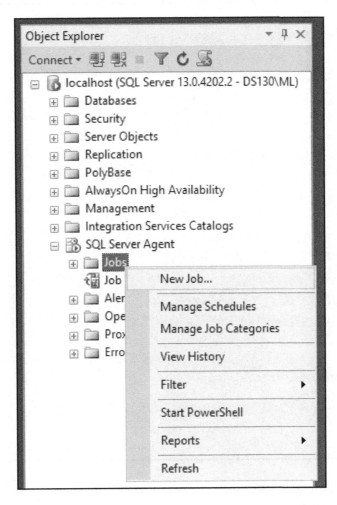

3. On the **General** page of the **New Job** wizard, enter `Chapter06Scheduled` as the **Name** of the job, as shown here:

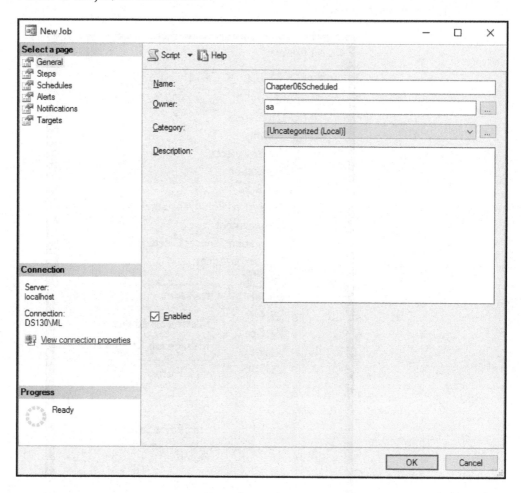

4. On the **Steps** page, click **New...** to add a new job step, and use the following settings to configure it:

Setting	Value
Step name	Chapter06
Type	SQL Server Integration Services Package

5. In the lower part of the **Steps** page, in the **Package** tab, use the following settings:

Setting	Value
Package source	SSIS catalog
Server	localhost
Log on to the server	Windows authentication

6. To select the package, click on the ellipsis icon on the far-right side of the **Package** text box, and in the **Select an SSIS Package** dialog locate the CustomLogging.dtsx package in the CustomLogging project of the CustomLogging folder, as shown here:

7. Click **OK** to confirm the selection. Use the following screenshot to verify your settings:

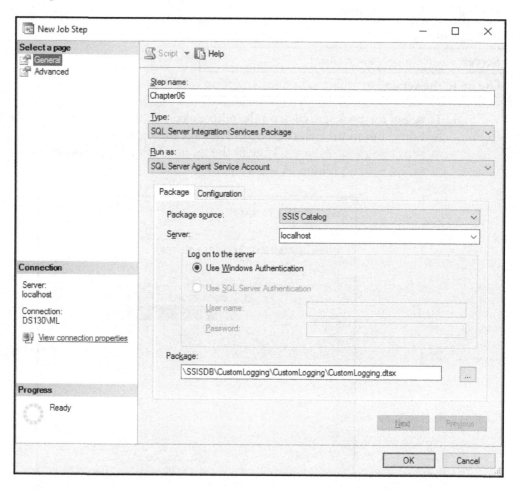

8. On the **Configuration** tab of the **General** page, under **Parameters**, check the **Environment** option and make sure that the **Chapter06** environment is selected in the selection box to the right.

9. Under **Connection Managers**, verify that the correct variable is used for the connection string of the **cmgr_TestCustomLogging** connection manager, as shown in the following screenshot:

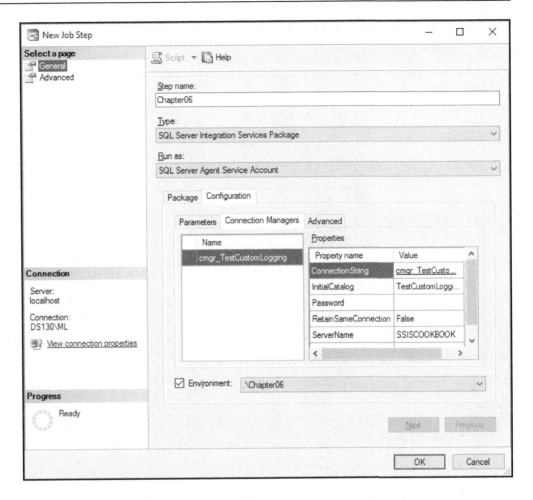

10. On the **Advanced** page of the **New Job** wizard, use the following settings to configure the rest of the step properties:

Setting	Value
On success action	Quit the job reporting success
On failure action	Quit the job reporting failure
Log to table	Checked
Include step in job history	Checked

11. Leave other settings unchanged; refer to the following screenshot to verify your settings:

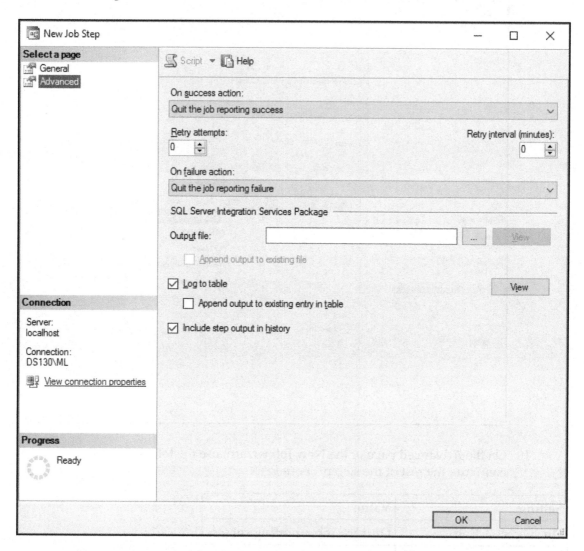

12. Click **OK** to confirm the step configuration.
13. The expected result is shown in the following screenshot:

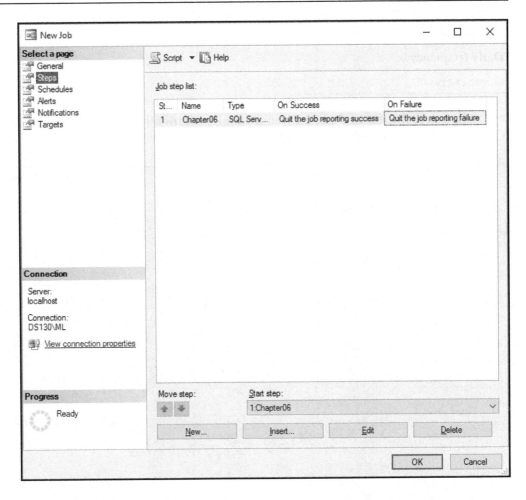

14. On the **Schedules** page, click **New...** to create a new schedule by using the following settings:

Setting	Value
Name	TestSchedule
Schedule type	Recurring
Enabled	Checked
Frequency	
Occurs	Daily

Recurs every	1
Daily frequency	
Occur every	1

15. Leave the rest of the settings unchanged; refer to the following screenshot to verify the schedule configuration:

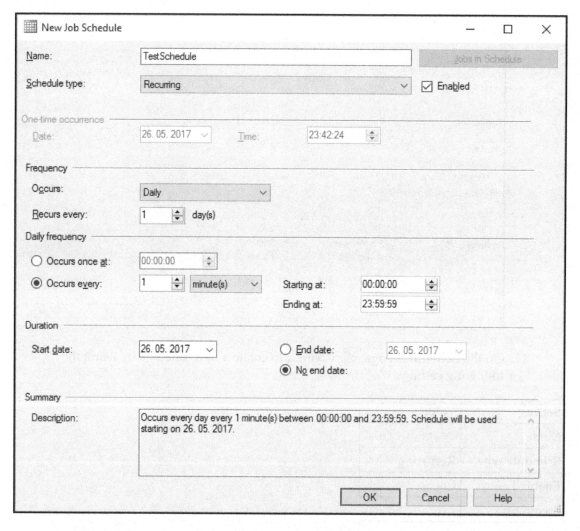

16. Click **OK** to confirm the schedule, and then click **OK** once more to complete the creation of a new SQL Server Agent job.

How it works...

As long as the SQL Server Agent service is running, and the job has not been disabled, the execution begins automatically at the scheduled time. Recurring jobs run continuously in the defined intervals between the **Start date** (by default the date when the schedule was created) and the **End date** of the schedule. When no end date is specified, the schedule will be used until you disable it.

Using the cascading lookup pattern

Typically, the structure and the semantics of a data flow source correspond to the data model used in the source data store; this structure, or the semantics used to represent data in the source system, might not be aligned with the structure or the semantics of the destination system.

For instance, the client entity in the source system might be represented by a single set, but the data warehouse might have to distinguish between a client, who is a person, and a client that represents a company. To correctly interpret the source data, you would need appropriate logic in the data flow to differentiate between source rows representing persons, and source rows representing companies, before loading the data correctly into the data destination data store.

How to do it...

1. In SSDT, open the `AdventureWorksETL.sln` solution located in the `C:\SSIS2016Cookbook\Chapter06\Starter\AdventureWorksETL\` folder.
2. Make sure that the `CascadingLookup.dtsx` SSIS package is open, locate the **Resolve Client Data** task in the control flow, and open it in the data flow designer.
3. The data flow contains one source component named **Source Client Data** that extracts client data from a flat file.
4. Double-click the source component to open the **Flat File Source** editor, and on the **Connection Manager** page, click **Preview...** to inspect the source data.

The source contains a single column with a list of clients, and no other information about them.

5. Click **Close** to close the **Data View** window, and then click **Cancel** to close the **Flat File Source** editor.
6. From the **SSIS Toolbox** drag a **Lookup** transformation to the data flow designer, and change its name to "Person Lookup".
7. Connect the regular data path from the **Source Client Data** source to the **Person Lookup**, and then double-click the Lookup transformation to open the **Lookup Transformation Editor**.

8. On the General page, change the **Specify how to handle rows with no matching entries** setting to **Redirect rows to no match output**, as shown here:

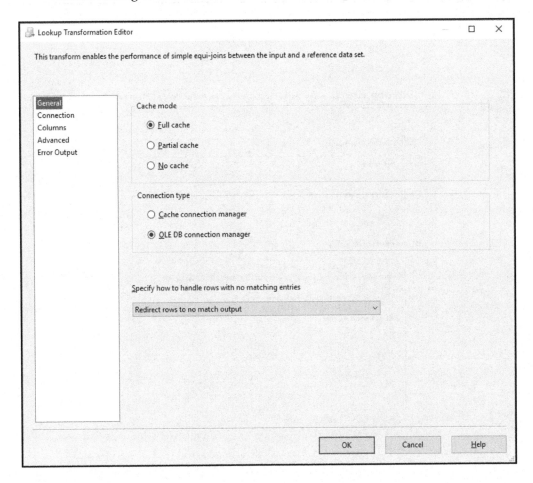

9. On the **Connection** page, select `cmgr_Reference` in the **OLE DB connection manager** selection box, select the **Use results of an SQL query** option, and enter the following query in the text box:

```
SELECT CAST(Person.LastName + COALESCE(N' ' + Person.MiddleName,
N'') + N', ' + Person.FirstName AS NVARCHAR(256)) as ClientName,
Person.BusinessEntityID AS BusinessEntityID, CAST(1 AS BIT) AS
IsPerson
FROM Person.Person;
```

10. Use the following screenshot to verify your settings:

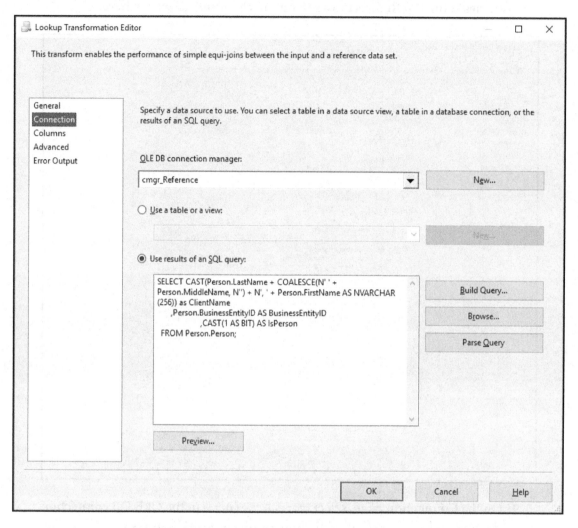

11. On the **Columns** page, connect the **ClientName** column in the **Available Input Columns** list to the **ClientName** column in the **Available Lookup Columns** list.

12. Check the **BusinessEntityID** and **IsPerson** columns in the **Available Lookup Columns** list, as shown in the following screenshot:

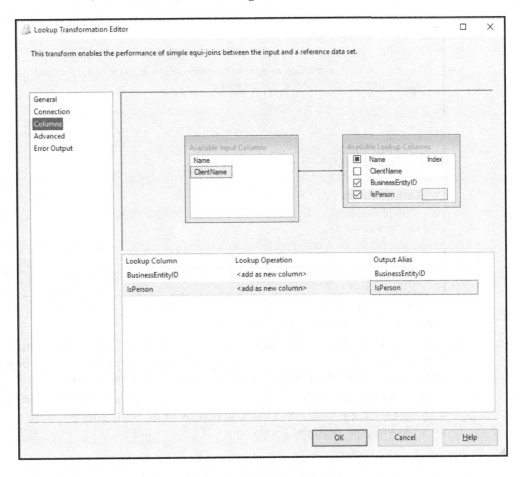

13. Click **OK** to confirm the configuration.
14. From the SSIS Toolbox, drag another Lookup transformation to the data flow designer, and change its name to `Company Lookup`.
15. Connect the regular data path from the **Person Lookup** transformation to the **Company Lookup** transformation.

16. In the **Input Output Selection** dialog, under **Output**, select **Lookup No Match Output**, as shown in the following screenshot:

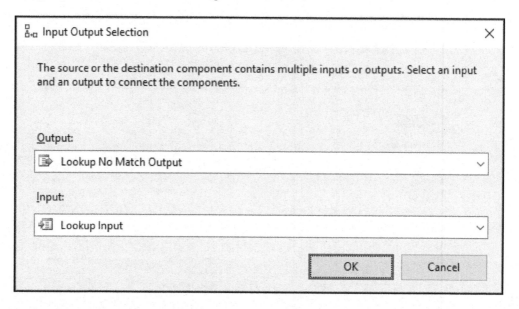

17. Click **OK** to confirm the selection.
18. Double-click the **Company Lookup** transformation to open the **Lookup Transformation Editor**, and on the **General** page change the **Specify how to handle rows with no matching entries** setting to **Ignore failure**.
19. On the **Connection** page, select cmgr_Reference in the **OLE DB connection manager** selection box, select the **Use results of an SQL query** option, and enter the following query in the text box:

```
SELECT CAST(Vendor.Name AS NVARCHAR(256)) AS ClientName
      ,Vendor.BusinessEntityID AS BusinessEntityID
      ,CAST(0 AS BIT) AS IsPerson
  FROM Purchasing.Vendor;
```

20. On the **Columns** page, connect the **ClientName** column in the **Available Input Columns** list to the **ClientName** column in the **Available Lookup Columns** list.
21. Check the **BusinessEntityID** and **IsPerson** columns in the **Available Lookup Columns** list, as you did in Step 9 for the **Person Lookup** transformation.
22. Click **OK** to complete the configuration.
23. From the SSIS Toolbox, drag a **Union All** transformation to the data flow designer.

24. Connect the regular data path from the **Person Lookup** transformation to the **Union All** transformation, and then do the same with the regular data path from the **Company Lookup** transformation.

25. In the **Input Output Selection** dialog, under **Output**, select **Lookup Match Output**, as shown in the following screenshot:

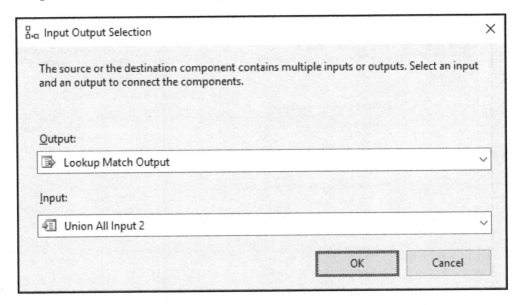

26. Click **OK** to confirm the selection.

27. From the SSIS Toolbox, drag an **OLE DB Destination** component to the data flow designer, and change its name to `Resolved Client`.

28. Double-click the **Resolved Client** destination to open the **OLE DB Destination Editor**, and on the **Connection Manager** page use the following settings to configure the destination:

Property	Value
OLE DB connection manager	`cmgr_Reference`
Name of the table or the view	`[dbo].[ResolvedClient]`

29. Leave the rest of the settings unchanged; refer to the following screenshot to verify your settings:

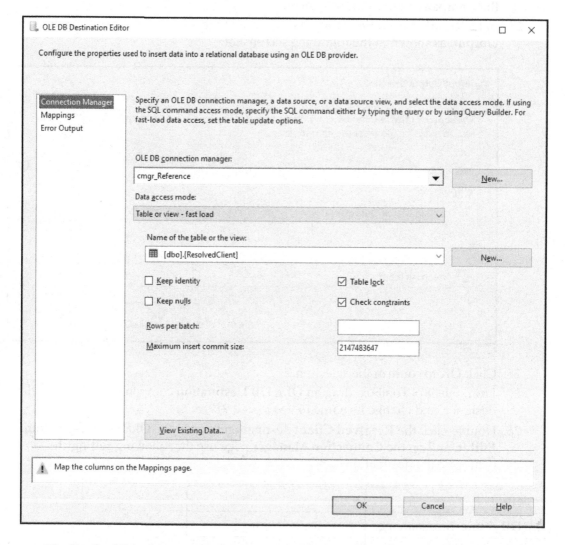

30. On the **Mappings** page, make sure that all the source columns are mapped to the corresponding destination columns, and then click **OK** to complete the configuration.

31. Save the solution, execute it in debug mode, and observe the results of the data flow task. Out of **19,905 rows, 122 rows** should not be recognized as persons.

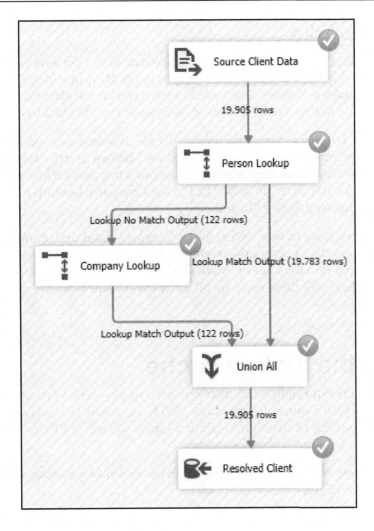

32. Stop the debug mode execution.

33. In SSMS, use the following query to inspect the results:

```
SELECT ResolvedClient.IsPerson AS IsPerson
      ,COUNT(*) AS ClientCount
  FROM dbo.ResolvedClient
GROUP BY ResolvedClient.IsPerson
ORDER BY ClientCount DESC;
```

How it works...

At the beginning of the execution, all reference data about persons and companies is loaded into memory; this is reflected by the messages in the **Output** window: **Company Lookup** and **Person Lookup.** Reference sets are extracted during the data flow's **Pre-Execute** phase. Data processing in this data flow cannot commence until the lookup data is cached.

After the data is extracted from the source flat file, it is first checked in the **Person Lookup** transformation: matching rows are placed in the **Lookup Match Output**, and non-matching rows are placed in the **Lookup No Match Output**. Only unmatched rows from the **Person Lookup** transformation are then checked in the **Company Lookup** transformation and placed in the **Lookup Match Output**.

Because of the **Ignore failure** setting in the **Company Lookup** transformation, 18 additional unmatched rows (that is, rows that were resolved neither as persons, nor as companies) were also placed into the **Lookup Match Output**; however, the `BusinessEntityID` and `IsPerson` columns of these rows are NULL, as is evident from the results of the query you used in Step 29.

Using the lookup cache

The **Lookup Transformation** can use two different connection types: the **OLE DB connection**, which requires the reference data to be stored in a data store that can be accessed by the OLE DB data provider, or a **Cache connection** that requires thee data to be available in an SSIS cache object.

In essence, there are three different modes of operation (depending on how the reference data is made available):

- In **full cache** mode, the reference data needs to be loaded completely into memory (cached) before the transformation can be used. Data is either loaded automatically (when an OLE DB connection is used to retrieve the lookup set), or needs to be loaded before the data flow, in which the lookup set is needed, and starts executing (when the cache connection is used to access the reference set).
- With **partial cache**, the reference data is loaded into memory at run time, while the pipeline rows are being processed, and the execution engine determines automatically (based on the reference query) which rows, and how many, are loaded into cache.
- Under **no cache** mode, no data is loaded into cache, and the reference query is called for each row in the pipeline.

All three modes of operation are supported when the OLE DB connection is used, but only the full cache mode is supported when the cache connection is used.

In this recipe, you will learn how to make the data available in an SSIS cache object, and how to configure the Lookup Transformation to use it.

How to do it...

1. Make sure that the AdventureWorksETL.sln solution is open in SSDT, and that the LookupCache.dtsx package is active in the control flow designer. The solution is located in the C:\SSIS2016Cookbook\Chapter06\Starter\AdventureWorksETL\ folder.

   This package is a variation of the package you developed in the preceding recipe; instead of processing a single source file, it uses the Foreach loop container to traverse a folder in the filesystem and process one or more files that correspond to the search criteria.

2. From the SSIS Toolbox, drag a **Data Flow** component to the control flow designer, and change its name to Load Person Cache.

3. Remove the precedence constraint leading from the **Truncate Resolved Client** task to the **Foreach File** container, and establish a new sequence:
   - Truncate Resolved Client
   - Load Person Cache
   - Foreach File

4. Open the **Load Person Cache** task in the data flow designer.

5. From the SSIS Toolbox, drag an **OLE DB Source** component to the data flow designer and change its name to **Person Data**.

6. Edit the **Person Data** source, and on the **Connection Manager** page use the following settings:

Property	Value
OLE DB connection manager	cmgr_Reference
Data access mode	**SQL command**

7. Enter the following query into the SQL command text box:

```
SELECT CAST(Person.LastName + COALESCE(N' ' + Person.MiddleName, N'') +
N', ' + Person.FirstName AS NVARCHAR(256)) as ClientName
        ,Person.BusinessEntityID AS BusinessEntityID
          ,CAST(1 AS BIT) AS IsPerson
    FROM Person.Person;
```

Refer to the following screenshot to verify your settings:

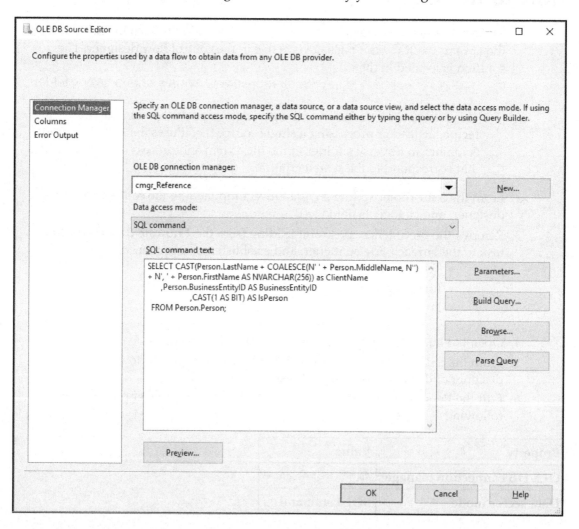

8. On the **Columns** page, make sure that all the source columns are selected, and then click **OK** to complete the configuration.

9. From the SSIS Toolbox, drag a **Cache Transform** component to the data flow designer, and change its name to `Person Cache`.

10. Connect the regular data path from the **Person Data** source to the **Person Cache** transformation.

11. Double-click the **Person Cache** component to open the **Cache Transform Editor**.

12. On the **Connection Manager** page, on the right-hand side of the **Cache Connection Manager** selection box, click **New...** to open the **Cache Connection Manager Editor**.

13. In the **Cache Connection Manager Editor**, on the **General** tab, use `PersonCache` as the **Connection manager name** property, as shown here:

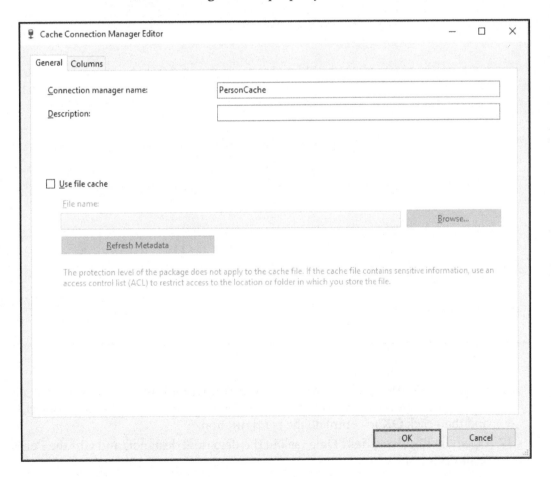

14. On the **Columns** tab, set the **Index Position** property of the **ClientName** column to **1**. This will instruct the transformation to create an index on the **ClientName** column.

Refer to the following screenshot to verify your settings:

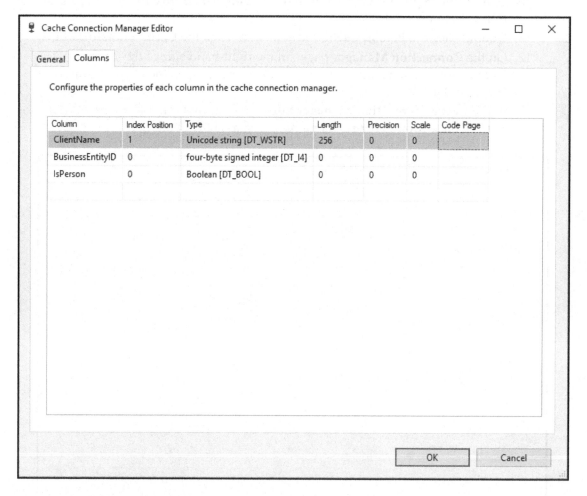

15. Click **OK** to complete the configuration.
16. On the **Mappings** page of the **Cache Transformation Editor**, make sure that all source columns are mapped to the corresponding columns of the cache object, and then click **OK** to complete the configuration.
17. Open the **Resolve Client Data** task in the data flow designer, and edit the **Person Lookup** transformation.

18. On the General page of the **Person Lookup** transformation editor, change the Connection type to the **Cache connection manager**. A warning should appear at the bottom of the editor, prompting you to continue the configuration on the **Connection** page.

19. On the **Connection** page, make sure that the **PersonCache** object is selected in the **Cache connection manager** selection box, as shown here:

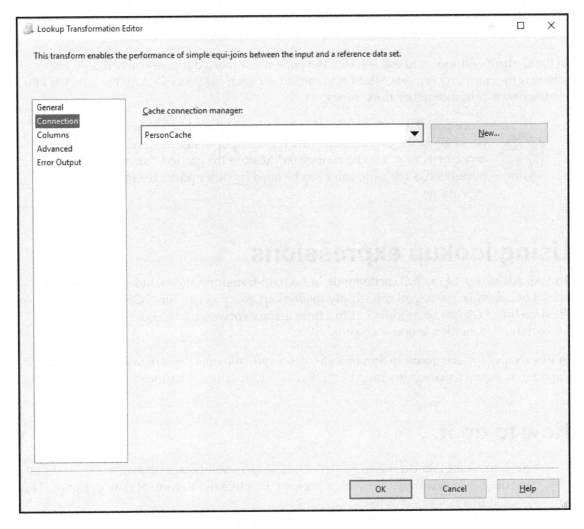

20. On the **Columns** page, make sure that all the settings have remained as they were set in steps 8 through 9 of the preceding recipe, and then click **OK** to complete the configuration.

21. Save the solution, and then execute it in debug mode. Observe the control flow, and inspect the messages in the **Output** window.

How it works...

In the control flow of the LookupCache.dtsx SSIS package, you changed the way the person reference data is cached; instead of relying on the **Person Lookup** transformation to load the data into cache, you decided when the data is going to be cached.

In the **Output** window, you can see that the person reference data was cached only once, whereas the company reference data was cached for each file processed by the Foreach File container—that is, altogether three times.

 Once populated, the cache object can be used multiple times in the same package, in the execution in which it was populated. Alternatively, the cache object can also be configured to store the cached data in a file; once populated, such a file can even be used by other packages in separate executions.

Using lookup expressions

To take advantage of the full cache mode in Lookup transformations, but only retrieve a subset of reference rows, you can supply the lookup query at run time. Certain properties of the data flow task can be modified at run time using expressions; the query used in a Lookup transformation is one such property.

In this recipe, you are going to dynamically determine the query restrictions and prepare the reference query in each iteration of the Foreach loop container processing the input files.

How to do it...

1. Make sure that the AdventureWorksETL.sln solution is open in SSDT, and that the LookupExpression.dtsx package is active in the control flow designer. The solution is located in the C:\SSIS2016Cookbook\Chapter06\Starter\AdventureWorksETL\ folder.
2. Create three new package variables using the following information; the **Variables** window can be opened by selecting **Variables** in the **SSIS** menu when an SSIS package is active in the control flow designer:

Name	Data type
lowerBoundary	String
upperBoundary	String
personLookupQuery	String

3. Make sure the **personLookupQuery** variable is selected in the **Variables** window, and click the **Move Variable** icon (the second from the left) to change the variable's scope.

4. In the **Select New Scope** dialog, locate and select the **Foreach File** object in the package's object tree, as shown here:

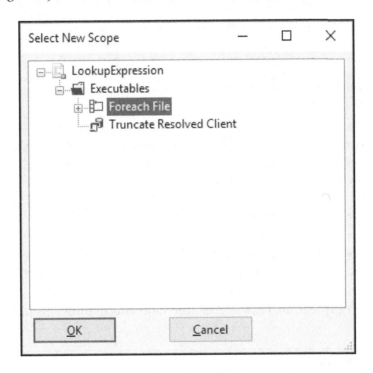

5. Click OK to confirm the move, and repeat steps 4 and 5 for the other two variables created in step 2.

6. The **currentFileName** variable must remain scoped to the package level. Refer to the following screenshot to verify your settings:

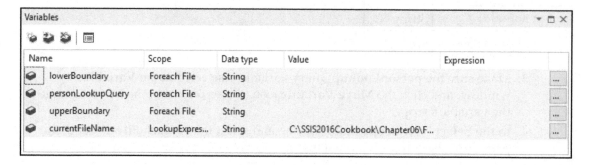

7. Use the following query as the value of the `personLookupQuery` variable:

```
SELECT CAST(Person.LastName + COALESCE(N' ' + Person.MiddleName, N'') +
N', ' + Person.FirstName AS NVARCHAR(256)) as ClientName
    ,Person.BusinessEntityID AS BusinessEntityID
    ,CAST(1 AS BIT) AS IsPerson
FROM Person.Person;
```

8. In the control flow designer, drag three **Expression Tasks** from the SSIS Toolbox to the **Foreach File** container, and name them Lower Boundary, Upper Boundary, and Person Lookup Query, respectively.

9. Establish the following sequence of operations inside the `Foreach` file container:
   - Lower Boundary
   - Upper Boundary
   - Person Lookup Query
   - Resolve Client Data

10. Edit each **Expression Task** and use the following expressions in their Expression text boxes:

Expression Task	Expression

Lower Boundary	`@[User::lowerBoundary] := SUBSTRING(`
	`@[User::currentFileName] , FINDSTRING(`
	`@[User::currentFileName] , "_", 1) + 1 , 1 )`

Upper Boundary	`@[User::upperBoundary]:=REPLICATE(SUBSTRING(`
	`@[User::currentFileName] , FINDSTRING(`
	`@[User::currentFileName] , "-", 1) +1 , 1 ), 256)`

Person Lookup Query	`@[User::personLookupQuery]:="SELECT *`
	
	`FROM`
	
	`(`
	
	`SELECT CAST(Person.LastName + COALESCE(N' ' +`
	`Person.MiddleName, N'') + N', ' + Person.FirstName AS`
	`NVARCHAR(256)) as ClientName`
	
	`,Person.BusinessEntityID AS BusinessEntityID`
	
	`,CAST(1 AS BIT) AS IsPerson`
	
	`FROM Person.Person`
	
	`) RefTable`
	
	`WHERE (RefTable.ClientName BETWEEN '" +`
	`@[User::lowerBoundary] + "' AND '" +`
	`@[User::upperBoundary] + "');"`

11. Select the **Resolve Client Data** task in the control flow designer and in the **Properties** pane locate the **Expressions** property and click inside the empty text box on the right.

12. Click on the ellipsis icon on the far-right side to open the **Property Expression Editor**.

13. In the **Property** column, select the `[Person Lookup].[SqlCommand]` property, and then click the ellipsis icon on the far-right side of the corresponding row to open the **Expression Editor**.

14. Drag the **User::personLookupQuery** variable from the `Variables and Parameters` tree to the **Expression** text box, and click **Evaluate** to validate the expression.

Refer to the following screenshot to verify your settings:

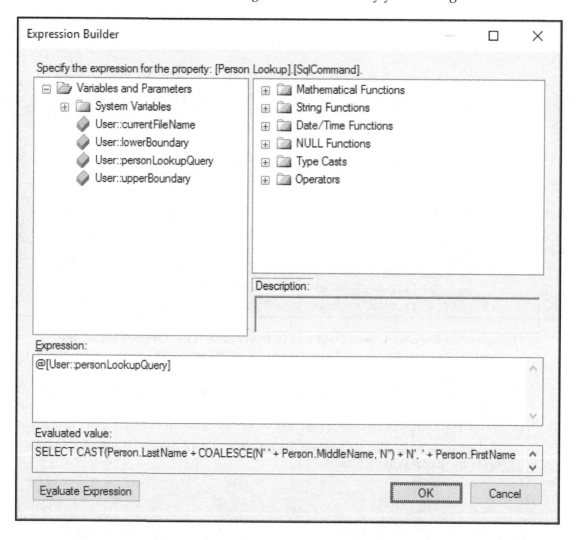

15. Click **OK** to confirm the configuration of the expression, and refer to the following screenshot to verify the settings in the **Property Expression Editor**:

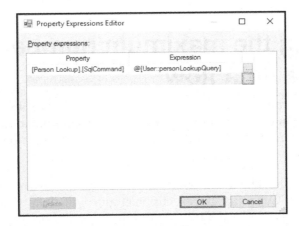

16. Click **OK** to confirm the property configuration.
17. The **Resolve Client Data** task should now have a new *fx* mark in the upper left corner; this means that the task is configured using property expressions.
18. Save the package, execute it in debug mode, and observe the execution.

How it works...

As in the preceding recipe, the package traverses the specified folder and processes multiple files. In this particular case, each filename also contains the information about which clients it contains; for instance, the Clients_H-R.csv file contains data for clients whose names start with letters H to R. This information is used to prepare the person lookup query by storing the first letter in the lowerBoundary variable, and the last letter of the range in the upperBoundary variable. Both variables are referenced in the expression used to determine the value of the personLookupQuery variable, which is then used to configure the **Person Lookup** transformation at run time.

In each iteration of the **Foreach File** container, a new pair of lowerBoundary and upperBoundary variable values is extracted from the currentFileName variable; as a consequence, in each iteration the **Person Lookup** transformation loads a different subset of reference data into cache. You can also observe this in the **Output** window; three different sets of Person data are cached in each iteration.

As long as the reference set is aligned with the expected values in the pipeline, the entities will be resolved correctly.

Determining the maximum number of worker threads in a data flow

Generally, multiple operations can be performed concurrently in SSIS, as long as sufficient resources are available in the environment hosting the execution. Parallelism can be achieved at several different levels, depending on the nature of the operations and the availability of resources.

Inside a data flow task, the data movements and transformations can be performed on one or more worker threads. Generally, the execution engine will always attempt to parallelize as many of the operations of a particular data flow as possible—in line with the nature of the transformations, and restricted by the available resources.

For instance, provided that enough worker threads are available for a particular transformation, and enough system memory can be allocated for the pipeline buffers, more than one instance of the same transformation can run concurrently. By setting the **EngineThreads** data flow property, you can restrict the number of concurrent data flow instances.

In this recipe, you are going to restrict the number of worker threads in a data flow task to the minimum, thus preventing the data flow from being parallelized. This is useful in cases where you know at design time that the data flow cannot be parallelized due to the nature of its transformations, the sources, or destinations used in it. Disabling parallelism at design time is also recommended when you know that one or more transformations in the data flow (typically, script or custom transformations) should only run as a single instance.

How to do it...

1. In SSDT, open the `SSISCookbook.sln` solution, located in the `C:\SSIS2016Cookbook\Chapter06\Starter\SSISCookbook\` folder.
2. Open the `StgAddress.dtsx` package, locate the `dft_Staging_StgAddress` data flow task in the control flow, and open it in the data flow designer.
3. Click on the empty canvas of the data flow designer to make sure that the data flow as a whole is selected.

4. In the **Properties** pane, you should now have access to the data flow properties.

5. Locate the **EngineThreads** property, and set its value to the minimum number of **2**, as shown in the following screenshot:

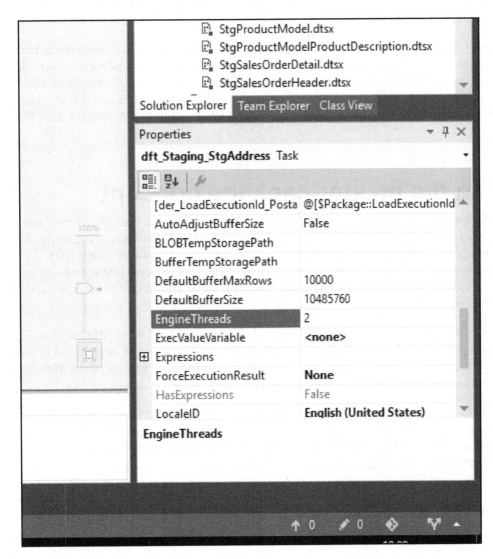

6. Save the package.

How it works...

By setting the number of worker threads to its minimum value, you have made certain that this data flow will not be parallelized. By using a number greater than 2, you instruct the SSIS execution engine to try to assign more than one thread to the data flow.

Note though, that at run time the SSIS engine might assign fewer (or more) threads than specified at design time—it takes into account the actual needs of a particular data flow (for instance, the size of the data, the complexity of the transformations, and so on), and it also considers the availability of resources (that is, the actual number of available worker threads, the actual amount of memory that can be allocated to this particular data flow, and so on).

Using the master package concept

By using the master package concept, it is possible to parallelize the execution of multiple child packages as determined in the control flow of the master package. Typically, this approach is used to parallelize packages that use separate data sources and data destinations (for instance, processing separate dimension tables in data warehousing scenarios), or to parallelize packages with CPU-intensive operations to run concurrently with packages with I/O-intensive operations.

In the control flow, you use precedence constraints and containers to determine which operations can be performed in parallel, and which of them must be performed in sequence. Through the `MaxConcurrentExecutables` package property, you can determine the maximum number of tasks to be performed simultaneously.

For instance, in data warehousing scenarios, fact tables are processed after the associated dimension tables have been processed successfully. Prior to fact processing, most dimension tables, or even all of them, can be processed concurrently as long as their data sources can be accessed independently of one another.

In this recipe, you are going to learn about the master package concept; you are going to orchestrate the execution of multiple child packages from within a single master package.

How to do it...

1. Make sure that the SSISCookbook.sln solution from the
   C:\SSIS2016Cookbook\Chapter06\Starter\SSISCookbook\ folder is open
   in SSDT.
2. Open the EP_Staging.dtsx package; this package implements the master
   package design—most of the child packages are already configured.
3. From the SSIS Toolbox, drag an **Execute Package Task** to the **seqc_Dimensions**
   sequence container. Change the task name to ept_StgAddress.
4. Double-click the newly added task to open the **Execute Package Task Editor**, and
   on the **Package** page use the following settings to configure the task:

Property	Value
ReferenceType	Project Reference
PackageNameFromProjectReference	StgAddress.dtsx
ExecuteOutOfProcess	False

5. Leave the **Password** property unchanged; no passwords are used in these
   packages.
6. On the **Parameter bindings** page, click **Add** to add a new child package
   parameter, and use the following settings to configure the parameter:

Property	Value
Child package parameter	LoadExecutionId
Binding parameter or variable	System::LoadExecutionId

7. Click **OK** to complete the configuration.

8. Change the sequence of the operations in the `seqc_Dimensions` container so that:

   - The `ept_StgAddress` and `ept_StgCustomer` tasks are completed successfully before the `ept_StgCustomerAddress` task starts
   - The `ept_StgProductCategory`, `ept_StgProductDescription`, `ept_StgProductModel`, and `ept_StgProductModelProductDescription` tasks are completed successfully before the `ept_StgProduct` task starts

9. Save the package.

10. In the following screenshot, you can observe one way of implementing the sequence described in step 7:

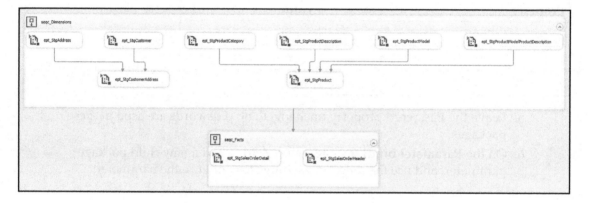

11. Click the empty canvas of the control flow designer, so that the **Properties** pane displays the package properties.

12. Locate the **MaxConcurrentExecutables** property, and set its value to **4**, as shown here:

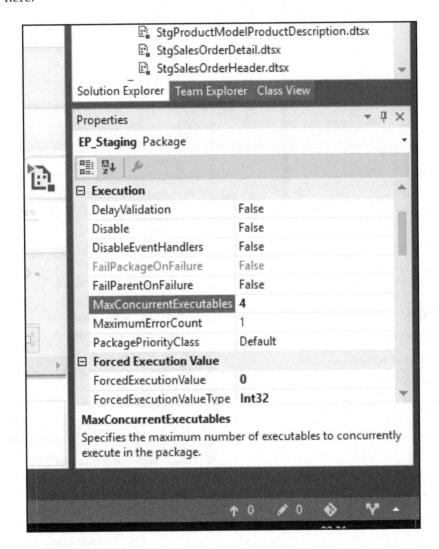

13. Save the package.
14. In the **Solution Explorer**, right-click each package, and make sure that the **Entry-point Package** setting in the shortcut menu is checked only for the `EP_Staging.dtsx` master package, and uncheck it for all the child packages, as shown in the following screenshot:

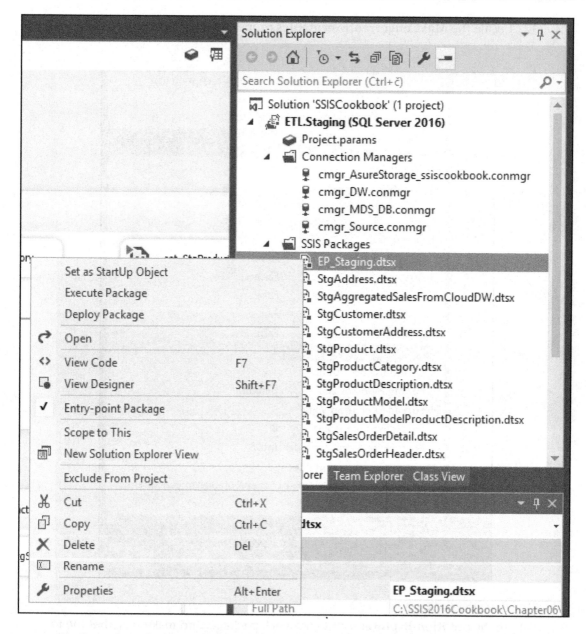

15. Save the solution, and then execute the master package in debug mode. Observe how each individual child package is activated and executed.

How it works...

The master package concept allows you to divide the work among the members of the development team, so that multiple packages, representing individual units of work, can be developed at the same time. This modular approach to SSIS development also means that the same package, since it facilitates only a very specific process, can be reused in another project.

The master package concept also allows you to determine the best way to orchestrate the execution of the complete work, because all the individual packages can be controlled from a single point—both in the ability to specify what moment, and under what circumstances, a specific operation will be performed, as well as in the ability to centralize the configuration of the child packages.

By setting the `MaxConcurrentExecutables` package property to a specific value, you instruct the SSIS execution engine as to how many control flow tasks should be running concurrently. By keeping this number lower than the total number of CPUs available for SSIS executions, you effectively make room for other operations that might have to run in the production environment on the same server, and at the same time. By keeping this number close to the total number of CPUs, you can improve the utilization of server resources during the maintenance window.

The **Entry-point Package** property allows you, at design time, to specify which of the multiple packages in the same SSIS project will actually be exposed for configuration. This allows you to hide the child packages from the production environment administrators, so that they only need to configure the project properties, and the properties exposed through the entry-point (master) package. This way all child (non-entry-point) package properties can be under full control of the master package.

Requesting an execution tree in SSDT

Every time the execution of an SSIS package is started, the SSIS execution engine first prepares the execution plan. This plan contains the package metadata used by the execution engine to determine the range of resources that are going to be needed to perform the operations defined by the package.

The **Execution Tree** of a given SSIS package, representing its execution plan, can be prepared on demand at design time. The functionality is available when the SSIS package is being edited in SSDT. The purpose of the Execution Tree is to provide you with the same information the execution engine uses to determine resource usage. By examining the Execution Trees, you can understand the expected behavior of the package in terms of resource usage, and become familiar with resource requirements before the SSIS package is deployed, or used, in the destination environment.

In this recipe, you are going to configure an SSIS package to capture two special events during an execution in debug mode in SSDT. You are then going to inspect the captured event data.

The following events can be used at design time to help you understand the resource requirements of your data flows:

- The `PipelineExecutionPlan` event provides access to the execution plan of the data flow—how the pipeline buffers will be managed
- The `PipelineExecutionTrees` event provides the information about how the operations are going to be executed—how the buffers will be used

Typically, you would capture these events at design time so that you can get a good estimate of how many resources will be required by a particular data flow, and how the execution of one data flow might affect the concurrent executions of other data flows.

How to do it...

1. In SSDT, open the `AdventureWorksETL.sln` solution located in the `C:\SSIS2016Cookbook\Chapter06\Starter\AdventureWorksETL\` folder.
2. Open the `ExecutionTrees.dtsx` package in the control flow designer.
3. Right-click on the empty canvas of the control flow designer, and select **Logging...** from the shortcut menu to open the **Configure SSIS Logs** editor, as shown in the following screenshot:

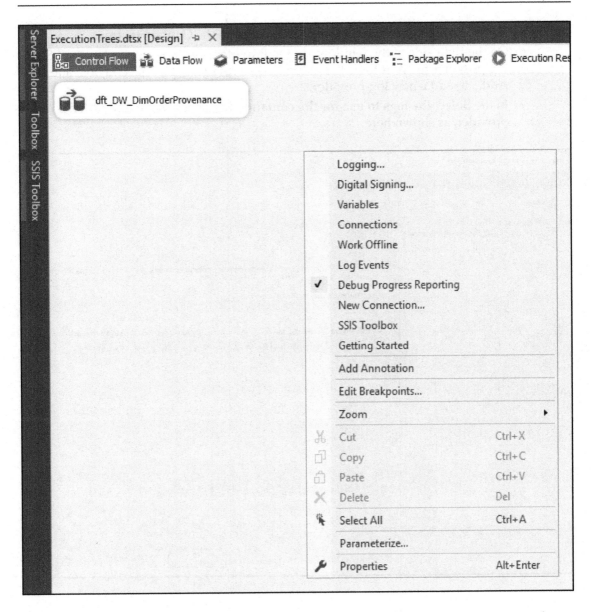

4. In the **Containers** tree on the left-hand side, check the ExecutionTrees package, and the dft_DW_DimOrderProvenance data flow task, to enable logging on both objects.

5. Select (but do not uncheck!) the package node in the **Containers** tree.

6. On the right side of the window, on the **Providers and Logs** tab, select the **SSIS log provider for Windows Event log** in the **Provider type** selection box, and click **Add...** to add a new log provider.

7. In the **Select the logs to use for the container** list, check the newly added SSIS log provider, as shown here:

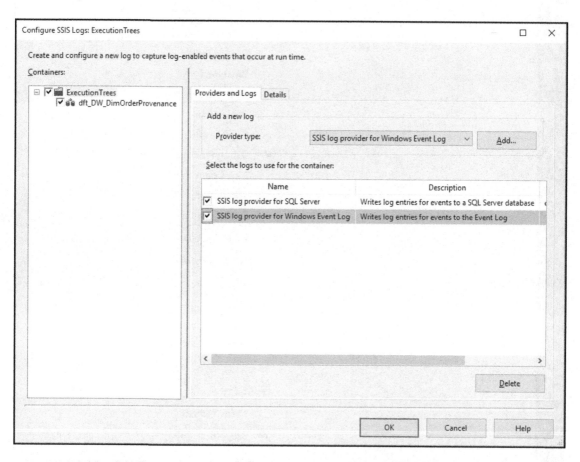

8. In the **Containers** list, now select the data flow.
9. In the **Select the logs to use for the container** list, check the **SSIS log provider for Windows Event logs**, as shown here:

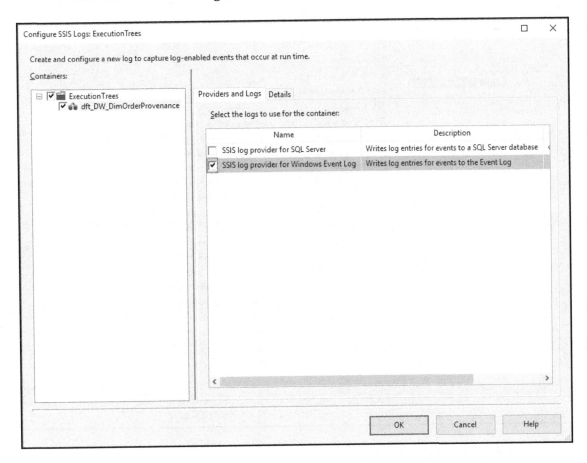

10. On the **Details** tab, check the **PipelineExecutionPlan** and the **PipelineExecutionTrees** events, as shown in the following screenshot:

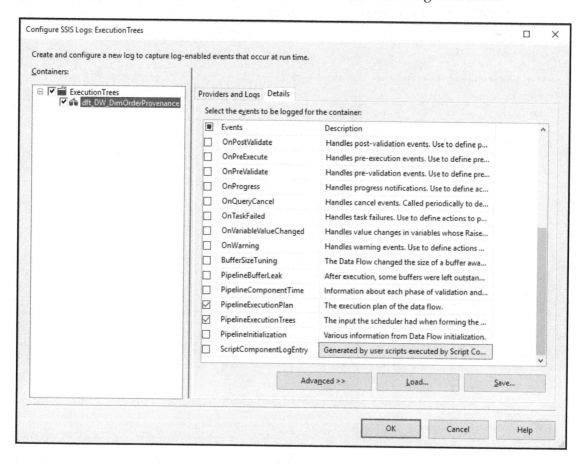

11. Click **OK** to confirm the configuration.

12. In the **View** menu, expand the **Other Windows** sub-menu, and select **Log Events** to open the **Log Events** pane, as shown in the following screenshot:

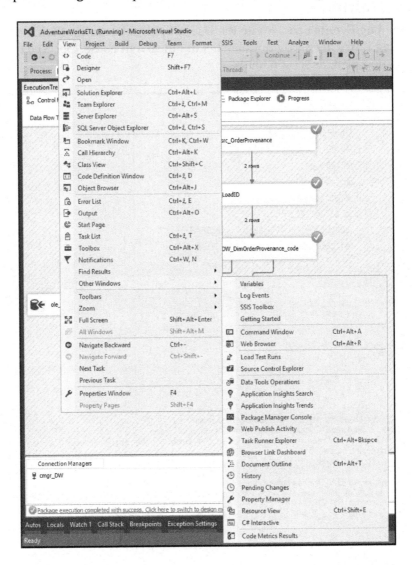

13. Execute the package in debug mode; as the execution progresses, events are captured and displayed in the **Log Events** pane.

14. Do not stop the execution.

15. In the **Log Events** pane, locate the **User::PipelineExecutionPlan** event, and open the **Log Entry** details by double-clicking the event name. Observe the data flow execution plan, as shown here:

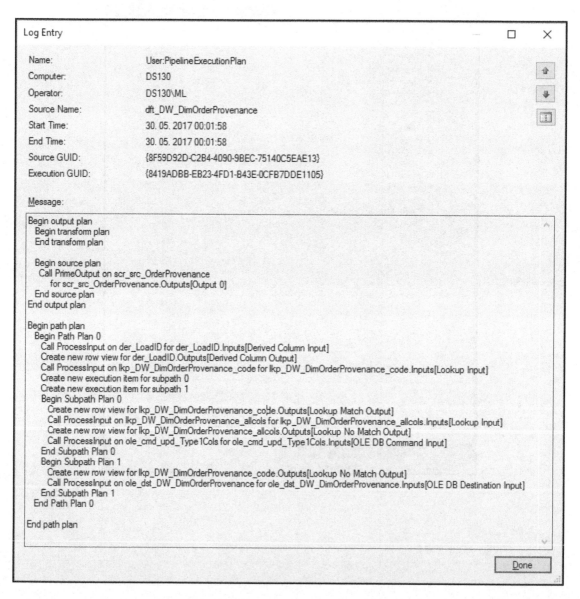

16. In the **Log Entry** window, you can navigate between the events by using the icons with the up and down arrows in the top right corner of the window.

17. In the following screenshot, you can observe the **PipelineExecutionTrees** event data:

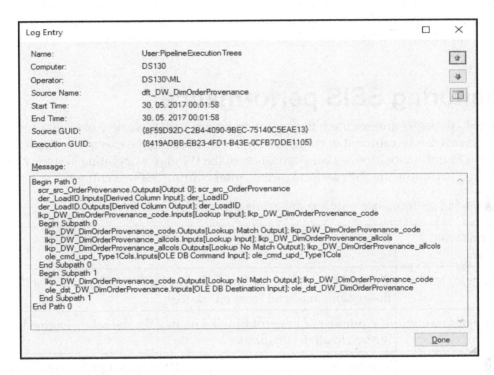

18. When you are done inspecting the event data, click **Done** to close the **Log Entry** window.

19. Stop the package execution.

How it works...

By inspecting the event data of the **PipelineExecutionTrees** event, you can see how the data will flow from the source components through the transformations, all the way to the destination components. In the preceding example, one main data path is used throughout the data flow, with two additional sub-paths for the two Lookup transformations.

The **PipelineExecutionPlan** event shows the individual operations that will be performed in order to facilitate the data movement through the pipeline. In the previous example, you can see that the buffers created in the source component (represented by the main data path in the execution tree) will be *reused* throughout this particular data flow. Because only non-blocking transformations are used in this data flow, the buffers can be shared by downstream components—by using views to access the buffers created in upstream components (these are represented by the sub-paths in the execution tree).

Monitoring SSIS performance

When SSIS packages are executed, the execution engine emits a variety of events and messages that can be captured in the operating system hosting the execution. Typically, Windows Performance Monitor, an application of the Windows operating system, can be configured to capture the SSIS performance counters during SSIS executions.

The following performance counters are available in SQL Server 2016:

Performance counter	Description
BLOB bytes read	The number of bytes of binary large object (BLOB) data that the data flow engine has read from all sources.
BLOB bytes written	The number of bytes of BLOB data that the data flow engine has written to all destinations.
BLOB files in use	The number of BLOB files that the data flow engine currently is using for spooling.
Buffer memory	The amount of memory that is in use. This may include both physical and virtual memory. When this number is larger than the amount of physical memory, the Buffers Spooled count rises as an indication that memory swapping is increasing. Increased memory swapping slows performance of the data flow engine.
Buffers in use	The number of buffer objects, of all types, that all data flow components and the data flow engine is currently using.
Buffers spooled	The number of buffers currently written to the disk. If the data flow engine runs low on physical memory, buffers not currently used are written to the disk and are then reloaded when needed.

Flat buffer memory	The total amount of memory, in bytes, that all flat buffers use. Flat buffers are blocks of memory that a component uses to store data. A flat buffer is a large block of bytes that is accessed byte by byte.
Flat buffers in use	The number of flat buffers that the data flow engine uses. All flat buffers are private buffers.
Private buffer memory	The total amount of memory in use by all private buffers. A buffer is not private if the data flow engine creates it to support data flow. A private buffer is a buffer that a transformation uses for temporary work only. For example, the Aggregation transformation uses private buffers to do its work.
Private buffers in use	The number of buffers that transformations use.
Rows read	The number of rows that a source produces. The number does not include rows read from reference tables by the Lookup transformation.
Rows written	The number of rows offered to a destination. The number does not reflect rows written to the destination data store.

You can find more information about the SSIS performance counters in the book's online article entitled **Performance Counters**, at https://docs.microsoft.com/en-us/sql/integration-services/perfor mance/performance-counters.

The Performance Monitor can be used to establish an ad-hoc monitoring session, where the performance counters are observed for the duration of the monitoring session, or by configuring a data collector set to be run automatically on a schedule. After the data collection has completed, you can use the Performance Monitor to inspect the behavior of the server during the execution.

Establishing a performance monitor session

In this recipe, you are going to prepare an ad-hoc performance monitoring session by using the Performance Monitor, a component of the Windows operating system.

How to do it...

1. In the Windows **Start** menu, locate the Performance Monitor and open it.
2. In the tree on the left, expand the **Monitoring Tools** node, and select the **Performance Monitor** node.
3. In the command ribbon on the right side of the window, click the **Add** icon, marked by the green plus sign, to open the **Add Counters** dialog.
4. In the Available counters list, locate the **SQL Server SSIS Pipeline 13.0** group, and expand it by clicking the tiny downward arrow to the right of the group name.
5. With the help of the ctrl button on your keyboard, and the mouse, select the following counters:
   - Buffer memory
   - Buffers in use
   - Buffers spooled
   - Flat buffer memory
   - Flat buffers in use
   - Private buffer memory
   - Private buffers in use

6. Click **Add >>** below the list. The counters should now be listed in the **Added counters** list on the right, as shown in the following screenshot:

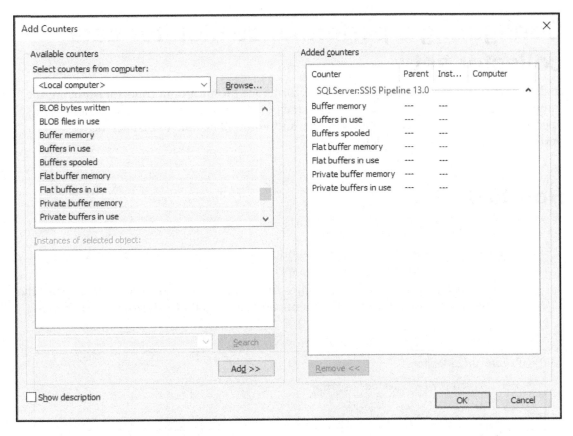

7. Click OK to complete the configuration. As soon as you add the counters, the **Performance Monitor** should start collecting data and displaying it in the graph.

8. If the **Performance Monitor** is not running, click the **Unfreeze display** icon in the command ribbon, marked by a green arrow.

9. In SSDT, open the AdventureWorksETL.sln solution, located in the C:\SSIS2016Cookbook\Chapter06\Solution\AdventureWorksETL\ folder.

10. Open the LookupExpression.dtsx package, and execute it in debug mode.

11. Observe the activity in the **Performance Monitor** window.

How it works...

While the performance monitor session is running, the selected counters, emitted by the SSIS execution engine, are captured by the Performance Monitor and are displayed in a chart in the tool's graphical user interface.

Configuring a performance monitor data collector set

In this recipe, you are going to prepare a Performance Monitor data collector set using the same settings that you used in the previous recipe. This time the performance monitoring operation is going to run in the background, and you will be able to inspect the performance data after it completes.

How to do it...

1. Open the **Performance Monitor**.
2. In the tree on the left side of the window, navigate to the **Performance Monitor** node, as described in the previous recipe.
3. When the graph is visible, right-click the **Performance Monitor** node, expand the **New** sub-menu in the shortcut menu, and select **Data Collector Set**, as shown here:

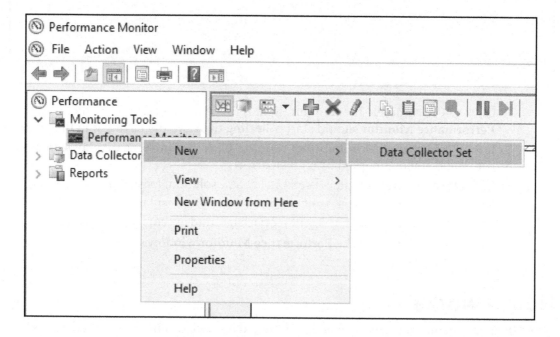

4. The **Data Collector Set** wizard starts. On the first page, enter `Chapter06` in the **Name** text box, and then click **Next**.

5. On page two, leave the default value of the **Root directory** property unchanged, and click **Next**.

6. On page three, leave the **<Default>** value of the **Run as** property unchanged, and make sure that the Save and close option is selected, as shown in the following screenshot:

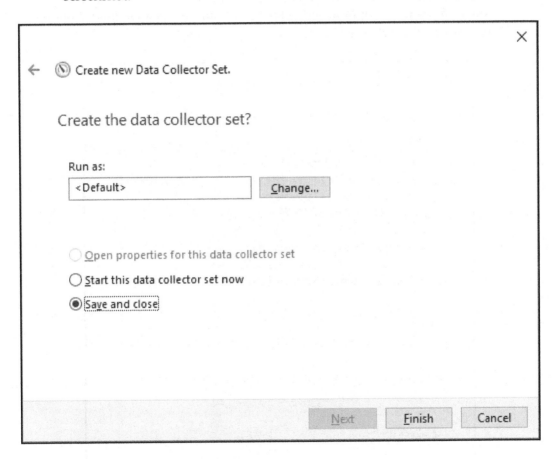

7. Click **Finish** to complete the configuration.

8. Locate the **Data Collector Set** that you just created in the tree on the left side of the window, under **Data Collector Sets / User Defined**.

9. Select the **Chapter06** node to open the data collector set contents on the right.

10. Right-click the **System Monitor Log** item, and select **Properties** from the shortcut menu.

11. On the **Performance Counters** tab, click **Add...** to add the SSIS performance counters, as described in steps 4 through 7 of the preceding recipe.

12. After the counters have been added and the System Monitor Log Properties dialog is active again, change the **Sample interval** to **1 second**, check the **Maximum samples** option, and enter **120** into the text box below this option.

13. Refer to the following screenshot to verify your settings:

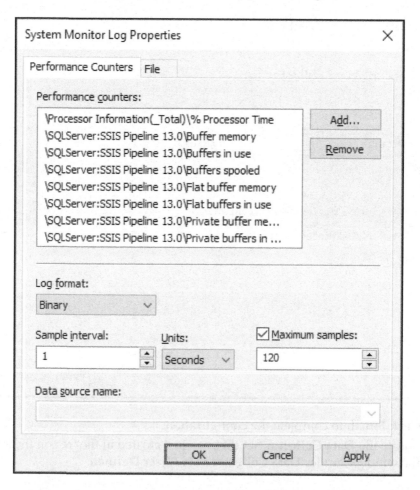

14. Click **OK** to complete the configuration.

15. In SSDT, make sure that the `AdventureWorksETL.sln` solution from the `C:\SSIS2016Cookbook\Chapter06\Solution\AdventureWorksETL\` folder is open, and that the `LookupExpression.dtsx` package is active.

16. In the **Performance Monitor**, in the tree on the left, right-click the **Chapter06** data collector set and select **Start** from the shortcut menu.

17. Switch to SSDT, and start the execution.

18. Switch back to the **Performance Monitor**, and either wait for the data collection to complete, or stop it manually by right-clicking the **Chapter06** node and selecting **Stop** from the shortcut menu.

19. To inspect the latest results, right-click the **Chapter06** node, and select **Latest Report** from the shortcut menu.

20. To access all of the collected results, navigate to the **Chapter06** node, under **Reports /User Defined**. The reports are listed under the **Data Collector Set** node; their names are made up of the server name, the date of the collection, and an ordinal number.

How it works....

Performance Monitor data collection can either be started on demand, or performed on a schedule. When data collection is started, the Performance Monitor begins capturing the configured counters and it saves the data to the location specified when the data collector set was configured.

The data can be inspected after the scheduled run is completed (or stopped manually).

7
Unleash the Power of SSIS Script Task and Component

In this chapter, we will cover the following recipes:

- Using variables in SSIS Script task
- Execute complex filesystem operations with the Script task
- Reading data profiling XML results with the Script task
- Correcting data with the Script component
- Validating data using regular expressions in a Script component
- Using the Script component as a source
- Using the Script component as a destination

Introduction

The **Script task** and **Script component** allow you to execute a custom Visual Basic or Visual C# code inside your SSIS package control flow or data flow. This way, you can perform complex operations beyond the capabilities of other built-in tasks and transformations. The Script task works like any other task in the control flow. You can use the Script component in the data flow as the **source, transformation**, or **destination**.

Both the Script task and the Script component have two design-time modes: you begin editing by specifying properties using the common editors for tasks and components that you are already familiar with, and then switch to a development environment to write the .NET code. The second environment is the **Microsoft Visual Studio Tools for Applications (VSTA)** environment.

The Script task provides the entire infrastructure for the custom code for you, letting you focus exclusively on the code. You can use any .NET class library and namespace in your code. In addition, from your code, you can interact with the containing SSIS package through the global **Dts object**. For example, the Dts object exposes package variables, and you can read and modify them in your custom code.

When you add the Script component to your data flow, you have to make the first decision immediately. You can use the Script component as a custom data source, a destination, or a transformation. When you add it to the data flow, you will be asked which Script component type you are creating.

The next step to designing a Script component, after you have determined its type, is to configure its metadata. In the metadata configuration part, you use the Script Component Editor to define the component's properties, such as the name and the language you will use. You also have to enlist the SSIS package variables you are going to use in the script in the `ReadOnlyVariables` and `ReadWriteVariables` properties. Note that, as always, variable names are case sensitive.

The Script component metadata configuration is slightly more complex than the Script task configuration. You need to define the input and output columns of the data flow buffers for the component as well. If you use the Script component as a data source, then you define the output columns only. The Script component is then responsible for creating the data flow buffers. If you use the component for a transformation, then you have to configure input and outputs. If you use it for a data destination, you configure the input only. You have to select which columns from the input buffers you are going to use in the script, and which columns you are going to send to the output buffers or to the data destination.

An output of an SSIS component can be **synchronous** or **asynchronous**, and thus the component can be non-blocking or blocking. Each output of the component has the `SynchronousInputID` property. If the value of this property is None, then the output is asynchronous, and you can completely redefine it. In addition, you can also define whether the output is sorted. If the value of the `SynchronousInputID` property is the component's input ID, then the output is synchronous. You process input row by row, and you cannot change the sort order of the input rows for the output. If you use synchronous outputs, then you can also configure the `ExclusionGroup` property to identify redirections of rows to different outputs. For example, you could redirect some of the rows to the regular output and some to the error output.

Using variables in SSIS Script task

The objective of this task is to teach you how to work with SSIS variables in a Script task.

You will learn two ways, a more complex one and a simpler one. You will typically use the latter in your packages.

Getting ready

There are no special prerequisites for this recipe, except, of course, SSIS 2016. In addition, you can use either your own text files for testing, or the three text files provided with the code for this chapter (Ch07_03.txt, Ch07_08.txt, and Ch07_10.txt).

 For your convenience, the VB and C# code snippets needed for this chapter are provided in the Chapter07.txt file.

How to do it...

1. Open SQL Server Data Tools (SSDT) and create a new project using the Integration Services Project template. Place the solution in the C:\SSIS2016Cookbook\Chapter07\Solution folder and name the project AdventureWorksETL.
2. Rename the default package UsingVariables.dtsx.
3. Create a intCounter variable with data type Int32 and a default value of 0.
4. Create a strFile variable of type String with the default value blank. Your **Variables** window should look like the following screenshot:

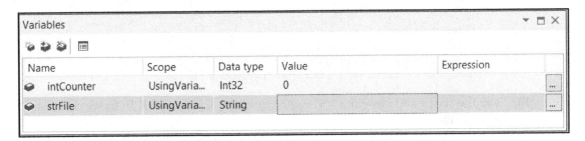

5. Add a For Loop container to the control flow. Rename it LoopThreeTimes.
6. Add a Foreach Loop container to the control flow. Rename it GetFileNames.

7. Connect the `GetFileNames` container with the `LoopThreeTimes` container with the **green (on success) arrow** from the LoopThreeTimes container. The `For Loop` container should finish with success before the Foreach Loop container starts executing.

8. Start editing the `LoopThreeTimes` container. Set the following properties:
   - **InitExpression** to @intCounter = 0
   - **EvalExpression** to @intCounter < 3
   - **AssignExpression** to @intCounter = @intCounter + 1

9. When you have finished setting the expressions, click on **OK**.

10. Add a Script task to the `LoopThreeTimes` container. Rename it `VariableDispenser`. You will use the `VariableDispenser` class from the `Microsoft.SqlServer.Dts.Runtime` namespace to handle a variable in the script. With this class, you have a detailed control over locking and unlocking variables during the script. You need to lock the variables inside the script either for reading or for writing before you use them, because the SSIS execution is parallelized, and some other thread might want to use the same variables at the same time.

11. Double-click the `VariableDispenser` task to open the Script Task editor. Change the default script language to Microsoft Visual Basic 2015. Leave the `ReadOnlyVariables` and `ReadWriteVariables` properties empty. Click the Edit Script button.

12. Expand the **Imports** region. Note that the `Microsoft.SqlServer.Dts.Runtime` namespace is already imported for you.

13. Locate the `Main()` method. Place the following script between the `Add your code here` comment and the `Dts.TaskResult = ScriptResults.Success` line:

```
Dim vars As Variables = Nothing
Dts.VariableDispenser.LockForRead("intCounter")
Dts.VariableDispenser.GetVariables(vars)
MsgBox("Iteration: " & CStr(vars(0).Value))
```

14. Save the script and close the VSTA environment. Click on **OK** in the Script task editor to close it.

15. Double-click the `GetFileNames` container to open the editor. Click the **Collection** tab.

16. Specify the **Foreach File Enumerator** in the **Enumerator** property.

17. Use the `C:\SSIS2016Cookbook\Chapter07\Files` folder (or any other folder you wish if you have put the text files provided in some other folder). Three text files, `Ch07_03.txt`, `Ch07_08.txt`, and `Ch07_10.txt` are provided with the code download for this book.

18. Specify the `Ch07*.txt` file pattern in the **Files** textbox. Retrieve the name and extension only.

19. Do not check the **Traverse subfolders** checkbox. The following screenshot shows what your settings should look like:

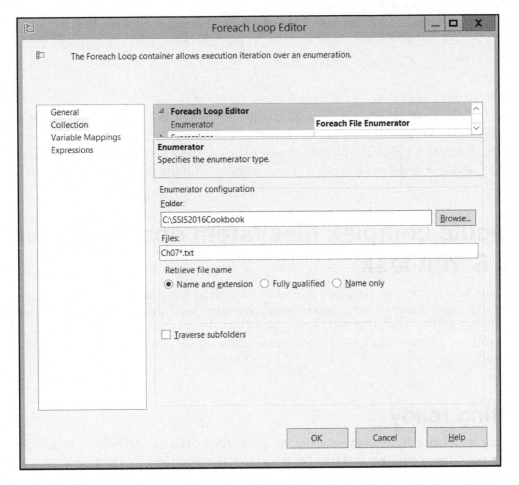

20. Click the **Variable Mappings** tab.

21. Map the `User::strFile` variable to Index 0. Click on **OK**.

22. Drag the **Script task** to the container. Rename it `ReadOnlyVariables`. Open the task editor.

23. In the **Script** tab, select **Microsoft Visual Basic 2015** as the scripting language.

24. Select the **User::strFile** variable in the **ReadOnlyVariables** property. When you define variables here, they are locked for the whole script. Lock and unlock happen automatically. This is a much simpler way to do the locking than with the VariableDispenser class, although you have more control, or control on a finer grain, with the VariableDispenser class.

25. Click the **Edit Script** button.

26. Locate the `Main()` method. Place the following script between the `Add your code here` comment and the `Dts.TaskResult = ScriptResults.Success` line:

```
MsgBox("File name: " & CStr(Dts.Variables("strFile").Value))
```

27. Save the script and close the VSTA environment. Click on **OK** in the Script task editor to close it.

28. Execute the package. Note how you see three iterations and three files. Save the solution, but don't exit SSDT if you want to continue with the next recipe.

Execute complex filesystem operations with the Script task

In the previous recipe, you retrieved filenames filtered by name and extension using the Foreach File enumerator of the Foreach Loop container. Sometimes you need more precise filters. For example, you might need to retrieve files with a larger size than a predefined value. You can get the collection of the filenames that satisfy your custom criteria with the Script task.

Getting ready

There are no special prerequisites for this recipe, except, of course, SSIS 2016. In addition, you can use either your own text files for testing, or the three text files provided with the code for this chapter (`Ch07_03.txt`, `Ch07_08.txt`, and `Ch07_10.txt`). Note that the length of the `Ch07_03.txt` file is 3 bytes, the `Ch07_08.txt` file is 8 bytes, and the `Ch07_10.txt` file is 10 bytes.

How to do it...

1. In **File Explorer**, right-click the Ch07_08.txt file and select **Properties**, as shown in the following screenshot:

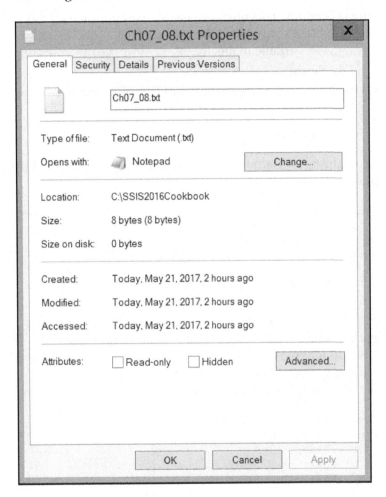

2. Note the file size, 8 bytes. Click **OK**.
3. In SSDT, add a new package to the Chapter07 project. Rename it FileSizes.dtsx.

4. Add two variables to the package:
   - intSize, with data type Int64, and default value 5
   - objList, with data type Object, default System.Object

5. Add a new **Script task** to the control flow. Rename it FilesBySize.

6. Open the task editor. This time, use the Microsoft Visual C# 2015 language. Add the User::intSize variable to the ReadOnlyVariables and the User::objList variable to the ReadWriteVariables collection.

7. Click on **Edit Script**.

8. Expand the **Namespaces** region and add the following two lines:

```
using System.IO;
using System.Collections;
```

9. Just before the Main method, add the following declarations of the constants and variables:

```
private const string FILE_PATH = "C:\\SSIS2016Cookbook";
private const string FILE_FILTER = "Ch07*.txt";
long fileSizeLimit;
private ArrayList listForEnumerator;
```

10. Please note that you might need to change the FILE_PATH and FILE_FILTER constants appropriately.

11. In the Main method, add the following code, that reads the file size limit from the package variable intSize, declares an array to store the names of the local files, a variable to store the file size, and an ArrayList, which will hold the filenames that will satisfy your custom criteria. The Directory.GetFiles method returns an array of the full names (including paths) for the files in the specified directory:

```
fileSizeLimit = (long)(Dts.Variables["intSize"].Value);
string[] localFiles;
long fileSize;
ArrayList listForEnumerator = new ArrayList();
localFiles = Directory.GetFiles(FILE_PATH, FILE_FILTER);
```

12. Add the following code to populate the **ArrayList** with the qualifying filenames:

```
foreach (string localFile in localFiles)
{
  FileInfo fi = new FileInfo(localFile);
  fileSize = fi.Length;
  if (fileSize >= fileSizeLimit)
  {
    listForEnumerator.Add(localFile);
  }
}
```

13. Finally, just before the `Dts.TaskResult = (int)ScriptResults.Success;` line, add the following code to show the number of matching files and to populate the `objList` package variable:

```
MessageBox.Show("Matching files: " + listForEnumerator.Count,
"Results",
    MessageBoxButtons.OK, MessageBoxIcon.Information);
    Dts.Variables["objList"].Value = listForEnumerator;
```

14. Save the code and exit the VSTA environment. Also exit the Script task editor.
15. Add a `Foreach` container to the control flow. Connect it with the FilesBySize Script task with the green arrow from the Script task. Rename the container `GetFileNameBySize`. Open the container editor.
16. In the **Collection** tab, specify the **Foreach From Variable Enumerator**. Use the `User::objList` variable.
17. In the **Variable Mappings** tab, map the `User::objList` variable to index 0. Click on **OK** to close the editor.
18. Add a **Script task** inside the container. Rename it `ShowFileNames`. Open the Script task editor.
19. Use the Microsoft Visual C# 2015 language. Define the `User::objList` variable as a read only variable. Click on **Edit Script**.
20. Add the following line of code to the `Main` method to show the names of the qualifying files:

```
MessageBox.Show(Dts.Variables["objList"].Value.ToString());.
```

21. Save the script and exit the task editor.
22. Run the package and observe the results.

Reading data profiling XML results with the Script task

In this recipe, you will read the XML file produced by the Data Profiling task and use the Script task to read the regular expressions extracted and store them in package variables.

Getting ready

This recipe assumes that you have finished the first recipe of Chapter 5, *Dealing with Data Quality*, and have the results of the Data Profiling task at your hand.

 For your convenience, the results of the Data Profiling task needed for this recipe are provided in the DataProfiling.xml file.

How to do it...

1. Add a new package to the AdventureWorksETL project. Rename the default package RegExValidation.dtsx.
2. Create two package variables. Name them EmailRegEx1 and EmailRegEx2. Use the **String** data type for both variables.
3. Drag the Script task to your control flow. Rename it ReadPatterns.
4. Open the editor for this task. On the Script page of the Script Task Editor, make sure that the Visual C# language is selected. Add the User::EmailRegEx1 and User::EmailRegEx2 variables to the ReadOnlyVariables property, as shown in the following screenshot:

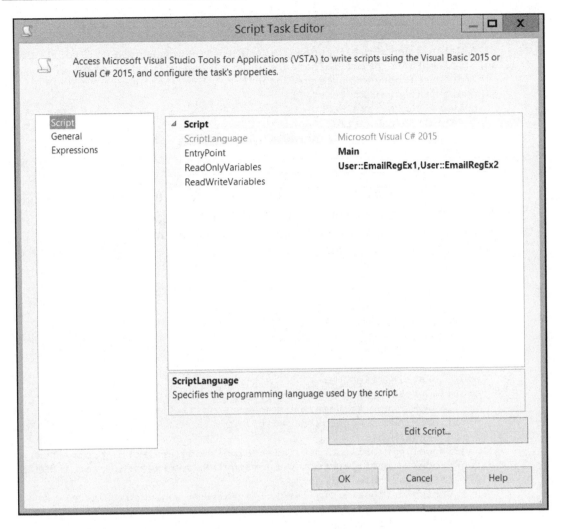

5. Click the **Edit Script** button. Expand the **Namespaces** region. Add the `System.Xml` namespace with the following code: `using System.Xml;`.

6. Declare private variables for the `ScriptMain` class. These private variables will point to the Data Profiling task result XML file, to the XML namespace URI for the Data Profiling task results, and to the two nodes in the XML file with the extracted regular expressions. Enter the following code right after the `ScriptMain` class definition and before the first help region in the class:

```
private string fileName =
@" C:\SSIS2016Cookbook\Chapter07\Files \DataProfiling.xml";
private string profileNamespaceUri =
```

```
        "http://schemas.microsoft.com/sqlserver/2008/DataDebugger/";
        private string erx1Path =
        "/default:DataProfile/default:DataProfileOutput/default:Profiles" +
"/default:ColumnPatternProfile[default:Column[@Name='EmailAddress']]" +
        "/default:TopRegexPatterns/default:PatternDistributionItem[1]
        /default:RegexText/text()";
        private string erx2Path =
        "/default:DataProfile/default:DataProfileOutput/default:Profiles" +
"/default:ColumnPatternProfile[default:Column[@Name='EmailAddress']]" +
        "/default:TopRegexPatterns/default:PatternDistributionItem[2]
        /default:RegexText/text()";
```

7. The previous part of the code looks ugly. This is due to the fact that XML is ugly.

8. Modify the `Main` method of the class. Add the following code after the // TODO:... comment and before the last command of the method, the Dts.TaskResult =... command.

```
        // Local variables
        string profilePath;
        XmlDocument profileOutput = new XmlDocument();
        XmlNamespaceManager profileNSM;
        XmlNode regExNode1;
        XmlNode regExNode2;
        // Open output file
        profilePath = fileName;
        profileOutput.Load(profilePath);
        profileNSM = new XmlNamespaceManager(profileOutput.NameTable);
        profileNSM.AddNamespace("default", profileNamespaceUri);
        // Get regExNodes
        regExNode1 = profileOutput.SelectSingleNode(erx1Path, profileNSM);
        regExNode2 = profileOutput.SelectSingleNode(erx2Path, profileNSM);
        // Assign variable values
        Dts.Variables["User::EmailRegEx1"].Value = regExNode1.Value;
        Dts.Variables["User::EmailRegEx2"].Value = regExNode2.Value;
        // Show variable values
MessageBox.Show(Dts.Variables["User::EmailRegEx1"].Value.ToString());
MessageBox.Show(Dts.Variables["User::EmailRegEx2"].Value.ToString());
```

9. Note that this code reads the data profiling results, loads the XML file, and then assigns the extracted regular expression patterns to the values of the two SSIS package variables you just created. Finally, the code shows the variable values in two message boxes.

10. Save the script and close the VSTA environment. In the Script Task Editor, click on the **OK** button to close the editor.

11. Right-click the **ReadPatterns** task and execute it. Check the two message boxes with the two regular expressions extracted by the Data Profiling task. Click on **OK** in each of the boxes to close them. Stop debugging the package.

Correcting data with the Script component

In this recipe, you will use the Script Component in the data flow as a transformation for advanced data cleansing. You will read an Excel file and do a custom transformation in order to make the output ready for further processing in the data flow.

Getting ready

In order to test this recipe, you need to have an Excel file prepared. In the file, there should be a single sheet with the following content:

OrderId	Date	Product	Quantity
1	20160915	ABC	1
		DEF	5
		GHI	3
2	20160916	GHI	2
		ABC	4

 For your convenience, an Excel file with the content needed is provided in the Ch07_Orders.xls file.

Note that the table represents simple orders with order details. However, the order info is added to the first order details line only. Your task is to add the appropriate order info to every single line.

How to do it...

1. Add a new package to the `AdventureWorksETL` project. Rename it `ProcessingExcel.dtsx`.

2. Add a new package-level Excel connection manager. Rename it `Excel_Ch07_Orders`. Point to your Excel file path and define your Excel version appropriately, as shown in the following screenshot:

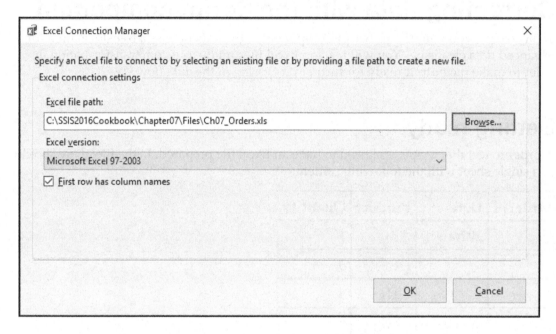

3. Add a **Data Flow task** to the control flow. Rename it to `ProcessExcelOrders`. Open the Data Flow tab.

4. Add an **Excel source**. Double-click it to open the editor.

5. Using the **Connection Manager** tab, define the **Excel connection manager**. Point to the `Excel_Ch07_Orders` connection manager you just created. Use the **Table or view data access** mode. Select `Sheet1$` in the name of the Excel sheer drop-down list. Click on the **Preview** button to preview the content of the file, as shown in the following screenshot:

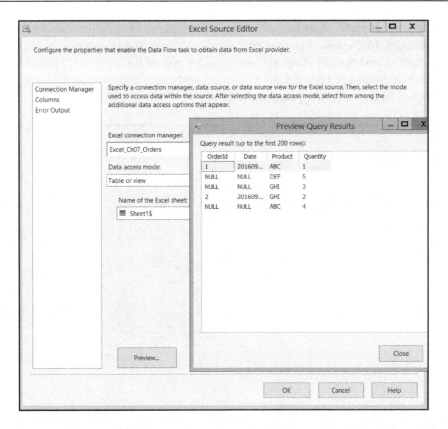

6. You can note in the data preview pop-up window that order info columns are NULL except for the first order detail of an order. When finished with the preview, click the Close button.

7. Click the **Columns** tab to check the columns mapping. Then click on **OK** to close the data source editor.

8. Add a **Script Component** to the data flow. In the **Select Script Component Type** pop-up window, make sure that **Transformation** option button is selected. Then click on **OK**.

9. Connect the Script component with the blue arrow (regular data flow) from the data source.

10. Double-click the Script component to open the editor. Note that the **Script** tab is more complex than the Script tab of the Script task. Nevertheless, you can easily find the `ScriptLanguage`, `ReadOnlyVariables`, and `ReadWriteVariables` properties. Leave all of them with their defaults, meaning you will use the Microsoft Visual C# 2015 language and that you don't need any variables in the script.

11. Click the **Input Columns** tab. In the `Available Input Columns` table, select all columns. In the lower part of the window, check the mappings between input columns and output aliases. Don't change any of the output aliases. However, change the usage type for the `OrderId` and `Date` columns to `ReadWrite`, as shown in the following screenshot:

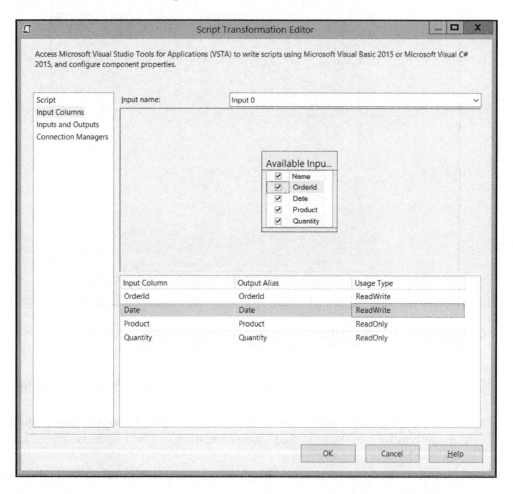

12. When setting up the columns correctly, click the **Script** tab and then the **Edit Script** button to open the VSTA environment.

13. In the script, find the `Input0_ProcessInputRow` method. Add the following two variables just before the method definition and after the comments, with the summary and parameters description of this method:

```
Double MyDate;
Double MyOrderId;
Add the following code to the method:
// Check if OrderId column is null
if (Row.OrderId_IsNull)
{
    // if null then replace value with variable value
    Row.OrderId = MyOrderId;
}
else
{
    // if not null then replace variable value with column value
    MyOrderId = Row.OrderId;
}
// Check if Date column is null
if (Row.Date_IsNull)
{
    // if null then replace value with variable value
    Row.Date = MyDate;
}
else
{
    // if not null then replace variable value with column value
    MyDate = Row.Date;
}
```

14. Save the code end exit the VSTA environment. In the Script Transformation Editor, click on **OK**.

15. Add a **Multicast** transformation to the data flow and connect it with the blue arrow from the Script component. This transformation serves as a placeholder only, in order to enable a Data Viewer after the Script transformation does its job.

16. Enable two **Data Viewers**, one on the path from the source to the Script component, and one from the **Script** component to the Multicast transformation. Your data flow should look as shown in the following screenshot:

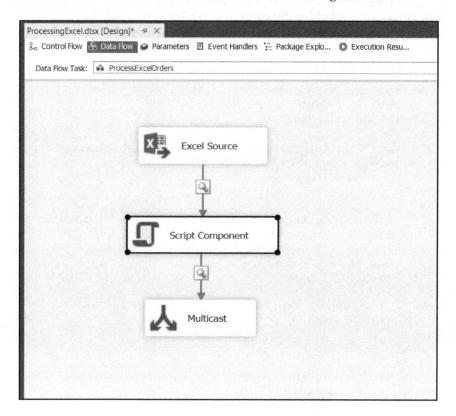

17. Note that, depending on the Excel version you are using, you might need to change the `Run64BitRuntime` property of your project to False before running the package, as shown in the following screenshot:

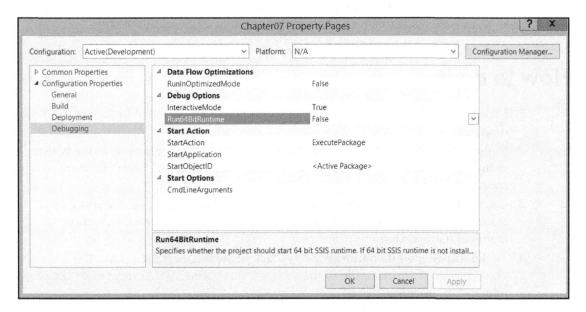

18. Save the package and run it. Observe the data before correction with the Script component and after it. When finished, stop debugging.

Validating data using regular expressions in a Script component

In this recipe, you will create a Script Component that will use the regular expressions in the `DataProfiling.xml` file to validate the emails of the personal data extracted from a flat file.

Getting ready

This recipe assumes that you successfully completed the *Reading data profiling XML results with Script task* recipe earlier in this chapter. If you did not complete that recipe, you can prepare an appropriate SSIS package simply by completing step 1 of that recipe.

How to do it...

1. Make sure that the `RegExValidation.dtsx` package is active in the control flow designer.
2. Right-click in the empty canvas of the **Connection Managers** pane at the bottom of the SSDT window and select **New Flat File Connection...** from the shortcut menu.
3. Use the **Flat File Connection Manager Editor** to create a new connection manager, and on the **General** page enter `PersonData` into the Connection manager name textbox.
4. To determine the **File name** property, click **Browse...**, and then select the `Ch07_PersonData.csv` file in the `C:\SSIS2016Cookbook\Chapter07\Files\` folder.

   The file should be recognized as a Unicode file automatically; otherwise, check the **Unicode** option below the **Browse...** button.

5. Leave the rest of the properties unchanged, as shown in the following screenshot:

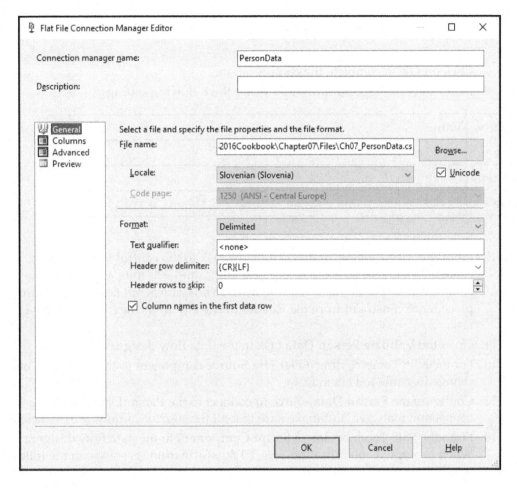

6. On the **Columns** page, verify that all the source columns have been recognized: Title, FirstName, MiddleName, LastName, Suffix, and EmailAddress.

> If any of the columns are missing, click **Reset Columns** below the columns list.

7. Click on **OK** to complete the configuration.
8. Add a new package parameter by using the following settings:

Property	Value
Name	DataProfileName
Data type	String
Value	C:\SSIS2016Cookbook\Chapter07\Files\DataProfiling.xml

9. Save the package.
10. From the SSIS Toolbox, drag a Data Flow task to the control flow designer, change its name to Validate Person Data, and—as long as you have completed the *Reading data profiling XML results with Script task*—connect the precedence constraint from the **ReadPatterns** task to the newly added data flow task.
11. Open the **Validate Person Data** task in the data flow designer.
12. For the SSIS Toolbox, drag a **Flat File Source** component to the data flow, and change its name to Person Data.
13. Configure the **Person Data** source to connect to the **PersonData** flat file connection manager, and make sure that all the source columns are extracted.
14. From the SSIS Toolbox, drag a **Script Component** to the data flow designer. When prompted about its type, select **Transformation**, as shown in the following screenshot:

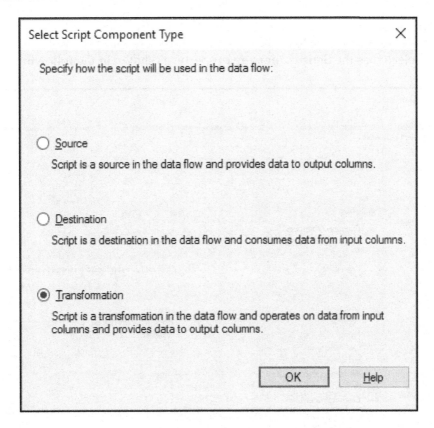

15. Click **OK** to confirm the component type, and then change its name to Validate Email.

16. Connect the regular data path from the **Person Data** source to the **Validate Email** transformation.

17. Double-click the **Validate Email** transformation to open the Script Task Editor.

18. On the Script page, add the **$Package::DataProfileName** package parameter to the **ReadOnlyVariables** collection, and make sure that Microsoft Visual C# 2015 is selected as the **ScriptLanguage** property, as shown in the following screenshot:

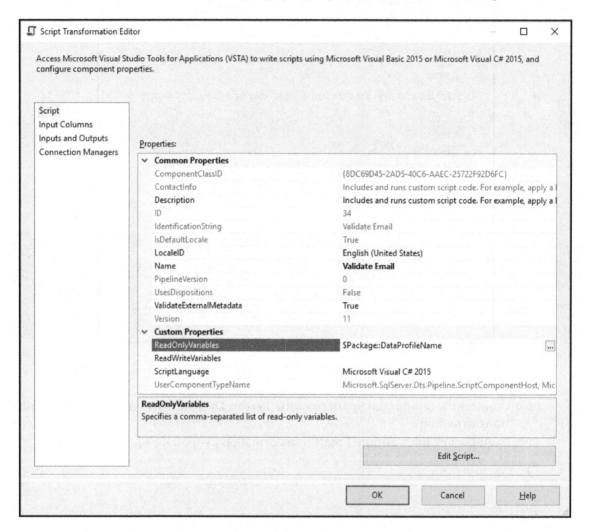

19. On the **Input Columns** page, make sure that all the input columns are selected; their usage type should be **ReadOnly**.

20. On the **Inputs and Outputs** page, in the **Inputs and outputs** list, select the **Input 0** input, and in the properties pane on the right-hand side of the editor, change its **Name** property to `PersonDataInput`.

21. Select the **Output 0** output, and change its name to `PersonDataOutput`.

22. In the `PersonDataOutput` properties, locate the `SyncronousInputID` property and make sure it references the `Validate Email.Inputs[PersonDataInput]` input.

    This means that the component's output is synchronous.

23. Expand the `PersonDataOutput` in the **Inputs and outputs** list and select the Output Columns node.

24. Click on **Add Column** to create a column in the output; use the following settings to configure it:

    ```
    Property Value
    Name IsValidEmail
    DataType Boolean [DT_BOOL]
    ```

25. Click on **OK** to confirm the component's configuration so far.

It is recommended to save all Script component settings, such as variables, inputs, outputs, and additional connection managers, before creating the script.

This way, if there are problems with the script that you cannot resolve during editing, the rest of the settings do not need to be set again.

26. Open the **Validate Email** transformation editor again, and on the Script page click **Edit Script...** to start **Visual Studio for Applications (VSTA)** IDE.

27. Locate the `Namespaces` region at the beginning of the component definition and add the following references to the region:

    ```
    using System.Collections.Generic;
    using System.Text.RegularExpressions;
    using System.Xml;
    ```

28. In the `ScriptMain` class definition, add the following constant and private variable declarations:

```
private const String DATA_PROFILE_NAMESPACE =
"http://schemas.microsoft.com/sqlserver/2008/DataDebugger/";
private const String DATA_PROFILE_NAMESPACE_ALIAS = "dp";

private String _regexElementXPath =
"/dp:DataProfile/dp:DataProfileOutput/dp:Profiles" +
"/dp:ColumnPatternProfile[dp:Column[@Name='EmailAddress']]" +
"/dp:TopRegexPatterns/dp:PatternDistributionItem/dp:RegexText/text()";

private List<String> _regexPatterns = new List<String>();
```

Typically, variable definitions are placed at the beginning of the class definition, right after the three `Help` regions.

29. At the end of the `ScriptMain` class definition (before the last closing brace) place the following function definition:

```
private List<String> LoadRegularExpressions(String dataProfileName)
{
  List<String> result = new List<String>();
  XmlDocument dataProfile = new XmlDocument();
  dataProfile.Load(dataProfileName);
  XmlNamespaceManager dataProfileNSM = new
  XmlNamespaceManager(dataProfile.NameTable);
  dataProfileNSM.AddNamespace(DATA_PROFILE_NAMESPACE_ALIAS,
  DATA_PROFILE_NAMESPACE);

  foreach (XmlNode regexPatternElement in
  dataProfile.SelectNodes(_regexElementXPath, dataProfileNSM))
  {
    String regexPattern = regexPatternElement.Value;
    if (!result.Contains(regexPattern))
    {
      result.Add(regexPattern);
    }
  }

  return result;
}
```

This function extracts all relevant regular expression patterns from the data profiling result and loads them into a variable.

30. Right after the `LoadRegularExpressions()` function, add another function:

```
private Boolean IsValidEmail(String emailAddress)
{
  Boolean result = false;
  if (!String.IsNullOrEmpty(emailAddress))
  {
    foreach (String regexPattern in _regexPatterns)
    {
      if (Regex.IsMatch(emailAddress, regexPattern,
      RegexOptions.IgnoreCase))
      {
        result = true;
        break;
      }
    }
  }
  return result;
}
```

This function tests the supplied email address against all available regular expressions, and returns `true` as soon as one of the patterns is matched; otherwise, it returns `false`.

31. Locate the `PreExecute()` method add the following command to its definition:

```
_regexPatterns.AddRange(this.LoadRegularExpressions(Variables.DataProfileNa
me));
```

The `PreExecute()` data flow component method is called at the beginning of the data flow execution, before the rows are acquired from the upstream pipeline. As the same set of regular expressions is going to be used throughout the data flow execution, it only needs to be loaded once, not for every row.

32. Locate the `PersonDataInput_ProcessInputRow()` method, and add the following command to its definition:

```
Row.IsValidEmail = this.IsValidEmail(Row.EmailAddress);
```

The `IsValidEmail()` function needs to be called for each row as it needs to validate each e-mail address extracted from the source.

33. Save the VSTA project and build it by selecting the **Build** command from the **Build** menu.

If you entered all the code correctly, the build should succeed; otherwise, you need to follow the error messages in the Error pane to resolve the errors.

34. After the successful build, close the VSTA window, and return to SSDT.
35. In the Script Transformation Editor, click on **OK**, to confirm and save the component script, and then save the package.
36. From the SSIS Toolbox, drag a **Conditional Split** transformation to the data flow designer, and change its name to `Valid or Invalid Email`.
37. Connect the regular data path from the **Validate Email** transformation to the **Conditional Split** transformation.
38. Double-click the newly added transformation to open the **Conditional Split Transformation Editor**.
39. Create a new output using the following settings:
    - **Property**: `Value`
    - **Output name**: `Valid Email`
    - **Condition**: `IsValidEmail`

Alternatively, to reduce typing, you can drag the `IsValidEmail` column from the **Columns** list in the top-left part of the **Conditional Split Transformation Editor**.

40. Change the **Default output name** to `Invalid Email`.

Refer to the following screenshot to verify your settings:

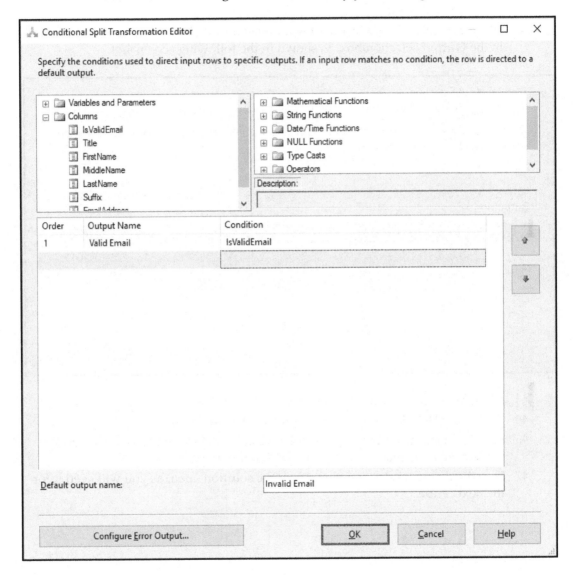

41. Click on **OK** to complete the configuration.

42. From the SSIS Toolbox, drag a **Multicast** transformation to the data flow designer and connect the regular data path from the **Valid** or **Invalid Email** transformation to it.

43. When prompted by the **Input Output Selection** dialog, select the **Invalid Email** in the **Output** selection box, as shown in the following screenshot:

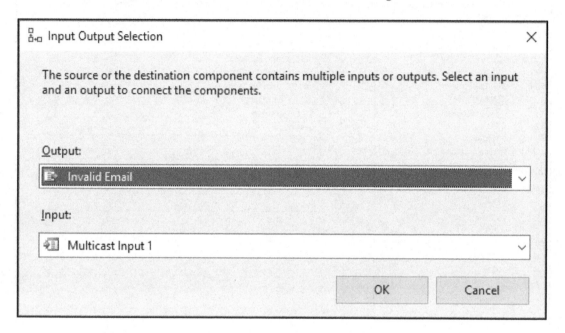

44. Click on **OK** to confirm the selection.

45. Enable the **Data Viewer** on the **Invalid Email** data path.

46. Save the package and execute it in debug mode. Observe the execution and inspect the rows placed in the **Invalid Email** data path.

47. Stop the debug mode execution; leave the solution open, as you will need it for the next recipe.

Using the Script component as a source

In this recipe, you will create a custom source by using the Script Component as a data flow source.

You will connect to a web service and retrieve the data from it, which you will then place into the data flow pipeline.

How to do it...

1. Add a new SSIS package to the **AdventureWorksETL** project you created at the beginning of this chapter.

2. Change the name of the newly created package to CustomWebServiceSource.dtsx and save it.

3. Make sure the **CustomWebServiceSource.dtsx** package is active, and then create a new package parameter using the following settings:
   - **Property**: Value
   - **Name**: CountryName
   - **Data type**: String
   - **Value**: France

4. Drag a **Data Flow** task to the control flow designer and change its name to Airport Information.

5. Open the **Airport Information** task in the data flow designer and drag a **Script Component** to the data flow designer.

6. In the **Select Script Component Type** dialog, select **Source**, as shown in the following screenshot:

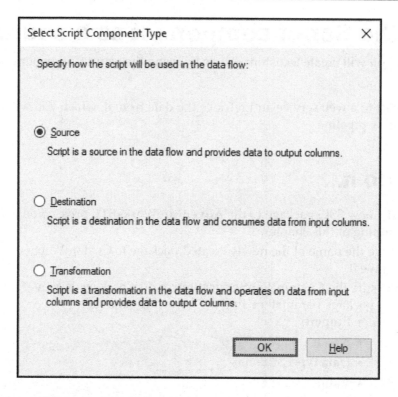

7. Click on **OK** to confirm the selection.

8. Change the name of the Script component to Airport Info by Country.

9. Double-click on the **Airport Info by Country** source to open the Script Transformation Editor.

10. On the **Script** page, add the `$Package::CountryName` parameter to the `ReadOnlyVariables` collection, and make sure that Microsoft Visual C# 2015 is selected as the **ScriptLanguage** property.

11. On the **Inputs and Outputs** page, select **Output 0** and change its name to `AirportInfoOutput.`

12. Add columns to the output's Column Collection using the following settings:

```
Name DataType Length
Country Unicode string [DT_WSTR] 50
AiportName Unicode string [DT_WSTR] 50
AirportCode Unicode string [DT_WSTR] 3
RunwayLengthFeet four-byte signed integer [DT_I4] /
```

Refer to the following screenshot to verify your settings:

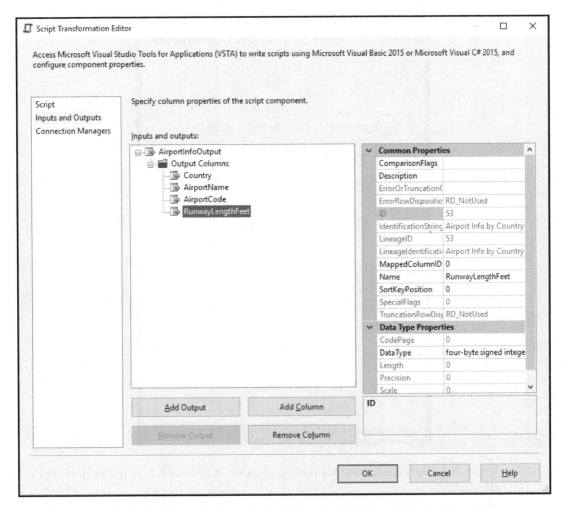

To ensure that each new column is added to the end of the list, click on the **Output Columns** node before adding the next column.

13. Click **OK** to confirm the configuration.
14. Open the **Airport Info by Country** transformation editor again, and this time click **Edit Script...** to start VSTA.

15. In the **Solution Explorer**, right-click the **References** node and select **Add Service Reference...** from the shortcut menu, as shown in the following screenshot:

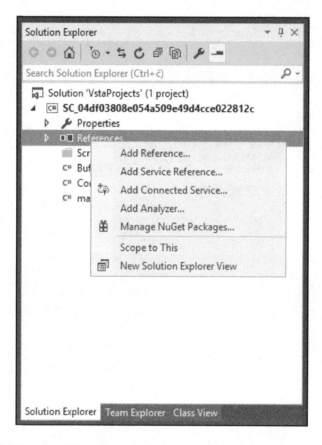

16. In the **Add Service Reference** dialog, click on **Advanced...** on the bottom-left of the dialog.
17. In the **Service Reference Settings** dialog, click on **Add Web Reference...** to open the **Add Web Reference** dialog.
18. Enter the following URL in the **URL** textbox:

    ```
    http://www.webservicex.net/airport.asmx?WSDL
    ```

19. Click the arrow pointing to the right, on the right-hand side of the textbox, to load the information from the web service.

20. Enter `AirportInfo` into the **Web reference name** textbox.

Refer to the following screenshot to verify your settings:

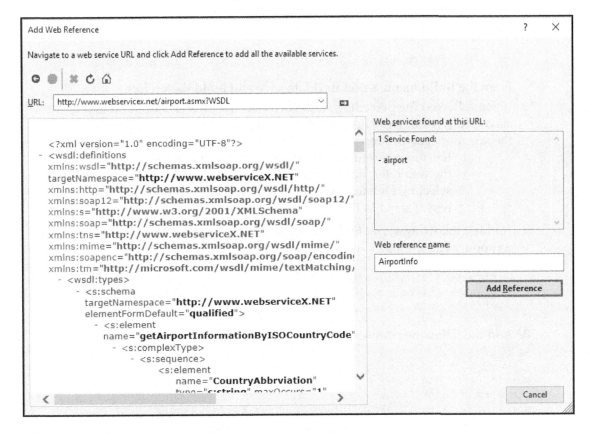

21. Click **Add Reference** to confirm the settings and create the reference.
22. Save the project.
23. In the component definition, at the beginning of the code, locate the `Namespaces` region and expand it to list the existing references.
24. Add another `using` command after the last one, and start typing the name of the project (it should be similar to `SC_04df03808e054a509e49d4cce022812c`); allow the Visual Studio *intellisense* to suggest the complete namespace, and then complete the reference to the `AirportInfo` namespace:

```
using SC_04df03808e054a509e49d4cce022812c.AirportInfo;
```

25. The `SC_04df03808e054a509e49d4cce022812c` value in this example is used for the name of the VSTA project and for its default namespace. When you add a web reference to the project, proxy classes, and functions are created automatically and placed in the project's default namespace.

26. Add the following reference as it will be needed later:

```
using System.Xml;
```

27. From the **Build** menu, select **Build**, to save and build the project.

28. If you followed the preceding steps correctly, the project should build successfully; otherwise, inspect the errors reported in the Error pane and make the necessary corrections.

   1. If errors are returned from the automatically generated code, remove the web reference by right-clicking it in the **Solution Explorer** and selecting **Delete** from the shortcut menu, then rebuild the project and repeat steps 14 through 21.

29. Add the following variable declarations to the `ScriptMain` class of the component definition:

```
private String _countryName;
private String _airportXPath = @"/NewDataSet/Table";
private XmlNodeList _airportXmlNodes;
```

30. Add the following commands to the `PreExecute()` method:

```
airport airportInfo = new airport();
String airportInfoByCountry =
airportInfo.GetAirportInformationByCountry(_countryName);
XmlDocument airportInfoByCountryXml = new XmlDocument();
airportInfoByCountryXml.LoadXml(airportInfoByCountry);
_airportXmlNodes = airportInfoByCountryXml.SelectNodes(_airportXPath);
```

31. The `GetAirportInformationByCountry` function of the given web service returns a list of airports and their properties for the supplied country name. This function only needs to be invoked once per data flow execution; therefore, you should place it in the `PreExecute()` method, which is invoked once, at the beginning of the data flow execution.

32. Add the following commands to the `CreateNewOutputRows()` method:

```
foreach (XmlNode airportXmlNode in _airportXmlNodes)
{
    AirportInfoOutputBuffer.AddRow();

    AirportInfoOutputBuffer.Country = _countryName;
    AirportInfoOutputBuffer.AirportName =
airportXmlNode.SelectSingleNode("CityOrAirportName").InnerText;
    AirportInfoOutputBuffer.AirportCode =
airportXmlNode.SelectSingleNode("AirportCode").InnerText;
    AirportInfoOutputBuffer.RunwayLengthFeet =
Int32.Parse(airportXmlNode.SelectSingleNode("RunwayLengthFeet").InnerText);
}
```

> This code will read all the items retrieved from the web service `GetAirportInformationByCountry()` function and place each one of them in the component's output.

33. Use the **Build** command from the **Build** menu to save and build the component project. In case of any errors, inspect the **Error** pane and resolve the problems.

34. After the project is built successfully, close the VSTA window and return to SSDT.

35. In the **Script Transformation Editor**, click **OK** to complete the configuration of the **Airport Info by Country** source component.

36. Save the package.

37. From the SSIS Toolbox, drag a **Multicast** transformation to the data flow designer.

38. Connect the regular data path from the **Airport Info by Country** source component to the **Multicast** transformation and activate the **Data Viewer** on this data path.

39. Save, and execute the package in debug mode. Observe the rows in the **Data Viewer**.

40. Stop the debug mode execution; leave the solution and the package open, as you will need them in the following recipe.

How it works...

The **Airport Info by Country** source component connects to a publicly available web service that provides information about airports in various countries. It retrieves the list of airports for the country specified by the **CountryName** package parameter.

Alternatively, the country name could also be supplied via a variable populated in a **Foreach Loop** container, so that the same data flow is executed multiple times for multiple countries.

After the data is retrieved from the web service, it is placed into a variable. When the component starts to generate rows, specific properties of each item retrieved from the web service are placed into the downstream pipeline. Each row in the components output represents one entity retrieved from the web service.

Using the Script component as a destination

In this recipe, you will design a custom data flow destination by using the Script Component.

You will use the data retrieved by using the source component created in the *Using the Script component as a source* recipe and export it in JSON format to one or more files.

The acronym JSON stands for JavaScript Object Notation, an open-source format for representing data in human-readable form that can also be consumed by automated processes.

Getting ready

Before you can complete this recipe, you need to complete the *Using the Script component as a source* recipe.

How to do it...

1. Make sure that the CustomWebServiceSource.dtsx package of the AdventureWorksETL solution from the C:\SSIS2016Cookbook\Chapter07\Solution\ folder is active in the control flow editor.
2. Add a package parameter using the following settings:
   - **Property**: Value
   - **Name**: JSONFilePath
   - **Data type**: String
   - **Value**: C:\SSIS2016Cookbook\Chapter07\Files
3. Add another package parameter using the following settings:
   - **Property**: Value
   - **Name**: JSONFileNameFormat
   - **Data type**: String
   - **Value**: AirportInfo_{0:D3}.JSON
4. Open the **Airport Information** data flow in the data flow designer.
5. Form the SSIS Toolbox, drag a Script Component to the data flow designer.

6. In the **Select Script Component Type** dialog, select **Destination**, as shown in the following screenshot:

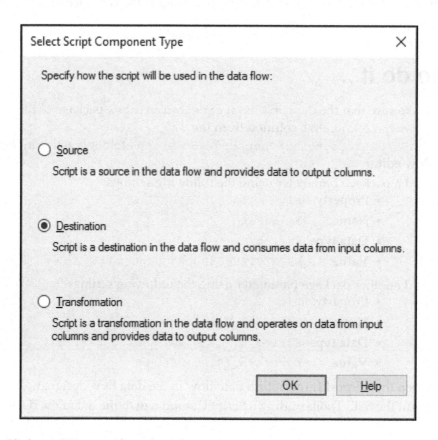

7. Click on **OK** to confirm the selection.
8. Change the name of the destination component to JSON File.
9. Connect the regular data path from the Multicast transformation to the **JSON File** destination.
10. Double-click the **JSON File** destination to open its editor, and on the **Script** page, add the `$Package::JSONFilePath` and `$Package::JSONFileNameFormat` parameters to the `ReadOnlyVariables` collection.
11. On the **Input Columns** page, make sure that all the input columns are selected. The usage type for all the columns can remain **ReadOnly**.
12. On the Inputs and Outputs page, rename the **Input 0** input to `JSONFileInput`.
13. Click **OK** to confirm the configuration.

14. Open the **JSON File** destination again, and on the **Script** page click **Edit Script...** to open the component's project in VSTA.

15. In the Solution Explorer, right-click **References** and select **Add Reference...** from the shortcut menu.

16. In the **Reference Manager**, in the navigator on the left, make sure that the **Assemblies / Framework** node is selected, and then in the list in the middle of the dialog, locate the **System.Web.Extensions** assembly and check it, as shown in the following screenshot:

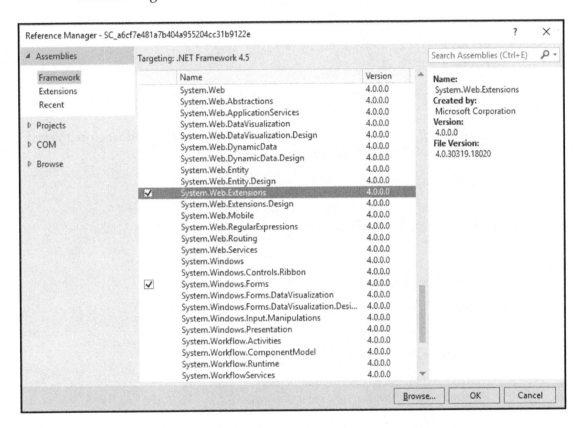

17. Click **OK** to confirm the selection.

18. At the beginning of the component definition, locate the `Namespaces` region and expand it to inspect the existing namespace references.

19. Add the following references below the existing ones:

```
using System.Web.Script.Serialization;
using System.Collections.Generic;
```

```
using System.IO;
```

The `System.Web.Script.Serialization` namespace contains the functionalities needed to create and consume JSON data. The `System.IO` namespace provides access to the functionalities needed to work with the Windows operating system filesystem.

20. In the `ScriptMain` class, add the following constant and variable declarations:

```
private const Int32 JSON_MAX_ITEM_COUNT = 50;

private String _jsonFilePath;
private String _jsonFileNameFormat;
private Int32 _fileCounter = 0;

private JavaScriptSerializer _jsonSerializer =
new JavaScriptSerializer();
```

21. Also inside the `ScriptMain` class, at the end of the existing code (before the last closing brace), add the following class definition:

```
public class AirportInfo
{
  public String CountryName { get; set; }
  public String AirportName { get; set; }
  public String AirportCode { get; set; }
  public Int32 RunwayLengthFeet { get; set; }

  public AirportInfo()
  {
  }

  public AirportInfo(String countryName, String airportName,
  String airportCode, Int32 runwayLengthFeet)
  {
    this.CountryName = countryName;
    this.AirportName = airportName;
    this.AirportCode = airportCode;
    this.RunwayLengthFeet = runwayLengthFeet;
  }
}
```

This class allows you to store the pipeline data during processing, and it provides the metadata to the `JavaScriptSerializer.Serialize()` method that creates the JSON documents.

TIP

Unless explicitly marked **public**, class members are, by default, marked **private**, and thus *inaccessible* to the caller. If the metadata for the JSON document cannot be determined, the serialization will *not* fail, but the resulting document will also not contain any data for which the metadata was not available during serialization.

22. Before the `AirportInfo` class definition, place the definition of the function that will be used to write the data to the file:

```
private void WriteJSONFile(List<AirportInfo> airportInfo,
Int32 fileCount)
{
   String airportInfoJSON = _jsonSerializer.Serialize(airportInfo);

   String jsonFileName = Path.Combine(_jsonFilePath,
   String.Format(_jsonFileNameFormat, fileCount));

   using (StreamWriter jsonStreamWriter = new
StreamWriter(jsonFileName))
      {
        jsonStreamWriter.Write(airportInfoJSON);
        jsonStreamWriter.Flush();
      }
}
```

23. Add the following variable assignments to the `PreExecute()` method:

```
_jsonFilePath = Variables.JSONFilePath;
_jsonFileNameFormat = Variables.JSONFileNameFormat;
```

24. Remove the `JSONFileInput_ProcessInputRows` method, as this component will not process individual rows in the traditional way.

25. Instead, just after the `PostExecute()` method definition, enter a new line, and start typing the `override` directive. Visual Studio will list the overridable methods of the component; select the `JSONFileInput_ProcessInput` method to override, and add the following code to its definition:

```
List<AirportInfo> airportInfo = new List<AirportInfo>();

Int32 index = 0;
while (Buffer.NextRow())
{
  airportInfo.Add
  (
    new AirportInfo
```

```
        (
          Buffer.Country,
          Buffer.AirportName,
          Buffer.AirportCode,
          Buffer.RunwayLengthFeet
        )
      );
      index++;
      if (index % JSON_MAX_ITEM_COUNT == 0)
      {
        _fileCounter++;
        this.WriteJSONFile(airportInfo, _fileCounter);
        airportInfo.Clear();
      }
    }
    if (airportInfo.Count > 0)
    {
      _fileCounter++;
      this.WriteJSONFile(airportInfo, _fileCounter);
      airportInfo.Clear();
    }
```

26. Build the project by selecting the **Build** command from the **Build** menu.
27. Close VSTA and return to SSDT.
28. In the Script Transformation Editor, click OK to complete the configuration of the **JSON File** destination.
29. Save the package and execute it in debug mode. The **JSON File** destination loads the rows from the pipeline into files, 50 rows at a time.
30. In Windows Explorer, navigate to the **C:\SSIS2016Cookbook\Chapter07\Files** folder; it should contain six additional files, named **AirportInfo_001.JSON** through **AirportInfo_006.JSON**.
31. Right-click one of the files and use the **Open With** command to open the file in Notepad. Inspect the file; it should contain the JSON representation of the information about the airports.
32. Return to SSDT, stop the debug mode execution, and close SSDT.

How it works...

The **JSON File** destination receives the rows from the upstream component, stores them in a variable (50 rows at a time), and converts the row set into a JSON document, which it then loads into a file in the file system.

The `JSONFileInput_ProcessInput` method contains all the logic needed to process the incoming pipeline data; it creates batches of up to 50 rows so that no resulting JSON document contains more than 50 items.

The `WriteJSONFile` function uses the `Serialize()` method of the `JavaScriptSerializer` class to create a JSON document from the row set, and the metadata needed to create the document's structure is provided by the `AirportInfo` class.

8

SSIS and Advanced Analytics

In this chapter, we will cover the following recipes:

- Splitting a dataset into a training and test set
- Testing the randomness of the split with a SSAS decision tree model
- Preparing a Naive Bayes SSAS data mining model
- Querying the SSAS data mining model with the data mining query transformation
- Creating an R data mining model
- Using the R data mining model in SSIS
- Text mining with term extraction and term lookup transformations

Introduction

Advanced analytics, including statistics, data mining, and machine learning, has become very popular in recent years. You can use SSIS to prepare the data you need for further analysis. Often, you need to prepare a sample of your data. The sample has to be random. For predictive algorithms, you typically split the data into a training set, used to train multiple models, and a test set, used to perform predictions on it, and see which model gives you the best results. You can use the row sampling and the percentage sampling transformations to create random samples.

In the SQL Server suite, you can use **SQL Server Analysis Services (SSAS)**, installed in multidimensional and data mining mode, to create data mining models. In addition, from SQL Server 2016, you can also use the R language to do nearly any kind of advanced analysis you want. You will learn in this chapter how you can use both SSAS and R models in the SSIS data flow.

You will use the data mining query transformation for predictions from the SSAS mining model, and SQL Server source to execute the R code inside SQL Server with the `sys.sp_execute_external_script` system procedure.

Analyzing texts is also an important part of advanced analytics. In SSIS, you can use two transformations, term extraction and term lookup, for this task.

Splitting a dataset into a training and test set

In this recipe, you will split the data into training and test sets using the SSIS percentage sampling transformation. You will use 70 percent of the data for the training set and 3 percent for the test set.

Getting ready

There are no special prerequisites for this recipe, except, of course, SSIS 2016 installed, and the `AdventureWorksDW2014` database available in your SQL Server instance.

How to do it...

Open **SQL Server Data Tools** (**SSDT**) and create a new project using the integration services project template. Place the solution in the `C:\SSIS2016Cookbook` folder and name the project `Chapter08`:

1. Rename the default package to `SplitData.dtsx`.
2. In the **Control Flow** tab in the **Package Designer**, add a new data flow task by dragging and dropping it from the SSIS toolbox.
3. Right-click the task and select **Rename** from the pop-up menu. Change the task's name to `SplitData`.
4. Click the **Data Flow** tab.
5. Create a new OLE DB source. Name it `AW_DW_Source`.
6. Double-click the `AW_DW_Source` data source.
7. On the **General** tab, create a new connection manager.
8. Prepare the connection to the `AdventureWorksDW2014` database on your SQL Server instance.
9. Select the **Table or view** option in the **Data access** mode drop-down list.
10. Select the **vTargetMail** view.

11. Click the **Columns** row in the left-hand list to check the mapping between input and output columns. Leave the default mappings. Click **OK** to close the **OLE DB Source Editor**.

12. Add the percentage sampling transformation and name it `SplitData`. Connect it to the source with the gray arrow that goes out from the source connection object. Set the following properties for the new transformation and then click **OK** to close the **Percentage Sampling Transformation Editor**:

Property	Value
Percentage of rows	70
Sample output name	TrainingSet
Unselected output name	TestSet
Use the following random seed	Leave unchecked

13. The following screenshot shows how you should set up the properties of the percentage sampling transformation:

14. Add two derived column transformations.

15. Name the first transformation `IdentifyTrainingSet` and the second one `IdentifyTestSet`.

16. Drag the first blue arrow from the percentage sampling transformation to the identify training set transformation. Select the `TrainingSet` output.

17. Drag the second blue arrow from the percentage sampling transformation to the identify test set transformation. Make sure that the `TestSet` output is selected.

18. Double-click the `IdentifyTrainingSet` transformation. Add a new column, called `TrainTest`, with a constant expression of one and a datatype of signed 4-byte integer.

19. Double-click the `IdentifyTestSet` transformation. Add a new column, called `TrainTest`, with a constant expression of two and a datatype of signed 4-byte integer.

20. Add two OLE DB destinations. Name the first destination `TMTrainingSet`, and the second one `TMTestSet`.

21. Connect the `TMTrainingSet` destination to the output of the `IdentifyTrainingSet` transformation, and connect the `TMTestSet` destination to the output of the `IdentifyTestSet` transformation.

22. Double-click the `TMTrainingSet` destination. Select the connection manager you created to connect to your `AdventureWorksDW2014` database. Click the **New** button near the name of the table, or the view drop-down menu, to create a new table. Check the columns and click **OK**.

23. Click **Mappings** to get the mapping page of the **OLE DB Destination Editor**. Check the mappings between input and output columns. Click **OK** to close the **OLE DB Destination Editor**.

24. Repeat the last two steps for the `TMTestSet` destination. Make sure that your data flow looks as follows:

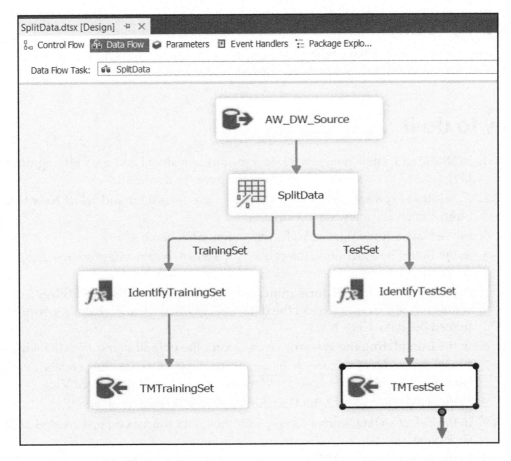

25. In solution explorer, right-click the `SplitData` package and execute it. After the package has executed, stop the debugging.
26. Save the project. Do not exit SSDT.

Testing the randomness of the split with a SSAS decision trees model

You need to test the randomness of the split from the previous recipe. You will use the SSAS decision trees algorithm to check whether you can predict a set membership with input variables. You should get a very shallow tree, meaning there are no patterns that could explain the set membership.

Getting ready

For this recipe, you need to have SSAS installed in multidimensional and data mining mode. You also need to finish the previous recipe.

How to do it...

1. In SSDT, add a new analysis services multidimensional and data mining project to the Chapter08 solution and name the project Ch08SSAS.
2. In solution explorer, right-click the Data Sources folder and select **New Data Source** to create a new data source.
3. In the **Data Source Wizard** welcome screen, click **Next**.
4. In the **Select** how to define the connection screen, create a data source using a connection AdventureWorksDW2014 database. Click **Next**.
5. In the **Impersonation Information** screen, you need to define how SSAS will connect to SQL Server to read the data. Use a Windows user that has permission to read the data. Click **Next**.
6. In the **Completing the Wizard** screen, accept the default name and click **Finish**.
7. Create a new data source view based on the data source you just created. Right-click the Data Source Views folder and select **New Data Source View**.
8. In the welcome screen of the **Data Source View Wizard**, click **Next**.
9. In the **Select a Data Source** screen, select the data source you just created and click **Next**.
10. In the **Select Table and Views** screen, do not select any tables or views, just click **Next**.
11. In the **Completing the Wizard** screen, accept the default name and click **Finish**.
12. In the **Data Source View Editor**, right-click somewhere in the main working pane and select **New Names Query** option.
13. In the **Create Named Query** pop-up window, name the named query TrainTest. This query will combine the test and training sets you created in the previous recipe.
14. In the **Query definition** part of the window, in the bottom area, write the following query:

```
SELECT *
FROM TMTrainingSet
UNION ALL
SELECT *
```

```
FROM TMTestSet;
```

15. Note that using an asterisk (*) to select all columns (SELECT *) is usually not recommended in production. However, in this case, it is not a problem because the **Create Named Query** editor spells out column names explicitly and thus corrects your queries. The **Create Named Query** editor should look like the following screenshot. Then click **OK**:

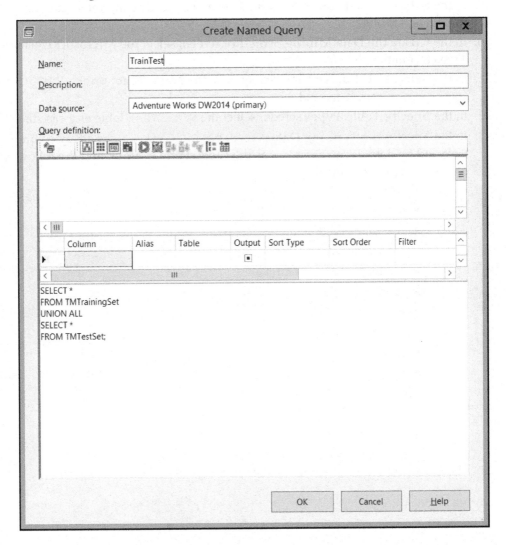

16. Use `CustomerKey` as a logical primary key. In the **Data Source View** editor, right-click the `CustomerKey` column in the named query you just created, and select the **Set Logical Primary Key** option.

17. In solution explorer, right-click the `Mining Structures` folder and select **New Mining Structure**.

18. In the **Data Mining Wizard** welcome screen, click **Next**.

19. In the **Select the Definition Method** screen, use the existing relational database or data warehouse.

20. In the **Create the Data Mining Structure** screen, select the **Microsoft Decision Trees** technique.

21. In the **Select Data Source View** screen, use the `Adventure Works DW2014` data source view you just created.

22. In the **Specify Table Types** screen, select the `TrainTest` table as a case table.

23. In the **Specify the Training Data** screen, use `CustomerKey` as a **Key** column (selected by default), `TrainTest` as the **Predictable** column, and the following columns as **Input** columns:
    - Age
    - BikeBuyer
    - CommuteDistance
    - EnglishEducation
    - EnglishOccupation
    - Gender
    - HouseOwnerFlag
    - MaritalStatus
    - NumberCarsOwned
    - NumberChildrenAtHome
    - Region
    - TotalChildren
    - YearlyIncome

24. The following screenshot shows how your columns should be selected:

Tables/Columns	Key	Input	Predic...
AddressLine1			
AddressLine2			
Age		☑	
BikeBuyer		☑	
BirthDate			
CommuteDistance		☑	
CustomerAlternateKey			
CustomerKey	☑		
DateFirstPurchase			
EmailAddress			
EnglishEducation		☑	
EnglishOccupation		☑	
FirstName			
FrenchEducation			
FrenchOccupation			
Gender		☑	
GeographyKey			
HouseOwnerFlag		☑	
LastName			
MaritalStatus		☑	
MiddleName			
NameStyle			
NumberCarsOwned		☑	
NumberChildrenAtHome		☑	
Phone			
Region		☑	
SpanishEducation			
SpanishOccupation			
Suffix			
Title			
TotalChildren		☑	
TrainTest			☑
YearlyIncome		☑	

25. In the **Specify Columns' Content and Data Type** screen, click the **Detect** button. Change the `Age` and `YearlyIncome` content type to discretized (they are continuous variables, and you will use SSAS discretization).

26. In the **Create Testing Set** screen, change the **Percentage of data for testing** option to `0`.

27. Name the structure `Train Test`, and name the model `Train Test` (these should be the default names). Then click **Finish**.

28. In the **Mining Structure** window, click the `Age` column. Open the **Properties** window for this column if it is closed. (The **Properties** window is open by default. If you have closed it, you can open it from the **View** menu or with the *F4* key.) Set the **DiscretizationBucketCount** property to `5` and the **DiscretizationMethod** property to `EqualAreas`.

29. Repeat the previous step for the `YearlyIncome` attribute.

30. Click the **Mining Models** tab. Right-click the `Train Test` model and select the **Set Algorithm Parameters** option.

31. Refine the model parameters so it can find fine patterns. Use `0.01` for `COMPLEXITY_PENALTY` and `5` for `MINIMUM_SUPPORT`, and then click **OK**. By setting low values for these two parameters, you are forcing the splitting of the decision tree. You are also forcing SSAS to find any patterns. Note that the patterns should be clear. Otherwise, the data split between the training and test sets would not be random. The following screenshot shows how the parameters should be set:

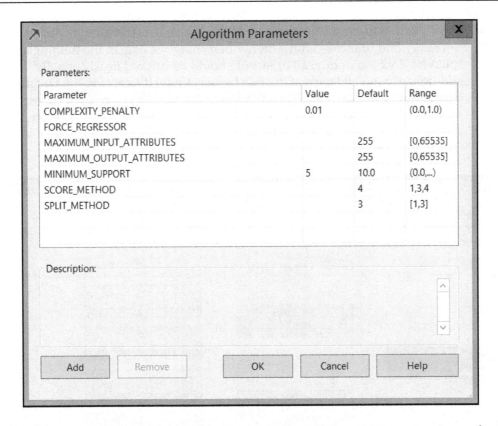

32. Save the project. In solution explorer, right-click the Ch08SSAS project and select **Deploy**. Wait until the deployment is finished.
33. Click the **Mining Model Viewer** tab. Use the default **Decision Tree** view.

34. Color the background using value 1 of the `Train Test` attribute. This way, you can easily find branches with a higher percentage of data in the training set. If the split was done randomly, all branches should be colored nearly equally. In addition, expand all levels of the tree by selecting **All Levels** in the **Default Expansion** drop-down list. You shouldn't get a very deep tree. For example, you should get a tree like the one in the following screenshot. As you can see, in this case, it has only three levels, with a nearly equal percentage of training and test data in each branch:

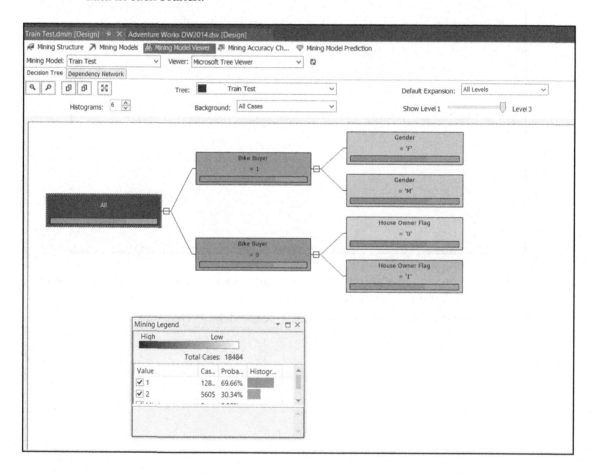

35. Note that your tree should differ slightly from the tree in the screenshot. This is because the SSIS package splits the data randomly.

36. Although the tree found a few patterns, none of them is significant. Either the distributions between the training and test sets do not vary significantly, and/or the support of the nodes is low. This is a good split, as you could expect from a SSIS sampling transformation.

37. Save the solution.

Preparing a Naive Bayes SSAS data mining model

In this recipe, you will determine the factors that influence buying bikes. You will use the Naive Bayes algorithm with the training set you prepared in the previous recipe.

Getting ready

For this recipe, you need to have SSAS installed in multidimensional and data mining mode. You also need to finish the first recipe in this chapter.

How to do it...

1. In SSDT, add a new analysis services multidimensional and data mining project to the Chpater08 solution. Name it Ch08NaiveBayes.

2. Create a new data source using the AdventureWorksDW2014 database. Use the Native OLE DB\SQL Server Native Client 11.0 provider. Use a Windows user that has permission to read the data. Use the default name for the data source.

3. Create a new data source view based on the data source created in step 2. Select the TMTrainingSet and TMTestSet tables created in the first recipe of this chapter for the training and test sets. Use the default name for the data source view.

4. Set the CustomerKey column as the logical primary key for both tables.

5. In solution explorer, right-click the Mining Structures folder and select **New Mining Structure**.

6. Use the existing relational database or data warehouse.

7. Select the **Microsoft Naive Bayes** data mining technique.

8. Use `Adventure Works DW2014` **data source view.**

9. Specify `TMTrainingSet` **as the case table.**

10. Use `Customer Key` **as the** `Key` **column (selected by default),** `Bike Buyer` **as the** `Predictable` **attribute, and the following columns as the** `Input` **columns:**

    - Age
    - Commute Distance
    - English Education
    - English Occupation
    - Gender
    - House Owner Flag
    - Marital Status
    - Number Cars Owned
    - Number Children At Home
    - Region
    - Total Children
    - Yearly Income

11. In the **Specify Columns' Content and Data** Type screen, click the **Detect** button. Change the **Content Type** of all the columns to `Discrete`, except for the `Customer Key` column, which should be `Key`, and the `Age` and `Yearly Income` columns, which should be `Discretized`, as shown in the following screenshot:

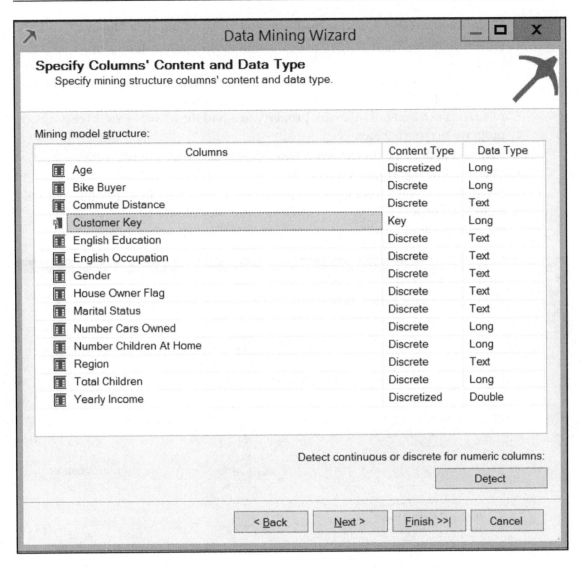

12. In the **Create Testing Set** screen, change the percentage of data for testing to 0. You already created the test set, so you do not need SSAS to create it.

13. Name the structure `TM`, and name the model `TM_NB`. Then click **Finish**.

14. Discretize the `Age` and `Yearly Income` mining structure columns into five groups using the `EqualAreas` method. On the **Mining Structure** tab of the Data Mining Designer, open the **Properties** window of each column. Make sure that the **Content** property is set to `Discretized`, and change the `DiscretizationBucketCount` property to `5` and the `DiscretizationMethod` property to `EqualAreas`.

15. Save and deploy the project. Processing should also start automatically.

16. Click the **Mining Model Viewer** tab.

17. The first view you get is **Dependency Network**. Find the three attributes with the highest influence on `Bike Buyer`. These attributes should be `Number Cars Owned`, `Age`, and `Commute Distance`, as the following screenshot shows:

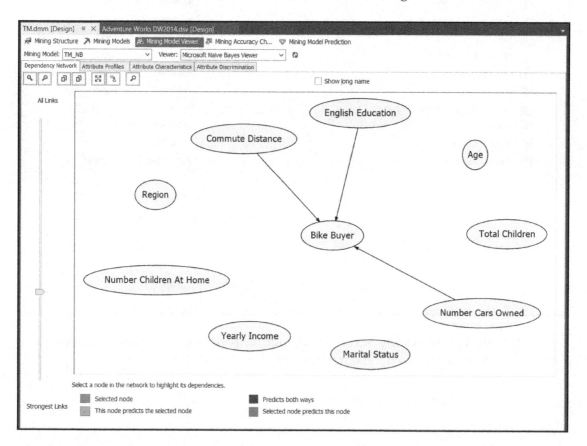

18. Click the **Attribute Profiles** tab. Check how the Region attribute is distributed between customers that do not buy bikes.

19. Click the **Attribute Characteristics** tab. Check the characteristics for bike buyers (value 1 of the Bike Buyer attribute). You should see that they typically do not have children at home, are either married or single, and are from North America.

20. Finally, check the **Attribute Discrimination** tab. Find out what factors influence buying a bike.

21. Save the project.

Querying the SSAS data mining model with the data mining query transformation

In this recipe, you are going to use the data mining query transformation. Based on the Naive Bayes model built in the previous recipe, you will use a (**Data Mining Extensions (DMX)** prediction query to get predictions from the SSAS mining model for the test dataset you created in the first recipe of this chapter.

Getting ready

In order to test this recipe, you need to have SSAS installed in multidimensional and data mining mode. In addition, you need to finish the first and third recipes of this chapter.

For your convenience, the SSIS and SSAS projects needed here are provided in the Chapter08 solution.

How to do it...

1. Add a new package to the `Chapter08` project. Rename it `DataMining.dtsx`.
2. In the control flow of the package, add a new data flow task by dragging it from the SSIS toolbox to the control flow work area.
3. Click the **Data Flow** tab to open the **Data Flow Designer**.
4. Create a new OLE DB source. Name it `TMTestSet`. Double-click the `TMTestSet` data source.
5. On the **General** tab, create a new connection manager. Use the `AdventureWorksDW2014` database on your SQL Server instance.
6. Select the **Table or view** option in the **Data access** mode drop-down list.
7. Select the `dbo.TMTestSet` table.
8. Click the **Columns** row in the left-hand list to check the mapping between the input and output columns. Leave the default mappings.
9. Add the data mining query transformation and name it `NBPrediction`. Connect it to the source with the blue arrow that goes out from the source connection object.
10. Double-click the `NBPrediction` transformation to open the **Data Mining Query Transformation Editor**.
11. On the **Mining Model** tab, create a new connection manager. Click the button **New** near the **Connection Manager** drop-down list.
12. In the **Add Analysis Services Connection Manager** pop-up window, click the **Edit** button.

13. Use your SSAS server, and use Windows integrated security. Select
    `Ch08NaiveBayes` for the **Initial catalog**. Make sure that the **Microsoft OLE DB
    Provider for Analysis Services 13.0** is used for the provider, as shown in the
    following screenshot. Then click **OK**:

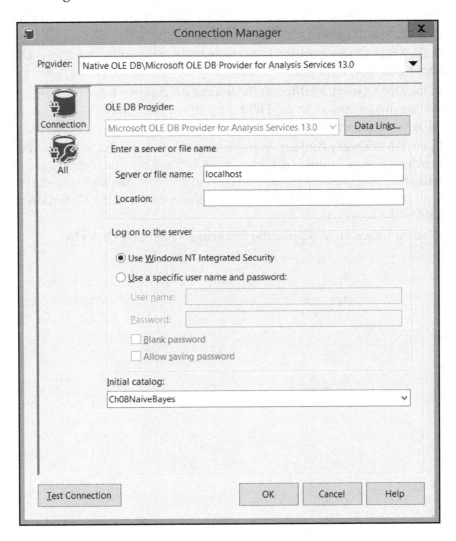

14. Click **OK** twice to get back to the **Data Mining Query Transformation Editor**.

15. In the **Mining structure** drop-down list, select the TM mining structure.

16. In the **Mining models** box at the bottom of the editor, select the TM_NB mining model.

17. Click the **Query** tab. Click the **Build New Query** button to use the **DMX Query Builder** to build a new prediction query.

18. In the **DMX Query Builder**, in the **Source** drop-down list, select the **Data Flow Input Columns** option. In the **Field** drop-down list, select CustomerKey.

19. In the **DMX Query Builder**, in the **Source** drop-down list, select the TM_NB mining model option. In the **Field** drop-down list, select Bike Buyer. In the **Alias** text box, write SSASPrediction.

20. In the **DMX Query Builder**, in the **Source** drop-down list, select the **Prediction function** option. In the **Field** drop-down list, select PredictProbability. In the **Alias** text box, write SSASPredictProbability. Drag the Bike Buyer column from the mining model at the top left of the window to the **Criteria/Argument** field of the function.

21. When your screen looks like the following screenshot, click **OK**:

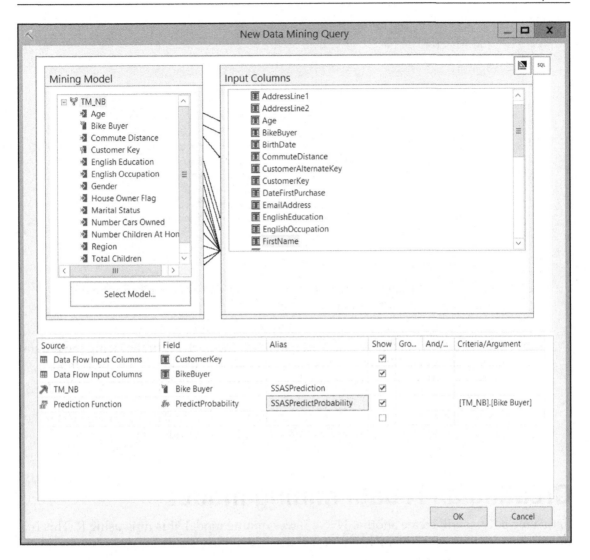

22. Your query should be like the following. Click **OK** when you're finished with the DMX query to close the **Data Mining Query Transformation Editor**:

```
SELECT FLATTENED
  t.[CustomerKey],
  t.[BikeBuyer],
  ([TM_NB].[Bike Buyer]) as [SSASPrediction],
  (PredictProbability([TM_NB].[Bike Buyer])) as
[SSASPredictProbability]
From
```

```
     [TM_NB]
PREDICTION JOIN
  @InputRowset AS t
ON
     [TM_NB].[Marital Status] = t.[MaritalStatus] AND
     [TM_NB].[Gender] = t.[Gender] AND
     [TM_NB].[Yearly Income] = t.[YearlyIncome] AND
     [TM_NB].[Total Children] = t.[TotalChildren] AND
     [TM_NB].[Number Children At Home] = t.[NumberChildrenAtHome] AND
     [TM_NB].[English Education] = t.[EnglishEducation] AND
     [TM_NB].[English Occupation] = t.[EnglishOccupation] AND
     [TM_NB].[House Owner Flag] = t.[HouseOwnerFlag] AND
     [TM_NB].[Number Cars Owned] = t.[NumberCarsOwned] AND
     [TM_NB].[Commute Distance] = t.[CommuteDistance] AND
     [TM_NB].[Region] = t.[Region] AND
     [TM_NB].[Age] = t.[Age] AND
     [TM_NB].[Bike Buyer] = t.[BikeBuyer]
```

23. Add a new sort transformation. Connect it with the blue line from the data mining query transformation.
24. Sort the data by the CustomerKey column, in ascending order.
25. You are done with this recipe. You will finish the package in the Using the R data mining model in SSIS recipe, when you will add predictions from the R model. Then you will be able to compare the quality of the predictions from different models.
26. If you want to test the data flow you created, you can enable a data viewer on the last path. Don't forget to disable it when you finish with testing.

Creating an R data mining model

In this recipe, you will create another Naive Bayes mining model, this time using R. This is a preparation for the next recipe, when you will use R in SSIS.

Getting ready

You can download R from the **Comprehensive R Archive Network (CRAN)** site at http://cran.r-project.org. You can get the R engine for Windows, Linux, or macOS. After installation, you start working in an interactive mode. You can use the R console client tool to write the code line by line. However, the most widely used free tool for writing and executing R code is RStudio IDE. It is a free tool, and you can download it from https://www.rstudio.com/.

This section assumes you use RStudio for the code examples. In addition, you need to have a web connection in order to install additional R packages you need for this recipe.

Note that if you are not interested in R, you can completely skip this recipe. The R code developed here is used in the next recipe as a parameter of the `sys.so_execute_external_script` SQL Server system procedure, so you can switch to the next recipe immediately.

For your convenience, the R code for this recipe is provided in the `Chapter08.R` file.

How to do it...

1. In RStudio, open a new script file (**File | New File | R Script**). Save the file in the `Chapter08.R` file.

2. Install the RODBC package and load the library to memory. You can use the following code for this task. Highlight the code in RStudio and press *Ctrl + Enter* to execute the code. Note that you need to have a web connection in order to install a package:

   ```
   # Install RODBC library
   install.packages("RODBC");
   # Load RODBC library
   library(RODBC);
   ```

3. In SQL Server, create a SQL Server login named RUser, with the password Pa$$w0rd. Create a database user in the `AdventureWorksDW2014` database for this user and add it to the `db_datareader` role. You can execute the following code in SSMS to create this login and user:

   ```
   -- Add Ruser
   USE master;
   GO
   CREATE LOGIN RUser WITH PASSWORD=N'Pa$$w0rd';
   GO
   USE AdventureworksDW2014;
   GO
   CREATE USER RUser FOR LOGIN RUser;
   GO
   ALTER ROLE db_datareader ADD MEMBER RUser;
   ```

```
GO
```

4. In the ODBC Data Source Administrator tool, create a new system DSN, name it
   AWDW, and connect to the AdventureWorksDW2014 database of your SQL Server
   instance. Log in with the RUser login you just created.

5. Back in RStudio, use the following code to connect to your SQL Server:

```
# Connect to AWDW
# AWDW system DSN created in advance
con <- odbcConnect("AWDW", uid="RUser", pwd="Pa$$w0rd");
Union the data from both tables you created in the first recipe of
this chapter, the dbo.TMTrainingSet and dbo.TMTestSet tables. Use
the following code to send the query to SQL Server and read the
data in an R data frame:
TM <- as.data.frame(sqlQuery(con,
"SELECT CustomerKey, MaritalStatus, Gender,
  TotalChildren, NumberChildrenAtHome,
  EnglishEducation AS Education,
  EnglishOccupation AS Occupation,
  HouseOwnerFlag, NumberCarsOwned, CommuteDistance,
  Region, TrainTest, BikeBuyer
 FROM dbo.TMTrainingSet
 UNION
 SELECT CustomerKey, MaritalStatus, Gender,
  TotalChildren, NumberChildrenAtHome,
  EnglishEducation AS Education,
  EnglishOccupation AS Occupation,
  HouseOwnerFlag, NumberCarsOwned, CommuteDistance,
  Region, TrainTest, BikeBuyer
 FROM dbo.TMTestSet;"),
 stringsAsFactors = TRUE);
```

6. Close the connection with the following code:

```
# Close the connection
close(con);
```

7. The Education and the Occupation columns are ordered. You need to inform R
   about the order by creating a factor from each one of them. Use the following
   code:

```
# Education and Occupation are ordered
TM$Education =
  factor(TM$Education, order=TRUE,
         levels=c("Partial High School",
                  "High School","Partial College",
                  "Bachelors", "Graduate Degree"));
```

```
TM$Occupation =
   factor(TM$Occupation, order=TRUE,
          levels=c("Manual", "Skilled Manual",
"Professional", "Clerical", "Management"));
```

8. You can check whether you defined the order correctly by quickly plotting the two ordered variables. The following code shows how to create a plot for `Education`:

```
# A quick plot of Education
plot(TM$Education, main = 'TM$Education',
     xlab='TM$Education', ylab ='Number of Cases',
     col="purple");
```

9. The following screenshot shows the `Education` plot:

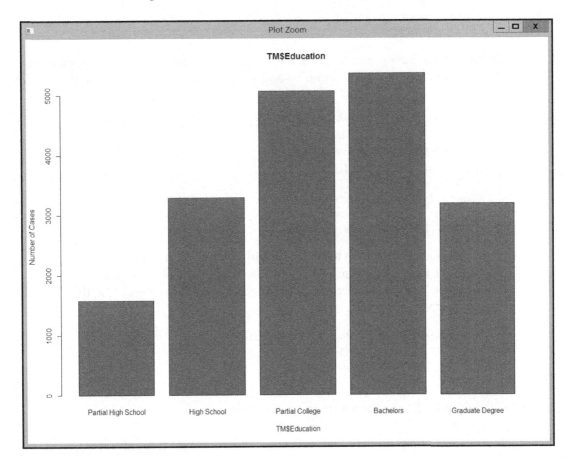

10. You need to split the data into training and test sets again. Note that you could also read the data from the two tables into two separate data frames immediately. However, the `sys.sp_execute_external_script` system stored procedure in SQL Server accepts only a single input query. Therefore, this code will be directly used in the next recipe. Use the following code to do the split:

```
# Split the data to the training and test set
TMTrain <- TM[TM$TrainTest==1,];
TMTest <- TM[TM$TrainTest==2,];
```

11. You will use the Naive Bayes algorithm from the `e1071` package. Install the package and load it to memory:

```
# Naive Bayes
# Package e1071 (Naive Bayes)
install.packages("e1071", dependencies = TRUE);
library(e1071);
```

12. Build a Naive Bayes model with the `naiveBayes()` function. Use columns 2 to 11 as input columns and column 13 as a predictable one. Use the following code:

```
# Build the Naive Bayes model
TMNB <- naiveBayes(TMTrain[,2:11], TMTrain[,13]);
```

13. Make predictions on the test set with the `predict()` function and store the predictions in a new data frame:

```
# Data frame with predictions for all rows
TM_PR <- as.data.frame(predict(
  TMNB, TMTest, type = "raw"));
```

14. Bind the predictions to the test dataset with the `cbind()` function and store the result to the new data frame. View the new data frame and check a few predictions. You may notice that some predictions are incorrect. Use the following code:

```
# Combine original data with predictions
df_TM_PR <- cbind(TMTest[,-(2:12)], TM_PR);
# View the original data with the predictions
View(df_TM_PR);
```

15. When finished, save the script and exit RStudio.

Using the R data mining model in SSIS

The R code developed in the previous recipe can be used directly in the
`sys.sp_execute_external_script` system stored procedure. You will test this in SSMS.
Then you will use the procedure in an OLE DB source inside a SSIS data flow.

Getting ready

In order to continue with this recipe, you need to have R Services (In-Database). This is the
installation that integrates R in SQL Server. It includes a database service that runs outside
the SQL Server database engine and provides a communication channel between the
database engine and R runtime. You install it with SQL Server setup. The R engine includes
the open-source R components, and in addition, a set of scalable R packages.

How to do it...

1. First, you need to enable external scripts in SQL Server. In SSMS, execute the
following code:

```
-- Allow external scripts
USE master;
EXEC sp_configure 'show advanced options', 1;
RECONFIGURE
EXEC sp_configure 'external scripts enabled', 1;
RECONFIGURE;
GO
```

 For your convenience, the T-SQL code for this and the previous recipe
is provided in the `Chapter08.sql` file.

2. Then you need to install the `e1071` package. You need to run as administrator `R.exe` the R Command Prompt from the `C:\Program Files\Microsoft SQL Server\MSSQL13.MSSQLSERVER\R_SERVICES\bin` folder and execute the following commands:

```
install.packages("e1071");
q();
```

3. In SSMS, use the following code to create an R Naive Bayes model and make predictions on a test set. Note that the code that is used as parameters for the `sys.sp_execute_external_script` procedure is copied from the previous recipe:

```
-- Use SQL Server data and analyze it in R
USE AdventureWorksDW2014;
EXECUTE sys.sp_execute_external_script
  @language = N'R'
 ,@script = N'
   # Education and Occupation are ordered
   TM$Education =
     factor(TM$Education, order=TRUE,
            levels=c("Partial High School",
                     "High School","Partial College",
                     "Bachelors", "Graduate Degree"));
   TM$Occupation =
     factor(TM$Occupation, order=TRUE,
            levels=c("Manual", "Skilled Manual",
                     "Professional", "Clerical",
                     "Management"));
   # Split the data to the training and test set
   TMTrain <- TM[TM$TrainTest==1,];
   TMTest <- TM[TM$TrainTest==2,];
   # Package e1071 (Naive Bayes)
   library(e1071);
   # Build the Naive Bayes model
   TMNB <- naiveBayes(TMTrain[,2:11], TMTrain[,13]);
   # Data frame with predictions for all rows
   TM_PR <- as.data.frame(predict(TMNB, TMTest, type = "raw"));
   # Combine original data with predictions
   df_TM_PR <- cbind(TMTest[,-(2:12)], TM_PR);'
 ,@input_data_1 = N'
   SELECT CustomerKey, MaritalStatus, Gender,
    TotalChildren, NumberChildrenAtHome,
    EnglishEducation AS Education,
    EnglishOccupation AS Occupation,
    HouseOwnerFlag, NumberCarsOwned, CommuteDistance,
    Region, TrainTest, BikeBuyer
```

```
    FROM dbo.TMTrainingSet
    UNION
    SELECT CustomerKey, MaritalStatus, Gender,
     TotalChildren, NumberChildrenAtHome,
     EnglishEducation AS Education,
     EnglishOccupation AS Occupation,
     HouseOwnerFlag, NumberCarsOwned, CommuteDistance,
     Region, TrainTest, BikeBuyer
     FROM dbo.TMTestSet;'
  , @input_data_1_name =  N'TM'
  , @output_data_1_name = N'df_TM_PR'
WITH RESULT SETS
(
  ("CustomerKey"             INT   NOT NULL,
   "BikeBuyer"               INT   NOT NULL,
   "Predicted_0_Probability" FLOAT NOT NULL,
   "Predicted_1_Probability" FLOAT NOT NULL)
);
GO
```

4. Check whether the results are the same as you got in RStudio.

5. Switch back to SSDT. You will continue to develop the DataMining.dtsx package you created in the fourth recipe of this chapter. Open the data flow editor.

6. Create a new OLE DB source. Name it RModel. Double-click the RModel data source.

7. Use the AdventureWorksDW2014 connection manager.

8. Select the **SQL Command** option in the **Data access** mode drop-down list.

9. In the **SQL Command** text, copy and paste the code that executes the sys.sp_execute_external_script system procedure from SSMS.

10. Click the **Columns** row in the left-hand list to check the mapping between the input and output columns. Leave the default mappings.

11. Add a Derived Column transformation and connect it with the blue arrow from the RModel data source.

   1. Add a new derived column, with 4-byte signed integer datatype. Name it RPrediction. Use the following formula for the expression:

```
Predicted_1_Probability >= 0.50 ? 1 : 0
```

12. Add another derived column. Name it `RPredictProbability`. Use the double-precision float datatype. Use the following formula for the expression:

```
Predicted_1_Probability < 0.50 ? Predicted_0_Probability :
Predicted_1_Probability
```

14. Add a new `Sort` transformation. Connect it with the blue line from the `Derived Column` transformation.

15. Sort the data by the `CustomerKey` column, in ascending order.

16. Add a `Merge Join` transformation. Use the first **Sort** transformation as the left input, and the second `Sort` transformation as the right input. Use the **Inner join** as the join type. Select the `CustomerKey`, `BikeBuyer`, `SSASPrediction`, and `SSASPredictProbability` columns from the left input, and the `RPrediction` and the `RPredictProbability` columns from the right input. Close the Merge Join Transformation Editor.

17. Add a `Multicast` transformation and connect it with the blue line from the `Merge Join` transformation. This transformation will serve just as a placeholder for enabling a data viewer.

18. Enable the **Data Viewer** on the path between the `Merge Join` and the `Multicast` transformations. Your data flow should look like the following screenshot:

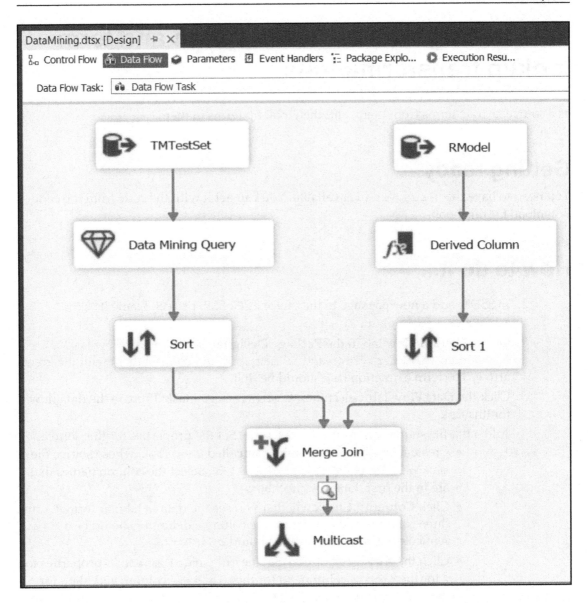

19. Save the package and execute it. Observe the actual value of the `BikeBuyer` column, and the predictions from SSAS and R.

Text mining with term extraction and term lookup transformations

In this recipe, you will see how text mining works. You will use a text file with some blogs as a source, extract terms from them, and then look up terms in them.

Getting ready

You need to have the `Blogs.txt` file available. You can get it with the code from the code download for this book.

How to do it...

1. In SSDT, add a new package to the `Chapter08` SSIS project. Name it `TermExtactionLookup`.
2. On the **Control Flow** tab in the **Package Designer**, add two data flow tasks. Name them `TermExtraction` and `TermLookup` and connect them with the green arrow. The term extraction task should be first.
3. Click the **Data Flow** tab. Select the `TermExtraction` task. Prepare the data flow for this task.
4. Add a flat file source. Name it `ImportBlogs`. Set the properties for this source:
   - Create a new connection manager called `BlogsTxt`, whose source file is `C:\SSIS2016Cookbook\Blogs.txt`. Select the column names that are in the first data row checkbox.
   - Click **Columns**. Check whether you see the data in tabular format with three columns and five rows. The columns delimiter should be a semicolon. The row delimiter should be <CR><LF>.
   - Click the **Advanced** option. Set the `OutputColumnWidth` properties to 2 for the `blogid` column, 70 for the `blogname` column and 3500 for the `blogbody` column. Click **OK**.

5. Click the **Columns** tab of the **Flat File Source Editor**. Click **OK** twice to close the **Flat File Source Editor**.

6. Add the `Multicast` transformation. Name it `MulticastBlogs`. Connect it with the source transformation with the gray arrow. You will save the imported blogs into a SQL Server table, which will feed the term extraction transformation.

7. Add an OLE DB destination. Name it `Blogs`. Connect it with the `Multicast` transformation with the blue arrow. Create a new OLE DB connection manager to the `AdventureWorksDW2014` database, and then create a new table named `Blogs` in the `AdventureWorksDW2014` database.

8. Click the **Mappings** tab to map the input and the destination columns (the mappings between columns should happen automatically because the input and the destination columns have the same names). Click **OK**.

9. Add a `Term Extraction` transformation. Connect it with the second blue arrow from the `Multicast` transformation. Configure it:
   - Specify the `blogbody` column for the input column.
   - Keep the default names for the output columns (`Term` and `Score`).
   - Configure the error output to ignore failures.
   - Check what you can configure on other tabs (exclusion table and advanced options). Click **OK**.

10. Add an OLE DB destination. Name it `Terms`. Connect it with the `Term Extraction` transformation. Use the connection manager to your local `AdventureWorksDW2014` database. Create a new table, `Terms`, in the `AdventureWorksDW2014` database.

11. Click the **Mappings** tab to map the input and the destination columns. Click **OK**.

12. Make sure your `TermExtraction` data flow looks as follows:

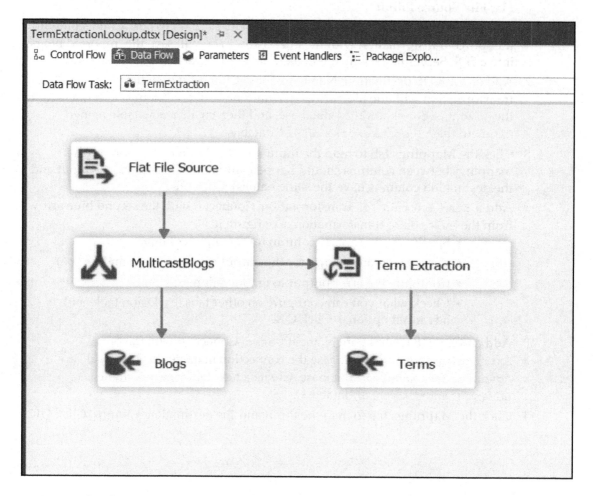

13. Configure the term lookup data flow.
14. Add a new OLE DB source. Name it `Blog`. Use the `dbo.Blogs` table created in the previous data flow from the `AdventureWorksDW2014` database.
15. Add a `Term Lookup` transformation and connect it with the blue arrow from the source. Configure it:
    - Use the `dbo.Terms` table as the reference table.
    - Click the `Term Lookup` tab. Connect the `blogbody` input column with the `Term` reference column.
    - Make `blogid` and `blogname` **Pass-Through Columns**.

16. Your term lookup configuration should look like the following screenshot:

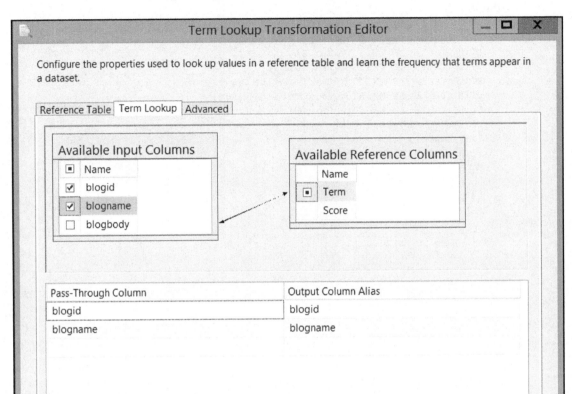

17. Add an OLE DB destination. Name it `TermsInBlogs`. Connect it with the `Term Extraction` transformation. Use the connection manager to your local `AdventureWorksDW2014` database. Create a new table named `TermsInBlogs` in the `AdventureWorksDW2014` database.

18. Click the **Mappings** tab to map the input and the destination columns. Click **OK**.

19. In solution explorer, right-click the `TermExtractionLookup` package and execute it. Follow the execution. After the package is executed, stop the debugging. If you have to repeat the execution of the package, you might have to delete the tables created in the package and recreate them.

20. Check the output of the package by querying the tables created in the package:

```
USE AdventureWorksDW2014 GO SELECT * FROM dbo.Blogs;
SELECT * FROM dbo.Terms;
SELECT * FROM dbo.TermsInBlogs;
GO
```

21. You can use the following code to clean up the AdventureWorksDW2014 database:

```
USE AdventureWorksDW2014;
DROP TABLE IF EXISTS dbo.Blogs;
DROP TABLE IF EXISTS dbo.Terms;
DROP TABLE IF EXISTS dbo.TermsInBlogs;
DROP TABLE IF EXISTS dbo.TMTrainingSet;
DROP TABLE IF EXISTS dbo.TMTestSet;
DROP USER RUser;
USE master;
DROP LOGIN RUser;
GO
```

9
On-Premises and Azure Big Data Integration

This chapter will cover the following recipes:

- Azure Blob storage data management
- Installing a Hortonworks cluster
- Copying data to an on-premises cluster
- Using Hive – creating a database
- Transforming the data with Hive
- Transferring data between Hadoop and Azure
- Leveraging a HDInsight big data cluster
- Managing data with Pig Latin
- Importing Azure Blob storage data

Introduction

Data warehouse architects are facing the need to integrate many types of data. Cloud data integration can be a real challenge for on-premises data warehouses for the following reasons:

- The data sources are obviously not stored on-premises and the data stores differ a lot from what ETL tools such as SSIS are usually made for. As we saw earlier, the out-of-the-box SSIS toolbox has sources, destinations, and transformation tools that deal with on-premises data only.

- The data transformation toolset is quite different to the cloud one. In the cloud, we don't necessarily use SSIS to transform data. There are specific data transformation languages such as Hive and Pig that are used by the cloud developers. The reason for this is that the volume of data may be huge and these languages are running on clusters. as opposed to SSIS, which is running on a single machine.

While there are many cloud-based solutions on the market, the recipes in this chapter will talk about the Microsoft Azure ecosystem.

Azure Blob storage data management

This recipe will cover the following topics:

- Creating a Blob storage in Azure
- Using SSIS to connect to a Blob storage in Azure
- Using SSIS to upload and download files
- Using SSIS to loop through the file using a for each loop task

Getting ready

This recipe assumes that you have a Microsoft Azure account. You can always create a trial account by registering at `https://azure.microsoft.com`.

How to do it...

1. In the Azure portal, create a new storage account and name it `ssiscookbook`.
2. Add a new package in the `ETL.Staging` project and call it `AggregatedSalesFromCloudDW`.
3. Right-click in the **Connection Manager** pane and select **New file connection** from the contextual menu that appears.
4. The **Add SSIS Connection Manager** window appears. Select **Azure Srorage** and click on the **Add...** button.

5. Fill the **Storage account name** textbox, as shown the following screenshot:

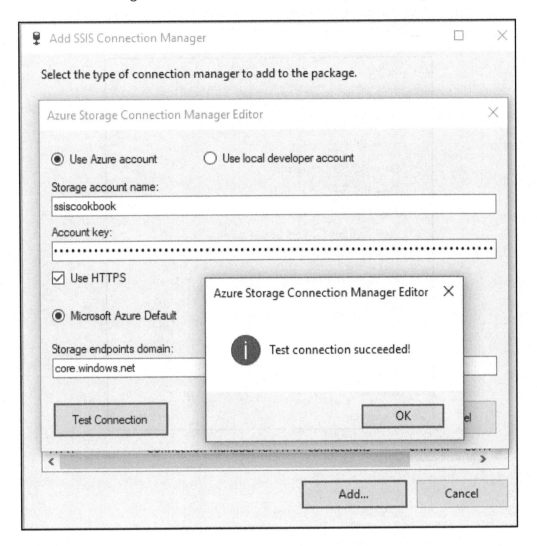

6. Rename the connection manager `cmgr_AzureStorage_ssiscookbook`.

7. Right-click on the newly created connection manager and select **Convert to Project Connection**, as shown in the following screenshot:

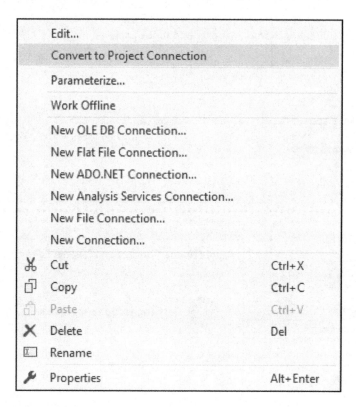

8. Parameterize the `AccountKey`, as shown in the following screenshot:

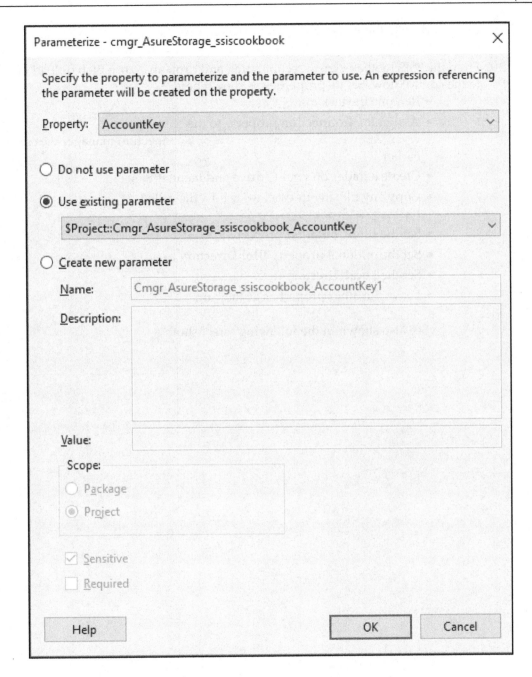

9. Copy and paste the Azure Blob storage key in the `Cmgr_AzureStorage_ssiscookbook_AccountKey` parameter.

10. From the SSIS toolbox-Azure section, drag and drop an Azure Blob upload task to the control flow. Set its properties as shown here:
    - Rename the task `abut_test`
    - Assign the **Connection** property to the `cmgr_AzureStorage_ssiscookbook` connection manager we created earlier.
    - Create a folder on your C drive and name it `test`.
    - Copy any file; in our case, we used a file called `ExtendedProperties.sql`.
    - Set the **BlobContainer** property to `test`.
    - Set the optional property **BlobDirectory** to `uploadfiletest/`.
    - Set the **LocalDirectory** to `C:\test`.
    - Leave the other properties as they are.

    See also shown in the following screenshot:

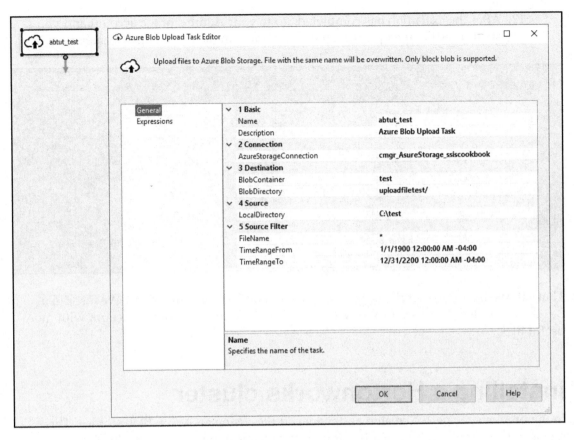

11. Now, right-click on the package to execute it.

12. After the execution has completed, go to your Azure storage account and you should see the file uploaded there, as shown in the following screenshot:

That's it. We have successfully uploaded a file to a Blob storage with SSIS. We just did a `Hello world` test. The next recipes with Azure will fill out this storage account with more useful files.

Installing a Hortonworks cluster

In the previous recipe, we created and managed files using an Azure Blob storage. This recipe will do similar actions but this time using an on-premises Hadoop cluster.

Getting ready

This recipe assumes that you can download and install a virtual machine on your PC.

How to do it...

1. You will need to download and install a Hortonworks sandbox for this recipe. Go to `https://hortonworks.com/downloads/` to download a Docker version of the sandbox. You can choose the sandbox you want, as shown in the following screenshot:

2. Download the VM you want; in our case, we used the last one, **DOWNLOAD FOR DOCKER**. Once done, follow the instructions to configure it and make sure you have added the following entry to the `%systemroot%\system32\drivers\etc\hosts` file:

```
127.0.0.1 sandbox.hortonworks.com
```

This is shown in the following screenshot:

```
# Additionally, comments (such as these) may be inserted on individual
# lines or following the machine name denoted by a '#' symbol.
#
# For example:
#
#      102.54.94.97     rhino.acme.com          # source server
#      38.25.63.10      x.acme.com              # x client host

# localhost name resolution is handled within DNS itself.
#      127.0.0.1        localhost
#      ::1              localhost
127.0.0.1 sandbox.hortonworks.com
```

3. Open your browser and navigate to
   `http://sandbox.hortonworks.com:8888`. Your browser screen should look
   like the following screenshot:

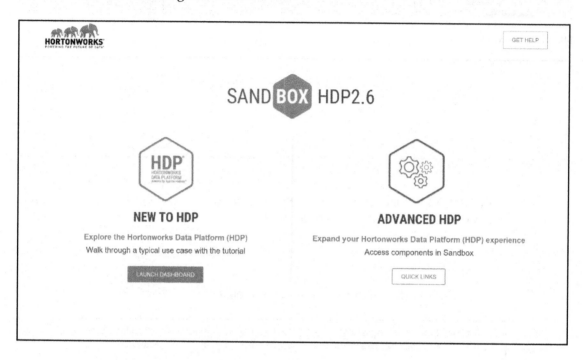

4. Click on **NEW TO HDP**. The **Ambari** screen will appear. Now, click the more
   icon, as shown in the following screenshot, and select **Files View**:

5. The following screen appears. Click on **New Folder** and type `SSISCookBook` as shown in the following screenshot. Click on the **+Add** button to add the folder:

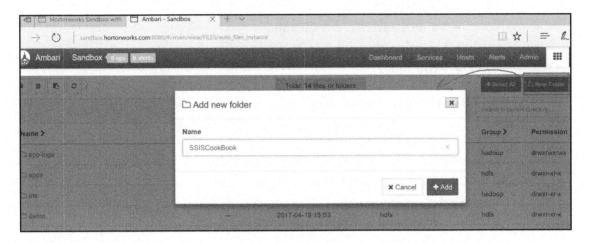

That's it! We're now ready to interact with our local cluster using SSIS.

Copying data to an on-premises cluster

In this recipe, we'll add a package that will copy local data to the local cluster.

Getting ready

This recipe assumes that you have access to an on-premises cluster and have created a folder to hold the files in it from the previous recipe.

How to do it...

1. In the solution explorer, open (expand) the `ETL.DW` project and right-click on it to add a new package. Name it `FactOrdersToHDPCuster.dtsx`.

2. Go to the **Parameters** tab and add a new parameter:
    - **Name**: LoadExecutionId
    - **Data type**: Int64
    - **Value**: Leave the default value 0
    - **Sensitive**: Leave the default value False
    - **Required**: True

3. Add a data flow task on the control flow and name it dft_FactOrders.

4. In the data flow task, drag and drop an OLE DB source. Name it ole_src_DW_vwFactOrders.

5. Double-click on it to open the OLE DB source editor.

6. Set the OLE DB connection manager to cmgr_DW.

7. For data access mode, use the SQL command.

8. Set the SQL command text to the following:

```
SELECT          OrderDate, FirstName, LastName, CompanyName,
Category, ProductName, ProvenanceCode, ProvenanceDescription,
EnglishDescription, OrderQy, UnitPrice, Discount, TaxAmount,
Freight, SalesOrderNumber, PurchareOrderNumber
FROM            DW.vwFactOrders
```

9. Click on **OK** to close the **OLE DB Source Editor**.

10. Drag and drop a **Derived Column** transform from the SSIS toolbox.

11. Name it der_LoadExecutionId and tie it to the ole_src_DW_vwFactOrders.

12. Open it and assign the following properties:
    - **Derived Column Name**: LoadExecutionId
    - **Derived Colum**: Leave the default (add as new column)
    - **Expression**: @[$Package::LoadExecutionId]

13. Click on **OK** to close the derived column editor.

14. Right-click on the **Connection Manager** pane and select **New Connection...** from the contextual menu that appears. The **ADD SSIS Connection Manager** window opens.

15. Select **Hadoop** from the **Type** column as shown in the following screenshot and click on **Add...**:

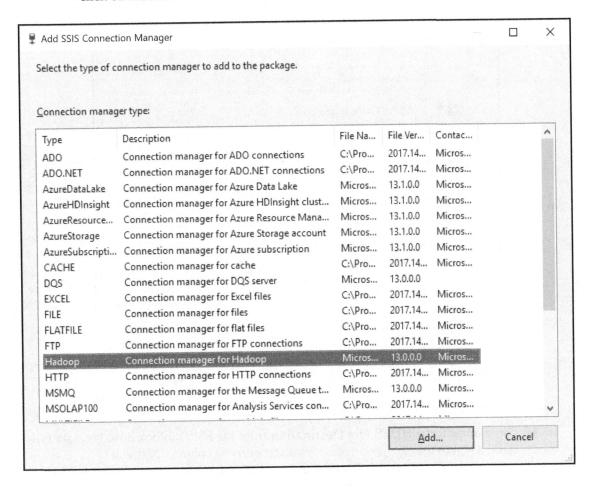

16. The Hadoop connection manager editor opens. Set the properties as shown in the following screenshot. Make sure the connection works and click on **OK** to close the window.

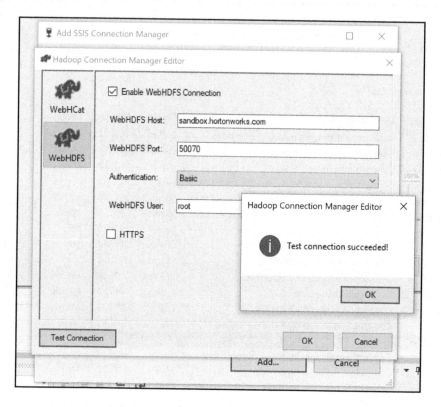

17. Drag and drop a **HDFS File Destination** from the SSIS toolbox onto the data flow task. Tie it to the `der_LoadExecutionId` derived column. Name it `hdfs_dst_FactOrders`. Double-click on **OK** and set the properties as follows:
    - In the **Hadoop Connection Manager** select `cmgr_Hadoop_Sandbox`
    - Set the **File path** to `/SSISCookBook/Import/FactOrders.txt`
    - Select mappings from the left-hand pane to set the mapping between the source and destination columns

18. Click on **OK** to close the **HDFS File Destination Editor**.

19. Now, as usual, make sure that the transforms are the same size and aligned properly. Your data flow task should look like the following screenshot:

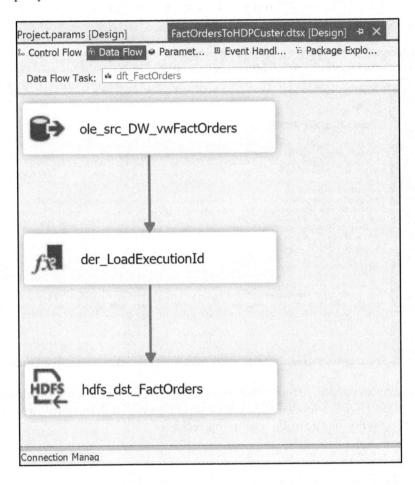

20. Now we can run the package. Once done, we can see that a file has been created in the cluster in the `/SSISCookBook/Import/` folder, as shown in the following screenshot. Go to **Ambari | Files View** and browse to the `SSISCookBook/Import` folder. You can open the file as shown in the following screenshot:

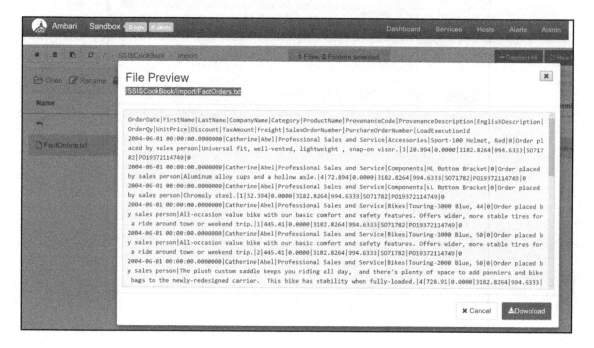

That's it! We have successfully transferred data from SQL Server to our Hortonworks sandbox cluster on HDFS, a totally different OS and filesystem than Windows. We'll continue working with the file in the following recipes.

Using Hive – creating a database

Hive is one of the languages used in Hadoop to interact with large volumes of data. It is very easy to learn since it uses SQL commands. This recipe will show you how we can use Hive to transform data from our source. Although we have only 542 lines of data in our file, we can still use it to learn Hadoop services calls.

In this recipe, we're going to create a database in Hive.

Getting ready

This recipe assumes that you have access to a Hortonworks sandbox on-premises or in Azure. It is also assumed that you have executed the previous recipe.

How to do it...

1. Open Ambari and navigate to `http://Sandbox.Hortonworks.com:8080`. Use `raj_ops` for both the username and password to log in.

2. Click on the more icon (nine-squares button near `raj_ops`) in the toolbar and select **Hive View 2.0**, as shown in the following screenshot:

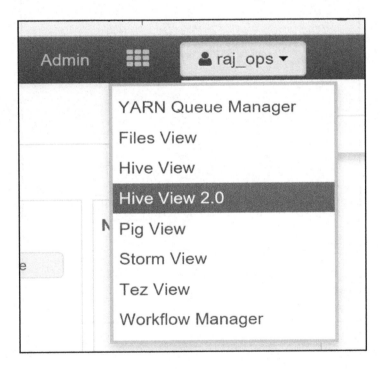

3. Type `create database SSISCookBook` in **Worksheet1** and click on **Execute**, as shown in the following screenshot:

4. Refresh your browser and click on **Browse**, as shown in the following screenshot. The database has been created.

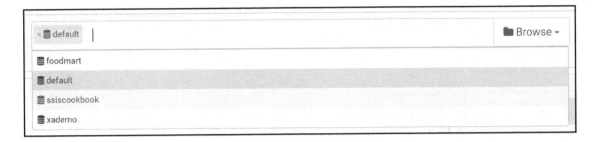

There's more...

The first step is done; we have created the database. We'll interact with the data in the following recipe.

Transforming the data with Hive

The data is now in the cluster in HDFS. We'll now transform it using a SQL script. The program we're using is Hive. This program interacts with the data using SQL statements.

With most Hadoop programs (Hive, Pig, Sparks, and so on), source is read-only. It means that we cannot modify the data in the file that we transferred in the previous recipe. Some languages such as HBase allow us to modify the source data though. But for our purpose, we'll use Hive, a well-known program in the Hadoop ecosystem.

Getting ready

This recipe assumes that you have access to a Hortonworks cluster and that you have transferred data to it following the previous recipe.

How to do it...

1. If not already done, open the package created in the previous recipe, `FactOrdersToHDPCuster.dtsx`.

2. Add a Hadoop Hive task and rename it `hht_HDPDWHiveTable`.

3. Double-click on it to open the **Hadoop Hive Task Editor,** as shown in the following screenshot:

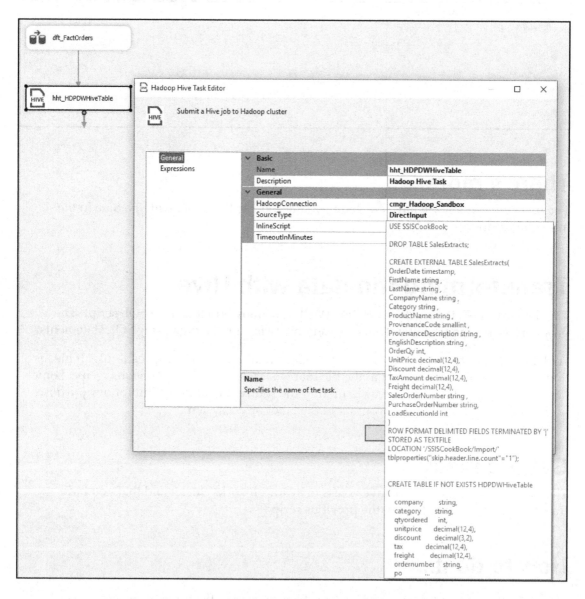

Update the following parameters:

HadoopConnection: cmgr_Hadoop_Sandbox

SourceType: DirectInput

InlineScript: Use the following script:

```
USE SSISCookBook;

DROP TABLE SalesExtracts;

CREATE EXTERNAL TABLE SalesExtracts(
OrderDate timestamp,
FirstName string ,
LastName string ,
CompanyName string ,
Category string ,
ProductName string ,
ProvenanceCode smallint ,
ProvenanceDescription string ,
EnglishDescription string ,
OrderQy int,
UnitPrice decimal(12,4),
Discount decimal(12,4),
TaxAmount decimal(12,4),
Freight decimal(12,4),
SalesOrderNumber string ,
PurchaseOrderNumber string,
LoadExecutionId int
)
ROW FORMAT DELIMITED FIELDS TERMINATED BY '|'
STORED AS TEXTFILE
LOCATION '/SSISCookBook/Import/'
tblproperties("skip.header.line.count"="1");


CREATE TABLE IF NOT EXISTS HDPDWHiveTable
(
    company        string,
    category       string,
    qtyordered     int,
    unitprice      decimal(12,4),
    discount       decimal(3,2),
    tax            decimal(12,4),
    freight        decimal(12,4),
    ordernumber    string,
    po             string
```

```
)
ROW FORMAT DELIMITED FIELDS TERMINATED BY ',' LINES TERMINATED
BY '10' STORED AS TEXTFILE
LOCATION '/SSISCookBook/Export/';


INSERT OVERWRITE TABLE HDPDWHiveTable
SELECT CompanyName, Category ,   SUM(OrderQy) AS OrderQy,
AVG(UnitPrice) AS UnitPrice, SUM(Discount) AS Discount,
SUM(TaxAmount) AS TaxAmount, SUM(Freight) AS Freight,
            SalesOrderNumber, PurchaseOrderNumber
FROM   SalesExtracts
GROUP BY CompanyName, Category, SalesOrderNumber,
PurchaseOrderNumber;
```

The preceding script does the following:

- Switches context to the `SSISCookBook` database we created in a preceding recipe.
- Creates an external table, that is, a table stored outside Hive. These tables have the characteristic that, whether we drop the table in Hive, the data file will not be dropped. Regular (internal) tables will drop the files underneath when dropped.
- The external table created has the same structure as the data we copied over in a preceding recipe. The command `skip.header.line.count` skips one line, the header line of the file.
- Then, another external table is created but this time in another folder: `Export`. It will create a file called `000000_0`. The trailing `0` is the reducer number that created the file. If we had a large volume of data and were using a real cluster that would create the result in parallel we would have many files (`000000_1`, `000000_2`, and so on). You will notice that a comma is now used as the column delimiter.
- Lastly, we insert into the table previously created. The overwrite clause will overwrite the table content as opposed to appending it, like a regular `INSERT` command would have done.

There's more...

The recipe, as simplistic as it is, was a quick introduction to Hive in Hadoop. This language mainly transforms the data by creating structures on top of others. In a further recipe later in this chapter, we'll use another program to transform the data: Pig Latin. But now, we'll leave the on-premises big data world to go into Azure.

Transferring data between Hadoop and Azure

Now that we have some data created by Hadoop Hive on-premises, we're going to transfer this data to a cloud storage on Azure. Then, we'll do several transformations to it using Hadoop Pig Latin. Once done, we'll transfer the data to an on-premises table in the staging schema of our `AdventureWorksLTDW2016` database.

In this recipe, we're going to copy the data processed by the local Hortonworks cluster to an Azure Blob storage. Once the data is copied over, we can transform it using Azure compute resources, as we'll see in the following recipes.

Getting ready

This recipe assumes that you have created a storage space in Azure as described in the previous recipe.

How to do it...

1. Open the `ETL.Staging SSIS` project and add a new package to it. Rename it `StgAggregateSalesFromCloud.dtsx`.
2. Add a Hadoop connection manager called `cmgr_Hadoop_Sandbox` like we did in the previous recipe.
3. Add another connection manager, which will connect to the Azure storage like the `cmgr_AsureStorage_ssiscookbook` we did in a previous recipe in this chapter.
4. Add a **Foreach Loop** container to the control flow and rename it `felc_HDP_Export`.

5. Double-click on it to open the **Foreach Loop** editor. Set the **Collection** properties, as shown in the following screenshot:

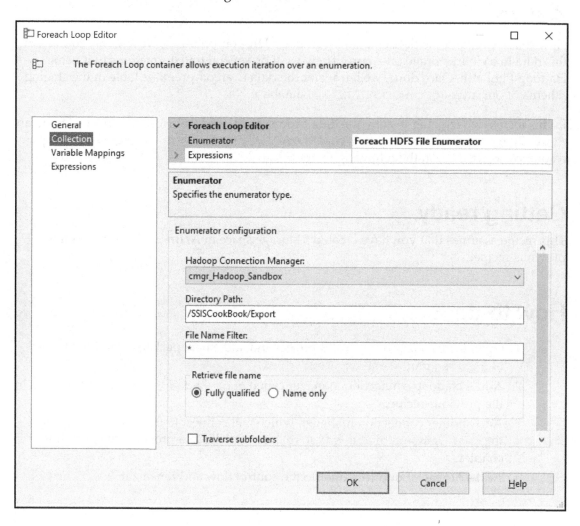

6. Click on the **Variable Mappings**, create a new variable at the package level, and name it `HDPFileNamePath`, as shown in the following screenshot:

General	Select variables to map to the collection value.	
Collection		
Variable Mappings	Variable	Index
Expressions	User::HDPFileNamePath	0

7. Click **OK** to close the **Foreach Loop** editor.
8. Go to the **Variables** pane and set the value of the `HDPFileNamePath` to `/SSISCookBook/Export/000000_0`.
9. From the SSIS toolbox, drag and drop a HDFS file source into the `felc_HDP_Export` Foreach Loop container. Rename it `hfs_src_SSISCookBook_Export`.
10. Click anywhere in the data flow task background and go to the **Properties** pane (or press F4 to display it). Scroll down to **Expressions** and click on the ellipsis (...) button.
11. From the drop-down list, click on the ellipsis button to the right of the `hfs_src_SSISCookBook_Export.FilePath` expression. Fill the **Expression Builder**, as shown in the following screenshot. Click on **OK** to close the **Expression Builder**:

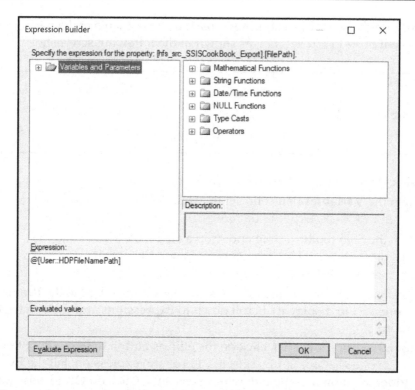

12. Close and reopen the package to force the expression to be considered.

13. Double-click on it to open the **HDF File Source** editor and assign the following:

- **Hadoop Connection Manager**: Select the `cmgr_Hadoop_Sandbox` from the drop-down list.
- **File Path**: It should be `/SSISCookBook/Export/000000_0`. This is the value of the variable expression we set earlier.
- **File format**: Leave the default, `Text`.
- **Column delimiter character**: Use the vertical bar (|).

14. Click on the **Columns** tab and set the columns at the left of the editor and rename them, as shown in the following screenshot. Once done, click on **OK** to close the **HDFS File Source Editor**:

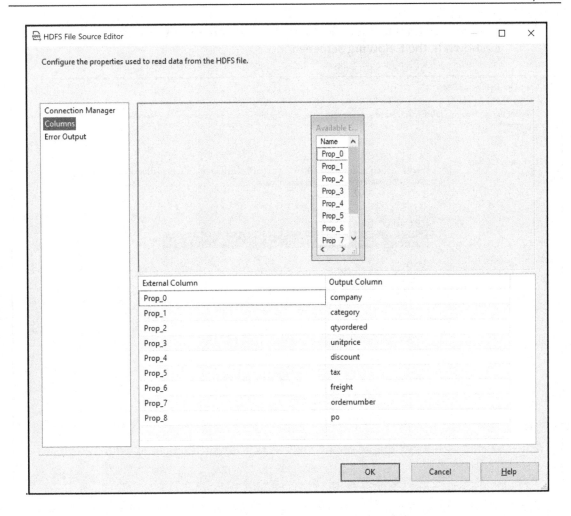

15. Add a **Derived Column** to the data flow task and link it to
    `hfs_src_SSISCookBook_Export.FilePath`. Rename it
    `der_LoadExecutionId`. Open the **Derived Column Editor** and add a column
    called `LoadExecutionId`. Set the value to the **Package::LoadExecutionId**
    package parameter.
16. Add an **Azure Blob Destination** to the data flow task and rename it
    `abd_dst_ssiscookbook_import_FactOrdersAggregated`. Link it to the
    `der_LoadExecutionId` transform.

17. Double-click on it to open the **Azure Blob Destination Editor**. Set its properties as shown in the following screenshot:

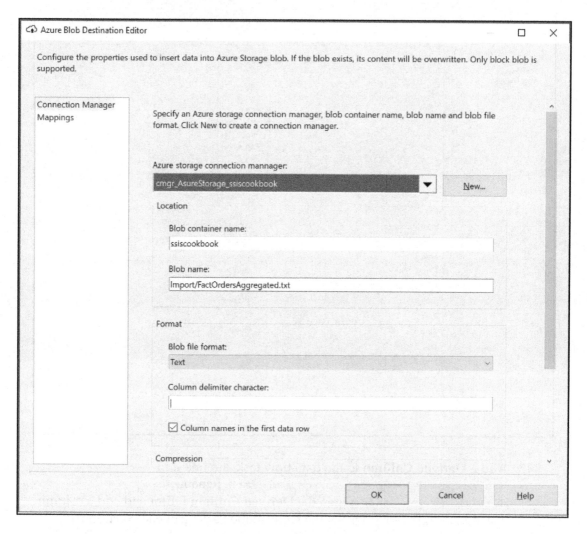

18. Click on the column mapping and verify that our input columns are mapped.
19. The final data flow task should look like the following screenshot:

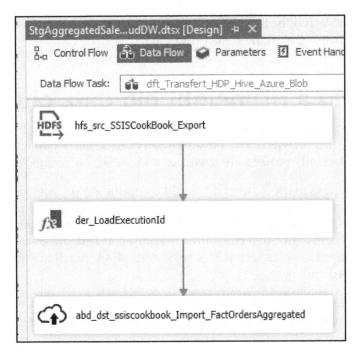

20. Execute the data flow task. Once completed, go to the Azure portal
    (`portal.azure.com`), go into your **HDInsight cluster** | **Storage accounts** | **Blob
    service**, and click on **Import Blob**. You should have a screen similar to the
    following screenshot:

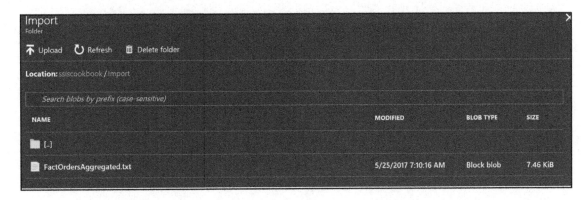

21. Right-click on the `FactOrdersAggergated.txt` file and select **Download**. The
    content of the file will open in your browser.

That's it! We've transferred the local HDP cluster data to another one. In the following recipe, we'll do something with the transferred data.

Leveraging a HDInsight big data cluster

So far, we've managed Blobs data using SSIS. In this case, the data was at rest and SSIS was used to manipulate it. SSIS was the orchestration service in Azure parlance. As stated in the introduction, SSIS can only be used on- premises and, so far, on a single machine.

The goal of this recipe is to use Azure HDInsight computation services. These services allow us to use (rent) powerful resources as a cluster of machines. These machines can run Linux or Windows according to user choice, but be aware that Windows will be deprecated for the newest version of HDInsight. Such clusters or machines, as fast and powerful as they can be, are very expensive to use. In fact, this is quite normal; we're talking about a potentially large amount of hardware here.

For this reason, unless we want to have these computing resource running continuously, SSIS has a way to create and drop a cluster on demand. The following recipe will show you how to do it.

Getting ready

You will need to have access to an Azure subscription to do this recipe.

How to do it...

1. If not open, open the package we're using from the previous recipe:
   `ETL_Staging.StgAggregatedSales.dtsx`.
2. Right-click on the **Connection Manager** pane, add **New Connection...**, and select `AzureResourceManager`. Fill out the properties following the instructions provided at the following link:
   `https://docs.microsoft.com/en-us/azure/azure-resource-manager/resource -group-create-service-principal-portal`.

3. Your connection manager should look like the one in the following screenshot:

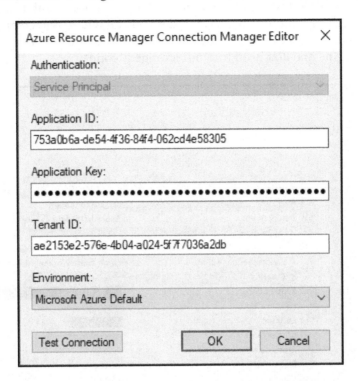

4. Drag and drop an **Azure Create Cluster** task from the SSIS toolbox on the control flow and attach it to the felc_HDP_Export Foreach Loop container. Rename the task acc_ssiscookbook for **Azure Create Cluster** as ssiscookbook.

5. Double-click on it to open the **Azure HDInsight Create Cluster Editor**. Fill the properties as shown in the following screenshot. For the **SubsciptionId**, use your Azure subscription ID. The location depends on where you created your storage account. To avoid extra fees, you should have your cluster created in the same region as the one you used for your storage account:

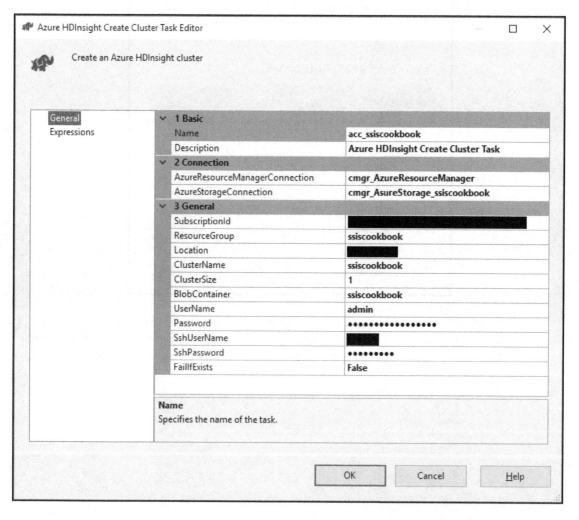

6. Now, for this task to work correctly, you have to parameterize both passwords: cluster password and SSH password.

7. Now we'll test if the cluster creation works. Right-click on the task and select **Execute Task**. The cluster creation starts. This task might take several minutes to complete. In our case, it takes up to 15 minutes.

8. Once completed, open a bash terminal. We will use the one that comes with Windows 10. Go to the Azure portal and look for the HDInsight cluster that has been created. In the overview, there is an option to connect using SSH. Click on it and copy the SSH command. Paste it in the bash terminal. It should consist of a command similar to the following:

```
ssh User@yourcluster-ssh.azurehdinsight.net
```

It is also shown in the following screenshot:

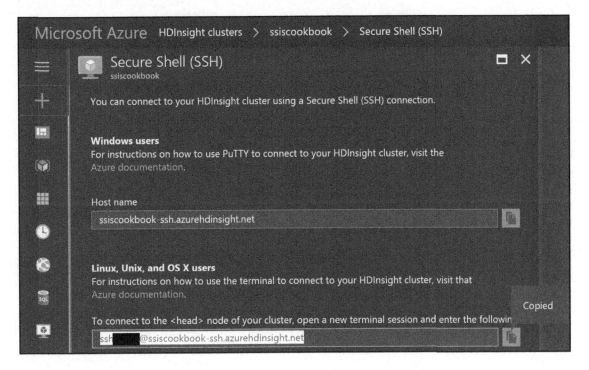

9. Next, we'll add a task to drop the cluster once we've finished with it. From the SSIS toolbox, drag and drop an **Azure HDInsight Delete Cluster Task** on the control flow. Rename it `adc_ssiscookbook`. Double-click on it and set the properties as shown in the following screenshot:

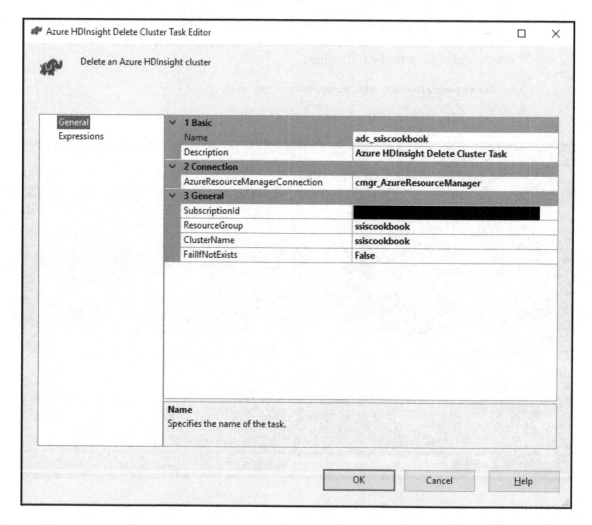

10. Click **OK** to close the `adc_ssiscookbook` task. Right-click on it and select **Execute Task** from the contextual menu that appears. Once executed successfully, go to the Azure portal and verify that the cluster has been dropped.

There's more...

That's it! We can now create and drop clusters on demand. The following recipe will show how we can use the cluster with Pig.

Managing data with Pig Latin

Pig Latin is one of the programs available in big data clusters. The purpose of this program is to run scripts that can accept any type of data. "Pig can eat everything," as the mantra of the creators states.

This recipe is just meant to show you how to call a simple Pig script. No transformations are done. The purpose of the script is to show you how we can use an Azure Pig task with SSIS.

Getting ready

This recipe assumes that you have created a HDInsight cluster successfully.

How to do it...

1. In the `StgAggregatedSales.dtsx` SSIS package, drag and drop an **Azure Pig Task** onto the control flow. Rename it `apt_AggregateData`.

2. Double-click on it to open the **Azure HDInsight Pig Task Editor** and set the properties as shown in the following screenshot:

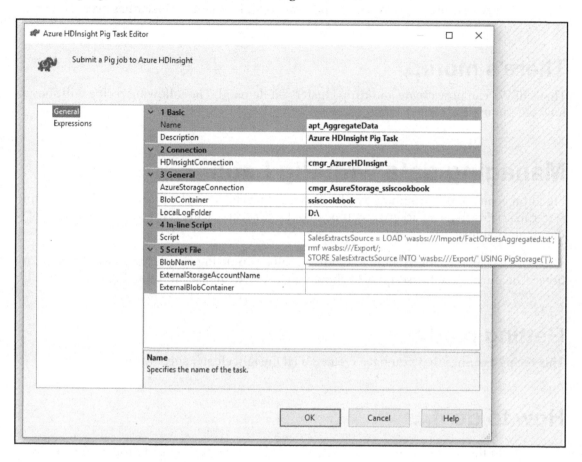

3. In the script property, insert the following code:

```
SalesExtractsSource = LOAD
'wasbs:///Import/FactOrdersAggregated.txt';
rmf wasbs:///Export/;
STORE SalesExtractsSource INTO 'wasbs:///Export/' USING
PigStorage('|');
```

4. The first line holds a reference to the `Import/FactOrdersAggregated.txt` file. The second line removes (deleting) the directory `/Export`. Finally, the data is copied over to a new file in the `/Export` folder using a vertical bar (|) as a delimiter.

5. Right-click on the `apt_AggregateData` and select **Execute Task** from the contextual menu that appears to run the script.

6. Once done successfully, go to the Blob storage in the Azure portal to check that the file has been created.

7. If any error occurs, go to the log file located in the directory that you specified in `apt_AggregateData`.

8. Your package should now look like the following screenshot:

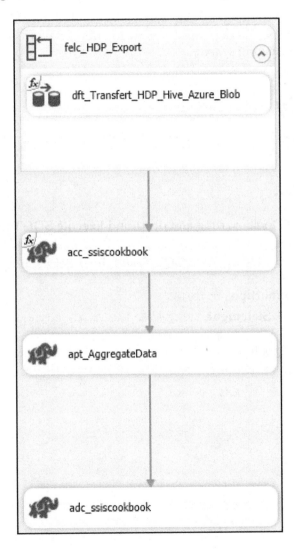

There's more...

You'll notice that the data hasn't been modified, as the purpose of the recipe was to show how to call a Pig script from SSIS.

Importing Azure Blob storage data

So far, we've created and dropped a HDInsight cluster and called a Pig script using the Azure Pig task. This recipe will demonstrate how to import data from an Azure Blob storage to a table in the staging schema.

Getting ready

This recipe assumes that you have completed the previous one.

How to do it...

1. From the SSIS toolbox, drag and drop, and **Execute SQL Task** on the control flow, and rename it `sql_truncate_Staging_StgCloudSales`.

2. Double-click on it to open the **SQL Task Editor**. Set the properties as follows and click on OK:
   - **Connection:** `cmgr_DW`
   - **SQL Statement:** `TRUNCATE TABLE [Staging].[StgCloudSales];`

3. From the SSIS toolbox, drag a **Foreach Loop Container** and rename it `felc_StgCloudSales`.

4. Double-click on it to open the **Foreach Loop Editor**, and assign the properties in the **Collection** pane, as shown in the following screenshot:

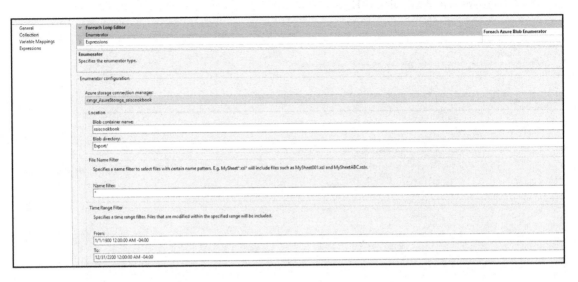

5. Now go to the **Variable Mappings** pane and add a string variable called User::AzureAggregatedData. Make sure the scope is at the package level.

6. Drag a **Data Flow Task** into the felc_StgCloudSales and rename it dft_StgCloudSales.

7. Go into the **Data Flow Task** and drag an **Azure Blob Source** from the SSIS toolbox. Rename it azure_blob_src_ExportBlob.

8. Click anywhere on the background of the data flow and go to the **Properties** pane. Select **Expressions**. Click on the ellipsis button (...) and select [azure_blob_src_ExportBlob].[Blob Name] from the list. Assign @[User::AzureAggregatedData] as the value.

9. Double-click on the `azure_blob_src_ExportBlob` to open the **Azure Blob Source Editor**, and assign the various properties as shown in the following screenshot. And click **OK**.

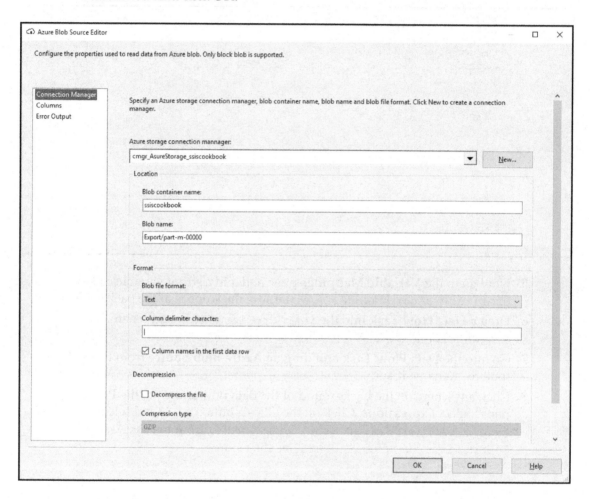

10. Drag an **OLE DB Destination** to the **Data Flow Task** and rename it `ole_dst_Staging_StgCloudSales`. Attach it to `azure_blob_src_ExportBlob`.

11. Double-click on it and set the properties as follows:
    - **OLE DB connection manager**: `c,mgr_DW`
    - **Name of the table or view**: `[Staging].[StgCloudSales]`

12. Go into the **Mappings** panes and make sure that all columns are mapped. Click **OK** to close the editor. Your screen should look like the following screenshot:

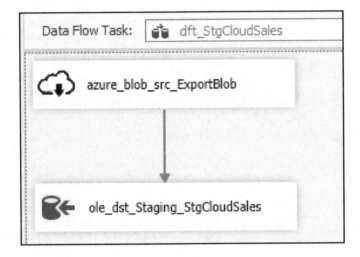

13. Go back to the control flow and right-click on `felc_StgCloudSales`. Select **Execute** from the contextual menu to execute the container.

14. Attach `felc_StgCloudSales` to both the
    `sql_truncate_Staging_StgCloudSales` and the `apt_AggregateData` tasks.
    Your final package should look like the following screenshot:

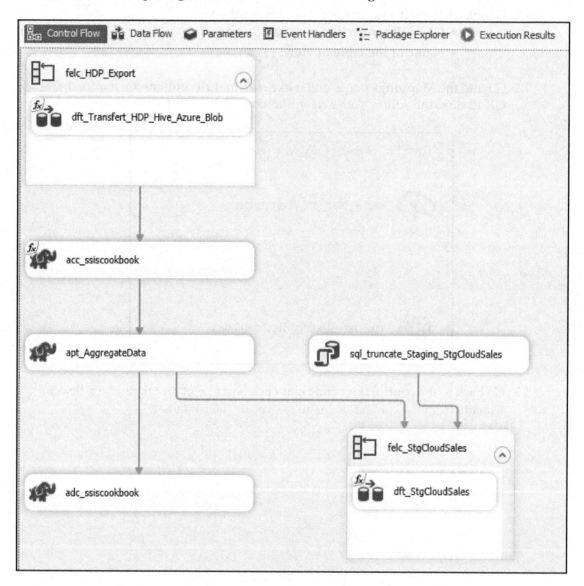

That's it! We now have a package that can read from a local Hadoop cluster, transfer data to and from Azure, and execute Azure HDInsight tasks.

There's more...

This chapter gave a 360° overview of how SSIS can interact with the big data world, be it on- premises or in the clouds. The next section will consist of a brief discussion on the difference between SSIS and the Azure Data Factory.

There is a service available in Azure that can do about as much as SSIS can do with Azure data. In fact, if your data is only in Azure, this is the service you should use in conjunction with SSIS.

Azure Data Factory and SSIS

Azure Data Factory (ADF) is a service that orchestrate data integration using different services available in Azure. Like SSIS, it can move data from one location to another. The main differences are the following:

- SSIS needs a windows machine to run. Even to copy data, the service runs on a windows server. ADF doesn't needs anything to accomplish copy data tasks since the service runs in Azure
- SSIS has a rich toolset integrated into it to transform data; the dataflow task. ADF has nothing that come close to it built-in.
- ADF relies on compute services like HDInsight clusters that can run Hive and Pig scripts to transform data.
- SSIS can transform data on without leaving the package and, without necessarily staging it. It can transform and load data immediately to the destination. ADF calls a service that will transform the data but this service might not be able to load the data directly in a destination.

For example, we need to load data from Oracle, transform and load it into SQL Server. SSIS can do it in one single package. ADF would have to copy the data to an intermediately storage, call a service to transform the data and finally load it into the destination. SSIS 2016 service runs on a Windows OS based machine; ADF runs in Azure where there's no OS to consider.

Generally, when most of your enterprise data is in Azure ecosystem and you barely use data on premises, it makes sense to use ADF. In that case, you are probable making the ETL using ADF and/or TSQL be it stored procedure or DML statements.

But, if your enterprise data is mostly on premises and some of it is in Azure, it makes more sense to use SSIS. Same statement if you're using on-premises Big Data cluster as you saw earlier in this chapter. SSIS now has a lot of connectors to leverage big data clusters on premises as well as in Azure.

10

Extending SSIS Custom Tasks and Transformations

This chapter covers the following recipes:

- Designing a custom task
- Designing a custom transformation
- Managing custom components versions

Introduction

This chapter discusses SSIS customization-the built-in capability of the SSIS platform that allows you to extend the natively provided programmatic elements. In addition to the system-provided tasks and components, including the script task and the script component, the SSIS programming model allows you to implement your own programmatic logic by designing your own control flow tasks (custom tasks) or your own data flow components (custom components).

Typically, a custom task would be needed when none of the system-provided tasks facilitate the specific operation that you need to implement in your SSIS solution; for instance, the built-in **File Transfer Protocol (FTP)** task does not support Secure FTP, so if you need to access remote file locations using the **Secure File Transfer Protocol (SSH FTP)**, you need to design a custom task.

The most frequent uses of the custom component are custom transformations that either provide operations that are not provided by the built-in components, or they encapsulate a series of transformations within a single one. In the latter case, you might also implement the operations by using multiple built-in transformations, but you would prefer to reduce the complexity of the data flow by implementing them as a single component.

Script tasks and components are discussed in more detail in Chapter 7, *Unleash the Power of SSIS Script Tasks and Components*. In both cases, the custom code is embedded in the SSIS package definition; you can create and modify it during package development, and it is deployed together with the package.

When using custom tasks or components, the custom code is developed in a separate Visual Studio project. You should create a separate assembly for each custom task, or component; this allows you to develop, modify, and deploy them without having to redeploy any of the packages in which they are used, and independently of any other custom tasks or components.

To decide whether to use scripting, or whether to design a custom task or component, you can use the following rule: use scripting if the complete logic of the task or component can be encapsulated into a single script and if the same script does not need to be used in multiple packages. Otherwise, you are encouraged to consider using custom tasks or components, especially in situations where the same custom logic needs to be implemented in numerous packages.

Designing a custom task

To design a custom control flow task, you create a DOT.NET assembly based on the Class Library Visual Studio template; the task's definition must be placed in a class derived from the `Task` base class, of the `Microsoft.SqlServer.Dts.Runtime` namespace (located in the `Microsoft.SqlServer.ManagedDTS.dll` assembly). This class also needs to implement the `DtsTaskAttribute` that is used to identify the class as an SSIS task and provide the elementary properties used when implementing the custom task in SSIS control flows.

Optionally, you can provide a custom graphical user interface for the custom task, which will be used as the task editor when the task is configured during SSIS package development. If a custom editor is not provided, the custom task can be edited by using the built-in advanced editor.

The task base class provides two methods that you need to override, and in them provide your custom code to:

- Validate the configuration of the task. This method is called automatically by the SSIS control flow designer whenever the task settings are changed, and allows you to communicate with the SSIS package developers to help them understand the task's configuration and help them configure it correctly before it can be used.
- You also need to provide the logic needed to execute the task. This method will be called at runtime, when the package execution reaches the task in the control flow sequence. This method also allows access to various SSIS package resources:
  - The SSIS variables can be read or written
  - The connections accessible to the package can be used to connect to various data sources
  - The custom task may send log entries to the event log
  - You are encouraged to implement events in your custom task, so that its performance can be captured by SSDT at design time, and by the SSIS server after the packages implementing the task have been deployed
  - In the custom task, you can also detect whether the operation is participating in a transaction, and use this information when connecting to a data source

Both the preceding methods return a DTSExecResult value specifying the result of the validation, or the execution; this communicates the outcome of each method to the SSIS package developer, as well as the SSIS execution engine. The following values are supported by the DTSExecResult enumeration:

- Success is used to specify that the validation, or the execution, completed successfully.
- Failure specifies that the validation, or the execution, has failed. Generally, in case of failure, additional events should be returned from the task to provide more information about the failure to the SSIS package developer, or to the administrator of the deployment environment.
- Completion can be used for executions when either Success or Failure are not relevant results, or not specific enough. For instance, if a task completes its work successfully it returns Success, if it fails, it returns Failure, but if no work was performed, even though the configuration was in order, the task might return Completion to communicate a specific result that is neither a success nor failure.

- `Canceled` is used to report to the SSIS execution engine that the execution had to be interrupted; for instance, before even reaching the point in its execution that could be interpreted as any of the other three results.

Normally, only `Success` and `Failure` should be used in the `Validate()` method.

To deploy a custom task - either to the development workstation used in SSIS package development, or to the environment, in which it is going to be used - the assemblies containing the task need to be copied to the following folders:

- `%ProgramFiles%\Microsoft SQL Server\130\DTS\Tasks` - for the 64-bit edition of the assembly
- `%ProgramFiles(x86)%\Microsoft SQL Server\130\DTS\Tasks` - for the 32-bit edition of the assembly

If the assembly is platform-independent, the file needs to be copied to both folders.

The assembly, and all of the assemblies it references, must also be registered in the **Global Assembly Cache (GAC)**. To register the assemblies on the SSIS development workstation, you can use the `gacutil.exe` command-line utility (it is installed together with Visual Studio); however, on a production server `gacutil.exe` might not be available. You can also use an appropriate Windows PowerShell script to perform the registration.

In this recipe, you are going to develop a custom task, deploy it to your development workstation, and use it in an SSIS package.

This custom task is going to use an external library to allow you to perform FTP tasks in SSIS using the (SSH FTP).

 For your convenience, the C# code snippets needed for this chapter are provided in the `Chapter10.txt` file.

Getting ready

Before you begin, you need to install the `WinSCP` class library from the `https://winscp.net/` website; WinSCP is a free tool that you can use in your own solutions, under the terms of the GNU General Public License as published by the Free Software Foundation (`https://www.gnu.org/licenses/gpl.html`).

Please review the WinSCP GNU license, at
https://winscp.net/eng/docs/license.

To install and register the external library on your workstation, follow these steps:

1. Download version **5.9.5** of the **Installation package,** or the **.NET assembly / COM library** of WinSCP from https://winscp.net/eng/download.php.

2. We recommend that you use the installation package, which will install the application and the necessary assemblies in a folder expected by the recipes in this chapter.

3. If you decided on using the installation package, run it, and then follow the instructions in the installation wizard to complete the installation.

4. If you prefer to download only the assembly, download the archive file, and then unzip it into the C:\Program Files (x86)\WinSCP\ folder.

5. After the installation has completed successfully, or after you placed the files in the specified folder, use Windows Explorer to navigate to the C:\SSIS2016Cookbook\Chapter10\Scripts folder.

6. Locate the Chapter10_GAC_WinSCPnet.bat command file, and open it in Notepad.

7. Inspect the file, and then close it.

8. In Windows Explorer, right-click the command file, and select **Execute as administrator...** from the shortcut menu.

9. In the **User Account Control** dialog click **OK** to allow the execution.

10. After the execution completes, press any key to close the command prompt window.

You are now ready to design the custom task.

How to do it...

1. Start Visual Studio 2015 and create a new project.
2. In the **New Project** dialog, make sure that **.NET Framework 4.5.2** is selected, and then under **Templates \ Visual C#**, select the **Class Library** template. Use SSISCustomTasks as the project name, place it in the C:\SSIS2016Cookbook\Chapter10\Starter folder, check **Create directory for solution**, and use SSISCustomization as the solution name. Refer to the following screenshot to verify your settings:

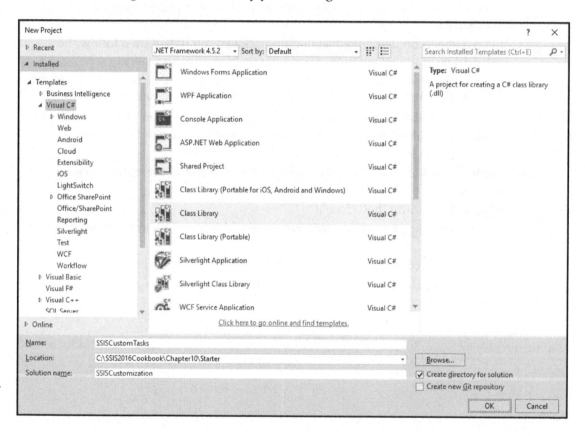

3. Click **OK** to confirm the configuration and create the solution.

4. In the **Solution Explorer**, right-click the newly created SSISCustomTasks project, and select **Properties** from the shortcut menu to open the SSISCustomTasks properties pane.

5. On the **Application** page, change the default namespace value to SSIS2016Cookbook.

6. On the **Signing** page, check **Sign the assembly**, and select **<Browse...>** in the **Choose a strong name key file** selection box.

7. In the **Select File** dialog, navigate to the C:\SSIS2016Cookbook\Chapter10\Scripts folder, and select the SSIS2016Cookbook.snk strong name key file, as shown in the following screenshot:

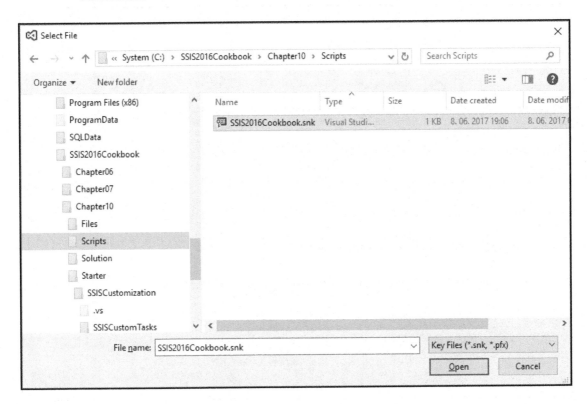

8. Click **Open** to confirm the selection.

9. Save the solution, and then close the project properties pane.

10. In the `Class1.cs` designer pane, change the namespace of the class to `SSIS2016Cookbook`, and change the `Class1` name to `SecureFTP`.

11. In the **Solution Explorer**, change the `Class1.cs` file name to `SecureFTP.cs`, and then save the solution.

12. In the **Solution Explorer**, right-click **References**, and then select **Add Reference...** from the shortcut menu to open the **Reference Manager** dialog.

13. Under **Assemblies / Extensions**, check the `Microsoft.SqlServer.Dts.Design`, `Microsoft.SqlServer.ManagedDTS`, and **WinSCPnet** assemblies, as shown in the following screenshot:

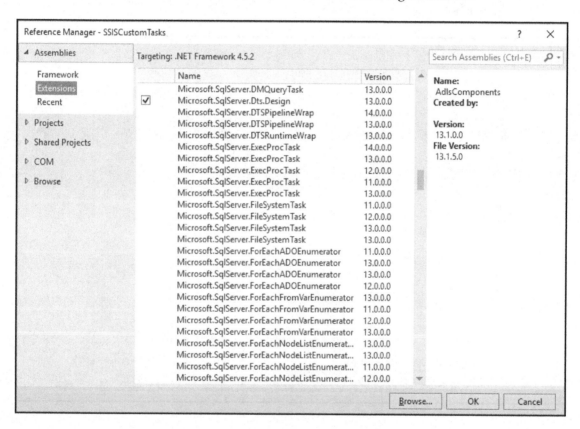

14. Click **OK** to confirm the selection.

15. In the `SecureFTP.cs` file, at the top of the source code, replace all existing namespace references with the following ones:

```
using System;
using Microsoft.SqlServer.Dts.Runtime;
using WinSCP;
```

16. The `SecureFTP` class must be derived from `Microsoft.SqlServer.Dts.Runtime.Task` base class, and it must also implement the `DtsTaskAttribute`:

```
[DtsTaskAttribute
    (
    Description = "Perform FTP operations securely, by using SSH.",
    DisplayName = "Secure FTP Task"
    )]
public class SecureFTP : Task
{
    ...
}
```

The `Microsoft.SqlServer.Dts.Runtime.Task` base class provides the functionalities necessary in any SSIS control flow task, and the `DtsTaskAttribute` allows you to configure some principal properties of the custom task. Together they allow the class in the assembly to be recognized as an SSIS Task, which in turn allows it to be used in an SSIS package.

17. Add the following private constants to the `SecureFTP` class:

```
private const String TASK_NAME = "Secure FTP Task";
private const String FtpProtocolName_MISSING_MESAGE =
"FtpProtocolName has not been set.";
private const String FtpHostName_MISSING_MESAGE = "FtpHostName has
not been set.";
private const String FtpUserName_MISSING_MESAGE = "FtpUserName has
not been set.";
private const String FtpPassword_MISSING_MESAGE = "FtpPassword has
not been set.";
private const String FtpSshHostKeyFingerprint_MISSING_MESAGE =
"FtpSshHostKeyFingerprint has not been set.";
private const String FtpOperationName_MISSING_MESAGE =
"FtpOperationName has not been set.";
private const String FtpLocalPath_MISSING_MESAGE = "FtpLocalPath
has not been set.";
private const String FtpRemotePath_MISSING_MESAGE = "FtpRemotePath
```

```
has not been set.";
private const String REMOVE_ENABLED_MESSAGE = "FtpRemove is set to
TRUE, which means that the file is going to be removed from the
source.";
private const String SESSION_OPEN_MESSAGE = "Session opened
succesfully.";
private const String REMOTE_DIRECTORY_MISSING_MESSAGE_PATTERN =
"The specified remote [{0}] directory is missing.\r\nIt will be
created.";
private const String REMOTE_DIRECTORY_CREATED_MESSAGE_PATTERN =
"The specified remote [{0}] directory has been created.";
private const String REMOTE_FILES_MISSING_MESSAGE_PATTERN = "The
specified remote file(s) [{0}] cannot be found.";
private const String EXCEPTION_MESSAGE_PATTERN = "An error has
occurred:\r\n\r\n{0}";
private const String UNKNOWN_EXCEPTION_MESSAGE = "(No other
information available.)";
```

These constants are going to be used by the custom task's methods to convey information about the state of the task to the SSIS package developers when configuring the task.

18. Create the following public members of the `SecureFTP` class:

```
public String FtpProtocolName { get; set; }
public String FtpHostName { get; set; }
public Int32 FtpPortNumber { get; set; }
public String FtpUserName { get; set; }
public String FtpPassword { get; set; }
public String FtpSshHostKeyFingerprint { get; set; }
public String FtpOperationName { get; set; }
public String FtpLocalPath { get; set; }
public String FtpRemotePath { get; set; }
public Boolean FtpRemove { get; set; }
```

These public members of the `SecureFTP` class will be accessible in the SSDT as task properties, and will allow the SSIS package developers to configure the custom task; in SSDT, the values can be supplied as literal values or by using expressions.

19. Add the following enumeration to the class definition:

```
public enum OperationMode
{
    GetFiles,
    PutFiles
}
```

This enumeration lists the supported modes of operation of the **Secure FTP Task**; two of them are implemented using the code in this recipe: `GetFiles` receives the files from and `PutFiles` sends the files to the specified FTP site. Of course, the enumeration itself does not contain the complete programmatic logic needed to perform these operations.

You can extend the range by implementing additional functions available in the WinSCP library. You can find more information about the library at `https://winscp.net/eng/docs/start`.

20. Add the following private function to the `SecureFTP` class:

```
private Session EstablishSession()
{
    Session winScpSession = new Session();

    Protocol ftpProtocol = (Protocol)Enum.Parse(typeof(Protocol),
this.FtpProtocolName);

    SessionOptions winScpSessionOptions = new SessionOptions
    {
        Protocol = ftpProtocol,
        HostName = this.FtpHostName,
        PortNumber = this.FtpPortNumber,
        UserName = this.FtpUserName,
        Password = this.FtpPassword,
        SshHostKeyFingerprint = this.FtpSshHostKeyFingerprint
    };

    winScpSession.Open(winScpSessionOptions);

    return winScpSession;
}
```

This function creates an instance of the `WinSCP Session` class; it connects to the FTP server, establishes the appropriate security context, and allows the operations to be performed against the remote site.

21. Add another private function to the `SecureFTP` class:

```
private DTSExecResult ValidateProperties(ref IDTSComponentEvents
componentEvents)
{
    DTSExecResult result = DTSExecResult.Success;
```

```
    if (String.IsNullOrEmpty(this.FtpProtocolName))
    {
        componentEvents.FireError(0, TASK_NAME,
FtpProtocolName_MISSING_MESAGE, String.Empty, 0);
        result = DTSExecResult.Failure;
    }

    if (String.IsNullOrEmpty(this.FtpHostName))
    {
        componentEvents.FireError(0, TASK_NAME,
FtpHostName_MISSING_MESAGE, String.Empty, 0);
        result = DTSExecResult.Failure;
    }

    if (String.IsNullOrEmpty(this.FtpUserName))
    {
        componentEvents.FireError(0, TASK_NAME,
FtpUserName_MISSING_MESAGE, String.Empty, 0);
        result = DTSExecResult.Failure;
    }

    if (String.IsNullOrEmpty(this.FtpPassword))
    {
        componentEvents.FireError(0, TASK_NAME,
FtpPassword_MISSING_MESAGE, String.Empty, 0);
        result = DTSExecResult.Failure;
    }

    if (String.IsNullOrEmpty(this.FtpSshHostKeyFingerprint))
    {
        componentEvents.FireError(0, TASK_NAME,
FtpSshHostKeyFingerprint_MISSING_MESAGE, String.Empty, 0);
        result = DTSExecResult.Failure;
    }

    if (String.IsNullOrEmpty(this.FtpOperationName))
    {
        componentEvents.FireError(0, TASK_NAME,
FtpOperationName_MISSING_MESAGE, String.Empty, 0);
        result = DTSExecResult.Failure;
    }

    if (String.IsNullOrEmpty(this.FtpLocalPath))
    {
        componentEvents.FireError(0, TASK_NAME,
FtpLocalPath_MISSING_MESAGE, String.Empty, 0);
        result = DTSExecResult.Failure;
    }
```

```
        if (String.IsNullOrEmpty(this.FtpRemotePath))
        {
            componentEvents.FireError(0, TASK_NAME,
FtpRemotePath_MISSING_MESAGE, String.Empty, 0);
            result = DTSExecResult.Failure;
        }

        return result;
}
```

This function extends the `Validate()` method of the `Task` base class by encapsulating additional validation rules that need to be performed on the string properties of this particular task. The function reports any string properties that do not have their values set, through SSIS events.

22. Below the `SecureFTP` class public member declarations, create some space, and start typing the `override` directive; Visual Studio Intellisense should list the `Task` base class methods that you can override; select the `Validate()` method.

23. Replace the default definition of the newly overridden method with the following code:

```
Boolean fireAgain = false;

try
{
    // Validate mandatory String properties.
    DTSExecResult propertyValidationResult =
this.ValidateProperties(ref componentEvents);
    if (propertyValidationResult != DTSExecResult.Success)
    {
        return propertyValidationResult;
    }

    // The package developer should know that files will be removed
from the source.
    if (this.FtpRemove)
    {
        componentEvents.FireInformation(0, TASK_NAME,
REMOVE_ENABLED_MESSAGE, String.Empty, 0, ref fireAgain);
    }

    // Verify the connection.
    using (Session winScpSession = this.EstablishSession())
    {
        componentEvents.FireInformation(0, TASK_NAME,
SESSION_OPEN_MESSAGE, String.Empty, 0, ref fireAgain);
```

```csharp
            // Verify the remote resources.
            OperationMode operation =
(OperationMode)Enum.Parse(typeof(OperationMode),
this.FtpOperationName);
            switch (operation)
            {
                case OperationMode.PutFiles:
                    Boolean remoteDirectoryExists =
winScpSession.FileExists(this.FtpRemotePath);
                    if (!remoteDirectoryExists)
                    {
                        componentEvents.FireInformation(0, TASK_NAME,
String.Format(REMOTE_DIRECTORY_MISSING_MESSAGE_PATTERN,
this.FtpRemotePath), String.Empty, 0, ref fireAgain);
                    }
                    break;
                case OperationMode.GetFiles:
                default:
                    Boolean remoteFileExists =
winScpSession.FileExists(this.FtpRemotePath);
                    if (!remoteFileExists)
                    {
                        componentEvents.FireInformation(0, TASK_NAME,
String.Format(REMOTE_FILES_MISSING_MESSAGE_PATTERN,
this.FtpRemotePath), String.Empty, 0, ref fireAgain);
                    }
                    break;
            }
        }

    return DTSExecResult.Success;
}
catch (Exception exc)
{
    String exceptionMessage = exc != null ? exc.Message :
UNKNOWN_EXCEPTION_MESSAGE;
    componentEvents.FireError(0, TASK_NAME,
String.Format(EXCEPTION_MESSAGE_PATTERN, exceptionMessage),
String.Empty, 0);
    return DTSExecResult.Failure;
}
```

The `Validate()` method is going to be used whenever the SSIS package, in which the task is used, is validated or executed, and will report any incorrect or missing settings, as well as notify the caller of any exceptions returned by the `WinSCP` library. This method also invokes the `ValidateProperties()` method created in step 21.

24. Make some more room below the `Validate()` method definition, and start typing the `override` directive again; this time select the `Execute()` method to override, and replace its default definition with the following code:

```
Boolean fireAgain = false;

try
{
    // Create a new FTP session.
    using (Session winScpSession = this.EstablishSession())
    {
        componentEvents.FireInformation(0, TASK_NAME,
SESSION_OPEN_MESSAGE, String.Empty, 0, ref fireAgain);

        // Determine the operation mode.
        OperationMode operation =
(OperationMode)Enum.Parse(typeof(OperationMode),
this.FtpOperationName);
        switch (operation)
        {
            case OperationMode.PutFiles:
                // When uploading files, make sure that the
destination directory exists.
                Boolean remoteDirectoryExists =
winScpSession.FileExists(this.FtpRemotePath);
                if (!remoteDirectoryExists)
                {
winScpSession.CreateDirectory(this.FtpRemotePath);
                    componentEvents.FireInformation(0, TASK_NAME,
String.Format(REMOTE_DIRECTORY_CREATED_MESSAGE_PATTERN,
this.FtpRemotePath), String.Empty, 0, ref fireAgain);
                }
                winScpSession.PutFiles(this.FtpLocalPath,
this.FtpRemotePath, this.FtpRemove);
                break;
            case OperationMode.GetFiles:
            default:
                winScpSession.GetFiles(this.FtpRemotePath,
this.FtpLocalPath, this.FtpRemove);
                break;
        }

        return DTSExecResult.Success;
    }
}
catch (Exception exc)
{
```

```
    String exceptionMessage = exc == null ?
UNKNOWN_EXCEPTION_MESSAGE : exc.Message;
    componentEvents.FireError(0, TASK_NAME,
String.Format(EXCEPTION_MESSAGE_PATTERN, exceptionMessage),
String.Empty, 0);
    return DTSExecResult.Failure;
}
```

25. Save the class file and build the SSISCustomTasks project. If you followed the preceding instructions correctly, the build should succeed. If the build fails, inspect the **Error List** pane, and check whether any errors have occurred. Investigate each error and resolve it accordingly.

26. In the Visual Studio toolbar, select **Release** in the **Solution Configuration** selection box, as shown in the following screenshot:

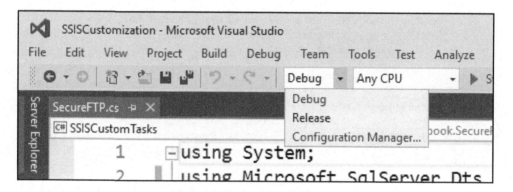

27. Build the SSISCustomTasks project again. The files are now created in the release folder and are ready to be deployed.

28. Use Window Explorer to locate the Chapter10_Deploy_CustomTask.bat command file in the C:\SSIS2016Cookbook\Chapter10\Starter\ folder.

29. Run the command file as the administrator. This will copy the custom task assembly to the appropriate folders, and register the assemblies in the Windows GAC, SSDT (at design time), and the SSIS runtime (at runtime), and it needs the relevant assemblies to be registered in GAC.

30. In SSDT, open the AdventureWorksETL.sln solution, located in the C:\SSIS2016Cookbook\Chapter10\Starter\AdventureWorksETL\ folder.

31. Open the `SecureFtpTask.dtsx` SSIS package in the control flow designer.

32. Inspect the package properties and the variables; this package contains most information needed to configure the **Secure FTP Task** that you created earlier in this recipe.

33. Make sure that the control flow designer is active, and inspect the **SSIS Toolbox**. The **Secure FTP Task** should be listed in the **Common** section. If the task is missing, right-click the **SSIS Toolbox**, and select **Refresh Toolbox** from the shortcut menu. If that doesn't help, close SSDT and open the solution again. If not even that helped, close SSDT, and repeat steps 26 to 33.

34. From the **SSIS Toolbox**, drag the **Secure FTP Task** to the control flow designer, and change its name to **Download Files**.

35. Double-click the task to open its editor; the following warning should pop up:

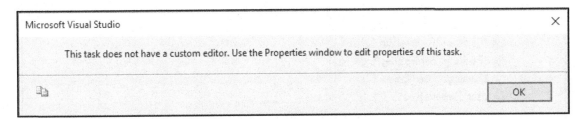

You did not design a custom editor for your custom task; therefore, in order to use the task, you need to configure its properties in the **Properties** pane.

36. While the **Secure FTP Task** is selected in the control flow, inspect its properties in the **Properties** pane. In addition to the base task properties, all of the public members of the `SecureFTP` class that you created in step 18 should be listed in the **Misc** section.

37. Locate the **Expressions** collection, click its text box, and then click the ellipsis icon on the far-right side to start the **Property Expression Editor**.

38. In the **Property Expression Editor**, in the **Property** column select the `FtpHostName` property.

39. Click the ellipsis icon on the far right in the same row to open the **Expression Builder** dialog.

40. In the **Expression Builder**, drag the `$Package::HostName` parameter to the **Expression** text box, and then click **Evaluate** to validate the expression, as shown in the following screenshot:

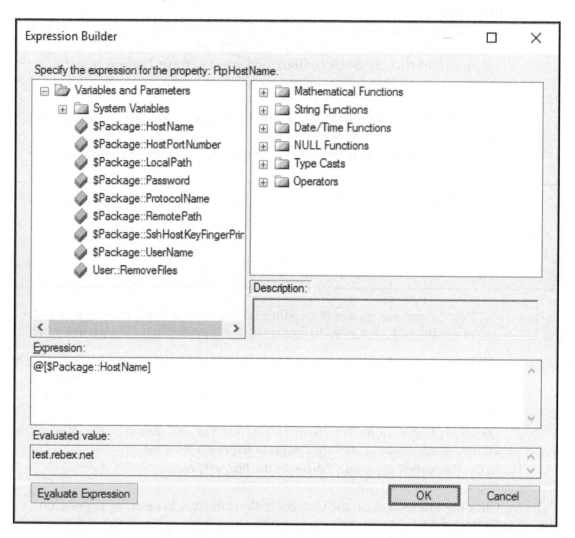

41. Click **OK** to confirm the expression.

42. Repeat steps 38 through 41 for the rest of the properties; use the following settings:

Property	Parameter or variable
FtpLocalPath	$Package::LocalPath
FtpPassword	$Package::Password
FtpPortNumber	$Package::HostPortNumber
FtpProtocolName	$Package::ProtocolName
FtpRemotePath	$Package::RemotePath
FtpRemove	User::RemoveFiles
FtpSshHostKeyFingerprint	$Package::SshHostKeyFingerprint
FtpUserName	$Package::UserName

Use the following screenshot to verify your settings:

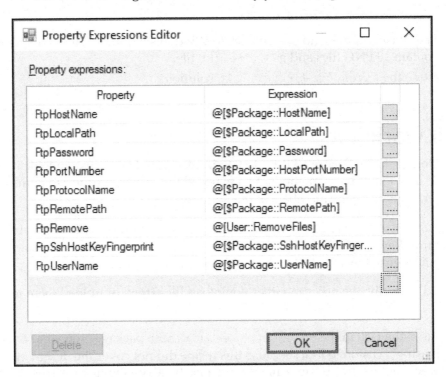

43. Click **OK** to confirm the property expressions.

44. In the **Secure FTP TaskProperties** pane, locate the **FtpOperationName** property and set its value to `GetFiles` (without the quotation marks).

45. Save the package.

46. Use Windows Explorer to navigate to the `C:\SSIS2016Cookbook\Chapter10\Files` folder; the folder should not contain any files.

47. In SSDT, execute the `SecureFtpTask.dtsx` SSIS package in debug mode. Observe its execution, and inspect the messages in the **Progress** pane.

> The public FTP site used in this example is hosted on `test.rebex.net`; the site exposes one folder with read-only permissions for the purposes of FTP testing. Several file transfer protocols are supported, and a few files are available in the folder for testing purposes.
> As file access is restricted to read-only, the site cannot be used to upload files. Therefore, in order to test the `PutFiles` operation mode, you need to connect to another site - for instance, create your own FTP server.
> You can find additional information on the Rebex company website, at `http://www.rebex.net/`.

48. Stop the execution and switch back to Windows Explorer. The folder should now contain 18 PNG files and a `Readme.txt` file.

49. Close the `AdventureWorksETL.sln` solution.

How it works...

In your custom task, the **Secure FTP Task**, you implemented your custom logic in the `Validate()` and `Execute()` methods. You exposed the settings needed to perform the file transfer operations as public members of the `SecureFTP` class.

The `Microsoft.SqlServer.Dts.Runtime.Task` base class allows the task to be used in an SSIS control flow, its public properties are accessible from SSDT, and the custom programmatic logic allows the task to be validated and executed.

If configured correctly, the task can either download files from, or upload them to, an FTP site.

When you used the task in the `SecureFtpTask.dtsx` SSIS package, you were not able to configure it using a custom editor, because this recipe did not cover the design of such an editor. However, you were able to configure the task by accessing its properties directly.

All of the properties were passed into the task using property expressions, except for the `FtpOperationName` property, for which you used a literal value.

When you executed the package, the **Secure FTP Task** connected to the remote server, traversed the files in the remote folder, and downloaded them to the local folder.

Designing a custom transformation

To design a Custom Data Flow Component, you need to create a .NET assembly based on the Class Library Visual Studio template; the class with the component's definition must be derived from the `PipelineComponent` base class of the `Microsoft.SqlServer.Dts.Pipeline` namespace. The class also needs to implement the `DtsPipelineComponentAttribute` that allows the class to be identified as an SSIS component and to provide the essential properties of the component used in the development of SSIS data flows.

If you want to simplify the configuration of the component, you can provide a custom graphical user interface; otherwise, the **Advanced Transformation Editor** will be used to configure the component during SSIS package development.

The component also needs access to the interfaces and classes of the `Microsoft.SqlServer.Dts.Pipeline.Wrapper` namespace. Depending on the functionalities provided by the component, additional references might be needed to the `Microsoft.SqlServer.Dts.Runtime` and `Microsoft.SqlServer.Dts.Runtime.Wrapper` namespaces.

The custom component, be it a source, a destination, or a transformation, must implement two sets of methods of the base class:

- **Design time** methods are used, as the name suggests, at design time; they are called during SSIS package development when the custom component is implemented in the data flow. These methods provide a way for the SSIS package developer to correctly configure the component. They also provide a way for the developer of the component to communicate with the package developers, making sure that they understand how the component is to be used, and to configure it correctly.
- **Run time** methods are used by the execution engine at run time, when the SSIS packages are being executed. These methods provide the programmatic logic needed to perform the operations against the data flow pipeline.

The following design time methods must be provided in order for the custom component to be available and configurable in an SSIS package:

- The `ProvideComponentPorperties()` method is invoked when the component is dropped into the data flow designer. In this method, you provide the configuration of the component's inputs and/or outputs, its custom properties, and any other settings that must be set for the component to be ready for design time configuration.
- The `Validate()` method is used to validate the component and its settings; it is invoked every time the SSIS package developer confirms (or attempts to confirm) the settings during data flow development. Therefore, this method also provides a way for you, the component developer, to communicate with the package developers and to help them configure the component correctly. Use the `FireError()`, `FireWarning()`, and `FireInformation()` methods to notify the package developer of any missing or incorrect settings by using the appropriate error messages or warnings.
- The `ReinitializeMetaData()` method is invoked when, based on the result of the validation, the component's metadata needs to be reset and reinitialized.

The following run time methods are used to provide the principal programmatic logic of the custom component:

- The `PrepareForExecute()` method is used to determine the values of any settings that need to be set before the rows are received from any upstream components, and for any processing that needs, and can be, performed before the rows have been placed into the pipeline. When this method is executed, no additional connections are available yet.
- The `AcquireConnections()` and `ReleaseConnections()` methods are used to manage connections to any additional data sources that are needed in the component and are not provided by any of the component's inputs. Use the former to establish connections to external data sources, and the latter to release them. `AcquireConnections()` is invoked during validation, and again at the beginning of the execution, whereas `ReleaseConnections()` is invoked at the end of the validation, and again at the end of the execution.

- When the `PreExecute()` method is invoked, the rows are already available in the pipeline, and any external connections are also ready, which means that this method can be used to determine any settings that depend on the pipeline data, or the data from the external data sources. If the data acquired from any external sources can be cached (for instance, because its size allows it to be placed completely in memory), this method is also a good alternative to the `ReleaseConnections()` method when you need to close the external connections early to save on resources.

- The `PrimeOutput()` method is used in source components, and in transformations that use asynchronous outputs; it allows these outputs to start consuming data. If the component implements multiple outputs, the method must be capable of preparing each one of them - rows can only be placed into primed outputs. In a source component, this is the principal data processing method.

- The `ProcessInput()` method represents the principal data processing method in transformation and destination components; it is used to consume the data received from the upstream components.

- The rows in the current buffer need to be consumed in a `while` loop with the aid of the `NextRow()` method of the `PipelineBuffer` instance.

    In SSIS data flows, the data is placed into one or more buffers; therefore, the `ProcessInput()` method may be invoked multiple times. In addition, depending on the complexity of the data flow and the availability of resources, the SSIS execution engine can also parallelize the execution of data flow components.

    To make sure that all the upstream rows have been consumed, and to complete the processing of any asynchronous outputs correctly, you also need to check whether more buffers are available with the help of the `EndOfRows()` method of the `PipelineBuffer` instance. This check needs to be made after all the rows of the given buffer instance have been received.

    Synchronous outputs will be closed automatically after all input buffers have been consumed, but asynchronous outputs must be closed explicitly. When no more rows are to be placed into any asynchronous output, you must state this by invoking the `SetEndOfRowset()` method of the output `PipelineBuffer` instance.

    If the component uses multiple inputs, it must also be capable of processing each one of them.

- The `PostExecute()` and `Cleanup()` methods are invoked at the end of the data flow execution; the former is called as soon as all the pipeline data has been consumed, and the latter is invoked last. You should use them to assign values to any writable variables, and complete any unfinished operations.

- The `ReleaseConnections()` method is called after the `PostExecute()` method; therefore, in the `PostExecute()` method you might still have access to any external data sources that you haven't released up to this point in the execution.

- Use the `Cleanup()` method to release any remaining resources that were used in the data flow, in order to make a clean exit from the execution. This is also the last place where variable assignments can be made.

To deploy a custom component - either to the development workstation used in SSIS package development, or to the environment in which it is going to be used - the assemblies containing the component need to be copied to the following folders:

- `%ProgramFiles%\Microsoft SQL Server\130\DTS\PipelineComponents` - for the 64-bit edition of the assembly

- `%ProgramFiles(x86)%\Microsoft SQL Server\130\DTS\PipelineComponents` - for the 32-bit edition of the assembly

If the assembly is platform-independent, the file needs to be copied to both folders.

The assembly, and all of the assemblies it references, must also be registered in the GAC. To register the assemblies on the SSIS development workstation, you can use the `gacutil.exe` command-line utility (it is installed together with Visual Studio); however, on a production server `gacutil.exe` might not be available. You can also use an appropriate Windows PowerShell script to perform the registration.

In this recipe, you are going to port the logic from a script transformation that you developed in Chapter 7, *Unleash the Power of SSIS Script Tasks and Components*, into a custom transformation, deploy it to your development workstation, and use it in an SSIS package.

How to do it...

1. In Visual Studio 2015, open the `SSISCustomization.sln` solution that you created in the previous recipe, *Designing a custom task*; it should be located in the `C:\SSIS2016Cookbook\Chapter10\Starter\SSISCustomization\` folder. In case you have not followed the previous recipe, follow steps 1 through 3 to create the solution.

2. In the **Solution Explorer**, right-click the **Solution** node, and select **Add New Project...** from the shortcut menu to add a new project.

3. In the **Add New Project** dialog, select the **Class Library** template, located in the **Visual C#** template group; use `SSISCustomComponents` as the project name. Refer to the following screenshot to verify your settings:

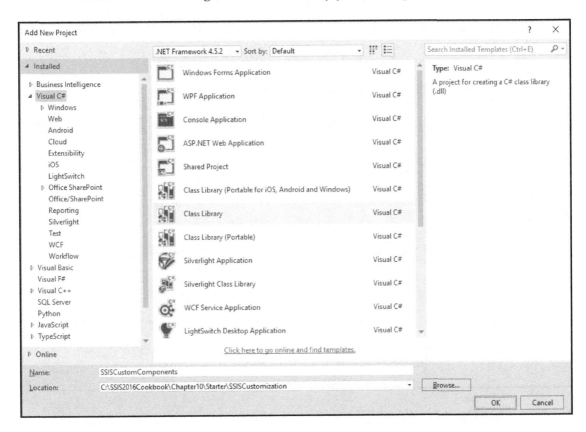

4. Click **OK** to confirm the configuration, and create the project.

5. In the **Solution Explorer**, right-click the newly created `SSISCustomComponents` project, and select **Properties** from the shortcut menu to open the `SSISCustomComponents` properties pane.

6. On the **Application** page, change the default namespace value to `SSIS2016Cookbook`.

7. On the **Signing** page, check **Sign the assembly**, and select **<Browse...>** in the **Choose a strong name key file** selection box.

8. In the **Select File** dialog, navigate to the `C:\SSIS2016Cookbook\Chapter10\Scripts` folder, and select the `SSIS2016Cookbook.snk` strong name key file, as shown in the following screenshot:

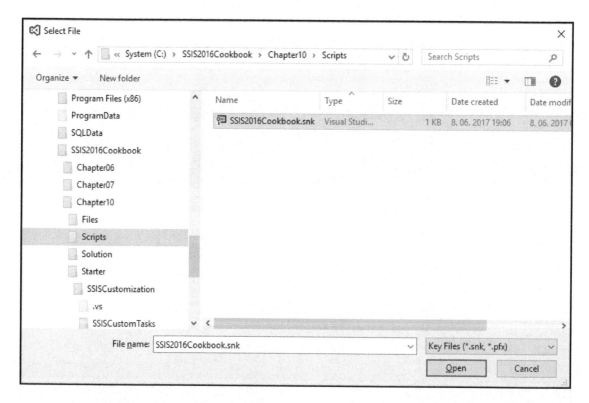

9. Click **Open** to confirm the selection.

10. Save the solution, and then close the project properties pane.

11. In the `Class1.cs` designer pane, change the namespace of the class to `SSIS2016Cookbook`, and change the `Class1` name to `ValidateEmail`.

12. In the **Solution Explorer**, change the `Class1.cs` file name to `ValidateEmail.cs`, and then save the solution.

13. In the **Solution Explorer**, right-click **References**, and then select **Add Reference...** from the shortcut menu to open the **Reference Manager** dialog.

14. Under **Assemblies | Extensions**, check the
    `Microsoft.SqlServer.PipelineHost,`
    `Microsoft.SqlServer.DTSPipelineWrap, and`
    `Microsoft.SQLServer.DTSRuntimeWrap` assemblies, as shown in the following screenshot:

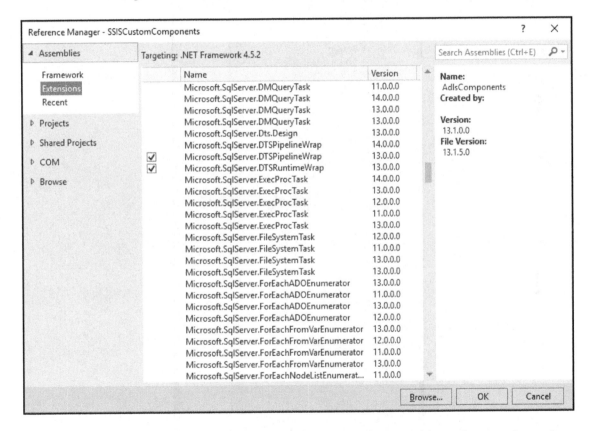

If multiple versions of the same assembly are available, make sure that only version **13.0.0.0** is checked.

15. Click **OK** to confirm the selection.

16. In the **Solution Explorer**, make sure that the **References** node is expanded.

17. Select the **Microsoft.SqlServer.DTSPipelineWrap** node, locate the Embed Interop Types setting in the assembly's properties, and make sure it is set to **False**, as shown in the following screenshot:

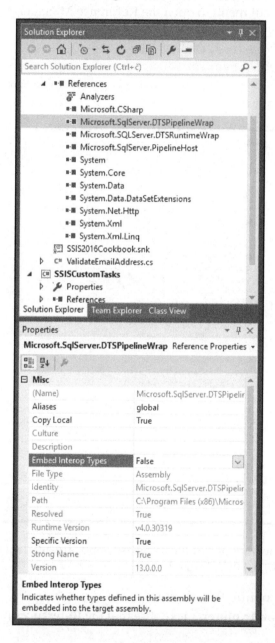

18. Do the same for the `Microsoft.SQLServer.DTSRuntimeWrap` assembly.

19. Save the project.

20. Make sure that `ValidateEmail.cs` is open in the designer, and replace the existing list of assembly references at the top of the definition with the following references:

```
using Microsoft.SqlServer.Dts.Pipeline;
using Microsoft.SqlServer.Dts.Pipeline.Wrapper;
using Microsoft.SqlServer.Dts.Runtime.Wrapper;
using System;
using System.Collections.Generic;
using System.IO;
using System.Linq;
using System.Text;
using System.Text.RegularExpressions;
using System.Xml;
```

The references provide the functionalities needed to develop a complete SSIS component, and to perform its operations.

21. Modify the `ValidateEmail` class definition so that it is derived from the `Microsoft.SqlServer.Dts.Pipeline.PipelineComponent` base class, and implement the `DtsPipelineComponent` attribute:

```
[DtsPipelineComponent
    (
    ComponentType = ComponentType.Transform,
    DisplayName = "Validate Email",
    Description = "Validates email addresses using the
corresponding rule in a data profile file.",
    NoEditor = false
    )]
public class ValidateEmail : PipelineComponent
{
}
```

The base class provides the design-time and run-time functionalities that every SSIS component needs to implement, and the `DtsPipelineComponent` attribute allows the class to be recognized as an SSIS component - at design time as well as run time.

22. Add the following private constant declarations to the `ValidateEmail` class definition:

```
private const String DATA_PROFILE_FILE_NAME_PROPERTY_NAME = "Data
Profile File Name";
private const String DATA_PROFILE_FILE_NAME_PROPERTY_DESCRIPTION =
"Data profile file name (fully qualified).";
private const String DATA_PROFILE_COLUMN_NAME_PROPERTY_NAME = "Data
Profile Column Name";
private const String DATA_PROFILE_COLUMN_NAME_PROPERTY_DESCRIPTION
= "The name of the columns in the data profile.";
private const String INPUT_NAME = "ValidateEmailInput";
private const String INPUT_COLUMN_NAME = "Input Column Name";
private const String INPUT_COLUMN_DESCRIPTION = "The name of the
column to be validated.";
private const String OUTPUT_NAME = "ValidateEmailOutput";
private const String IS_VALID_COLUMN_NAME = "IsValidEmail";
private const String IS_VALID_COLUMN_DESCRIPTION = "True, if the
value of the selected column is a valid email address; otherwise,
False.";
private const String IS_INTERNAL_OBJECT_PROPERTY_NAME =
"isInternal";

private const String TOO_MANY_INPUTS_MESSAGE = "Only a single input
is supported.";
private const String TOO_MANY_OUTPUTS_MESSAGE = "Only a single
output is supported.";
private const String DEFAULT_OUTPUT_MUST_EXIST_MESSAGE = "The
built-in synchronous output cannot be removed.";
private const String USER_DEFINED_COLUMNS_NOT_SUPPORTED = "User-
defined columns are not supported.";
private const String DEFAULT_COLUMNS_MUST_EXIST = "Built-in output
columns cannot be removed";
private const String DATA_PROFILE_FILE_NOT_FOUND_MESSAGE_PATTERN =
"The file [{0}] could not be located.";
private const String DATA_PROFILE_FILE_FOUND_MESSAGE_PATTERN = "The
file [{0}] exists.";
private const String REGEX_PATTERNS_LOADED_MESSAGE_PATTERN = "{0}
Regular Expression patterns loaded.";
private const String DATA_PROFILE_COLUMN_NOT_FOUND_MESSAGE_PATTERN
= "The file [{0}] does not contain a column named [{1}].";
private const String REGEX_PATTERNS_NOT_FOUND_MESSAGE_PATTERN =
"The file [{0}] does not contain any Regular Expressions patterns
data for a column named [{1}].";
private const String INPUT_COLUMN_NOT_SET_MESSAGE = "The input
column has not been set.";
private const String INPUT_COLUMN_NOT_FOUND_MESSAGE_PATTERN = "An
input column named [{0}] cannot be found.";
```

```
private const String INPUT_COLUMN_FOUND_MESSAGE_PATTERN = "The
input column named [{0}] was found.";
private const String
INPUT_COLUMN_DATATYPE_NOT_SUPPORTED_MESSAGE_PATTERN = "The data
type [{0}] of the selected input column [{1}] is not
supported.\r\nPlease, use a column with a supported data type:
DT_NTEXT, DT_TEXT, DT_STR, or DT_WSTR.";

private const String DATA_PROFILE_NAMESPACE =
"http://schemas.microsoft.com/sqlserver/2008/DataDebugger/";
private const String DATA_PROFILE_NAMESPACE_ALIAS = "dp";

private const String DATA_PROFILE_COLUMN_XPATH_PATTERN
    = "/dp:DataProfile/dp:DataProfileOutput/dp:Profiles" +
    "/dp:ColumnPatternProfile[dp:Column[@Name='{0}']]";

private const String REGEX_ELEMENT_XPATH_PATTERN
    = DATA_PROFILE_COLUMN_XPATH_PATTERN +
"/dp:TopRegexPatterns/dp:PatternDistributionItem/dp:RegexText/text(
)";
```

Object names and descriptions are defined in these constants, as well as all the messages used in communicating the current state of the component to the SSIS package developers.

23. Add the following private variables to the `ValidateEmail` class:

```
private String _dataProfileFileName;
private String _dataProfileColumnName;
private String _emailAddressInputColumnName;
private List<String> _regexPatterns = new List<String>();
```

These variables allow the principal settings of the component to be set once, and reused as many times as needed during validation and execution.

24. At the bottom of the `ValidateEmail` class definition, add the following private functions:

```
private Boolean DataProfileColumnExists(String dataProfileName,
String columnName)
{
    Boolean result = true;

    XmlDocument dataProfile = new XmlDocument();
    dataProfile.Load(dataProfileName);
    XmlNamespaceManager dataProfileNSM = new
XmlNamespaceManager(dataProfile.NameTable);
```

```
    dataProfileNSM.AddNamespace(DATA_PROFILE_NAMESPACE_ALIAS,
DATA_PROFILE_NAMESPACE);

    String regexElementXPath =
String.Format(DATA_PROFILE_COLUMN_XPATH_PATTERN, columnName);
    XmlNode dataProfileColumn =
dataProfile.SelectSingleNode(regexElementXPath, dataProfileNSM);
    if (dataProfileColumn == null)
    {
        result = false;
    }

    return result;
}
```

25. This function checks whether the data profile file contains the profile information about the specified column:

```
private List<String> LoadRegularExpressions(String dataProfileName,
String columnName)
{
    List<String> result = new List<String>();

    if (!String.IsNullOrEmpty(dataProfileName) &&
        !String.IsNullOrEmpty(columnName))
    {
        XmlDocument dataProfile = new XmlDocument();
        dataProfile.Load(dataProfileName);
        XmlNamespaceManager dataProfileNSM = new
XmlNamespaceManager(dataProfile.NameTable);
        dataProfileNSM.AddNamespace(DATA_PROFILE_NAMESPACE_ALIAS,
DATA_PROFILE_NAMESPACE);

        String regexElementXPath =
String.Format(REGEX_ELEMENT_XPATH_PATTERN, columnName);
        foreach (XmlNode regexPatternElement in
dataProfile.SelectNodes(regexElementXPath, dataProfileNSM))
        {
            String regexPattern = regexPatternElement.Value;
            if (!result.Contains(regexPattern))
            {
                result.Add(regexPattern);
            }
        }
    }

    return result;
}
```

26. This function extracts the regular expressions patterns for the specified column from the data profile file that can be used to validate the column values:

```
private void ResolveComponentCustomProperties()
{
    _dataProfileFileName =
ComponentMetaData.CustomPropertyCollection[DATA_PROFILE_FILE_NAME_P
ROPERTY_NAME].Value.ToString();
    if (VariableDispenser.Contains(_dataProfileFileName))
    {
        IDTSVariables100 variables = null;
        VariableDispenser.LockOneForRead(_dataProfileFileName, ref
variables);
        _dataProfileFileName = (String)variables[0].Value;
    }

    _dataProfileColumnName =
ComponentMetaData.CustomPropertyCollection[DATA_PROFILE_COLUMN_NAME
_PROPERTY_NAME].Value.ToString();
    if (VariableDispenser.Contains(_dataProfileColumnName))
    {
        IDTSVariables100 variables = null;
        VariableDispenser.LockOneForRead(_dataProfileColumnName,
ref variables);
        _dataProfileColumnName = (String)variables[0].Value;
    }

    _regexPatterns.Clear();
    _regexPatterns =
this.LoadRegularExpressions(_dataProfileFileName,
_dataProfileColumnName);

    _emailAddressInputColumnName =
ComponentMetaData.InputCollection[INPUT_NAME].CustomPropertyCollect
ion[INPUT_COLUMN_NAME].Value.ToString();
}
```

This last private function reads the component properties configured by the SSIS package developer, and stores them in private variables for later use. The function is invoked at package validation and at execution.

Observe the _dataProfileFileName and
_dataProfileColumnName variable assignments; if the custom
property contains the name of a variable or a parameter, the
actual value is retrieved from the corresponding variable or
parameter; otherwise, the literal value is used.

27. Immediately before the functions you just added, add the following private
function that is going to be used to validate the email addresses:

```
private Boolean IsValidEmail(String emailAddress)
{
    Boolean result = false;

    if (!String.IsNullOrEmpty(emailAddress))
    {
        foreach (String regexPattern in _regexPatterns)
        {
            if (Regex.IsMatch(emailAddress, regexPattern,
RegexOptions.IgnoreCase))
            {
                result = true;
                break;
            }
        }
    }

    return result;
}
```

The IsValidEmail() function in this component is the same as the one used
in the *Validating data using regular expressions in a script component* recipe
presented in Chapter 7, *Unleash the Power of SSIS Script Tasks and Components*.
Compared to the rest of the code of the ValidateEmail class, it might
appear insignificant; a lot of programmatic logic is needed to make custom
components behave correctly at design and at runtime.

28. Make some space just below the private variable declarations and start typing the
override directive; from the list of suggested
Microsoft.SqlServer.Dts.Pipeline.PipelineComponent base class
overridable methods, select ProvideComponentProperties() and replace its
default definition with the following code:

```
base.ProvideComponentProperties();

// Data Profile File name
```

```
IDTSCustomProperty100 dataProfileFileName =
ComponentMetaData.CustomPropertyCollection.New();
dataProfileFileName.Name = DATA_PROFILE_FILE_NAME_PROPERTY_NAME;
dataProfileFileName.Description =
DATA_PROFILE_FILE_NAME_PROPERTY_DESCRIPTION;
dataProfileFileName.State = DTSPersistState.PS_PERSISTASCDATA;
dataProfileFileName.TypeConverter =
typeof(String).AssemblyQualifiedName;
dataProfileFileName.Value = String.Empty;

// Data Profile Column name
IDTSCustomProperty100 dataProfileColumnName =
ComponentMetaData.CustomPropertyCollection.New();
dataProfileColumnName.Name =
DATA_PROFILE_COLUMN_NAME_PROPERTY_NAME;
dataProfileColumnName.Description =
DATA_PROFILE_COLUMN_NAME_PROPERTY_DESCRIPTION;
dataProfileColumnName.State = DTSPersistState.PS_DEFAULT;
dataProfileColumnName.TypeConverter =
typeof(String).AssemblyQualifiedName;
dataProfileColumnName.Value = String.Empty;

// Input
IDTSInput100 input = ComponentMetaData.InputCollection[0];
input.Name = INPUT_NAME;
// Input Column Name
IDTSCustomProperty100 inputColumnName =
input.CustomPropertyCollection.New();
inputColumnName.Name = INPUT_COLUMN_NAME;
inputColumnName.Description = INPUT_COLUMN_DESCRIPTION;
inputColumnName.State = DTSPersistState.PS_DEFAULT;
inputColumnName.TypeConverter =
typeof(String).AssemblyQualifiedName;
inputColumnName.Value = String.Empty;

IDTSCustomProperty100 isInternal;
// Synchronous Output
IDTSOutput100 output = ComponentMetaData.OutputCollection[0];
output.Name = OUTPUT_NAME;
output.SynchronousInputID =
ComponentMetaData.InputCollection[0].ID;
isInternal = output.CustomPropertyCollection.New();
isInternal.Name = IS_INTERNAL_OBJECT_PROPERTY_NAME;
isInternal.State = DTSPersistState.PS_DEFAULT;
isInternal.TypeConverter = typeof(Boolean).AssemblyQualifiedName;
isInternal.Value = true;
// Output column
IDTSOutputColumn100 isVaildEmailColumn =
```

```
output.OutputColumnCollection.New();
isVaildEmailColumn.Name = IS_VALID_COLUMN_NAME;
isVaildEmailColumn.Description = IS_VALID_COLUMN_DESCRIPTION;
isVaildEmailColumn.SetDataTypeProperties(DataType.DT_BOOL, 0, 0, 0,
0);
isInternal = isVaildEmailColumn.CustomPropertyCollection.New();
isInternal.Name = IS_INTERNAL_OBJECT_PROPERTY_NAME;
isInternal.State = DTSPersistState.PS_DEFAULT;
isInternal.TypeConverter = typeof(Boolean).AssemblyQualifiedName;
isInternal.Value = true;
```

The component is defined by the `ProvideComponentProperties()` method—its custom properties, its inputs, and outputs. This method is invoked when the component is placed in the data flow designer during SSIS package development.

29. Below the `ProvideComponentProperties()` method definition you just created, create some more space, and start typing the `override` directive again; this time select the `Validate()` method to override, and replace its default definition with the following commands:

```
Boolean isCanceled = false;
Boolean fireAgain = false;

// Only one input is supported.
if (ComponentMetaData.InputCollection.Count > 1)
{
    ComponentMetaData.FireError(0, ComponentMetaData.Name,
TOO_MANY_INPUTS_MESSAGE, String.Empty, 0, out isCanceled);
    return DTSValidationStatus.VS_ISCORRUPT;
}

// Only one output is supported.
if (ComponentMetaData.OutputCollection.Count > 1)
{
    ComponentMetaData.FireError(0, ComponentMetaData.Name,
TOO_MANY_OUTPUTS_MESSAGE, String.Empty, 0, out isCanceled);
    return DTSValidationStatus.VS_ISCORRUPT;
}

this.ResolveComponentCustomProperties();

// Data profile file must exist.
if (!File.Exists(_dataProfileFileName))
{
    ComponentMetaData.FireError(0, ComponentMetaData.Name,
String.Format(DATA_PROFILE_FILE_NOT_FOUND_MESSAGE_PATTERN,
```

```
_dataProfileFileName), String.Empty, 0, out isCanceled);
    return DTSValidationStatus.VS_ISBROKEN;
}
else
{
    ComponentMetaData.FireInformation(0, ComponentMetaData.Name,
String.Format(DATA_PROFILE_FILE_FOUND_MESSAGE_PATTERN,
_dataProfileFileName), String.Empty, 0, ref fireAgain);

    // Data profile file must contain at least one Regular
Expressions pattern for the specified column name.
    Int32 regexPatternCount = _regexPatterns.Count();
    if (regexPatternCount > 0)
    {
        ComponentMetaData.FireInformation(0,
ComponentMetaData.Name,
String.Format(REGEX_PATTERNS_LOADED_MESSAGE_PATTERN,
regexPatternCount), String.Empty, 0, ref fireAgain);
    }
    else
    {
        if (!this.DataProfileColumnExists(_dataProfileFileName,
_dataProfileColumnName))
        {
            ComponentMetaData.FireWarning(0,
ComponentMetaData.Name,
String.Format(DATA_PROFILE_COLUMN_NOT_FOUND_MESSAGE_PATTERN,
_dataProfileFileName, _dataProfileColumnName), String.Empty, 0);
            return DTSValidationStatus.VS_ISBROKEN;
        }
        else
        {
            ComponentMetaData.FireWarning(0,
ComponentMetaData.Name,
String.Format(REGEX_PATTERNS_NOT_FOUND_MESSAGE_PATTERN,
_dataProfileFileName, _dataProfileColumnName), String.Empty, 0);
            return DTSValidationStatus.VS_ISBROKEN;
        }
    }
}

// The input column must exist and must be of a supported data
type.
if (String.IsNullOrEmpty(_emailAddressInputColumnName))
{
    ComponentMetaData.FireError(0, ComponentMetaData.Name,
INPUT_COLUMN_NOT_SET_MESSAGE, String.Empty, 0, out isCanceled);
    return DTSValidationStatus.VS_ISBROKEN;
```

```
    }
    else
    {

        IDTSInputColumn100 inputColumn =
    ComponentMetaData.InputCollection[INPUT_NAME].InputColumnCollection
    [_emailAddressInputColumnName];
        if (inputColumn == null)
        {
            ComponentMetaData.FireError(0, ComponentMetaData.Name,
        String.Format(INPUT_COLUMN_NOT_FOUND_MESSAGE_PATTERN,
        inputColumn.Name), String.Empty, 0, out isCanceled);
            return DTSValidationStatus.VS_ISBROKEN;
        }
        else
        {
            ComponentMetaData.FireInformation(0,
        ComponentMetaData.Name,
        String.Format(INPUT_COLUMN_FOUND_MESSAGE_PATTERN,
        inputColumn.Name), String.Empty, 0, ref fireAgain);

            if (inputColumn.DataType != DataType.DT_NTEXT &&
                inputColumn.DataType != DataType.DT_TEXT &&
                inputColumn.DataType != DataType.DT_STR &&
                inputColumn.DataType != DataType.DT_WSTR)
            {
                ComponentMetaData.FireError(0, ComponentMetaData.Name,
        String.Format(INPUT_COLUMN_DATATYPE_NOT_SUPPORTED_MESSAGE_PATTERN,
        inputColumn.DataType.ToString(), inputColumn.Name), String.Empty,
        0, out isCanceled);
                return DTSValidationStatus.VS_ISBROKEN;
            }
        }
    }
    return base.Validate();
```

Components are validated whenever the package is loaded in SSDT, when the SSIS developer confirms the component's configuration at the beginning of the execution, and whenever deployed packages are validated explicitly.

30. To guide the SSIS package developers, and prevent them from inadvertently corrupting the component's configuration, add the following overrides to the ValidateEmail class definition:

```
public override IDTSInput100 InsertInput(DTSInsertPlacement
insertPlacement, Int32 inputID)
{
    // Only one input is supported.
```

```
      throw new NotSupportedException(TOO_MANY_INPUTS_MESSAGE);
}
```

This method will prevent the SSIS developers from creating any additional inputs:

```
public override IDTSOutput100 InsertOutput(DTSInsertPlacement
insertPlacement, Int32 outputID)
{
    // Only one output is supported.
    throw new NotSupportedException(TOO_MANY_OUTPUTS_MESSAGE);
}
```

This method will prevent the SSIS developers from creating any additional outputs:

```
public override IDTSOutputColumn100 InsertOutputColumnAt(Int32
outputID, Int32 outputColumnIndex, String name, String
description)
{
    // No additional Output Columns can be added.
    throw new
NotSupportedException(USER_DEFINED_COLUMNS_NOT_SUPPORTED);
}
```

This method will prevent the SSIS developers from adding any additional columns to the default output:

```
public override void DeleteOutput(Int32 outputID)
{
    // The built-in output cannot be removed.
    Boolean isInternal =
(Boolean)(ComponentMetaData.OutputCollection.GetObjectByID(outp
utID).CustomPropertyCollection[IS_INTERNAL_OBJECT_PROPERTY_NAME
].Value);
    if (isInternal)
    {
        throw new
InvalidOperationException(DEFAULT_OUTPUT_MUST_EXIST_MESSAGE);
    }
    else
    {
        base.DeleteOutput(outputID);
    }
}
```

This method will prevent the SSIS developers from removing the default output; it will allow them to remove other outputs, but only theoretically, because adding an output is already prevented by the preceding `InsertOutput()` method override:

```
public override void DeleteOutputColumn(Int32 outputID, Int32
outputColumnID)
{
    // Built-in output columns cannot be removed.
    Boolean isInternal =
(Boolean)(ComponentMetaData.OutputCollection.GetObjectByID(outp
utID).OutputColumnCollection.GetObjectByID(outputColumnID).Cust
omPropertyCollection[IS_INTERNAL_OBJECT_PROPERTY_NAME].Value);
    if (isInternal)
    {
        throw new
InvalidOperationException(DEFAULT_COLUMNS_MUST_EXIST);
    }
    else
    {
        base.DeleteOutputColumn(outputID, outputColumnID);
    }
}
```

This last override will prevent SSIS developers from removing the built-in output columns. Theoretically, it will allow them to remove user-defined columns; however, the overridden `InsertOutputColumnAt()` method prevents them from being added at all.

31. By using the same technique as in steps 26 and 27, override the `PreExecute()` base class method, and use the following code as its definition:

```
base.PreExecute();

this.ResolveComponentCustomProperties();
```

All the settings needed to process the pipeline data are determined in the `PreExecute()` method.

32. Next, override the `ProcessInput()` method and replace its default definition with the following commands:

```
IDTSInput100 input =
ComponentMetaData.InputCollection.GetObjectByID(inputID);
Int32 emailAddressInputColumnId =
input.InputColumnCollection[_emailAddressInputColumnName].ID;
IDTSInputColumn100 emailAddressInputColumn =
input.InputColumnCollection.GetObjectByID(emailAddressInputColumnId
);
Int32 emailAddressInputColumnIndex =
input.InputColumnCollection.GetObjectIndexByID(emailAddressInputCol
umnId);

IDTSOutput100 output =
ComponentMetaData.OutputCollection[OUTPUT_NAME];
Int32 isValidColumnId =
output.OutputColumnCollection[IS_VALID_COLUMN_NAME].ID;
IDTSOutputColumn100 isValidColumn =
output.OutputColumnCollection.GetObjectByID(isValidColumnId);
Int32 isValidColumnIndex =
BufferManager.FindColumnByLineageID(input.Buffer,
isValidColumn.LineageID);

while (buffer.NextRow())
{
    String emailAddress;
    switch (emailAddressInputColumn.DataType)
    {
        case DataType.DT_NTEXT:
            emailAddress =
Encoding.Unicode.GetString(buffer.GetBlobData(emailAddressInputColu
mnIndex, 0,
(Int32)buffer.GetBlobLength(emailAddressInputColumnIndex)));
            break;
        case DataType.DT_TEXT:
            emailAddress =
Encoding.GetEncoding(emailAddressInputColumn.CodePage).GetString(bu
ffer.GetBlobData(emailAddressInputColumnIndex, 0,
emailAddressInputColumn.Length));
            break;
        default:
            emailAddress =
buffer.GetString(emailAddressInputColumnIndex);
            break;
    }

    buffer.SetBoolean(isValidColumnIndex,
```

```
this.IsValidEmail(emailAddress));
}
```

Column value validation is performed in the `ProcessInput()` method. The data is retrieved from the specified column based on the input column data type - `DT_TEXT` and `DT_NTEXT` large object (LOB) data types require special handling, whereas the data in `DT_STR` and `DT_WSTR` can be read simply with the `GetString()` method.

33. In the overridden `PostExecute()` method, use the following commands:

```
_regexPatterns.Clear();

base.PostExecute();
```

After the rows have been processed, the `PostExecute()` method releases the resources; it clears the regular expressions collection, as it is no longer needed.

34. Save the solution, and build the project by selecting the **Build SSISCustomComponents** command from the **Build** menu - first using **Debug**, and then again using the **Release** solution configuration. If you followed the preceding instructions correctly, the project should build successfully. In case of any errors, inspect the messages in the **Error List** pane and make the appropriate corrections.

35. Use Windows Explorer to navigate to the `C:\SSIS2016Cookbook\Chapter10\Starter` folder, and locate the `Chapter10_Deploy_CustomComponent.bat` command file.

36. Execute the command file as the administrator, observe the messages returned in the **Command Prompt** window, and finally press any key to complete the deployment.

37. In SSDT, open the `AdventureWorksETL.sln` solution, located in the `C:\SSIS2016Cookbook\Chapter10\Starter\AdventureWorksETL\` folder.

38. Open the `RegExValidation.dtsx` package in the control flow; the package is based on a similar package with the same name that you created in the *Validating data using regular expressions in a script component* recipe of `Chapter 7`, *Unleash the Power of SSIS Script Tasks and Components*.

39. Open the **Validate Person Data** task in the data flow designer.

40. From the SSIS toolbox, drag the **Validate Email** transformation to the data flow designer; it should be located in the **Common** section. If the **Validate Email** transformation is not available in the SSIS Toolbox, right-click the toolbox, and select **Refresh Toolbox** from the shortcut menu. If that doesn't help, close SSDT, and open the `AdventureWorksETL.sln` solution again. If not even that resolves the problem, return to the Visual Studio instance with `SSISCustomization.sln` open, and repeat steps 32 through 34 to redeploy the assembly.

41. Connect the regular data path from the **Person Data** source component to the **Validate Email** transformation.

42. Double-click the **Validate Email** transformation to open the **Advanced Editor for Validate Email**.

43. On the **Component Properties** page, use the following settings to configure the component's custom properties:

Property	Value
Data Profile Column Name	EmailAddress
Data Profile File Name	$Package::DataProfileName

Refer to the following screenshot to verify your settings:

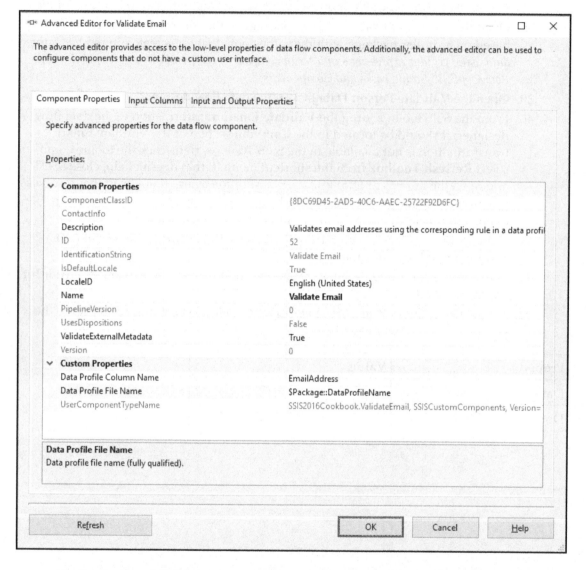

44. On the **Input Columns** page, make sure that all the input columns are selected; leave their **Usage Type** set to **READONLY**.

45. On the **Input and Output Properties** page, locate the **Input Column Name** custom property of the `ValidateEmailInput` input, and use `EmailAddress` as its value, as shown in the following screenshot:

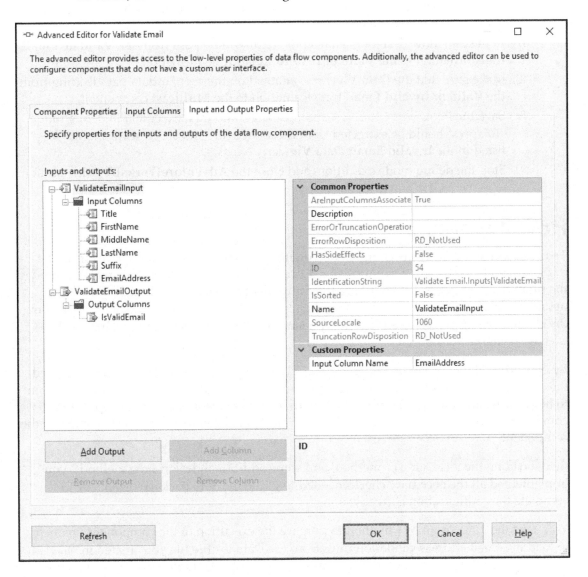

46. Click **OK** to confirm the configuration. If you followed the preceding instructions correctly, no validation errors should be reported. If the component is in error (marked by a red **X** mark), or if there are any warnings (marked by an exclamation mark), inspect the **Error List** pane, investigate each message, and resolve them accordingly.

47. In the data flow designer, connect the regular data path from the **Validate Email** transformation to the **Valid or Invalid Email** transformation.

48. Make sure that the **Data Viewer** is enabled on the regular data path leading from the **Valid or Invalid Email** transformation to the **Multicast** component.

49. Save the RegExValidation.dtsx package, and then execute it in debug mode. 107 rows should be extracted from the source file, and seven rows should be listed in the **Invalid Email Data Viewer**.

50. Stop the debug mode execution, and close the **AdventureWorksETL.sln** solution.

How it works...

To create a custom data flow component, you need to create a class that derives from the Microsoft.SqlServer.Dts.Pipeline.PipelineComponent base class, which provides the functionalities needed to configure the component at design time and perform the operations at run time. By implementing the DtsPipelineComponent attribute, you allow the class to be recognized as an SSIS component by SSDT at design time and by the SSIS execution engine at run time.

By overriding the ProvideComponentProperties() base class method, you established the essential elements of the component: the input, the output, and in it the output column to hold the result of the transformation. You defined the custom properties (two for the component and one for the input) that the SSIS package developers can use to configure the component.

By overriding the Validate() method, and some additional design-time methods, you implemented all the necessary checks needed to guide the SSIS package developer to complete the configuration correctly.

You used the PreExecute() method to prepare the execution of the component - namely, to load the email address validation rules from the Data Profile file you created in Chapter 5, *Dealing with Data Quality*, for the column specified in the **Data Profile Column Name** custom property. You used the PostExecute() method to release these resources after the execution completes.

The principal part of the transformation, however, is implemented in the `ProcessInput()` method, where each row received from the upstream pipeline is validated: data is read from the column specified by the **Input Column Name** custom input property and validated against the Regular Expressions patterns from the Data Profile file. Validation results are then placed in the **IsValidEmail** output column, to be consumed by the downstream components of the data flow.

Managing custom component versions

Over time you might need to make changes to a custom component, for instance because you needed to optimize or refactor the code, implement new features, or replace the external assemblies. As long as the interface of the component (its custom properties and its inputs and outputs) remain unchanged in a later version, you simply deploy the new version to the destination environments, register it in the GAC, and the new version of the component will be used the next time the package is executed or edited in SSDT. You do not even have to modify its version number.

However, if the change affects the components interface - for instance, if you need to add, remove, or modify any of its custom properties - you need to make the component upgradable. This upgrade is performed automatically - at design time or at run time - by invoking a special design-time method of the `Microsoft.SqlServer.Dts.Pipeline.PipelineComponent` base class, namely the `PerformUpgrade()` method. The method is invoked automatically in SSDT when the SSIS package is being designed or by the SSIS execution engine when the SSIS package is being executed, if the `CurrentVersion` property of the `DtsPipelineComponent` attribute was set in the component.

You use the `PerformUpgrade()` method in the later version of the component to make the necessary changes to the properties of the earlier version of the component, for instance by adding a property that was not available in the earlier version, by removing a property that is no longer used, or by modifying an existing property of the earlier version of the component so that it can be used by the later component.

In this recipe, you are going to create version two of the component that you created in the *Designing a custom transformation* recipe earlier in this chapter. The new version is going to use an additional custom parameter, and will allow the initial version to be upgraded automatically.

Getting ready

Before you can use this recipe, you need to design the custom component, as described in the *Designing a custom transformation* recipe earlier in this chapter.

Alternatively, you can use the **SSISCustomComponents** project of the SSISCustomization.sln solution, located in the C:\SSIS2016Cookbook\Chapter10\Solution\SSISCustomization\ folder.

How to do it...

1. Open the SSISCustomization.sln solution that you created in the *Designing a custom transformation* recipe, earlier in this chapter.

2. In the SSISCustomComponents project, locate the ValidateEmail.cs file, and open it in the designer.

3. Modify the DtsPipelineComponent attribute of the ValidateEmail class, and add the CurrentVersion property, as shown in the following example:

```
[DtsPipelineComponent
    (
    ComponentType = ComponentType.Transform,
    DisplayName = "Validate Email",
    Description = "Validates email addresses using the
corresponding rule in a data profile file.",
    NoEditor = false,
    CurrentVersion = 2
    )]
```

   Do not forget the comma after the NoEditor property declaration! When the CurrentVersion property is set, SSDT at design time and the SSIS execution engine at run time will invoke the PerformUpgrade() base class method, and attempt to upgrade an earlier version of the component used in an SSIS package to the current one registered in the GAC.

4. Add the following private constant declarations to the end of the current list of constants:

```
private const String REGEX_OPTIONS_PROPERTY_NAME = "Regular
Expressions Options";
private const String REGEX_OPTIONS_PROPERTY_DESCRIPTION = "The
Regular Expressions options to be used in email address
validation.";
```

```
private const Int64 REGEX_OPTIONS_UPGRADE_VALUE = 513;
private const String REGEX_OPTIONS_UNKNOWN_MESSAGE_PATTERN =
"The value of {0} does not represent a valid RegexOptions
value.";
```

These constants contain some of the settings needed by version two of the component: object names, descriptions, and messages.

5. Another private variable is required; place it next to the existing ones:

    ```
    private Int64 _regexOptionsNumber;
    ```

6. Modify the `ProvideComponentProperties()` method, and add the following new custom property declaration:

    ```
    // Regular Expressions Options
    IDTSCustomProperty100 regularExpressionsOptions =
    ComponentMetaData.CustomPropertyCollection.New();
    regularExpressionsOptions.Name = REGEX_OPTIONS_PROPERTY_NAME;
    regularExpressionsOptions.Description =
    REGEX_OPTIONS_PROPERTY_DESCRIPTION;
    regularExpressionsOptions.State = DTSPersistState.PS_DEFAULT;
    regularExpressionsOptions.TypeConverter =
    typeof(Int64).AssemblyQualifiedName;
    regularExpressionsOptions.Value = (Int64)0;
    ```

    This property will allow the SSIS package developers to not only specify which regular expressions patterns to use, and against which column, but also which regular expressions options to use for matching.

7. Extend the `Validate()` method by adding the following test at the end of the method's definition (before the `return` command):

    ```
    try
    {
        RegexOptions regexOptions = (RegexOptions)_regexOptionsNumber;
        Regex regex = new Regex(@".", regexOptions);
    }
    catch (ArgumentOutOfRangeException)
    {
        ComponentMetaData.FireError(0, ComponentMetaData.Name,
    String.Format(REGEX_OPTIONS_UNKNOWN_MESSAGE_PATTERN,
    _regexOptionsNumber.ToString()), String.Empty, 0, out isCanceled);
        return DTSValidationStatus.VS_ISBROKEN;
    }
    ```

8. Extend the `ResolveComponentCustomProperties()` private function by adding the following variable assignment to its definition:

```
_regexOptionsNumber =
(Int64)(ComponentMetaData.CustomPropertyCollection[REGEX_OPTIONS_PR
OPERTY_NAME].Value);
```

9. In the `IsValidEmail()` private function, amend the call to the `Regex.IsMatch()` method so that the Regular Expressions options can be passed to it dynamically, as shown in the following example:

```
if (Regex.IsMatch(emailAddress, regexPattern,
(RegexOptions)_regexOptionsNumber))
```

10. Make some space below the `PostExecute()` method definition, and start typing the override directive; from the list of possible overrides, select the `PerformUpgrade()` method. Use the following code to replace the method's default definition:

```
DtsPipelineComponentAttribute pipelineComponentAttribute =
(DtsPipelineComponentAttribute)Attribute.GetCustomAttribute(this.Ge
tType(), typeof(DtsPipelineComponentAttribute), false);
Int32 componentLatestVersion =
pipelineComponentAttribute.CurrentVersion;

Int32 activeComponentVersion = ComponentMetaData.Version;
if (activeComponentVersion < componentLatestVersion)
{
    try
    {
        IDTSCustomProperty100 existingRegularExpressionsOptions =
ComponentMetaData.CustomPropertyCollection[REGEX_OPTIONS_PROPERTY_N
AME];
    }
    catch (Exception)
    {
        IDTSCustomProperty100 regularExpressionsOptions =
ComponentMetaData.CustomPropertyCollection.New();
        regularExpressionsOptions.Name =
REGEX_OPTIONS_PROPERTY_NAME;
        regularExpressionsOptions.Description =
REGEX_OPTIONS_PROPERTY_DESCRIPTION;
        regularExpressionsOptions.State =
DTSPersistState.PS_DEFAULT;
        regularExpressionsOptions.TypeConverter =
typeof(Int64).AssemblyQualifiedName;
```

```
            regularExpressionsOptions.Value =
REGEX_OPTIONS_UPGRADE_VALUE;
        }
    }

    ComponentMetaData.Version = componentLatestVersion;
```

11. Save the project, and build it - first using the **Debug**, and then again using **Release** solution configuration. In case of any errors, inspect the messages in the **Error List** pane and make the appropriate corrections.

12. Use Windows Explorer to navigate to the `C:\SSIS2016Cookbook\Chapter10\Starter` folder, and locate the `Chapter10_Deploy_CustomComponent.bat` command file.

13. Execute the command file as the administrator, observe the messages returned in the **Command Prompt** window, and finally press any key to complete the deployment.

14. In SSDT, open the `AdventureWorksETL.sln` solution, located in the `C:\SSIS2016Cookbook\Chapter10\Starter\AdventureWorksETL\` folder.

15. Open the `RegExValidation.dtsx` package in the control flow, and then open the **Validate Person Data** task in the data flow designer. In case you did not use the previous recipe, follow steps 38 through 46 of the *Designing a custom transformation* recipe to complete the data flow; otherwise, the **Validate Email** transformation should already be in place.

16. In the **Advanced Editor for the Validate Email** transformation, under **Custom Properties**, the new **Regular Expressions Options** property should be available with the default value of 513 (the value represents the case-insensitive, and culture-invariant, regular expressions matching options). This value is applied during the upgrade. Refer to the following screenshot to verify your settings:

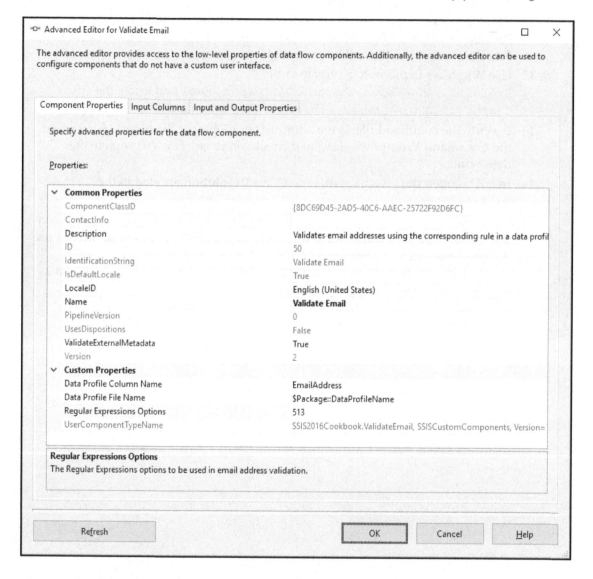

17. Click **OK** to confirm the configuration.

18. Save the package and execute it in debug mode. Out of 107 source rows, seven should fail the **EmailAddress** column validation.

19. Stop the debug mode execution.

20. Close the `AdventureWorksETL.sln` and `SSISCustomization.sln` solutions.

How it works...

By specifying the version number of the custom component, in the `DtsPipelineComponent` attribute, you mark the new version of the component; a new version is needed only if the exposed properties, inputs, and/or outputs, have been modified.

Of course, setting the new version number is not enough to allow the earlier versions of the component that are already in use in deployed SSIS packages to be upgraded accordingly. The upgrade is performed by overriding the `PerformUpgrade()` base class method. In the preceding example, a new component custom property is added.

After the upgrade, the component's version number is changed as well, to the version number of the component currently registered in the GAC.

When the new version of the component is deployed and registered, any SSIS package that uses the component will be upgraded, either the next time you edit it in SSDT or the next time it is executed.

11
Scale Out with SSIS 2017

This chapter will cover the following recipes:

- SQL Server 2017 download and setup
- SQL Server client tools setup
- SSIS configuration for scale out executions
- Scaling out a package execution

Introduction

Since its inception, SSIS was meant to execute on a single machine running Windows. The service by itself could not scale on multiple machines. Although it would have been possible to call package execution with custom orchestration mechanism, it didn't have anything built in. You needed to manually develop an orchestration service and that was tedious to do and maintain. See this article for a custom scale-out pattern with SSIS: https://msdn.microsoft.com/en-us/dn887191.aspx.

What lots of developers wanted was a way to use SSIS a bit like the way Hadoop works: call a package execution from a master server and scale it on multiple workers (servers). The SSIS team is delivering a similar functionality in 2017, enabling us to enhance scalability and performance in our package executions.

As mentioned before, the scale out functionality is like Hadoop. The difference is that we use tools we have more knowledge of. It's also a lot easier to work with SSIS since we are on the Windows filesystem. As we saw in Chapter 9, *On-Premises and Azure Big Data Integration*, on big data, we needed to use ssh to connect to the machine where the files were copied and produced. Another advantage is that we can consume data at the source. We don't have to copy it to another machine and SSIS can connect to lots of different sources.

We do not pretend that the SSIS scale out functionality is a replacement for Hadoop. In many situations, it might be a good option before exploring other solutions such as Hadoop/HDInsight or Azure SQL Data Warehouse.

SQL Server 2017 download and setup

This recipe will cover the following subtopics:

- Download SQL Server 2017
- Set up SQL Server with SSIS scale out options

Getting ready

This recipe assumes that you have the necessary permissions to install SQL Server on your machine.

How to do it...

1. Open your web browser and navigate to `https://www.microsoft.com/en-us/sql-server/sql-server-2017`.
2. Select **Download the preview**, as shown in the following screenshot:

3. On the page that appears, select **Windows** in the platform menus at the right and click on **Install on Windows**, as shown in this screenshot:

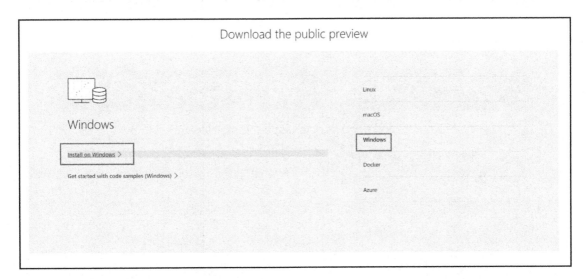

4. As shown in the following screenshot, fill in the form and click on **Continue**:

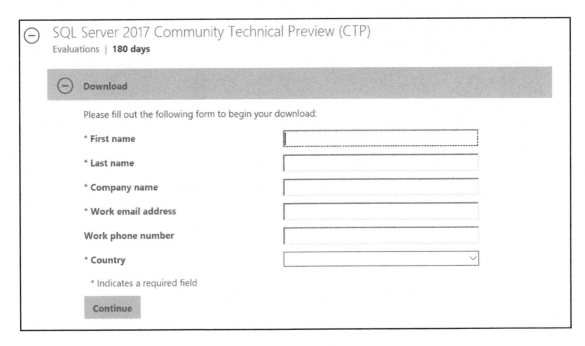

5. Choose **ISO** and click on **Continue**, as shown here:

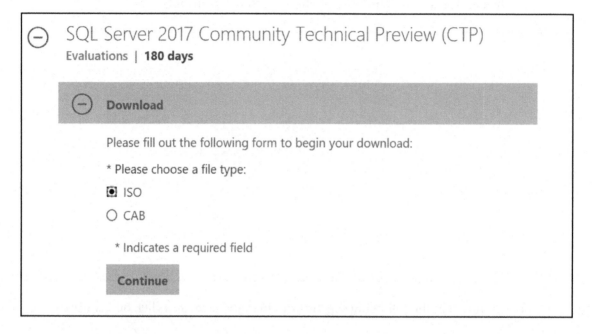

6. Choose the language (we selected **English**) and click on **Download**, as shown in the following screenshot:

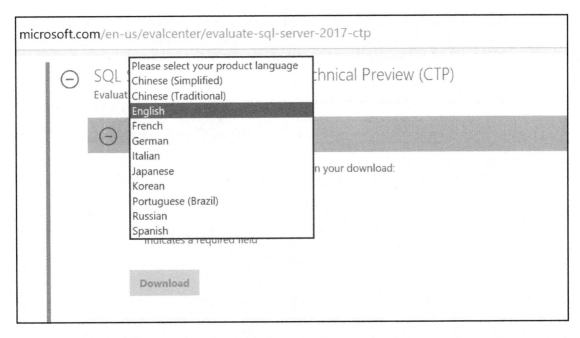

7. The download will now start. Once completed, navigate to the folder where you saved the file named `SQLServer2017CTP2.1-x64-ENU.iso` and double-click on it. Select **setup.exe** to proceed with the SQL Server 2017 CTP 2.1 installation, as shown in the following screenshot:

	Name	Date modified	Type	Size
	1033_ENU_LP	5/11/2017 1:02 AM	File folder	
	redist	5/11/2017 12:57 AM	File folder	
	resources	5/11/2017 12:57 AM	File folder	
	Tools	5/11/2017 12:57 AM	File folder	
	x64	5/11/2017 12:57 AM	File folder	
	autorun	4/7/2017 3:17 AM	Setup Information	1 KB
	MediaInfo	5/11/2017 1:00 AM	XML Document	1 KB
	setup	5/10/2017 7:20 PM	Application	107 KB
	setup.exe	4/12/2017 4:03 AM	XML Configuratio...	1 KB
	SqlSetupBootstrapper.dll	5/10/2017 7:11 PM	Application extens...	235 KB
	sqmapi.dll	4/7/2017 3:11 AM	Application extens...	131 KB

8. Once **SQL Server Installation Center** appears, click on **New SQL Server stand-alone installation or add features to an existing installation**. The **SQL Server 2017 CTP 2.1 Setup** window appears, as shown in the following screenshot. Click on **Next**.

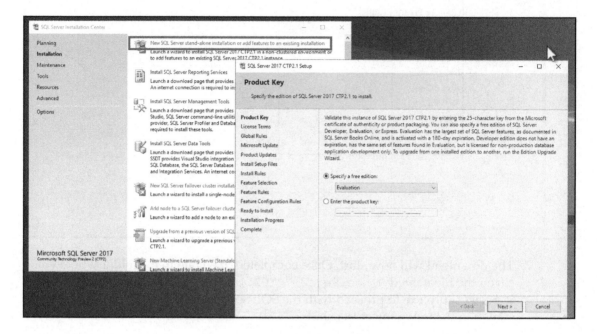

9. Accept the **License Terms** and click on **Next**:

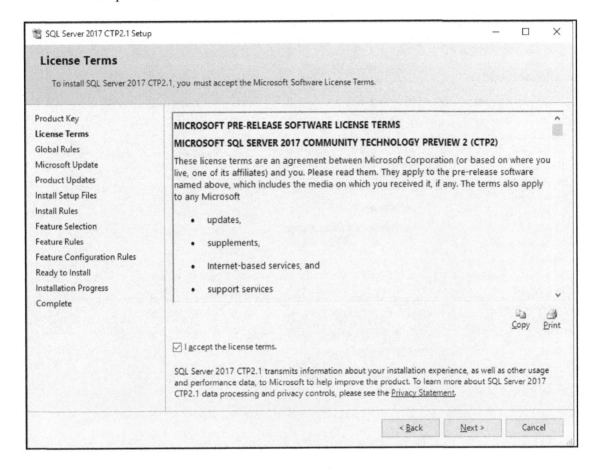

10. As shown in the following screenshot, allow **Microsoft Update** to run and click on **Next**:

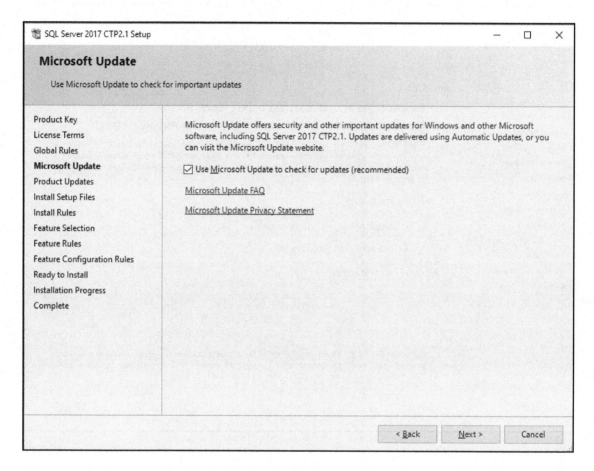

11. Once **Initial Setup Files** completes, as shown in this screenshot, click on **Next**:

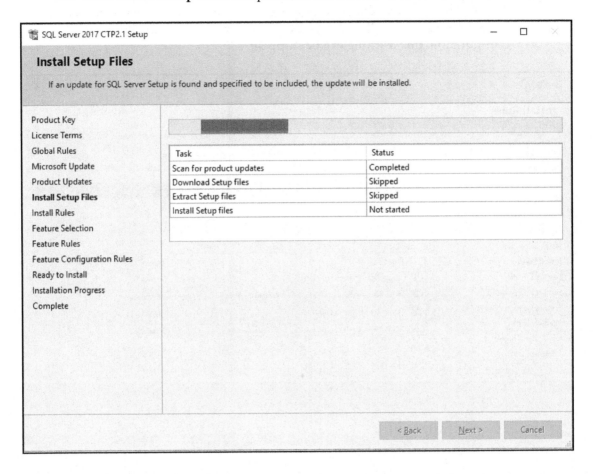

12. Once the updates are done, the **Install Rules** window appears; click on **Next** on this one once the rules check is completed. As shown in the next screenshot, there's always a firewall warning. Since we're working on an all-in-one configuration, this warning can be skipped:

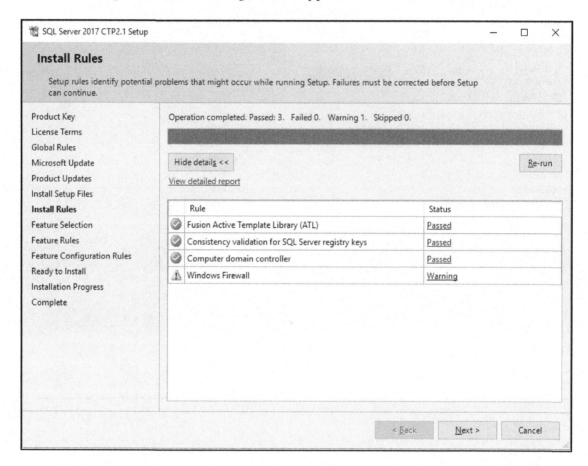

13. The **Feature Selection** window appears. In our case, we'll only install the database engine and SSIS. You'll notice that we select both **Scale Out Master** and **Worker** in **Integration Services**, the new features we're interested in. Select the features shown in the following screenshot and click on **Next**:

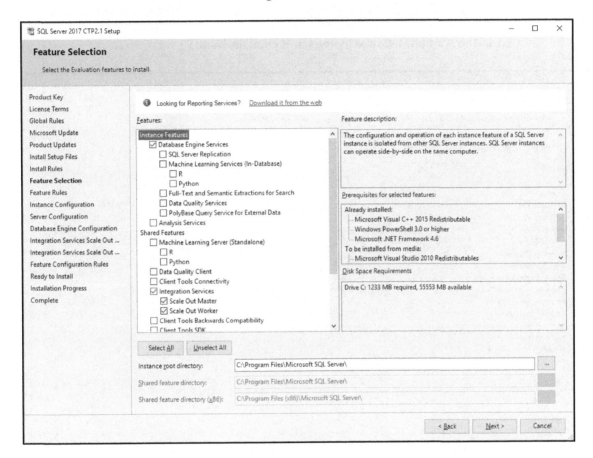

14. The **Instance Configuration** window appears; since we might have multiple instances of SQL Server 2017 until the final release, we'll use a named instance. This creates separate sets of services for each version of SQL Server installed on a machine. Be aware that each instance of SQL Server consumes resources, and the PC where it is installed might have performance issues if you install too many versions and run them at same time. Enter MSSQL2017_21 for MSSQL 2017 CTP 2.1 in the **Named instance** textbox and click on **Next**:

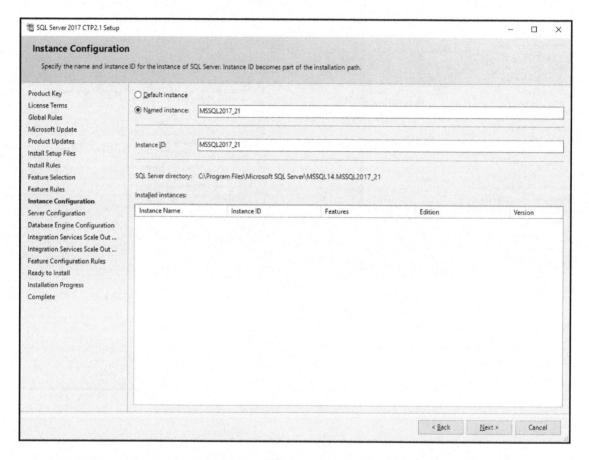

15. In the **Server Configuration** window, click on the **Collation** tab and set the collation to **Latin1_General_100_CI_AI**, as shown in the following screenshot. You might want to refer to Chapter 1, *SSIS Setup* for an explanation of the collation choice and definition. Click on **Next**:

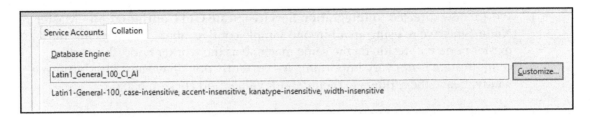

16. The **Database Engine Configuration** window appears. In the **Server Configuration** tab, select **Mixed Mode** as the authentication mode. Enter a password for the SA account. The **Mixed Mode** authentication is required by **Scale Out Workers (SSIS)** to be able to write into SSISDB. Add the current user (you) also as an SQL Server Administrator, as shown in the following screenshot. Leave the other settings as default and click on **Next**:

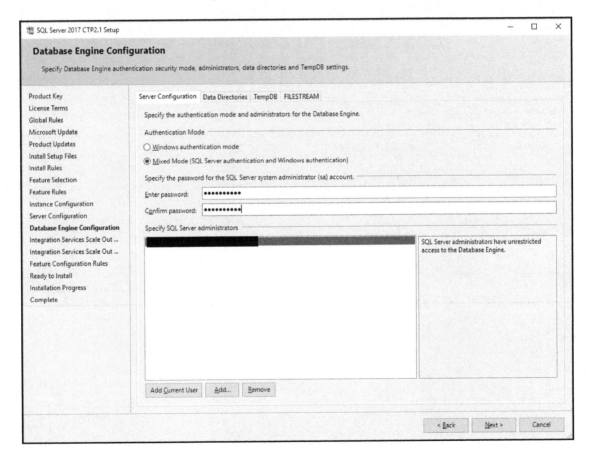

17. We are now directed to **Integration Services Scale Out Configuration - Master Node**. Since we're using an all-in-one sample configuration, which means the master node will reside on the same machine as the worker node, the port configuration is not very important. We currently don't have any SSL Certificate handy. Leave the settings to their default values and click on **Next**.

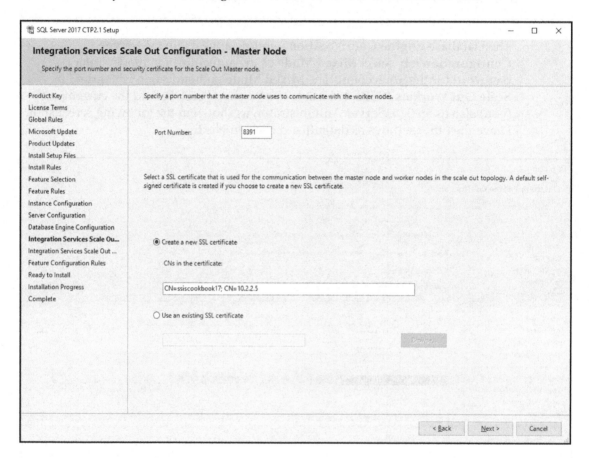

18. The **Integration Services Scale Out Configuration - Worker Node** window appears. As highlighted in the following screenshot, this step is useful when we install separate worker nodes on different machines. In these cases, we need to specify the trusted certificate used to authenticate to the master worker node. In an all-in-one configuration, this step is facultative. Click on **Next** to continue.

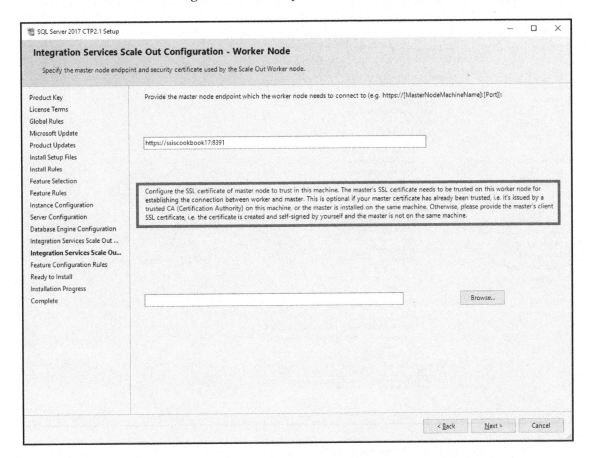

19. The **Ready to Install** window appears. As shown in the following screenshot, this step allows you to review what will be installed. We can always click on **< Back** to change anything that we selected before. In our case, everything is fine; click on **Install** to start installing SQL Server 2017 CTP1.

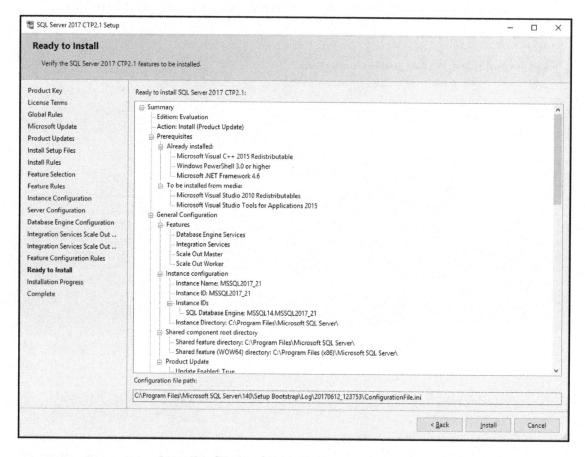

20. The **Installation Progress** window appears. It might take several minutes to complete. As shown in the following screenshot, there's a progress bar that tells us the progress of the installation:

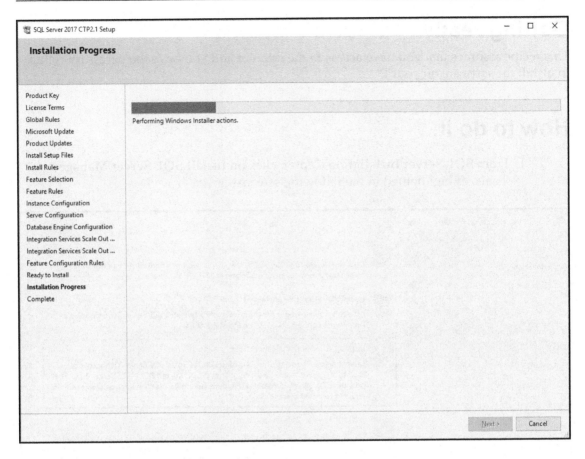

21. The last step will show you that the installation is complete.

There's more...

We have now installed the server portion of SQL Server. The next steps will show you how to install **SQL Server Management Studio (SSMS)** and **SQL Server Data Tools (SSDT)**.

SQL Server client tools setup

We will see how to setup SQL Server client tools.

Getting ready

This recipe assumes that you have access to the internet and you have the necessary rights to install the software on your PC.

How to do it...

1. From **SQL Server Installation Center**, click on **Install SQL Server Management Tools**, as highlighted in the following screenshot:

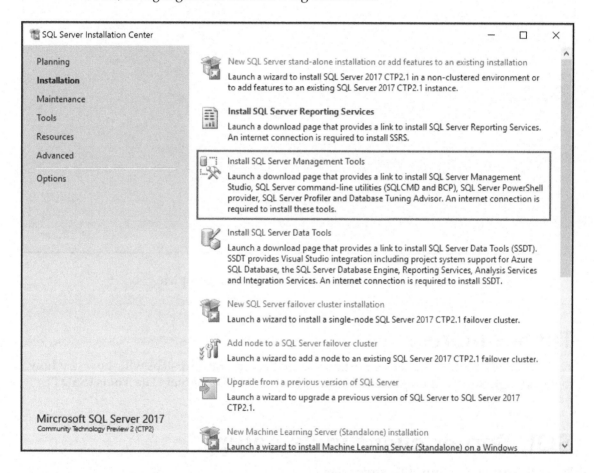

2. A browser opens and the following page opens. Select version 17.1 (the latest version available at the time of writing this book), highlighted in the following screenshot:

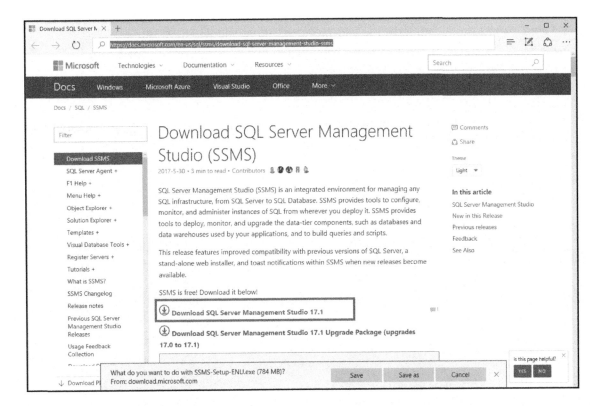

3. Once the download completes, double-click on the downloaded file to start the installation process. Once completed, you get a window similar as the one shown in the following screenshot:

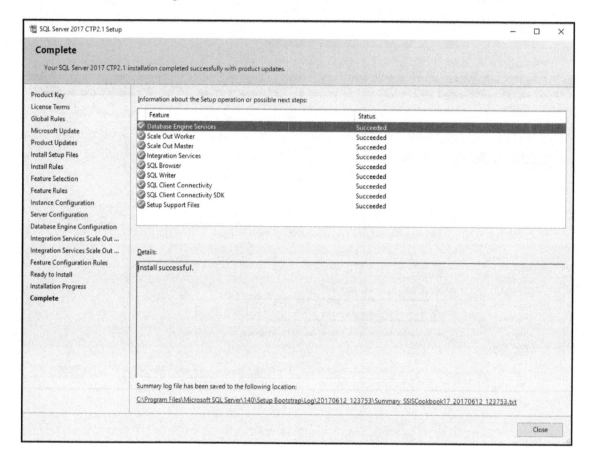

4. Go back to **SQL Server Installation Center**, and this time, click on **Install SQL Server Data Tools**, as highlighted in this screenshot:

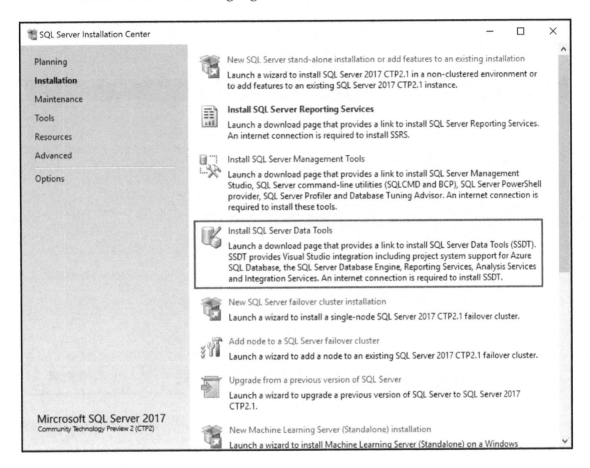

5. You are directed to the SSDT website. As shown in the following screenshot, download the latest version (17.1 at the time of writing) of SSDT:

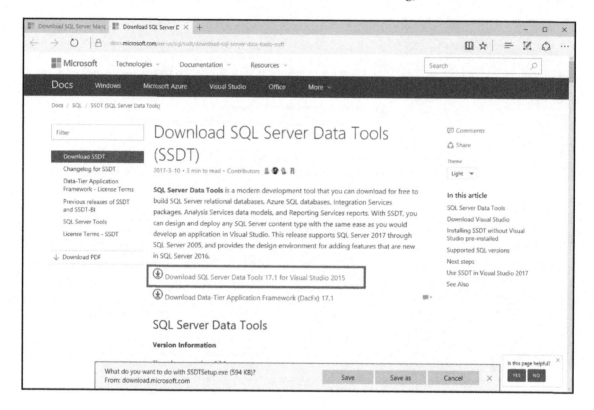

6. The SSDT installer appears as shown in the following screenshot. Although only **SQL Server Integration Services** is necessary for this chapter, it doesn't hurt to install the other component as you might want to use it later. Click on **Next** to start the installation:

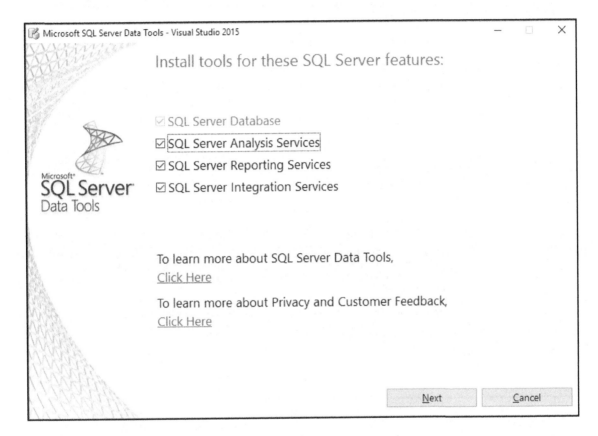

7. The **Microsoft Software License Terms** page appears. Check **I agree to the license terms and conditions** and click on the **Install** button, as shown in the following screenshot:

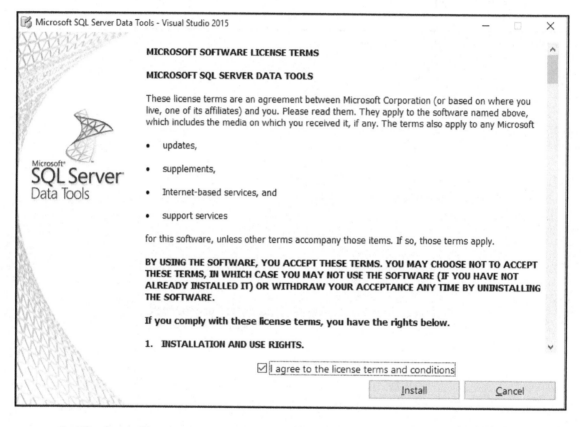

8. The **Setup Progress** page appears as SSTD gets installed, as shown in the following screenshot:

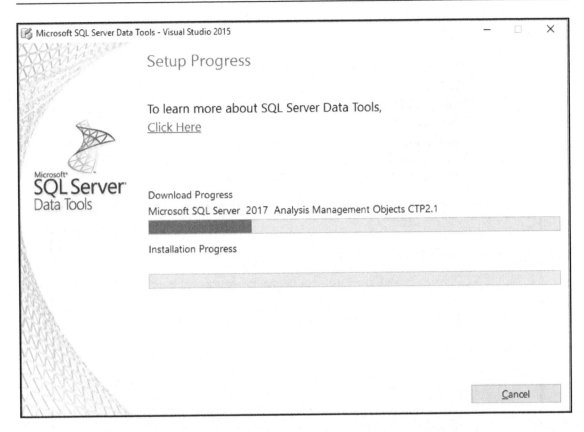

9. Once the installation completes, we're ready to proceed to the setup of SSIS to run in scale out mode.

Configuring SSIS for scale out executions

We'll now configure the SSIS catalog and workers to be able to use scale out executions with SSIS.

Getting ready

This recipe assumes that you've installed SQL Server 2017, SSIS in scale out mode as well as SSMS 17.1 or later.

How to do it...

1. Open **SQL Server Management Studio** and connect to the newly installed SQL Server 2017 instance.
2. In the **Object Explorer**, right-click on the **Integration Services Catalogs** node and select **Create Catalog**.
3. The **Create Catalog** window appears. As shown in the following screenshot, check the **Enable this server as SSIS scale out master** option as well as providing a password for the catalog. Click on **OK** when finished.

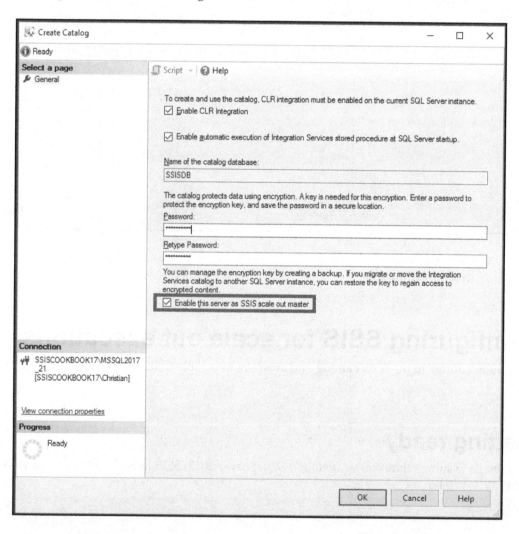

4. Still in SSMS, run the following SQL statements. The first statement lists the workers available. Copy the **WorkerAgentId** into the clipboard by right-clicking on the value in the grid and select **Copy**.
   Type the second SQL statement and use the clipboard's content as parameter (the grayed-out shape in the screenshot). This will enable this specific worker.

```
SQLQuery1.sql - DE...8PGJ3l\ccote (64))*   ⊕  ✕
  ⊟SELECT * FROM [SSISDB].[catalog].[worker_agents]


  EXEC [catalog].[enable_worker_agent] '
```

5. We'll now create a simple database to hold our test scale out data. In **SQL Server Object Explorer**, right-click on the **Databases** folder and select **Create Database**. Name it `TestSSISScaleOut` and click on **OK**.

6. By default, the workers run under the `NT Service\SSISScaleOutWorker140` Windows user. This user is not a login in SQL Server. In **SQL Server Object Explorer**, expand the **Security** folder and right-click on the **Logins** folder; select **New Login** from the contextual menu. The **Login - New** window appears. As shown in the following screenshot, type `NT SERVICE\SSISScaleOutWorker140` in the login name:

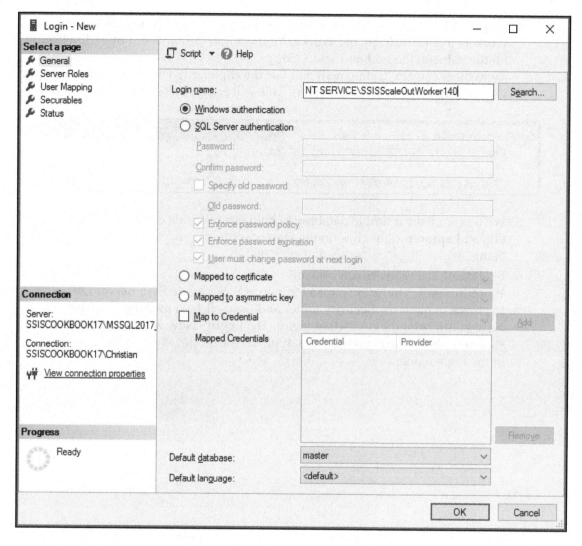

7. Click on **User Mapping** in the upper-left pane.

8. As shown in the following screenshot, select the **TestSSISScaleOut** database and assign both **db_datareader** and **db_datawriter** database roles to the login. Click on **OK** to complete the login creation.

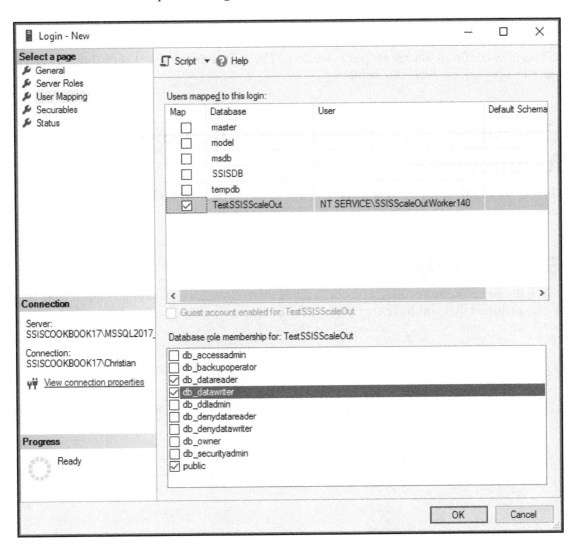

9. The last operation ensures that the worker will have access to the database objects in read/write mode.

There's more...

SSIS is now configured for scale out executions. The next recipe will just show how we can execute a package in scale out mode.

Executing a package using scale out functionality

Finally, we're able to do the real work: creating a simple package and execute it in scale out mode.

Getting ready

You will need SQL Server 2017, SSIS 2017, SSDT, and SSMS 2017 to complete this recipe. It is also assumed that you have configured SSIS in the previous recipe.

How to do it...

1. Open SSDT and create a new SSIS project named `SSISCookBookScaleOut`, as shown in the following screenshot. Click on **OK** to create it:

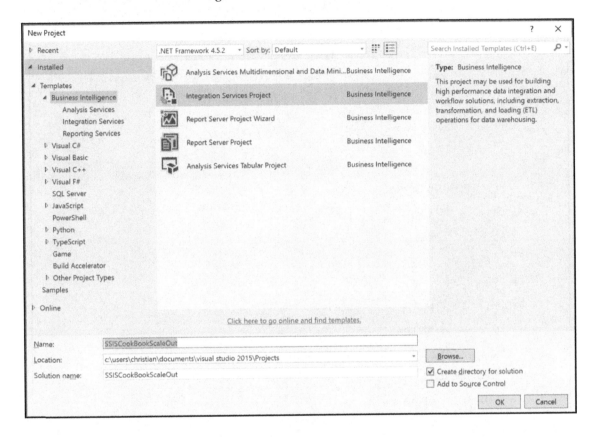

2. In the **Solution Explorer**, right-click on the **Package.dtsx** that is created with the project and select **Delete**, as shown in this screenshot:

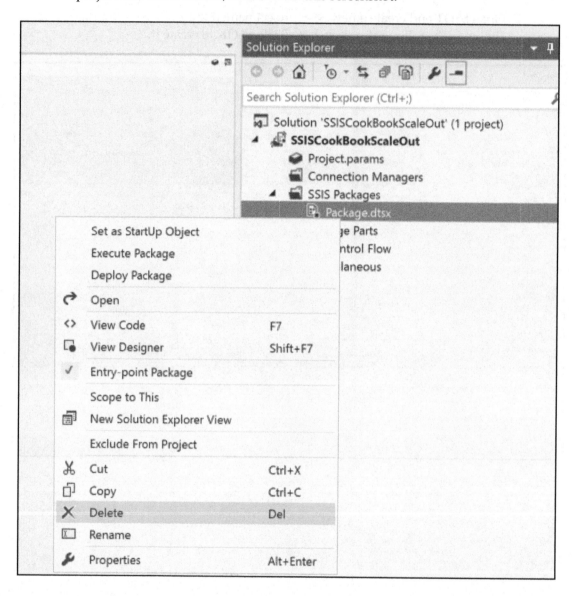

3. Right-click on the project and select **Properties** from the contextual menu. As shown in the following screenshot, change the **ProtectionLevel** property of the project to **Do not save sensitive data** and click on **OK** in both windows. You'll get a warning telling you that you'll have to do the same for all packages in the project. We don't have any, so we simply get rid of the warning dialog. Sensitive data means usernames and passwords. It's better to use parameters instead of relying on SSIS to keep this information. It doesn't hurt to leave this property as default, but we'll get annoying warnings at deployment time. So, the best practice is to use parameters and not the **Encrypt sensitive data with user key** setting.

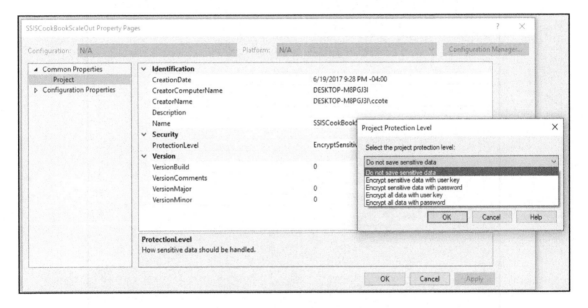

4. Now, right-click on the project and select **New SSIS package** from the contextual menu. Rename it `ScaleOut`.
5. From the SSIS toolbox, drag and drop a data flow task on the control flow of the package. Name it `dft_SSISScaleOut` and double-click on it to go into the data flow task.

6. From the connection managers pane, right-click and select **New OLEDB Connection Manager**. In the configure OLEDB **Connection Manager** window, click on **New** and set the properties as shown in the following screenshot:

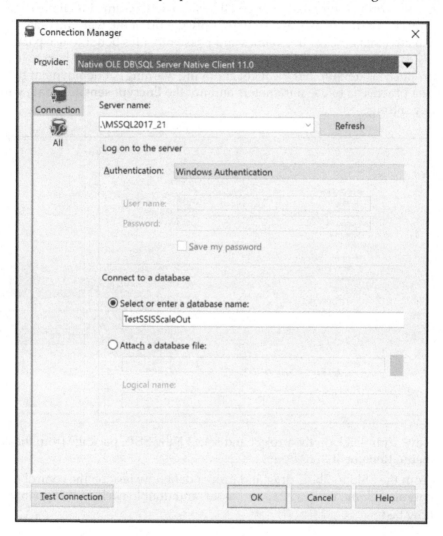

7. Click on the **Test Connection** button to test the connection. If everything is okay, get rid of the test dialog box and click on **OK** to create the connection manager.

8. Rename it as `cmgr_TestSSISScaleOut`.

9. From the **SSIS toolbox | Other sources**, drag and drop an OLEDB source. Rename it `ole_src_AddRows`. Double-click on it and enter the following query:

```
SELECT 1 AS Id, 'Test Scale out' AS ProcessName
```

10. Add a derived component to the data flow. Rename it to `der_ServerExecutionId` and tie it to the `ole_src_AddRow` source. Open it. Add a column, `ServerExecutionId`, and set its expression to `@[System::ServerExecutionID]`. Leave other columns as they are and click on **OK** to close the **Derived Column Transformation Editor**.

11. From the **SSIS toolbox | Other destinations**, drag and drop an OLEDB destination onto the data flow surface. Rename it as `ole_dst_SSISScaleOut`. Open it and click on the **New** button beside the table or view dropdown. Instead of choosing an existing table, since we don't have any yet, we'll create a new one.

12. As shown in the following screenshot, adapt the T-SQL, create the table script to remove the `ole_dst_`, and click on **OK**.

The query is as follows:

```
CREATE TABLE [SSISScaleOut] (
    [Id] int,
    [ProcessName] varchar(14),
    [ServerExecutionId] bigint
)
```

13. Click on the **Mappings** tab to set the links between pipeline and table columns. Click on **OK** in the **OLE DB Destination Editor** to close it. Your data flow should look like the following screenshot:

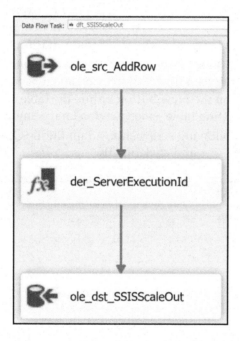

14. Test the package, ensuring that everything works correctly.
15. We'll now deploy the project. In the **Solution Explorer**, right-click on the SSIS and deploy it in the SSIS Catalog created in the previous recipe.
16. Once deployed, open SSMS; expand to the **Integration Services Catalogs** until you get to the **ScaleOut.dtsx** package. Right-click on it and select **Execute in Scale Out...** from the contextual menu, as shown in the following screenshot:

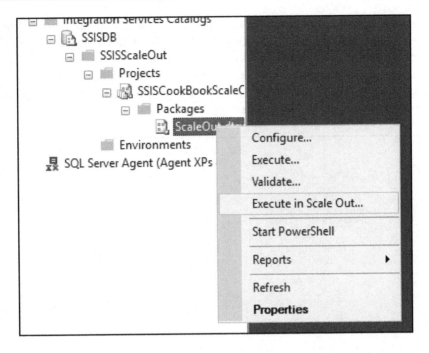

17. The **Execute Package In Scale Out** window opens, as shown here:

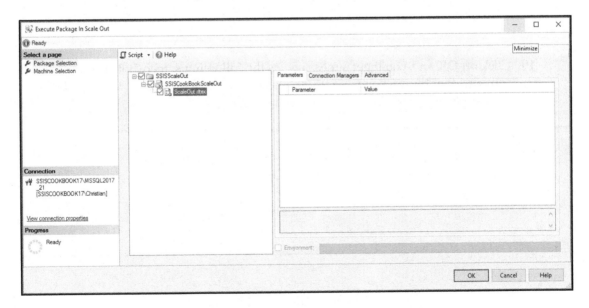

18. Click on **Machine Selection** in the upper-left pane. You can see that the worker we registered in the previous recipe is there. By default, **Allow any machine to execute the selected package** is checked. Since we have only one worker registered, we'll leave it checked. Modifying this setting would be useful if we had many workers and we'd like to be able to choose from among them the worker(s) to execute the package.

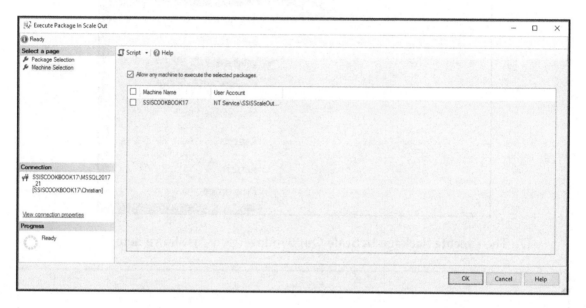

19. Click on **OK** and you'll get a message, as the following screenshot shows. This confirms that the package execution has been queued to execute. Click on **OK** to close this dialog box.

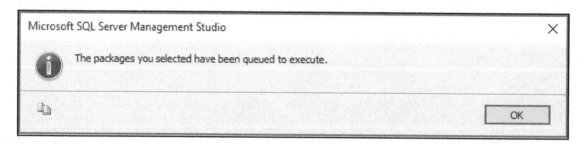

20. In the **SQL Server Object Explorer**, right-click again on the **ScaleOut.dtsx** package. As shown in the following screenshot, go to **Report | Standard Reports | All Executions** from the contextual menu:

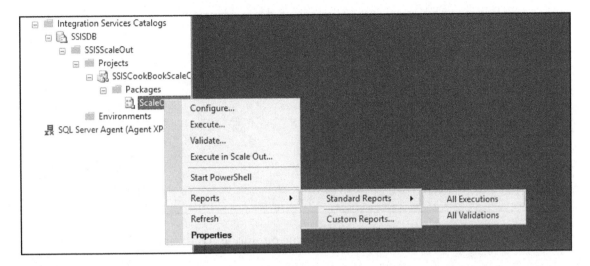

21. The report opens and you can see that the execution has succeeded, as shown in the following screenshot. Click on the **All Message** link under the **Report** column.

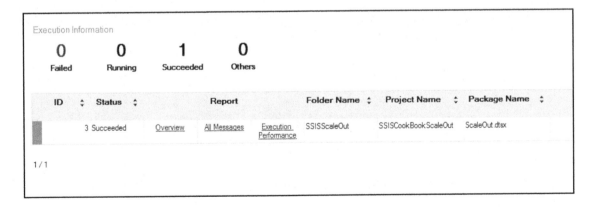

22. The report messages are now detailed. As highlighted in the following screenshot, we can see that SSIS tried to scale out the insertion in the destination, even though it was a very simple package.

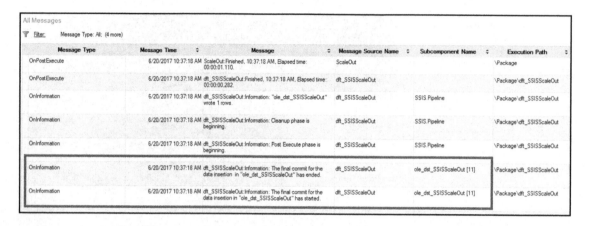

That's it! We've run the SSIS package using scale out mode. That completes the recipe.

Index

Made in the USA
Columbia, SC
08 May 2020